The Decline and Collapse of America

LCDR Tom McBride, USN/Ret.

Printed in USA
First edition September 2017
Second edition June 2018
Third edition August 2018

McBride, Thomas, 1922 -

The Decline and Collapse of America

ISBN-13: 978-1976148088

ISBN-10: 1976148081

Published in accordance with the standards of
The Thomas Jefferson Humanist Society
www.jefferson-society.com

The Decline and Collapse of America

Contents

About the Author

Readers of any politically sensitive book should have some idea of the political leanings of the author. Tom McBride is an American Patriot who served his country in four wars, including during as a Navy F4U Corsair fighter pilot aboard the USS Bennington during World War Two. After the war, he served as a test pilot. After retiring from the military, he became a successful businessman in the fields of real estate and property development.

So for the purpose of full disclosure: Tom was raised in a Republican family and voted the straight Republican ticket for many years. In the mid-1980s, he realized the Republican party was no longer the once "Grand Old Party" and had become what Senator Barry Goldwater supporters believed to be the new "GOP", "God's Own Party" [1]. He became a "RINO" - "Republican In Name Only". Sad to say, with the misogynist [2] Donald Trump as president, the term GOP has devolved to mean "grab our pussy". [3]

For many years, Tom was active in the church. In 1972, at the age of 50, he was the proud "Assistant Head Usher" of the prominent San Diego, California Point Loma United Presbyterian Church. He was then a conservative lifetime registered Republican.

One evening, he read a story in the San Diego newspaper about a prominent British mathematician, biologist, scientist and World War Two veteran visiting the University of California, San Diego and presenting an introductory presentation regarding the Jacob Bronowski adult course based on the book *Ascent of Man* being taught at the University of California. He attended the presentation. A few days later he enrolled in the program. This was a life changing experience. A few months after completing the one-semester course, he dropped out of the church and has never returned except for an occasional funeral service where he would sit quietly at the rear of the church.

Tom's studies of American history, Humanism, philosophy, and world religions have shaped his thinking. Now an Atheist and Humanist, these days, Tom only votes for politicians who speak and express ideas similar to the ideals held by the 1776 Founders of America - "Freedom of and Freedom from Religion". He believes every American should pay taxes to the federal government and in return, the federal government must provide the following for all citizens: a strong national military force, city and state police and fire protection, and federal health care similar to what American active duty military personnel currently receive (the same as what exists in Sweden and Taiwan). Tom says that it seems he's transformed from a Republican into a Socialist.

Why the footnotes? We live in strange times and some of the comments in this book may seem far-fetched. But they are true and well-researched.

---

1   http://www.washingtonpost.com/wp-dyn/content/article/2006/04/01/AR2006040100004.html
2   http://www.huffingtonpost.com/entry/donald-trump-misogyny-worse-thought_us_57edaa7be4b0c2407cdd1ca6
3   http://www.slate.com/blogs/the_slatest/2016/10/07/donald_trump_2005_tape_i_grab_women_by_the_pussy.html

Foreword

Politics, sex, religion: the trifecta of topics to avoid in polite conversation. Yet, they are intricately interwoven in the social and economic fabric of every nation. Each one affects the others, in different ways and proportions depending on the ethos of the age. In my book, *Religions...*, I outline the history of some of the world's religions and their impact on the political climate. In this book, my goal is to convince readers that politicians who base their decisions on the tenets of fictitious religions can cause significant harm to the country they are elected to serve.

In July 2017, the New York Times columnist David Brooks wrote, "Do you ever get the feeling we're all going to be judged for this moment? Historians, our grandchildren and we ourselves will look and ask: What did you do as the Trump/Scaramucci/Bannon administration dropped a nuclear bomb on the basic standards of decency in public life?"[4]

As of an early draft of this book, two of the three administration officials named above had left the administration as well as others too numerous to mention. [5,6] The revolving door of top White House personnel continues to this day, with a 48% turnover rate in the first 18 months of the Trump administration. [7,8] After only seven months in office, President Trump had made more than 1000 false or misleading claims. [9] That's 1000 lies in 200 days – averaging five lies per day. Some whoppers, some just ignorant. This is a presidency defined by blatant untruths and prevarications from a man who is unable to demonstrate presidential behavior.[10] As a result, everything the president says is immediately suspect, and the world has lost confidence in America's moral leadership and credibility. More than that, these behaviors strike fear and distrust. Is America headed to decline and collapse?

Every day, there are more news accounts of the ineptitude of the current administration and every day, I have to restrain myself from adding more of this information to this book. It has to stop somewhere, so I'm relying on the solid backing of the 1776 Founders of America and their wisdom in creating what is (and hopefully will continue to be) one of the greatest countries in the world.

This book, *The Decline and Collapse of America*, expands on the concepts introduced in the book by Kelle Metz and me titled *My Conversations with a WW-II Corsair Fighter*

---

4   https://www.nytimes.com/2017/07/28/opinion/columnists/jeff-flake-plants-a-flag.html?_r=0

5   https://www.nytimes.com/2017/07/31/us/politics/trump-white-house-obamacare-health.html?_r=0

6   https://www.nytimes.com/2017/08/18/us/politics/steve-bannon-trump-white-house.html

7   https://www.bostonglobe.com/news/politics/2017/07/31/look-trump-administration-revolving-door/fvLG5ibUdf8fGJIiJDeqcP/story.html

8   http://www.businessinsider.com/trump-turnover-rate-firings-resignations-compared-obama-bush-clinton-2018-3

9   https://www.washingtonpost.com/news/fact-checker/wp/2017/08/22/president-trumps-list-of-false-and-misleading-claims-tops-1000/?utm_term=.dffaba6d0bde

10   https://www.washingtonpost.com/blogs/right-turn/wp/2017/09/04/something-seriously-off-about-this-president/?utm_term=.47752da0296d

Pilot, first published in 2006. In that book, Kelle and I discussed the fact America had "an enemy within" causing difficulties and resulting in America declining to the standards of a third-world country. This makes me wonder and think: Is America the next great nation to decline and collapse? Why? If so, what can be done to halt or at least slow the decline?

Does it matter?

The Decline and Collapse of America

In this book, I share my thoughts and opinions of how to slow and possibly stop America's decline by encouraging all Americans to vote and elect leaders who are patriotic and "think out of the box" just as Benjamin Franklin and the 1776 Founders did when they founded this great nation more than two centuries ago.

In perusing the daily news in any form (online, television, print, etc.) the comments and activities to today's "religious conservative politicians" are truly startling. It seems to me that they may have missed the study of science, history, and political science altogether and don't have the background or education it takes to govern wisely, selflessly and with the best interests of the nation and its citizens at heart. I wonder if any one of them has ever read a science, economics, or history book? I wonder if any of them has ever heard of Charles Darwin or even heard of his famous 1859 book, *On the Origin of Species*?

Here in America, despite all the scientific information known worldwide, we have religious conservative politicians passing laws that take away the rights of innocent citizens. I cannot understand why any American would vote for such a person. These politicians are intent on denying rights to all Americans regardless if they are straight, gay or transgender. In my years of military service, my fellow officers and I knew that even though some of our very best troops were secretly gay or transgender, they were talented, patriotic warriors fighting for the nation they loved. The latest blow to American's rights is the decision to arm police forces with military equipment include tanks and grenade launchers. [11] Recently a nurse was arrested for refusing to draw blood from an unconscious patient even though the patient was not under arrest and there was no warrant. [12] We are watching our liberties being taken away wholesale.

11   https://www.nytimes.com/2017/08/28/us/politics/trump-police-military-surplus-equipment.html
12   http://www.cnn.com/2017/09/01/health/utah-nurse-arrest-police-video/index.html

It's a far cry from the sentiments expressed on the Statue of Liberty, which was given to America by the people of France in 1886. The statue has a plaque added in 1903, engraved with words from a sonnet by Emma Lazarus[13], "Give me your tired and poor; your huddled masses yearning to breathe free". America welcomed people from all over the world and America was a growing nation until the "moral majority religious conservative politicians" took control of the American government in 1981. Tragically, since the first printing of this book, the situation has worsened, with government forces separating more than 2000 children from their immigrant parents at the border.[14] Worse, the attorney general of the US, Jeff Sessions, used a Bible verse to justify these horrific actions, as did White House spokesperson Sara Huckabee Sanders. [15,16]

In November 2008, my wife, Karen and I were vacationing in Beijing, China. There I picked up a book called *Unrestricted Warfare: Thinking Out of the Box*, written by two military officers, Colonels Qiao Liang and Wang Xiangsui. Both colonels are graduates of the top senior military strategy staff college in China. Fortunately, the book was published in both Chinese and English. Their book covers a considerable amount of strategic military and historical information related to stealth, economic and internet types of unrestricted warfare.

Once I commenced reading the book I could no longer just be a Beijing tourist, so while Karen was sightseeing, I read the book from cover to cover and repeatedly reviewed specific parts. In 2008, I was 86 years old, a retired Navy LCDR, a graduate of the Navy Post Graduate School and a veteran of four wars. With this background, I realized these two young colonels were military geniuses. The book made it clear why some nations rise and become leading economic and military world powers and then collapse. It was shocking for me to realize what this book indicated for America. The prognosis was similar to what happened to the British Empire in the last 75 years. Based on their thinking, America is now on the way to decline and collapse in the next five or six decades as a significant or important economic and military world power. Their thinking correlated to much of what I posited in my first book, *Conversations with a WW-II Corsair Fighter Pilot.*

In 2017, I read *Unrestricted Warfare…* again and decided to write this book. This is simply the opinion of a 96 year old veteran who has witnessed how a few truly great American leaders of the past 75 years governed this great nation.

Nations ascend, nations decline, nations collapse. Throughout the recorded history of humankind, nations have been founded. Some become leading economic and military

---

13   https://en.wikipedia.org/wiki/The_New_Colossus

14   https://talkingpointsmemo.com/news/2000-migrant-minors-separated-border

15   https://www.huffingtonpost.com/entry/sarah-huckabee-sanders-cites-bible-as-reason-to-detain-immigrant-children_us_5b22c277e4b0d4fc01fc9b1d

16   https://www.huffingtonpost.com/entry/jeff-sessions-trump-immigration-family-separation-border_us_5b23ff24e4b0783ae128f90d

world powers and leaders. Inevitably, the rise is followed by eventual decline and then collapse – sometimes quickly, sometimes after centuries. The Roman Empire and British Empire are just two examples. You might even consider the Third Reich as another, albeit short-lived example.

A common thread running through the history of the decline and fall of nations and empires is a shift from the fundamental principles responsible for their initial success.

Of all the great powerful nations and empires since the collapse of the Roman Empire 2000 years ago, nothing is more startling and seemingly impossible to believe than the sudden meltdown and destruction of the once almighty British Empire. As a young man in the late 1920s and 30s, I remember my father, grandfather, uncles and important political and military leaders praising and admiring the mighty British Empire. In those days, the slogan "The Sun Never Sets on the British Empire" clearly explained that Britain held vast global territories and colonies. All day, every day, 24 hours a day, all across the globe, the sun would be shining on a part of the great British Empire, just as it had on the Spanish Empire before it. From the mid-1800s until 1914, the British Empire was the "world policeman". Then from 1914 to 1949, as a result of 35 years of wars and turmoil, the British Empire was reduced to nothing more than a few weak, struggling islands off the coast of Europe. By the end of World War II, Britain and Europe had been taken down as the leading economic and cultural continent of the world as a result of two world wars. In 2017, Britain left the European Union, possibly to its detriment and is now on the way to further decline and perhaps collapse in the next few decades as Scotland continues its attempts at independence.

After the end of World War II, the United States broke away from the isolationist stance put in place by the 1776 Founders and replaced Britain in the role of "world policeman". Since 1945, America has been engaging in expensive and often illegal interventions in the affairs of other nations. As a Navy aircraft carrier Corsair fighter pilot, I have been engaged in some of these conflicts. Often, the reason for these conflicts was due to jihad or other insurrection based on religious beliefs or disputes between various religious groups. These many interventions have resulted in a terrible waste of life and economic resources considering that military personnel were often fighting over fictitious religious beliefs. You can read more about this in my book, *Religions, The Curse of America and the Western World*.

America, the first modern nation in the world, was founded as a nation managed by its citizens rather than by principles of fictitious religions. But in the mid-1900s, a Christian political movement commonly referred to as the "moral majority" convinced Americans to elect politicians who referred to themselves as "conservative Christian politicians". Since the 1950s, America has departed from the goal and ambitions of the 1776 Founders to govern without the influence of a fictitious God and as a result America has become a declining nation in the last 60 years.

Obviously, since the presidential election in 1981, the political leaders of America shifted the manner America would be governed with the majority of the politicians elected by the so called "moral majority voters". I believe that since 1981, America has gradually declined as a major economic power because the fundamental principles for America's initial success suddenly shifted in that presidential election. Since 1981, American politicians who refer to themselves as "conservative religious politicians" and who have won elections by convincing voters they are closer to God than their political opponents have taken control of our government. When America was governed and led by intelligent politicians in the past years, the lives of all Americans were improving. People of color, gays, lesbians, transgender and so-called straight citizens were all beginning to enjoy a better life in America. Then came the sudden shift from a more tolerant and friendly America to the America we are living in as of 2017. This is a definite shift from the type of government envisioned by the 1776 Founders of America.

Engaging in illegal wars per the intent and ambitions of the so-called "moral majority" and by self-proclaimed patriotic "religious conservative politicians" elected to our Senate and House has weakened the country.

Consider the cost of the most recent illegal war in Iraq. Had it been avoided, the billions of dollars spent on the illegal war could have been used to provide university-level education for every child in America, along with free health care for all U.S. citizens similar to what exists in Sweden and a few other first class nations.

During the 2016 election campaign, the majority of American citizens were disappointed by the caliber of the presidential candidates. The 2016 campaign was an embarrassing display of the most ridiculous and most incompetent persons ever to campaign for the office of President of the United States. As a former Navy fighter pilot, veteran of four wars (two legal wars and two illegal wars) and a graduate of the Navy Post Graduate School, I realized regardless of which candidate won the election this nation would not be governed with the same level of intelligent leadership it has had in the past. It was obviously a blueprint for failure. It is indeed sad and disheartening to realize this once great nation formerly led by great political leaders and presidents such as Abraham Lincoln, Teddy Roosevelt, Woodrow Wilson, Franklin Roosevelt and Harry Truman could not produce a candidate of similar stature. In fact, in the Trump administration, many people in top federal positions have no governmental experience and little or no experience in the subject matter of the offices to which they have been appointed. Their disregard for truth and the order of law becomes more apparent and frightening every day. Recently a Fox News poll discovered that Americans think Donald Trump is an unstable, dishonest, immoral bully. And 56% of poll respondents said Trump was "tearing the country apart".[17]

Meanwhile, in the Far East, a struggling poor nation, China, commenced to grow

17   http://www.huffingtonpost.com/entry/donald-trump-unstable-bully-fox-news-poll_us_59a8d931e4b0dfaafcef376a

starting 75 years ago once it adopted principles similar to those of the founding of the United States in 1776. That is, a nation with no fictitious god; a nation led and governed by patriotic politicians.

Despite all the ridiculous American propaganda from our conservative Christian politicians – the self-called conservatives – the citizens of China enjoy living in a nation governed by humans who are not following the beliefs of a religion based on mythology. I know this because since retiring from the Navy in 1961, I have spent much of my life in China, Taiwan and Hong Kong. My youngest son John and I spent much of March 2017 in Hong Kong and Shanghai, China. I can assure you that the Chinese citizens are very proud of the fact their leaders have taken back Hong Kong from the British and now China has become the second greatest economy in the world. All of this has happened with without dependence on leaders who believe in fictitious gods. Unlike America, China is not governed by "religious conservative politicians".

My Important Message to All World Citizens

Now in 2018, I am 96 years old and I want to leave an important message to all intelligent world citizens. The three largest current global military powers should have no fear of having an old-fashioned war with bombs and guns like World Wars One and Two.

China's leaders should be aware America is no military threat to China. And America's leaders should know China is no military threat to America. The same thing is true regarding Russia. Leaders of these powerful nations know very well there is no winner in any kind of military bombing and shooting conflicts between "major nations" as was proven in World Wars One and Two.

All of this has been made very clear by the two of the most intelligent military strategists in China and the world, Colonels Qiao Liang and Wang Xiangsui who in their great book stated that "All future wars between major nations will be fought with intelligent, strategic economic and political strategy". Old fashioned gun and bomb type wars will be fought by the so-called and self-appointed "World Policeman" nation with small stupid rogue nations similar to North Korea and Iraq but there will never be another war similar to WW-Two between major nations. What our American political leaders are not aware of is there is and has been a war in progress for the past two or three decades. As I said in my first book, "All future wars between major nations will be fought economically and strategically". A perfect example of this is Russia's meddling in the 2016 presidential election. [18]

Over the past decades, China has been aggressively investing in nations all over the world, greatly increasing its influence in the United Nations while America has been busily

---

18   https://www.nytimes.com/news-event/russian-election-hacking

engaged in the useless bombings and military attacks of small nations in illegal wars not approved by the United Nations.

Current Christian and Islamic political leaders of the Western world are waging disastrous wars and spawning hatred. The question everyone must consider is, "Will our world collapse as a result of these 'God Wars' or is it possible that with education, science and common sense the Western world can be saved?" Obviously there can be peace when the adherents and proponents of Christian and Islamic religions are removed from the governments of all Western nations. Otherwise, one or another of the nations will eventually drop an atomic bomb and that may result in the collapse of the Western world. The best solution to bring about peace is for all nations of the Western world to be governed by politicians who believe in freedom of religion and freedom from religion "WITH ABSOLUTE SEPARATION OF CHURCH AND STATE".

Humanism and Why it Matters

Richard Dawkins (pictured with me below) is the famous Oxford University professor who is the world's foremost Humanist leader. In this role, Richard has all but eliminated the political power of the Christian leaders in Great Britain and most European nations.

People who attend the many seminars and conferences where Professor Dawkins speaks have noted that Professor Dawkins considers the 1776 Founders of our nation the foremost and most brilliant men of their time.

So what is Humanism and why does it matter?

The American Humanist Association's tagline "Good without a God" is another aspect of how America's founders viewed the basic tenets of the country. The association defines Humanism as a progressive life stance that, without supernaturalism, affirms our ability and responsibility to lead meaningful, ethical lives capable of adding to the greater good of humanity. Humanistic psychology is a psychological perspective that rose to prominence in Germany in the 1500s. Humanism is a progressive life stance that, without theism or other supernatural beliefs, affirms our ability and responsibility to lead meaningful, ethical lives capable of adding to the greater good of humanity.

Humanism is a rational philosophy informed by science, inspired by art, and motivated by compassion. Affirming the dignity of each human being, it supports the maximization of individual liberty and opportunity consonant with social and planetary responsibility. It advocates the extension of participatory democracy and the expansion of the open society, standing for human rights and social justice. Free of supernaturalism, it recognizes human beings as a part of nature and holds that values-be they religious, ethical, social, or political-have their source in human experience and culture. Humanism thus derives the goals of life from human need and interest rather than from theological or ideological abstractions, and asserts that humanity must take responsibility for its own destiny.

Humanism is a democratic and ethical life stance which affirms that human beings have the right and responsibility to give meaning and shape to their own lives. It stands for the building of a more humane society through an ethics based on human and other natural values in a spirit of reason and free inquiry through human capabilities. It is not theistic, and it does not accept supernatural views of reality.

Humanism is an approach to life based on reason and our common humanity, recognizing that moral values are properly founded on human nature and experience alone.[19]

With its roots running from Socrates through the Renaissance, this approach positively emphasizes individuals' inherent drive towards self-actualization, the process of realizing and expressing one's own capabilities and creativity. [20] It helps all people gain the belief that they are inherently good. It adopts a holistic approach to human existence and pays special attention to such phenomena as creativity, free will, and positive human potential. It encourages viewing ourselves as a "whole person" greater than the sum of our parts and encourages self-exploration rather than the study of behavior in other people. Humanistic thinking acknowledges spiritual aspiration as an integral part of the psyche. Primarily, this

---

19   https://americanhumanist.org/what-is-humanism/definition-of-humanism/
20   http://www.academia.edu/27658857/Humanistic_Psychology

Tom McBride and Richard Dawkins at the 2011 Boston Humanist Annual Convention

type of thinking encourages a self-awareness and mindfulness that helps people change their state of mind and behavior from one set of reactions to a healthier one with self-awareness that is more productive and thoughtful. Essentially, this approach allows the merging of mindfulness and behavioral therapy, with positive social support. More than any other thinking, Humanistic-Existential thinking models our 1776 Founders model of democracy.

America's Founders and Humanism

A subset of the 1776 Founders, Benjamin Franklin, Thomas Jefferson and Thomas Paine, were acquainted with the Humanist movement. Because of their understanding of Humanist ideals, they convinced the rest of the 1776 Founders to establish the first nation in the history of the world with "Freedom of Religion, Freedom from Religion with Absolute Separation of Church and State".

The 1776 Founders were led by George Washington, Benjamin Franklin, Thomas Jefferson and James Madison. They were well-educated men of the "Enlightened Age" and free of the Southern European and Irish "religious dogma" of society control. So they were well aware of the consequence of permitting religion to play any role in the Declaration of Independence. It was Thomas Jefferson who devised and documented the concept of the "Wall between religion and state". But fanatic Christian conservative politicians have been attempting to destroy that wall ever since the death of the last two 1776 Founders of America, Thomas Jefferson and John Adams in 1826. America's current religious conservative political leaders along with the majority of our federal political leaders are also attempting to destroy the wall by espousing the story that goes "I am closer to your God than my opponent or any other politician". What would Ben Franklin, Thomas Jefferson and Thomas Paine think of them?

The Early American Economy

When the brilliant, enlightened 1776 Founders of the United States (primarily led by Benjamin Franklin; author and brilliant philosopher, Thomas Paine; and 33-year old Thomas Jefferson) established the first nation in the modern world with no fictitious god, with Freedom of and Freedom from Religion, with absolute Separation of State and Religion, our Founding Fathers espoused the need for isolationism – to stay out of the conflicts of other nations. The new nation developed one of the top economies in the world in less than 75 years, just like what China has accomplished in the last 75 years. It is interesting to note that according to the Smithsonian Museum's archives, in 1776, only 17 percent of the new nation's citizens belonged to a church of any kind based on information from the first census. [21]

Former Presidents Thomas Jefferson and John Adams were the last surviving members of the original American revolutionaries who had stood up to the British Empire and forged a new political system in the former colonies. While they both believed in democracy and life, liberty and the pursuit of happiness, their opinions on how to achieve these ideals diverged over time. Thomas Jefferson and John Adams were the last surviving members of the original American revolutionaries who had stood up to the British Empire and forged a new political system in the former colonies. In 1826, on the same day, July 4th, these two remnants of the 1776 Founders died within five hours of each other.

After the deaths of Adams and Jefferson, in less than 74 years (1826 to 1901) Christian leaders changed America into a predominately Christian nation spending vast amounts of money influencing the voters of America to abandon the goals and ambitions of the Founders. Despite these efforts, by 1901, the Christians had not yet inserted their religious doctrine into the political governing of America. Our great nation prospered and became the leading economic nation of the world. But by the 1970s, the some politicians started referring to themselves as the moral majority - this group was associated with the Christian right and the Republican Party[22].

In 1981, the so called "Christian moral majority" won the presidential election and the gradual decline of America commenced.

The "Christian conservative politicians"[23] finally took control of the American government. Since 1981, slowly and surely as occurs in all nations where religious-oriented leaders become the nation's leaders, America has experienced the top 10 to 15 percent of the population controlling most of the wealth of the nation, the decline of the middle class and one in eight Americans is considered "officially poor". Nearly one-third of the American poor are children.[24] These are the typical conditions of third-world religiously-governed nations.

For a good example of how the religious conservative politicians have co-opted America's messaging, you need look no further than the story of the Pledge of Allegiance, which is recited by every school child every day and at public meetings such as city council meetings. The Pledge of Allegiance is an expression of allegiance to the flag of the United States and the republic of the United States of America. It was composed by Rear Admiral George Balch in 1887, later revised by Francis Bellamy in 1892 and formally adopted by Congress as the pledge in 1942.[25] The official name "The Pledge of Allegiance" was adopted in 1945. The last change in language came on Flag Day 1954 when the words "under

---

21   http://www.huffingtonpost.com/maria-mayo/religion-in-america-on-july-4-1776_b_3542203.html
22   https://en.wikipedia.org/wiki/Moral_Majority
23   http://talkingpointsmemo.com/cafe/brief-history-of-the-christian-right
24   http://poverty.umich.edu/about/poverty-facts/
25   https://en.wikipedia.org/wiki/Pledge_of_Allegiance

God" were added by "conservative Christian politicians".

The Thomas Jefferson Humanist Society, LLC is now campaigning for the government to modify the Pledge of Allegiance to again comply with the goals and ambitions of the America's founders. The latest 1954 statement "under God" must be replaced with "with Freedom of Religion and Freedom from Religion With Absolute Separation of State and Religion".

Great American Leaders

The government concept of America's founders resulted in a new nation that would rapidly grow and prosper and achieve economic prosperity for all common citizens. Let's take a look at what our country's early leaders proclaimed while governing our nation. George Washington and Thomas Jefferson are without a doubt among America's earliest great leaders. Others include James Madison and Benjamin Franklin.

I've always enjoyed studying history. In August 1945, President Truman had an atomic bomb dropped in Japan and a few weeks later the Second World War was over. At the time, I was a Navy F4U Corsair fighter pilot aboard the USS Bennington. Shortly thereafter our Air Group One returned to San Francisco. On my return to America, I was transferred to the Philadelphia Navy aircraft factory and the Patuxent Navy Air Base to serve as a test pilot, flying the latest fighter planes produced by America's aircraft firms.

While living in Philadelphia, I became fascinated with the history of all of the 1776 Founders of America and the historical sites in the city. Who was the actual team leader of the "1776 Founders of America"? I just had to know.

In less than a year of research, I realized who was the team leader who made certain the new nation would have no king, no religious leader and "Freedom of and Freedom from Religion with absolute Separation of Church and State". The father of the new nation, the team leader of the 1776 Founders of America obviously was the man who in his previous years had become a famous scientist, inventor of all types of gadgets, machines, the authority regarding the causes and means to defend persons from lightning strikes, discoverer of the Gulf Stream, the man who brought the French Navy to help the 13 colonies defeat the mighty British Empire, Benjamin Franklin (1706-1790). All of the 1776 Founders were intelligent patriotic individuals, but none had the genius, patience in planning all activities, projects and programs as Ben, who was the wealthiest, oldest, and most intelligent man on the team. Franklin lived his entire life in what is often referred to as the "Age of Reason" or "Age of Enlightenment". [26] The three major themes of this period were reason, deism (the belief that God is knowable through reason and nature instead of by divine revelation), and skepticism of religious dogma. The Enlightenment also included a range of ideas centered on reason as the primary source of authority and legitimacy, and advanced ideals such as

---

26   https://www.history.com/topics/enlightenment

liberty, progress, tolerance, fraternity, constitutional government, and separation of church and state.

How can I be sure Ben was the team leader? During my Navy career, the Navy sent me to the University of Mississippi where I graduated near the top of my class with a business degree. The Navy also sent me to the Navy Post Graduate School for a year where I was taught the technique of researching information for developing programs for missions and attacks. All the information I could gather while living in Philadelphia indicated Ben had been carefully developing close relationships with the top leaders of the 13 colonies and he also established a close relationship with the most popular man in the colonies, General George Washington.

In England, Franklin met Thomas Paine who was a well-known promoter of all facets of the Age of Enlightenment and Age of Reason. Franklin advised Paine to emigrate to America and gave him letters of recommendation.[27] Paine's famous 47-page pamphlet *Common Sense* was distributed throughout the 13 original American colonies and due to the many copies sold (500,000) Paine's influence on the Declaration of Independence of July 4, 1776 was profound. [28, 29]

When becoming acquainted with young Thomas Jefferson, Ben learned that Jefferson (young enough to be Ben's grandson) had the same opinion of kings, popes, religion and fictitious gods as he and Tom Paine. Ben made sure Thomas Jefferson, then at about age 33, was the person to prepare and write the document that later became the Constitution of the new nation. Then he had Jefferson present it to the members of the Congressional Congress in Philadelphia.

Just as Ben had gone about the establishment of libraries, fire departments, and a university, Ben (at this time of his late life suffering from old age problems) simply consulted and encouraged the younger and most energetic men of the 13 arguing jealous colonies to join together and found the new nation with no king, religious leader or god. They got it done.

In my opinion, after the founders of our country, there have been only a handful of great Republican leaders: Abe Lincoln, Teddy Roosevelt, FDR (FDR ran as a Democrat but he was actually a Republican just as his cousin Teddy); Franklin had to run as a Democrat as the New York Republicans would have nothing to do with FDR. Other great and patriotic leaders of my lifetime were Brigadier General/Senator Barry Goldwater and General George C. Marshall. It is important to compare political speeches and expressed political ideas of all future political candidates to what we know from the quotes of some of America's best and brightest.

---

27   http://www.let.rug.nl/usa/biographies/thomas-paine/
28   https://www.history.com/this-day-in-history/thomas-paine-publishes-common-sense
29   http://www.let.rug.nl/usa/biographies/thomas-paine/

On the pages that follow, I've included their portraits and some of their quotes which resonate even today, sometimes with my own comments.

President George Washington

The United States is in no sense founded upon the Christian Doctrine.

The Constitution is the guide which I never will abandon.

Truth will ultimately prevail where there is pains to bring it to light.

Benjamin Franklin

A lighthouse provides greater guidance than religion.

We are all born ignorant, but one must work hard to remain stupid.

To follow by faith alone is to follow blindly.

The way to see by Faith is to shut the Eye of Reason.

President Thomas Jefferson

On http://www.nobeliefs.com/jefferson.htm, you will find and read all of the quotes the great president had to say about the myths, legends, impossible to believe stories in the bible of the Christian religion. Jefferson was without question one of the most brilliant men of the 1776 Founders of America. These great men had the education, knowledge and patriotism to found the first nation in the world with no king, pope or belief in some fictitious god to direct and influence its governing.

I do not find in orthodox Christianity one redeeming feature.

In every country and every age, the priest had been hostile to Liberty.

Difference of opinion is advantageous in religion. The several sects perform the office of a Censor - over each other.

Question the boldness even the existence of God; because, if there be one, he must more approve of the homage of reason, than that of blindfolded fear.

The whole history of these books (the Gospels) is so defective and doubtful that it seems vain to attempt minute enquiry into it: and such tricks have been played with their text, and with the texts of other books relating to them, that we have a right, from that cause, to entertain much doubt what parts of them are genuine. In the New Testament there is internal evidence that parts of it have proceeded from an extraordinary man; and that other parts are of the fabric of very inferior minds. It is as easy to separate those parts, as to pick out diamonds from dunghills.

Thomas Paine

The following quotes are from Paine's *Age of Reason*.

It is from the Bible that man has learned cruelty, rapine, and murder; for the belief of a cruel God makes a cruel man.

One good schoolmaster is of more use than a hundred priests.

I do not believe in the creed professed by the Jewish church, by the Roman church, by the Greek church, by the Turkish church, by the Protestant church, not by any church that I know of. My own mind is my own church.

I have always strenuously supported the right of every man to his own opinion, however different that opinion might be to mine. He who denies to another this right, makes a slave of himself to his present opinion, because he precludes himself the right of changing it.

Of all the systems of religion that were ever invented, there is no more derogatory to the Almighty, more unedifying to man, more repugnant to reason, and more contradictory to itself than this thing called Christianity. Too absurd for belief, too impossible to convince, and too inconsistent for practice, it renders the heart torpid or produces only atheists or fanatics. As an engine of power, it serves the purpose of despotism, and as a means of wealth, the avarice of priests, but so far as respects the good of man in general it leads to nothing here or hereafter.

President John Adams

A government of laws, and not of men.

Fear is the foundation of most governments.

President James Madison

The purpose of separation of church and state is to keep forever from these shores the ceaseless strife that has soaked the soil of Europe with blood for centuries.

In no instance have... the churches been guardians of the liberties of the people.

Religion flourishes in greater purity, without than with the aid of Government.

Religious bondage shackles and debilitates the mind and unfits it for every noble enterprise, every expanded prospect.

President Abraham Lincoln

In my opinion, Abraham Lincoln was the greatest Republican president in history. If he were alive today, what would he do about how cleverly the right wing Republican politicians funded by the Koch brothers would be fooling American voters from about 1980 to the present time? Will patriotic Republican voters finally wake up????

My comments follow Lincoln's quotes which are italicized.

Tact is the ability to describe others "as they see themselves".

I dream of a place and a time where America will once again be seen as the last best hope of earth.

Character is like a tree and reputation like its shadow. The shadow is what we think of it; the tree is the real thing.

You can fool all the people some of the time, and some of the people all the time, but you cannot fool all the people all the time.

I want it said of me by those who knew me best, that I always plucked a thistle and planted a flower where I thought a flower would grow.

Let not him who is houseless pull down the house of another, but let him work diligently and build one for

himself, thus by example assuring that his own shall be safe from violence when built.
I don't think much of a man who is not wiser today than he was yesterday.

No matter how much the cats fight, there always seem to be plenty of kittens.

(What Abe meant of course was fight and argue but get it done. We should promote the idea that all Congress members and Senators should send a handwritten letter mentioning these quotes to the president every four months while serving in the Senate or House.)

We the people are the rightful masters of both Congress and the courts, not to overthrow the Constitution but to overthrow the men who pervert the Constitution.

(I wonder if in the upcoming 2018 elections and beyond whether patriotic American voters will vote the straight ticket for their party or vote for politicians who have ideals and dreams of our 1776 Founders for the future of America? Or will they vote for politicians heavily financed by special interest billionaires? All patriotic Americans must remember that the religious conservative politicians of the 1920s and 30s destroyed the League of Nations, thereby helping to bring on World War II. And now they are trying to destroy the United Nations set up by FDR, General Marshall, and Winston Churchill. As a registered Republican for more than 70 years, I will vote for anyone but a billionaire-financed so-called religious conservative politician regardless of their party affiliation.)

A house divided against itself cannot stand.

(Surely all "thinking voters" of any party have to be well aware that for the past four decades since the religious conservative billionaires took control of a significant segment of our now serving politicians now serving in the House and Senate on both sides of the will not negotiate in good faith, they will not adhere to normal legislative procedures of past generations, they will always commence political negotiations with people who have a different view on any subject in a combative tone. If all politicians in a meeting do not think just as the religious conservative politicians they simply walk out of the House or Senate or shut down the government.)

President Teddy Roosevelt

Theodore "Teddy" Roosevelt served first as a vice president and then president (1901 to 1909). Without a doubt, "Teddy" was second only to the Founder of the Republican Party, Abraham Lincoln, as one of the greatest Republican presidents.

In fact, history has proven there has never been a truly good Republican president since the passing of Teddy Roosevelt. Teddy was the president who crushed the corrupt corporations of America in the years 1901 to 1909. Teddy was the hero of the common hard-working people of America. Teddy was also the hero of my grandfather, my parents and all of my uncles.

My comments follow Teddy Roosevelt's quotes which are italicized.

It is not the critic who counts; not the man who points out how the strong man stumbles, or where the doer of deeds could have done them better. The credit belongs to the man who is actually in the arena, whose face is marred by dust and sweat and blood; who strives valiantly; who errs, who comes short again and again, because there is no effort without error and shortcoming; but who does actually strive to do the deeds; who knows great enthusiasms, the great devotions; who spends himself in a worthy cause; who at the best knows in the end the triumph of high achievement, and who at the worst, if he fails, at least fails while daring greatly, so that his place shall never be with those cold and timid souls who neither know victory nor defeat.

(Can you imagine any single one of the current right wing Senate or House Republican politicians even thinking about a "working man or woman"? The current Republican Senate and House politicians are now "owned and directed" by the anti-American billionaire Koch brothers. These current Republican politicians only think about how to vote to make sure their SEAT is bought and paid for again and again by the billionaire Koch brothers and other wealthy donors in the next election. These politicians do not dare to vote to the tune of the very best president of the last century, President Teddy Roosevelt.)

In any moment of decision, the best thing you can do is the right thing, the next best thing is the wrong thing, and the worst thing you can do is nothing.

(The current Republican right wing Koch brothers politicians do as directed and just shut down the government or do nothing. PERIOD. Their primary goal is to get Koch Brother Funds to win the next election.)

(OK, straight party ticket voters. Do you realize that you're voting for politicians who want to have no real government and who vote to shut down the government if they cannot have all believe as they believe. Who vote to keep the USA sliding toward the status of a third world nation whereby the top few percent of American billionaires purchase the politicians' seats in Congress and control the wealth of the nation, while we common folks wear their military uniforms, fight the wars and work hard and struggle to take care of their children and grandchildren?)

President Franklin Delano Roosevelt "FDR"

Franklin Delano Roosevelt, FDR, 32nd president of the United States was the only president ever elected to serve four straight terms (1933 to 1945). He is now regarded as one of the three greatest presidents in the history of the United States. He led the nation through the depression years (1933-38) and then along with Winston Churchill and General Marshall led the allies to victory over Germany and Japan. He was the nephew of the great Republican president Theodore Roosevelt. In my "Conversations..." book, I mention how I eventually learned the Republican Party had been taken over by corrupt politicians and had become the "Enemy Within" with regards to the welfare of the common people of America as well as the goals and ambitions of the 1776 Founders of America.

My comments follow FDR's quotes which are italicized.

The school is the last expenditure upon which America should be willing to economize.

(The right wing nuts hate this comment.)

A conservative is a man with two perfectly good legs who, however, has never learned how to walk forward.

(The Republican politicians now in Congress are not conservatives, they are right wing idiots.)

True individual freedom cannot exist without economic security and independence. People who are hungry and out of a job are the stuff of which dictatorships are made.

(Strange the conservative Christian politicians now in Congress have never been aware of this.)

Democracy cannot succeed unless those who express their choice are prepared to choose wisely. The real safeguard of democracy, therefore, is education.

(Think about the fact no current Republican politician will ever financially support significant educational programs.)

The only thing we have to fear is fear itself.

(Religious conservative politicians are afraid of the world so they just want to bomb nations they dislike.)

A nation that destroys its soils destroys itself. Forests are the lungs of our land, purifying the air and giving fresh strength to our people.

(In the 1930s, FDR could not have known what damage the right wing politicians would be doing to our nation's wellbeing since the election of Ronald Reagan in 1981 as they simply do not believe in the danger of global warming.)

The only sure bulwark of continuing liberty is a government strong enough to protect the interests of the people, and a people strong enough and well enough informed to maintain its sovereign control over the government.

(The multi-billions the right wing backers of the Republican Party have spent influencing the American people that government control of Wall Street and major financial institutions is a bad policy has been very successful over the last five decades.)

Here is my principle: Taxes shall be levied according to ability to pay. That is the only American principle.

(When right wing politicians hear statements such as this, they really get very angry.)

Don't forget what I discovered that over ninety percent of all national deficits from 1921 to 1939 were caused by payments for past, present, and future wars.

(Our right wing politicians "self-appointed world policeman" are never going to give up bombing other nations.)

I ask you to judge me by the enemies I have made.

(Me too.)

I am neither bitter nor cynical but I do wish there was less immaturity in political thinking.

(I do believe all Americans would like to see this come about in our capital but the right wing prefers to shut down the government rather than negotiate.)

Senator Barry Goldwater

Barry Goldwater was five-term United States Senator from Arizona (1953–65, 1969–87) and the Republican Party's nominee for president in the 1964 election. An articulate and charismatic figure during the first half of the 1960s, he was known as "Mr. Conservative".

Goldwater is most often credited for sparking the resurgence of the American conservative political movement in the 1960s. He also had a substantial impact on the libertarian movement.

My comments follow Goldwater's quote which is italicized.

On religious issues there can be little or no compromise. There is no position on which people are so immovable as their religious beliefs. There is no more powerful ally one can claim in a debate than Jesus Christ, or God, or Allah, or whatever one calls this Supreme Being. But like any powerful weapon, the use of God's name on one's behalf should be used sparingly. The religious factions that are growing throughout our land are not using their religious clout with wisdom. They are trying to force government leaders into following their position 100 percent. If you disagree with these religious groups on a particular moral issue, they complain, they threaten you with a loss of money or votes or both.

I'm frankly sick and tired of the political preachers across this country telling me as a citizen that if I want to be a moral person, I must believe in "A," "B," "C" and "D." Just who do they think they are? And from where do they presume to claim the right to dictate their moral beliefs to me?

And I am even angrier as a legislator who must endure the threats of every religious group who thinks it has some God-granted right to control my vote on every roll call in the Senate. I am warning them today: I will fight them every step of the way if they try to dictate their moral convictions to all Americans in the name of "conservatism."

General Goldwater was a military leader and spoke the truth, even after becoming a politician. Too bad none of the current Republican leaders ever wore a military uniform.

General George C. Marshall

General George C. Marshall, in my opinion, was America's greatest World War Two general and America's most brilliant Secretary of State. There has never been another general, admiral or secretary of state equal to him. PERIOD .

My comments follow Marshall's quotes which are italicized.

When a thing is done, it's done. Don't look back. Look forward to your next objective.

Don't fight the problem, decide it.

Passive inactivity, because you have not been given specific instructions to do this or to do that, is a serious deficiency.

Go right straight down the road, to do what is best, and to do it frankly and without evasion.

I will give you the best I have.

I was very careful to send Mr. Roosevelt every few days a statement of our casualties. I tried to keep before him all the time the casualty results because you get hardened to these things and you have to be very careful to keep them always in the forefront of your mind.

Albert Einstein, Carl Sagan, and Richard Dawkins are brilliant men who support the concept that religion is, as Donald Trump might say, "fake news".

Albert Einstein

I am a deeply religious nonbeliever - this is a somewhat new religion.

I do not believe in the God of Theology who rewards good and punishes evil.

Carl Sagan

For me, it is far better to grasp the Universe as it really is than to persist in delusion, however satisfying and reassuring.

Who are we? We find that we live on an insignificant planet of a humdrum star lost in a galaxy tucked away in some forgotten corner of a universe in which there are far more galaxies than people.

Richard Dawkins

Faith is the great cop-out, the great excuse to evade the need to think and evaluate evidence. Faith is belief in spite of, even perhaps because of, the lack of evidence.

I am against religion because it teaches us to be satisfied with not understanding the world.

Thomas Jefferson Humanist Society

At the time of the "invention" of all the Western World's religions, 99% of the population was illiterate. They had no idea the world was a round tiny spec in the vast universe or even that there was a universe, or what the small lights in the night sky were.

What Can We Do Now?

As a student at the Navy Post Graduate School in Monterey, CA, I was taught to never criticize an attack or a mission plan, the makeup of a command structure or the management program of an organization unless I also presented what I considered a more effective and efficient system and program. For that reason, I will present my beliefs and opinions as to how all Americans can pitch in and help save America from further decline and collapse. I do believe as a result of my extensive research and lengthy visits to the presidential homes, libraries, memorials and my reading all history books possible about the two greatest presidents of the past 125 years, Abe Lincoln and Franklin Roosevelt, I can pass on what I believe each of the great men would advise if they were alive today.

Even though you and I are no Teddy Roosevelt; FDR, Truman or General Marshall, there is much we can do to help bring America back to being the nation envisioned by its Founders.

Can America's decline and collapse be stopped? It's up patriotic Americans of all ages. All citizens need to **read and think critically, ask hard questions and demand answers**. Keep pushing. List your priorities and let your elected officials know what you think of their job performance and their positions on issues. Regardless of how well-funded they are, they are not psychic and need to hear from you, OFTEN.

Likewise, **talk to candidates for political office**; tell them about your concerns. Offer to help with campaigns for those candidates you think can reverse the decline and prevent the collapse of our country. To help save America, it is important to think about the goals and ambitions of the 1776 Founders for the future of the America and only vote for politicians who have the same beliefs.

VOTE! Think globally, vote locally. I live in California, which has the world's fifth largest economy.[30] The election for California's next governor has national and international implications and effects[31]. Of particular concern to me in 2018 is the race for California's governor. California voters will decide between John Cox, a Republican, and Lt. Gov. Gavin Newsom, a Democrat. WOW what a difference we will have from our current California government if John Cox, the Republican, wins the election. I have been a registered Republican for 76 years but have also been a dedicated Humanist for the past three decades. So why am I campaigning so aggressively for a Democrat? The reason is the Republican Party is no longer the "Grand OLD Party" of the common citizens of America. The GOP is now "God's Own Party". It is the party of the

---

30   http://www.latimes.com/business/la-fi-california-economy-gdp-20180504-story.html
31   https://www.politico.com/newsletters/california-playbook/2018/04/30/kamala-harris-builds-an-online-army-john-cox-gets-boost-from-outside-group-pence-heads-to-calexico-266615

billionaires promoting only their own interests. The platform of the current GOP now is informed by God-loving politicians led by Vice President Mike Pence, former Gov. of Indiana. Imagine a California governed by a politician so similar to the current US Vice President. California might become a state similar to Indiana. A state where the government dislikes Humanists, considers any women for her personal reasons not wanting another child to be a criminal[32]; lesbians, gay men and transgender persons as anti-Americans. [33]

In all get togethers I have attended, John Cox praises Vice President Pence and the State of Indiana as one of the best states of America. In my opinion, of all the Republican politicians in America, Mike Pence is the number one politician who hates the 1776 Founders for founding a Humanist nation "With Freedom of and Freedom from Religion, with absolute separation of Church and State".

In fact Mike Pence's brother stated publicly when his brother Mike was selected as Trump's running mate, "*Thankfully we will have a government governed in the manner God intended*". I do not think President Trump is of the same opinion as Vice President Mike Pence or John Cox. I believe that both Cox and Pence were brainwashed as youngsters in Sunday school just as I was. I wonder if either of them has ever read a history book or a book about Ben Franklin, Thomas Jefferson or Thomas Paine? I did not vote for Trump but now I live in fear that if anything should happen to Trump, this anti-American Pence would become our President.

Create a third party. In recent years I have realized the only patriotic American voters are independent voters who have no use for the platforms of either the GOP or the Democratic Party, Next year I no doubt will also become an independent voter. America should have a third party that I'd like to call "The America Founders Party". The "AFP" party with me at age 97 as its founder. The "AFP" party would mostly be led by former military persons who have served and fought for America.

Support education. Our youth, and even our adult and senior populations, need to understand civics, history, economics, and the basics of leadership. Support leadership education for our young people who will be tomorrow's leaders.

Volunteer. Surely you can find a few hours each week to work on programs important to you and your family's wellbeing, while making a difference to others.

---

32   https://www.cnn.com/2018/04/20/politics/mike-pence-indiana-abortion-law-court-unconstitutional/index.html

33   https://www.huffingtonpost.com/entry/mike-pence-religious-freedom-law-indiana_us_57c839b9e4b0a22de09446d8

Changes to the Tax Code

Most important of the changes I'd like to see is the subject of federal taxes. Presidents as great as Abraham Lincoln and FDR upon taking office would surely make tax reform the number one priority of their first term.

Priority should be given to eliminating all federal tax-free organizations of any type. If any foundation or organization earns money in any way, whether donations, gifts, collections of any kind, the organization should pay the federal government 10 percent of the income received each year. This means every religious organization, the Salvation Army, Red Cross; even Boy Scouts and Girl Scouts. There cannot be any tax-free organization in America. Period. Think about non-profits you're familiar with. Their executives are taking home enormous salaries. For example, the president of the Girl Scouts earns $383,380 annually. [34] And that's off the backs of little girls selling cookies. The head of the Red Cross was paid $561,210 in 2010. [35] Much of that compensation comes from people who think they're donating for disaster relief and from selling the blood that generous people donate to help others. Don't kid yourself, non-profits are big business and many pay big salaries.

Next: The federal tax system to remain as is with this exception. Regardless of the write-offs of the current federal tax system, no corporation in America will pay less than a 10 percent federal tax related to the total income earned each year. The fact many major corporations in America earn billions of dollars each year but pay little or no taxes due to ingenious loop holes invented by clever CPAs and attorneys really amounts to criminal theft.

Next is the pay scale of the executives of all corporations in America. The average pay earned per year by all common workers of any American corporation should be calculated each year. Any executive of the corporation earning more than 100 times the amount earned annually by the average employees will require the corporation to pay the Federal Government one dollar for each dollar paid the executive in excess of the 100 times figure. So if the president of a corporation is earning ten million dollars per year and 100 times the annual income of the average workers of the corporation is $60,000 per year, 100 times that would be $6 million. Therefore the corporation would owe the federal government $4 million per year.

The overwhelming and corrupt tax loopholes in America are beyond the scope of my book so I leave it to Americans to solve the problem by voting for honest patriotic politicians. Good luck!

Health Care

The United States has the most expensive and worst health care system of any of the so-called first-world nations. Surprisingly few Americans are aware of the fact the more or less "secret control of the number of physicians in America" (the method of the control and identity of the individuals is beyond the scope of this book) is the main reason for this problem. In the United

---

34   https://nypost.com/2013/06/09/shes-milking-the-scouts/
35   https://www.businessinsider.com.au/executive-compensation-at-the-red-cross-2012-11

States, any person with the ambition; education and motivation to become an attorney, CPA, engineer or any other profession can accomplish his or her goal. But not so to become an American doctor. No one has been able to really solve or bring to light how the number of doctors in America is controlled but for sure it is "controlled". A certain number of doctors "per million residents" is allowed by limiting the number of qualified applicants into medical schools.

The only way to solve this problem is to have the nation recruit any bilingual physician in any democratic nation in the world (as the United States Navy has been quietly doing for the past few decades) to come to America and attend one of our medical universities for evaluation and acceptance to be a doctor in America. And any medical school refusing to cooperate with the federal government to get this accomplished should be made to suffer severe financial and federal tax penalties if failing to cooperate with the federal government.

Another significant solution would be the establishment of a new very large federal medical training academy similar to our military academies and of course federally insuring the academy will not be controlled or managed by any organization or group of American doctors. The nations with the best health care systems have health taxation systems where all citizens with no exceptions pay a health care tax as a percent of their income. All citizens of these nations have federal health care similar to what exists in America for military persons when we are on active duty in the military.

I lived in Taiwan for almost a year in the 1980s and learned the health care system of Taiwan was based on the Franklin Roosevelt social security system for elder Americans. The intelligent Taiwan political leaders adopted FDR's program and modified it to apply to all Taiwan citizens from birth to death. A citizen of Taiwan had an ID card similar to an American military ID card. When a Taiwan citizen entered a doctor's office or hospital the citizen was met and treated the same as an active duty American service person entering a military medical facility (no bureaucratic, tedious insurance paper work) involved. I have not returned to Taiwan since 1992 and as of 2018 I am not sure if the 1980s Taiwan health care system remains the same or not. But I do know the Taiwan heath care system is still one of the best in the world.

Every study of our American health care system has revealed well over 50 percent of the cost of our American medical system is simple bureaucracy. (Plus considerable corruption activities of nearly all medical products in the developing, manufacturing and marketing of medical products.) Example, I have spent much of my life in foreign nations and have always noticed that medical products and services there are normally sold at about half the cost as the same items sold in America. Why? Corruption and bureaucracy. The only way the corrupt American health care industry can be changed is by patriotic American citizens demanding the political leaders of America get it done or are voted out of office.

The other reason health costs are so high is the insurance companies. Their executives enjoy six to seven-figure salaries while collecting ever-increasing premiums. A government-operated health insurance system would do away with much of the overhead of the private sector insurance companies.

The Military

We need to address the ridiculous method cadets are admitted into our three military academies. As a result of the poor quality of the average student entering our military academies as compared to the students entering the top great American universities, America has entered every war in the last century unprepared. The military leaders of America graduating from our academies have never been competitive with the brilliant leaders of Germany, Great Britain and many other foreign nations. In every war in the last century, America has been less prepared than the other leading nations.

I, of course, only experienced one major war, World War Two. Here are some examples from the start of WW Two and a few smaller following wars. At the start of WW Two no American submarine could dive one half the depth of a German submarine. None of our torpedoes actually worked. American tanks, guns, and airplanes were not equal to the quality and perfection of the German's equipment. With the exception of the US Marine Corps, no American military unit could compete with the German army. Although in the Navy we had a few great leaders like Admiral Nimitz, for the most part our Navy leaders were no match for the British Navy leaders.

I am totally familiar with one modern war weapon, the aircraft carrier. British Navy leaders invented the aircraft carrier, the arresting gear, the catapult and every modification of catapults as aviation technology changed, the armored carrier decks, the method to land jet aircraft on a carrier. In my first postwar assignment I was a test pilot at the Navy Aircraft Factory in Philadelphia in 1945 and at the Patuxent Navy test base. For the first time in my life I was associated with our former enemies: German fighter pilots and German aviation scientists. I also worked with some of the British military leaders. At that time we all believed we were going to eventually go to war with Stalin and Russia. With the exception of my test pilot group's commanding officer, a US Marine colonel (and a non-academy graduate) I cannot remember a single Navy Academy graduate being an equal to the British and German military personnel.

This is my recommendation to improve the quality of our future military leaders. Eliminate all political influence in the appointment of new cadets to the military academies. Eliminate any and all factors related to who attends the academies, such as "did my daddy go to the academy"? Each year every qualifying young person in America regardless of race or color or gender, ages 18 to 21 would get a copy of a document signed by the principal/top administrator of the school or college they attend. The document would state the student is one of the top ten percent in the school and therefore would be granted permission to apply to attend one of the military academies. All applicants would then have to pass a physical exam and take a common test in a carefully monitored manner covering history, science, math and other subjects. The completed tests would then be mailed to a military center to be reviewed by selected officials of our top American universities. The test would only have numbers to identify the students; there would be no way to know if the student had a foreign-sounding name, male or female. As a result of this exercise, the freshman class of each academy would all be intelligent students.

At the end of the freshman year, only the top 90 percent of students would remain as cadets. The bottom 10 percent would receive scholarships to attend any university of their choice that had an ROTC department entitling the student to become an officer in the military. History proves that this works. General Marshal, who was President Franklin Roosevelt's primary military strategic advisor was a graduate of Virginia Military Institute and the greatest military aviation genius of the post-WW One years was General Billy Mitchel, a graduate of George Washington University. If our three military academies had the same quality of students entering the academies as our civilian universities, America would have many brilliant military leaders in the future. In less than three decades, America would have military leaders the equal of Germany, Great Britain, China and all other leading nations of the world.

Federal Term Limits

In most major cities and state governments, there are term limits. As of 2017, America actually has no real government. Both the Senate and House are packed with "dead wood politicians", all determined to never again actually do anything other than spend the majority of their time fund raising for the next election.

The only way to have an effective government is to have term limits for both Senate and House politicians. Two six-year terms for senators and five two-year terms for the House of Representatives. With new fresh energetic blood in both the Senate and House, eventually the deadlock can be broken. I am confident term limits will bring about the development of a third party whereby the patriotic senators and house members will be free to run for seats in a third party. Hopefully the third party will not be named "Independents" but "American Patriots Party" - "APP". With three parties, the deadlock of our nation's political system will end and America will actually have a functioning government again.

Laws Relating to Drugs and Prostitution

And this will be "a very long author lecture". I realize all religious persons who have never had any interest in science or psychology will be shocked and outraged to learn this 96 year old college graduate with a master's degree would advise young Americans that every law of the federal government and every state in the Union related to drugs and prostitution is a combination of stupidity and foolishness. These silly laws are wasting billions of dollars of taxpayer money and also cause crime and loss of life.

Here's what I was aware of as a youth: in the late 1920s as I approached my teenage years, day after day I was hearing the horrible stories of the killing and murdering of Americans because of prohibition. It was illegal to manufacture, sell, or drink alcohol. My young Uncle Art at age of 18 or 19 and several of his young friends died because at a party they drank homemade drinks made with anti- freeze alcohol. It blinded some of the young men and killed my uncle and one or two other young men. The good, wise and patriotic conservative religious voters of America had decided no one in America should drink alcohol. And they elected politicians who were "Patriotic Conservative Religious Politicians".

Crime and murder of Americans were the leading stories in the newspapers and on the radio every day. As we approached the 1930s and the presidential election, my Republican family adults were shocked to hear that Democrat New York Governor Franklin, who my dad and uncles called, "That evil anti-American Socialist Communist" would legalize the manufacturing of beer and whiskey if he was elected president. Franklin Roosevelt was elected, legalized the manufacturing of beer and whiskey, and believe it or not, all the bootleggers and gangsters stopped killing people. Surprisingly, America did not become a nation of drunks.

In recent years thanks to the "religious conservative politicians" that have been elected billions of dollars are now spent as the Federal and state governments battle all these damn sinners who use drugs and these horrible people earning money as prostitutes. These religious conservative citizens are convinced the prostitutes are sinners and for sure, God hates them and is going to send them to hell for their sins when they die. But surprisingly in the intelligent small nations of the Netherlands in Europe, prostitution is legal, licensed, taxed and the prostitutes are protected by the government. Question? What if a brilliant president (man or woman) will someday take office and federally legalize the use of drugs and prostitution?

This is what I am positive would come about: billions of federal dollars would be saved. With the legalization of all types of drugs, drug users would have to be educated so they know what the use of drugs will do to their health. All users would have to be of age, get a license to use drugs and carry it. They would have to pass a test the same as to acquire a driver's license. At the same time, it would be legal for employers to prohibit drug use in the workplace and to perform random drug tests, dismissing those who violate their contracts to abstain from drug use.

Prostitution would be handled legally similar to what now exists in several European progressive nations and also in specific areas of the state of Nevada. The prostitutes would be protected and their pimps and gangster abusers would be gone. The states and federal government would be receiving taxes and the corrupt government anti-vice police now getting funds from the pimps and gangsters would then just concentrate on jailing real criminals.

Every so-called vice in the minds of our current so called "conservative religious politicians", and religious citizens has been practiced by humans of both sexes in the history of mankind. The intelligent political leaders of a few nations of the world are aware of this and have eliminated the corruption, chaos and the killing of their citizens by legalizing and taxing and protecting the activities of their citizens. Will the United States citizens ever elect similar political leaders? For sure not in my lifetime. So tomorrow and in my future days I will be hearing and reading about the continuing killing and arresting of people in America and the arresting of government agents and police accused of taking bribes from the illegal operators of drugs and prostitution. No different than the 1920 prohibition years. No different than what now exists in Mexico.

Robots and Employment

Centuries ago horses, mules and other animals gradually took over the tough work of humans. Then steam engines and other powered engines replaced the animals. Robots are now replacing humans in so many ways. We have a president who won a great majority of votes in one state claiming "He" would create jobs for coal miners; yet he had no idea "robot miners" have been replacing human coal miners in all mines in recent years.[36]

---

36   https://www.computerworld.com/article/3136675/it-careers/robotics-driverless-tech-are-taking-over-mining-jobs.html

The world has entered the "robot age" and our federal politicians are not adequately studying what this means to the economy and to the workforce.[37, 38] Each year more and more humans in every nation in the world are being replaced by robots. Example: each year fewer humans manufacture automobiles in America and all auto factories worldwide.

Globally, close to 39 percent of all assembly positions have been replaced by robots.[39] Robots are also now manufacturing robots.[40] In our Navy we now have robot firefighters no human can equal. In the aviation world, robot fighter pilots are so superior to human fighter pilots in test air battles, human pilots vs. robot pilots, no human pilot can compete[41]. In the game of chess, no human can defeat a robot player. Even trash trucks in our largest cities are beginning to be operated by robots with just one human on board[42]. In the past, several humans would be involved. Gradually cars are now robot operated. Soon a human will get into a car and punch in a destination or just say the destination to the robot driver (example McDonalds) and the robot takes the human to McDonalds where a robot will be preparing his or her hamburger.[43] I doubt that American federal politicians are willing to take time from their fund raising efforts to even think about this robot revolution in the evolution of civilization.

Where do we go from here in the "evolution of civilization"? This subject is beyond the scope of this book and the author. Hopefully a great political leader will be elected and possibly solve the problem. "Humans have to have jobs and earn income".

We Need Smart Political Leaders

Intelligent politicians who are similar in belief and goals of the 1776 Founders of our nation must be elected. They must share the same beliefs and goals of Abe Lincoln and Franklin Roosevelt.

The primary goal of authors and speech writers is to influence their audience to do what is best for the nation they love. That is what I am attempting to accomplish with this book. I want all Americans to become fully aware of what our dedicated intelligent past President Woodrow Wilson attempted to accomplish at the end of World War One - the establishment of a powerful

---

37   http://www.businessinsider.com/obama-warns-congress-about-robot-job-takeover-2016-3

38   https://www.brookings.edu/research/the-case-for-a-federal-robotics-commission/

39   https://www.theregister.co.uk/2017/03/28/robots_are_killing_jobs_after_all/

40   http://www.cnn.com/2015/02/12/tech/mci-saffir-robot/index.html

41   http://www.mirror.co.uk/news/world-news/robot-fighter-pilot-shoots-down-8306276

42   https://www.citylab.com/life/2016/03/the-robot-garbage-collectors-are-coming/471429/

43   https://www.ted.com/topics/driverless+cars

League of Nations with the political power to prevent any future great war. What was accomplished at the end of World War Two by our third greatest president, Franklin Roosevelt, who with the assistance of General Marshal established the United Nations.

America Needs to Drop its Role as World Policeman

The United States must give up its self-appointed role of "world policeman". Over the past 70 years the "conservative Christian politicians" have tried to destroy the United Nations in the same manner they destroyed the League of Nations prior to the commencement of World War Two. I am writing this book to pass on to all Americans my thoughts of how to make sure the United Nations becomes the "world policeman" and forces the United States to give up that role. First never vote for a federal politician who ever speaks unfavorably about the United Nations.

Send an email to all federal political candidates and demand their opinion about the United Nations. In the event the United States attacks a nation without the approval of the United Nations assembly, politically attack the American political leaders. Military personnel should refuse to serve in an illegal war until the United Nations approves the actions of the American leaders. Civilians should refuse to pay taxes or work in an armament firm of any kind until the United Nations approves the actions of American leaders. Also and most importantly, refuse to pay taxes during peace time if the United States ever misses its obligated annual payments to the United Nations.

Everyone must remember this: all the young people killed in the illegal "Iraq Bush War" died in an illegal war. Everyone who died in the Vietnam war died in an illegal war. I and many of my military friends joked during the Vietnam War, "We are fighting this war on behalf of the American fruit corporations associated with Secretary of State John Foster Dulles. [44] Few Americans were aware of the fact John Foster Dulles and the political leaders of France were confidentially working together to ensure France would continue to own Vietnam as a colony. If France lost Vietnam all of the major fruit corporations John Foster Dulles was associated with would lose their profitable properties. [45]

It is sad for an old veteran of four wars to know that no American alive today knows that the greatest speech ever made by a foreign leader praising America and its president, Franklin Roosevelt was made by Primer Ho Chi Minh of Vietnam a few months before Roosevelt died. In this speech I personally heard Ho Chi Minh say, "Thanks to the intelligence and leadership of President Roosevelt and the power of the United States at the conclusion of this war all small nations will be free of the control of powerful European nations." Roosevelt died and General Marshal was not able to continue the policies and intentions of our great president. As a result, many of my friends and thousands of patriotic Americans fought and died for the American owners of fruit corporations in Vietnam.

In the military all levels of command are taught the importance of discipline and the

---

44   https://www.ft.com/content/778739c4-f869-11db-a940-000b5df10621
45   https://en.wikipedia.org/wiki/United_Fruit_Company

importance of immediate action when action is needed. So now approaching my 96th birthday I am attempting to influence as many Americans as possible to take action and stop American's decline.

The Religion Issue and Why It Matters

In my last book, *Religions, the Curse of America and the Western World*, I presented an overview of world religions and summarized how they have been responsible for death, devastation, and disharmony rather than good and the betterment of mankind. I also made the case that all religions are male-created fiction intended to "control the herd". And of course this means that using and controlling the females of their herd is all important in the minds of the male leaders.

Skeptics like to claim that God was invented by men who were trying to explain things they didn't understand or couldn't rationalize. When something happens that requires an explanation, just say God did it. For example, when mankind didn't have an explanation for lightning, men created Thor and Zeus, the gods of lightning, to explain it away. Man has invented god out of his own imagination and due to his own ignorance![46]

My *Religions...* book gives details about many of the world's religions and some of these are excerpted below.

Today's religions have at least three concepts in common: the "one God theory", virgin birth, and guidance provided to religious leaders by angels or on tablets discovered under mysterious circumstances. The "one God theory" came from the extraordinary mind of the ancient Egyptian pharaoh Akhenaton in the year 1400 BCE. An intellectual genius and powerful political leader, Akhenaton strategically planned to make all of the Egyptian gods and their affiliated political leaders either non-gods or subsidiaries to his one Supreme Real GOD. True, he became the supreme leader of the Egyptian empire but this also caused centuries of Egyptian civil wars - "God wars" - that finally broke and destroyed the Egyptian empire.

With the decline and eventual collapse of the Egyptian empire, story tellers came up with a tale (see Genesis 12:1-2) of a covenant between God and Abraham, who is considered the father of the Jews. Like Akhenaton, Abraham promoted the idea of one god. Later, the tales were augmented with the stories of Moses, who was spoken to by a voice coming from a burning bush that commanded him to lead the Israelites out of Egypt and into Canaan. During that trip, he ascended a mountain (Mt. Sinai) and was handed tablets which contained rules for the Jews to follow. He told his group that God had written on the tablets. But even the biblical accounts are inconsistent about when, where, and how the tablets were found. (Exodus 19:1-34)

Eventually a storyteller who was not pleased with the much of the Moses story came up with the tale of a maiden having sex with God and after many years, the Christian religion came into being. Six hundred years later, a desert wanderer named Muhammad claimed to have received information from the angel Gabriel and the Islamic religion came into being. [47] The Qur'an and other

---

46   https://www.newyorkapologetics.com/man-invented-god-whattaya-do/

47   https://en.wikipedia.org/wiki/History_of_Islam#Islamic_origins

Islamic literature contain reports of a number of miraculous births.

The virgin birth is a familiar myth in many religions. [48], [49] Divine births were so commonly accepted among ancient people that whenever they heard of a greatly distinguished person, they immediately classified the person as having been born of supernatural lineage. The Egyptian sun god RA was said to have been born of a virgin mother. Classical mythology is also full of virgin births; for example, the Grecian god Dionysus was said to have been born to a virgin. It was said that Plato's mother told him that she had conceived him immaculately by the god Apollo. Buddha was considered to have been begotten of God and born of a virgin named Maya. The Siamese (Taiwan) had a God and savior called Codom who was said to be virgin-born. In this very ancient story, the beautiful virgin had been informed in advance that she was to become the mother of a great messenger of God, and one day during her usual time of meditation and prayer, she was impregnated by divine sun beams. When the boy was born, he grew up in a remarkable manner, became a protégé of wisdom and performed miracles. And so it goes.

The myths of virgin birth and information provided by angels are perpetuated today – a great example is Mormonism, which teaches that their sacred text, the Book of Mormon, was originally written in characters referred to as "reformed Egyptian" engraved on golden plates.[50] The religion's founder claimed that an angel revealed the location of the book to him and instructed him to translate it into English.

Current political leaders who base their actions on religious beliefs rather than the rule of law are causing disastrous wars and hatred. The question everyone must consider is, "Will our world collapse as a result of these 'God Wars' or is it possible that with education, science and common sense the Western world can be saved?" Obviously there can be peace when the adherents and proponents of the various religions are removed from the governments of all Western world nations. Otherwise, one or another of the nations will eventually drop an atomic bomb and that may result in the destruction of the Western world. The best solution to bring about peace is for all nations of the world to be governed by politicians who believe in freedom of religion and freedom from religion WITH ABSOLUTE SEPARATION OF CHURCH AND STATE.

Yet today, a political candidate with ideas similar to the founders of our nation without a proven affiliation to a major Christian denomination has trouble being elected. In fact, cannot get elected. Case in point, Abraham Lincoln never belonged to a church of any kind and never attended any churches in his life until "for political reasons" when he became president.

---

48   https://en.wikipedia.org/wiki/Miraculous_births#Islam
49   http://www.nairaland.com/193520/there-many-other-virgin-births
50   https://en.wikipedia.org/wiki/Book_of_Mormon

Why is religious affiliation a problem for humanist politicians hoping to achieve elected office? The reason is the Christian leaders in America over the past century have spent billions of dollars on propaganda convincing all voters that a humanist non-believer politician is not a good patriotic American. Yet the best candidate for office is always the one who can keep religious fantasies out of decision-making. I would like all Americans to get out and vote in every election, being sure to consider the quotes of the great leaders listed earlier and to remember the most important guiding principle of the 1776 Founders,

FREEDOM OF AND FREEDOM FROM RELIGION.

Tom McBride flying his Corsair in WW-Two.

First page of the first printing in 2006

My Conversations with a
WW-II Corsair Fighter Pilot

His Story Through the Decades

Kelle Metz

December 7, 1941. WOW! We are in a War!

Foreword

I have always been a history buff and love to tell stories. While doing historical research on my own father's wartime experience, I met retired fighter pilot Tom McBride. I thought we'd have some fascinating conversations, but I got more than I bargained for! This remarkable octogenarian doesn't miss a detail. Tom gave me amazing insights into his colorful fighter pilot experiences and life story, and then went on to share his extensive thoughts on wide ranging topics: philosophy, religion, the evolution and future of our country and all of mankind. This book chronicles our conversations over the years. Poignant, exuberant, strident, sometimes angry, then rational and even pedantic, Tom's memoir covers the gamut of emotions. I hope you'll enjoy getting to know Tom as much as I did. Get ready, you're in for an unusual adventure.

~Kelle Metz

A note about the photos: many of the photos in this book are official Navy photos, others were scanned from originals that are 60+ years old. They have been enhanced to the best of our ability.

Officers and men of the U.S.S. Bennington who made the supreme sacrifice in WW-II. The memory of their comradship and devotion to duty will remain forever in the hearts of their shipmates.

In Memoriam

EVERETT VYRON ALWARD
Major, USMC

CLAVIN MERRILL BARCHUS
Seaman Second Class, USNR

WILLIAM HENRY CARNEY
Ensign, USNR

JAMES FRANKLIN CARROLL
Lieutenant, USN

JOHN BLISS CHANDLER
Lieutenant (jg), USNR

ROBERT EDWARD CHRIST
Ensign, USNR

JOSEPH CHARLES CICCARELLI
Petty Officer Third Class, USNR

ROBERT MERVIN CIES
2nd Lieutenant, USMCR

TIMOTHY COVERT CLARK
2nd Lieutenant, USMCR

GEORGE ALBERT CLEGG, JR.
Petty Officer Third Class, USNR

ROBERT JAY COSBIE
Ensign, USNR

EDWARD GREGORY CURTIN
Petty Officer Second Class, USNR

HARRY JAMES DEAL
Captain, USMCR

GEORGE CHARLES DeFABIO
Captain. USMCR

EDWARD EMMET DeGARMO
Lieutenant Commander, USN

FRED DONINI
Petty Officer Third Class, USNR

JOEL COHN DRESSEL
Ensign, USNR

JAMES WESLEY DYE, JR.
Petty Officer Third Class, USN

WILLIAM FISHER EADIE
Commander, USN

RICHARD BOULIGNY EASON
Lieutenant, USNR

DEAN EDWARD ERICKSON
2nd Lieutenant, USMCR

OREN FLOYD FISHER
Ensign, USNR

HARRY EMGE FLICKINGER, JR.
Ensign, USNR

JACK CARL FULLER
Ensign, USNR

BERNARD EDWARD GALLAGHER
Petty Officer Third Class, USN

EDWARD JAMES GERBER
Petty Officer Third Class, USNR

LOUIS JOHN GERIG
Petty Officer Third Class. USNR

LEON J. GHARST
Petty Officer First Class, USN

GEORGE ADDISON GUSTIN
Lieutenant (jg), USNR

ROBERT BRUCE HAMILTON
2nd Lieutenant, USMCR

ANDREW BRITTE HAMM
Lieutenant Commander, USN

WALLACE REID HATHCOX, JR.
2nd Lieutenant, USMC

ROBERT HAUGHTON
Ensign, USNR

RICHARD THOMAS HAYES
Lieutenant (jg), USNR

In Memoriam

ELBERT STEWART HEIM
Lieutenant, USNR

ROBERT BRUCE HOPKINS
Petty Officer Third Class, USNR

MILO EDWARD HOUCK
Petty Officer Third Class, USNR

BENJAMIN ARTHUR INGHRAM
Lieutenant, USNR

VINCENT ARTHUR JACOBS
2nd Lieutenant, USMCR

STEPHEN KOMAR
Ensign, USNR

FRANKLIN RUDOLPH KURCHINSKI
1st Lieutenant, USMCR

VINCENT LAIRD LANDAU
Ensign, USNR

BENJAMIN PERRY LIMEHOUSE
Lieutenant, USNR

JAMES FIDELIS LUKINS
Petty Officer Second Class, USNR

ARTHUR WAYNE LUNDBLADE
Lieutenant, USNR

WILLIS MAYER
Lieutenant (jg), USNR

EARL ALDER MCALLISTER
Lieutenant (jg), USNR

HOWARD AUBRY MCBRIDE
Lieutenant (jg), USNR

JAMES ARTHUR MCCANN
Ensign, USNR

CHARLES REID MOXLEY, JR.
Lieutenant (jg), USNR

CARLYLE NEWTON
Lieutenant, USNR

CHARLES GILBERT OLIVER
Ensign, USN

DONALD COOK OWEN
Captain, USMCR

PETER PARTHEMOS
Ensign, USNR

RICHARD LESTER PFEIFER
Lieutenant (jg), USNR

JOSEPH TOWNSEND POLLOCK
Petty Officer Third Class, USNR

DAVID OLIVER PUCKETT, JR.
Leiutenant, USNR

GILBERT AURELIUS REYNOLDS, JR.
Petty Officer Second Class, USNR

ROBERT WILLIAMS RICHARDS
Petty Officer Third Class, USNR

EDWARD HUGO ROHRICHT
2nd Lieutenant, USMCR

WILLIAM ERNEST ROQUES
Captain, USMCR

VICTOR KENNETH RUSLING
2nd Lieutenant, USMCR

RALPH ALTON RUSSELL
2nd Lieutenant, USMCR

JACK RICHARD SESSIONS
Lieutenant, USNR

ROBERT JOSEPH SPECKMANN
Ensign, USNR

FRANK BRADY SPENCE
Petty Officer Third Class, USNR

PAUL KENNETH SPRADLING
Ensign, USNR

CHARLES JACKSON STETLER
Ensign, USNR

RODNEY CHARLES TABLER
Lieutenant, USNR

WILLIAM TROYAN
Ensign, USNR

WARREN EARL VAUGHN
2nd Lieutenant, USMCR

NORMAN FORREST WHITTREDGE
2nd Lieutenant, USMCR

CHARLES T. WILLIAMS, JR.
Petty Officer Third Class, USNR

GORDON KEITH WOOSTER
1st Lieutenant, USMCR

GRADY ALVAH YORK, JR.
Petty Officer Third Class, USN

A war bond poster Tom saw in the Navy recruiting office in the Pittsburgh, PA post office that influenced him to volunteer to be a Navy Aviation Cadet.

PROLOGUE

How did I become interested in the naval history of World War II? Like a chain reaction—my interest in history, the Navy, and World War II has gone from one link to another, and continues lengthening to this day. When I was in junior high school, and my family was among the affluent few, at least in my opinion, who was able to buy a black and white television—my favorite program was Victory At Sea. I watched this program every time it was broadcast—never missed it once. Here we have two links forming at the same time, my interest in history, and my love of the stories of the Navy ships that fought the Japanese during the war. Of course since my interest was piqued, I asked my father, who had served on an aircraft carrier in the Pacific during World War II, to tell me stories of his ship. This was when I first learned that the aircraft carrier's name was the USS Bennington, and my father was a Fire Controlman 2c. Of course being ignorant of the various rates in the Navy, I thought my dad was trained to fight fires onboard the ship, and I asked him how many fires he had put out.

Dad told me with a smile, that he didn't fight fires, he helped control the firing of the guns on the ship when enemy planes tried to attack it, or the task force it was assigned to. He, like most other WW-II veterans didn't really want to talk much about the war, but he related a few stories that have stuck with me through my life. One was a near miss —an attack a kamikaze plane made on the Bennington. In fact, it was shot down just in the nick of time and crashed into the sea at such close range that the plane's carburetor bounced up on the flight deck, where those in attendance looked at it in awe. Then there was the USS Franklin and the damage she sustained from two bombs dropped by a Japanese plane. Dad said fires raged on her for hours and hours. I could see in my imagination an aircraft carrier on fire, men jumping into the sea from all sides of the ship, and the overall horror of the event. Well, that's about all Dad said about his time in the Pacific, and due to my immaturity I was unable to come up with more pointed questions, or have the ability to get a reply from a man concerned with the ups and downs of family life and the process of earning a living, so the USS Bennington was put in my memory "dry dock" for many decades.

My father had a variety of health problems and toward the end of his life he was placed in a nursing home close to my mother's residence. Very early one morning, I received a call from a cousin telling me that Dad had passed away during the previous night. I was expecting something like this for several years, as Dad had come close to death many times in the past ten years, but like most people I never thought my father would die, but would live on and on . . . until who knew when. My mother wanted Dad to have a headstone from the Veteran's Administration, and along with it came a United States flag. She kept the flag tucked away in her apartment until near the end of her life, when she presented it to the local WW-II veteran's memorial to fly above Dad's name on a plaque, along with the names of others from his county who had served during the war.

Approximately six months after Dad died, I went to visit Mom. I made an oral history interview of her concerning her memories of WW-II. After we finished the interview, she asked me to get an old scrapbook for her from the closet. She opened the yellowed pages and

Photo of U.S.S. Bennington taken from plane
leaving flight deck on Oct. 20, 1944

started cutting out envelopes that had been pasted in the book some fifty-three years earlier. The envelopes contained all the letters Dad had written to her during his time in the Navy—from boot camp until the end of the war in September, 1945. Mom had lovingly pasted the letters in the scrapbook, and now she was lovingly cutting them from the pages. She told me that she wanted me to have the letters. Tears were in my eyes, but I fought hard to not let them well-up enough to run down my cheeks. I carefully put the letters in my carry-on baggage for the flight home, as I didn't want anything to happen to these precious documents of my parents' past. When I got home the letters stayed packed away for several weeks.

One night I was having trouble sleeping, and since reading was a sure way to get my eyelids to feel heavy, I decided to put Dad's letters in the order in which they had been written and start reading them. I ended up staying up most of the night, but still didn't finish all the letters. The next night I started reading them again and was able to finish them all. I noticed that there was a big hole in the time period the letters covered, and it was most of the time Dad spent on the USS Bennington. Another link in the chain started to form in my mind—I needed to find the history of the Bennington to complete my parents' WW-II history.

I found a website for the USS Bennington and some e-mail addresses for a few of the WW-II crew members. These men led me to more information, including a full roster of the men that had served on the Bennington during the war and a list of the ship's casualties and POWs. Now things really started rolling. Armed with the names on the Bennington's roster, I was able to contact more and more of the men who had served and were still living. I began mining their memories of the ship and items they had concerning her service from commissioning until the war ended. The stories I heard were so wonderful that I kept going, on and on, and before I knew it I was starting my fourth year of research regarding the carrier and her crew. I had at this point reams of info on the USS Bennington.

I noticed on a visit to the Bennington's website that they were gathering information for a book to be published by Turner Publishing Company of Paducah, Kentucky, and I decided to submit Dad's name, rank, and service dates on the ship for inclusion in the book, and of course I would have to have a copy when it was printed, so I also filled out an order form and sent that in too. Months passed without much more thought of the book because I had started a new in-depth project to find the dates, circumstances, and pictures of all the names listed on the Bennington's casualty list. In the late summer of 2004, I found the long forgotten book, USS Bennington (CV/CVA/CVS-20), in my mailbox.

I was delighted that several Bennington WW-II veterans had submitted not only their names, ranks, and dates of service on the ship, but also stories about their wartime experiences. I read these stories first, studying every word, and comparing them to the data I had collected. I was lucky to find some new answers to some of the questions I had about various incidents on the Bennington, and several circumstances of the deaths of some of the casualties.

One story was so wonderful concerning two Corsair fighter pilots conspiring against Navy regulations to enable one of the pilots to sneak home clear across the nation, from San Francisco to New York, to see his new baby daughter before the squadron deployed for combat. I simply had to see if I could locate and get the complete story from the surviving pilot of the

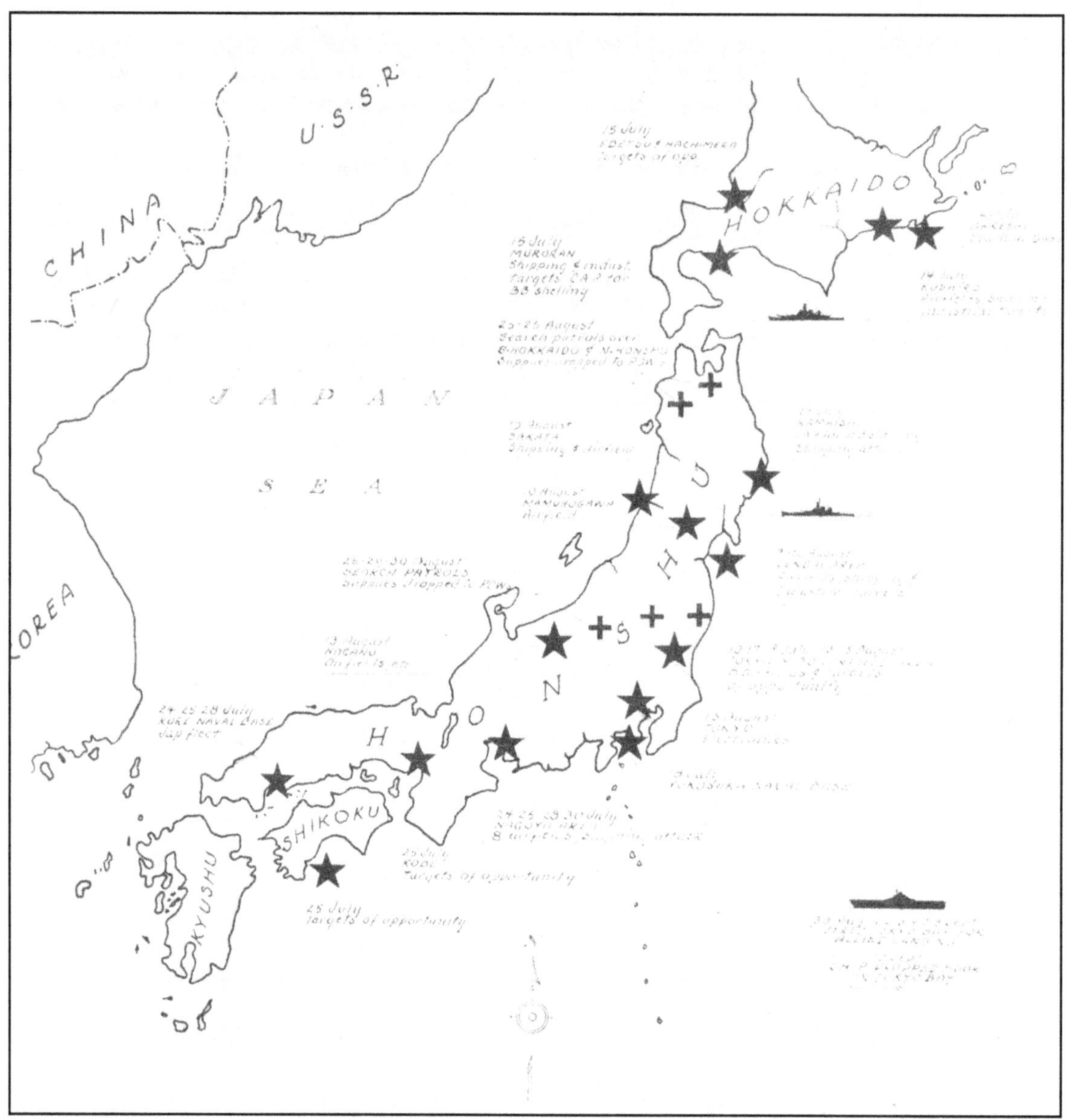

Map of Action. Stars represent strikes, crosses are POW camps.

escapade. I decided to try and find the narrator, Thomas McBride, a Navy Corsair fighter pilot from VBF-1. This wouldn't be too difficult, if the ex-pilot was still alive, and I hoped with all my might that he was.

I looked up Thomas McBride, or any variation of that name, on the internet telephone directory. Luckily the bio of Mr. McBride in the book mentioned where he lived. This allowed me to narrow the search to two possible phone numbers. I got the phone and started calling. The first number was not the Thomas McBride I was looking for, and the second number was a fax machine. I was stumped, but not down and out. I decided to contact the USS Bennington's web site's historian, Joe Pires, and ask if he might have information on Mr. McBride. Joe had been in charge of gathering all information for the Bennington book. Joe said that he'd have to do some searching and would get back to me. In a few days I found an e-mail from Joe in my in-box. He gave me three possible numbers for Mr. McBride. I noticed that one of the numbers was the one I had tried earlier, and reached the fax machine, so I called the other two. The first one was not Thomas McBride's residence—I called the last number on the list. When a gentleman answered the phone, I launched into my standard spiel. "Hello, I'm looking for a Thomas McBride who served on the USS Bennington during WW-II. Would this be the correct residence?" The answer was, "Yes, I am Tom McBride." I continued on without missing a beat, and asked if he had related the story about his friend, Charles Moxley in the USS Bennington (CV/CVA/CVS-20) book. To this Mr. McBride said, yes, his son, John, had transcribed that story and sent it in with several others. Mr. McBride said that he had not received his copy of the book yet, but was looking forward to it. I asked Mr. McBride if he had e-mail, and to my surprise he said yes. This always surprises me when I find a person in their eighties who has grit enough to venture into the electronic world that we now find ourselves living in. Mr. McBride and I exchanged e-mail addresses, and I said I would e-mail him soon.

Immediately I sat down and composed an e-mail and sent it off to Mr. McBride, asking him more about his friend, and fellow Corsair pilot, Lt. (jg) Moxley. Charles Moxley was the last Bennington casualty of the war, being killed two days before the Japanese surrendered. The story Mr. McBride told about his friendship with Charles Moxley, which will be related in detail later, but it struck home with me because Lt. (jg) Moxley had a baby girl, born just months before he was sent to the Pacific for attachment to the Bennington. His daughter would have been about a year younger than me. So many times I had wondered what would have happened to me had my father been killed in the war, and here was a story about a first child, a girl, of a Bennington pilot that had died during the war, just two days short of the end of hostilities.

It wasn't long before Mr. McBride and I were on a first name basis, exchanging e-mails several times a week. Tom McBride was a wealth of information about the Bennington and the war, and he had a philosophy that was so close to that of my father, that I felt I'd been given a second chance for an in-depth conversation very much like I would have had with my dad, were he still alive.

Tom sent me a long transcript of his memoir writings and I responded with questions about his life and his thoughts concerning the changes his world view had undergone over the past eight decades. In the spring of 2005, Tom and I arranged to meet in person at San Diego,

USS Bennington Aircraft of Air Groups One and Eighty-Two

Where's the Emperor's palace?

California, while I was visiting my youngest son. We enjoyed our get-together so much that we decided to put down, in book form, my "long-range" interviews with Tom. I hope that you will enjoy reading my Conversations with a WW-II Corsair Fighter Pilot: His Story Through the Decades. Remember, there are sages in your midst; don't wait until it is too late to have a conversation with one.

~ Kelle Metz

DEDICATION

I sincerely dedicate my work effort and time in writing my memoir to my departed close friend and shipmate aboard the USS Bennington who we lost in the last month of WW-II. He and I had shared many happy times together in flight training and at many fun parties. We double-dated many times and he married (a wartime verbal agreement) one of the ladies we partied with in San Francisco.

He has to remain nameless as this occurred almost 60 years ago and I am not in touch with his widow or his son (hard to believe that baby boy is now about 61 years old!) and don't even know if his widow remarried. I communicated with her for a brief few years with Christmas cards after the end of the war. I do not know if his family or son are believers or if his son may now be a Neocon supporter and not at all like the father he never got to know. Hopefully he is more like his father; I will never know.

There is the possibility that when I vacation at the Marine Memorial Club Hotel in San Francisco I have walked right by him on the street. My friend was one of three pilots in our squadron who was an openly confirmed atheist. All three were college men and senior to me. One of the three (not my friend addressed here) was the son of a minister. I had attended many of their bull sessions but did not argue or exchange views with them regarding religion. At that time I was a high school graduate and a firm believer that God would protect me if I said a prayer before I departed the carrier ready room to man my

Tom used much of the carefully researched information in *Genda's Blade*, a Japanese book, to refresh his memory of the details of the VBF-1 attacks on Japan, especially the July 24 encounter in the air battle when Tom's cabin mate LTjg. Robert Applegate was shot down by the pilots of the Kokutai #343 Japanese fighter squadron. Book cover with permission from Genda's Blade.

Japanese pilot and his "Kate" torpedo bomber meet their fate.

Air Group One - Destination Tokyo

F4U Corsair to go kill the Japanese.

About a month before the Pacific war ended my friend and I were, as usual, sitting next to each other in a pre-mission briefing in the VBF-1 pilots' ready room prior to a strike mission. The intelligence officer was briefing us for the mission. One of the ship's chaplains was intoning his long winded prayer on the very loud ship intercom system asking our God to keep us safe and to assist us in the mission of killing our enemy. He also intoned the usual religious thee and thou words asking God to see us through the flight over the ocean and a safe return the USS Bennington. My friend became very disruptive saying, "Knock off this bullshit, we have a war to fight and very little time to complete our briefing." Time of course, was always critical and there was always considerable tension before the "pilots man your planes" call. I then verbally assaulted him calling him a stupid son of a bitch, a nut and an idiot. I was tense getting ready to go while leaning back in my chair with my eyes closed and I desired the chaplain's assurance that God would be helping me on the mission. My friend was ruining my contemplation and the peacefulness the chaplain was dispersing. Later, while sitting in our F4U Corsair fighters on the carrier deck loaded with bombs and 5 inch rockets waiting for the launch, we did not exchange our usual thumbs up and smile to each other. On that mission we first attacked a Japanese ship anchored in a harbor and then strafed and bombed a Japanese airfield.

On our flight division's return to the USS Bennington, my friend was not one of the returning pilots. I never got to see him again. I never had the opportunity I was thinking about on my return to the ship, to apologize for my pre-launch behavior. He was senior to me and never said a word to me about being a junior officer insulting a senior officer when I lost my temper and insulted him. He did not live to see or enjoy his son as we had deployed from the states before his son was born. In the weeks previous to that mission, time after time, in the wardroom I would see him looking through a picture book of his wife and son that his wife had mailed to him. I did not learn the truth about the many fictitious man-made religions he had told me about until many, many years later. It still hurts. If the atheists are wrong, I hope he is happy somewhere out in the way beyond and will forgive me. Who knows, he may be out there somewhere with "SHE" a God who looks like Marilyn Monroe or former Ms. America, Mary Ann Mobley. I sure as hell hope so! Always remember, men wrote the Bible.

~ Tom McBride

SAN DIEGO, CALIFORNIA   MARCH 2005

On a pleasant Sunday morning sitting at a curbside café in beautiful San Diego, I had my first person-to-person meeting with my then longtime e-mail and phone friend,

One wheel landing F4U#15 #76720 Lt. (j.g.) McBride

One wheel landing F4U#15 #76720 Lt. (j.g.) McBride

Crash F4U#5 #88374 Lt. (j.g.) W. A. Henshaw

Crash F4U#5 #88374 Lt. (j.g.) W. A. Henshaw

Crash F4U#5 #88374 Lt. (j.g.) W. A. Henshaw

Barrier crash F4U#21 Kingston's

Crashes

the former USS Bennington Corsair fighter pilot, Tom McBride. I believe most adults including myself and Tom have fond thoughts of specific historical figures and role models with which they have mentally associated during their lifetime of studies and experiences. I have heard it said that each of us at one time or another will cross paths with an individual, an event or a subject gleaned from studying history that will substantially change our path and thoughts throughout our life.

In my first few minutes of conversation discussing Tom's past decades of research, studying and memoir writing, I learned that Tom's historical role models are America's 1776 forefathers, especially George Washington, Thomas Jefferson and Benjamin Franklin. In no uncertain terms I learned that in Tom's opinion, the 1776 forefathers were not only responsible for the existence of the greatest nation of the world, the United States of America, but also for changing the scenario of government of the majority of the nations in the world in less than 200 years.

Admiral Nimitz signs the instrument of Japanese surrender.

Victory Party

Contents

Our Thanks

Creating a book is not the solitary task you might think it is. We are grateful to so many people who contributed to make it possible. First of all, are the many people in our lives who shared adventures and helped shape our thoughts. Our families gave moral support and tolerated the many hours on the phone and computer. Our children helped gather photos and review old log books. And readers throughout the years since the first edition was published have given us lots of encouraging feedback.

~ Tom McBride and Kelle Metz

Tom McBride as a brand new ensign in 1943.
Ready to go and show the guys how to whip the Japanese.

Tom McBride at his retirement in 1961. A more sober and thoughtful pilot than in 1943. Followed orders, flew the missions assigned. When ordered to be a desk jockey after the war, transferred the paperwork from the in-basket to the out-basket. Lucky to still be around in 2014.

Boris (right) and Tom pondering some serious world problems. 2006

In 1776, all the nations of the world were ruled by kings, emperors, popes and their cardinals and bishops, ayatollahs, imams and other so called God-blessed dictators. But since that time and in less than 200 years, over 60 percent of the world's population has been converted to a form of democracy closely associated to the form of government designed by our 1776 forefathers. In Tom's opinion, our forefathers are not only responsible for the enjoyable lifestyle of citizens of this great nation but also for making it possible as of 2006 for over 60% of the world's population to now share many of the same freedoms and liberties we Americans enjoy.

Tom dislikes the word "sacred" but if there is one thing sacred in Tom's mind, it is the 1776 forefathers' wall of separation of state and religion. Tom is a firm believer that the lifestyle enjoyed by the citizens of the United States for the past 200 plus years as compared to the lifestyle of the citizens of the nations from the Mexican border to the southern tip of Argentina, the people of Ireland and the Latin nations of southern Europe over the past centuries is 100% due to the erection of that wall by our forefathers.

In his opinion, the freedom of and the freedom from religions is all important to the welfare of the citizens of any nation. In his opinion, no citizen of any nation should ever be required to believe in anything dictated by some self-appointed, so-called messenger from God. In his opinion, no individual on earth has ever had a conversation with God or any messengers representing "Her". (HER, because Tom never fails to mention that men wrote the Bible.) So I had to ask the question:

WHY ?

Kelle: (hereafter K:) Tom, what enticed you to do so much studying, writing and memorializing in your 80s rather than in your younger years?

Tom: (hereafter T:)   Well, being retired and not much to do other than to walk my dog Boris, read and travel a bit and attend shows, movies, operas and my senior classes at the California State University Long Beach Senior Center, I decided to put in writing my thoughts about my journey from Sunday school to age 83.

Until my retirement, I had lots to do working in real estate developments, taking care of my boat, a Columbia sloop, sailing to and from Catalina from our Long Beach marina and flying my Piper Comanche airplane about this country and Mexico. I no longer have either my boat or airplane. Now retired and without tax write-offs, the very enjoyable toys became too expensive.

The memoir starts in the 1920s, continues through the depression of the 1930s, then WW-II, then covers my service during a few other wars until my retirement from the Navy in 1961 and on to 2004. But here it is 2006 and I am still recalling events that I forgot to mention.

Several decades ago, I began to think about what a human is, where did we come from, why we are here and where will we be going. I decided I would like to know the truth, not answers based on fictitious stories, myths, fear and superstition. Of course we all know the biology, but I wanted to know more.

In writing this memoir, I have violated the professional advice about not editorializing, insulting people I don't like and at times writing as if I am speaking (shouting) from a soap box in a park. I tell it as I have seen it, witnessed and evaluated events over the past eight decades. If I have misinterpreted, have views contrary to those of others who observed the same events and if I come across as too opinionated...that's me.

I'm giving details of sources that helped shape my thinking and life. It may be from a book, from the internet, a visit with a person, an observation of an event or an experience I had. In each case, I note the years the individual lived and worked and cite references where readers can learn more about the individual.

K: So what is your objective or goal in writing this memoir? What are you trying to accomplish? What kind of people are your audience?

T:Kelle, any person who writes a book intends to deliver a message to influence one or maybe many people or in the case of a fiction writer, to entertain. I have several goals: one is to force myself to learn who I am and where I am going to go when I make my departure and the other is to attempt to influence people to think about reading about many of the interesting individuals of past and present generations who I quote here. My audience is any American who happens to come across my memoir. Hopefully at least a few individuals who read our book will begin to think about the danger if the wall

of separation of state and church is taken down and of our nation becoming a theocracy-controlled government.

I must admit the most important audience for my memoir and your book in my mind are my grandchildren, great grandchildren and their descendents. Hopefully, some of the copies of your/our book will be passed down through the generations of my family. I have often thought what a pleasure it would be if I could read a memoir written by one of my grandfathers or great grandfathers. What were their thoughts about their journey of life, what did they think about their American country and their 1776 forefathers? It would be so interesting to read such a memoir. Maybe our book will help them understand where we all came from and where they/we will be going at the end of life's journey based on knowledge and the understanding of the works of the many great scientists, philosophers and teachers of the past few centuries. I hope the book will encourage them to be doubters of unproven dogma, to be questioners of ancient sci-fi stories, to be aware of how the human species evolved as Dr. Charles Darwin scientifically proved. How in such a short time we evolved from a primitive hominoid animal to a modern human. And as genius scientist Dr. Jacob Bronowski taught how this human species of mammal conquered the world in a very brief time frame thanks to the mutational addition of the thumb and grip that grew the brain. To also alert them that this highly intelligent human tool-making animal has the capacity to reverse all of that progress in a matter of just a few hours by launching horrendous missiles of mass destruction. As Dr. Bronowski cautioned to never be persons of "absolute certainty," to always question and thoughtfully consider any "dogma of certainty" taught to them including dogma taught in Sunday school and church. Hopefully the book will help them to comprehend and realize religious leaders demand that religion is "certainty" that must never be questioned and that philosophy and science is related to "uncertainty" that may never be wholly answered. Hopefully they will be motivated to question, doubt and ceaselessly seek the truth.

A pleasant personal bonus I have received while focusing and reviewing my past 83 years and writing this memoir is the feeling of peace and comfort I have arrived at from learning about the true facts of life, about our planet and the universe, that comes from reading and studying the works of past great minds. Learning the truth about who we are, why we are here, how we arrived and where we will be going when we have completed our earthly journey really brings

Boris and friend.

Karen - my love, best friend and companion who makes my life enjoyable.

about a warm feeling. Having previously lived my life in a scenario of half truths, myths, superstition, sometimes fear of the invisible and passively following knowingly fictitious teachings "of certainty" was a miserable way to live this one and only journey I get to enjoy on earth.

K: You obviously are very emotionally charged to get your message into print. What is driving this ambition?

T: Why is this important to me? Kelle, as you will learn, I have a strong belief that citizens who question the fiction of the Christian leaders are less inclined to support the evil individuals who are attempting to break down the wall of separation of state and religion erected by our great 1776 forefathers. I know you refer to them as Founders which is literally correct but they are my role model heroes and I enjoy referring to them as my forefathers. Kelle, this 1776 forefathers' wall of separation of state and religion is the reason the USA has become the greatest nation in the world with freedom for all of our citizens; freedom of and freedom from religion. None of us has to believe in or live our lives according to the teachings of some self-appointed messenger of God thanks to our intelligent forefathers.

Fortunately a great deal of the information about the great geniuses of the past, their works, thoughts and discoveries are just a click away on Google (more about that later in the memoir).

These are some of the great men I mention in my story: Carl Van Doren, Carl Sagan, Charles Darwin, Charles Bradlaugh, Jacob Bronowski, the leading 1776 forefathers of America, (especially Thomas Jefferson and Benjamin Franklin), Leucippus of Miletus, (the Greek genius who in 495 BCE was the first to declare there is no supernatural power controlling the random actions of atoms). All of these great men have contributed to the improvement of the lifestyle and freedoms enjoyed by billions of people now experiencing their earth-journey. But the most important group of men who contributed to the lifestyle and freedom of over 60% of world's population in this century was that small handful of brilliant men we refer to as our 1776 forefathers.

After becoming aware of the works and thoughts of these individuals, you and others will come to believe that heaven is something for which we should work for now—each day of our lives—here on earth—for all men and women together to enjoy. We need to accept the fact that, as Leucippus of Miletus taught in 495 BCE, we can get no help through prayer. SHE is just too damned busy taking care of the vast universe.

K: OK Tom, I'm listening; let's get into the meat of your memoir which I am confident I will find both interesting and sometimes very controversial! I hope you are not going to be touchy about being challenged or questioned regarding some of the ideas and statements you express. I have some very strong feelings of my own on some of these subjects.

T: Kelle, are you familiar with what we refer to as down to earth "Navy lingo?" You challenge me on my opinions and I will not hesitate to challenge you on yours. Be sure to interrupt any time you want to make a comment or correct me if you think I am off base with some of my thoughts or should clarify some of my comments.

K: Be sure I intend to add my comments! This interview will become part of my storytelling collection.

T: Yes, I am aware that you devote much time as a professional storyteller. Kelle, during our conversation I occasionally mention an individual whose work or discovery I have become aware of and who has had significant influence on my thoughts about life, the universe, theocracy, society and government. To save our readers some confusion and frustration, their names appear in the index so that the reader can review the brief description of their significant work or scientific discovery that influenced me when I mention their name in our conversation. Learning about what Professor Carl Van Doren of Columbia University taught in the early 1900s before I was born really set me off on the path to write my memoir. Maybe the reader of your book should go to the index and read about Professor Van Doren at this part of the book. We have a good bit of information to discuss. Here we go. (See Van Doren on p. 291.)

Before the War

I was born in Carnegie, PA, 12 May 1922, the second son of Raymond H. and Permillia McBride, she was the former Ms. Permillia Davis. My parents had six children, five boys and one girl, Lois. All five sons served in the military. No sibling names were to be listed in this book without their permission to avoid embarrassment. I live in California, but some of the siblings now live in the "Bible belt" and do not agree with my thoughts about fictitious religion. But now I have changed my mind and a few will be mentioned later. My views about politics and religion are not shared by my surviving brothers or sister. My recently departed brother Donald who also served in WW-II and I have had pretty much the same views about these subjects for the past 40 years or so.

My family and I were fortunate not to have to suffer any of the American 1930s depression hardships that many of my childhood friends and their families experienced. My father worked his way up from being a laborer in the Jones & Laughlin Steel Corporation, (J&L), in Aliquippa, Pennsylvania to the position of a superintendent in the firm without

Repetition

T: In our conversation, we often repeat ourselves, especially me, and I am wondering how you are going to handle that when you write the book.

K: I think the readers will understand that in books based on conversation, repetition is bound to occur.

T: OK, so we will live with the repeated information. People like me in their 80s are prone to repeating the same topics. It's going to upset your readers.

Sergeant Raymond H. McBride Sr. age 21, serving in WW-I in the US Army Signal Corps, Aviation Department. Later named the US Army Air Corps and following WW-II, the Army Air Corps became the United States Air Force. During my teenage years, Dad was the commander of the Aliquippa American Legion.

Ray McBride, Sr. dressed in his Jones & Laughlin Steel Corp. superintendent's suit in the early 1950s.

Oil portrait of my mother and dad created from a 1955 photo.

ever being unemployed. From his discharge from the military service at the end of WW-I as a sergeant in 1918 until his death in 1958, except for a few months work with a construction company on his return from the war, he never worked for any firm other than J&L. Dad was never unemployed in his adult life. He was the typical and lifetime dedicated J&L company man. Dad's life was J&L, it was his work, career, hobby and next to his family, the most important entity in his life. When he became ill with a long term and painful illness in his early 60s as a result of his company loyalty, the executives of J&L made sure he was in the hands of the best physicians, medical specialists and was cared for in the top hospital in the Pittsburgh area. He died at the relatively young age of 63.

K: What was the cause of your father's early death?

T:It was a rare blood disease but I do not remember its medical name. I think it may have been a disease called multiple myeloma. The doctors told my mother they were sure it was caused by the environmental conditions in the huge Jones and Laughlin steel mill that stretched some 7 miles along the Ohio River in Aliquippa.

One of the top specialist doctors the J&L executives brought in to try and save Dad was Dr. Salk who a few years later became famous developing the polio vaccine.

I have no recollection of any contact or relationship with my dad for the first six years or so of my childhood. The reason for this was that we lived in Carnegie, some 28 miles from the J&L plant in Aliquippa as the crow flies but a considerably longer commute distance as my dad had to commute by street car and train prior to owning an automobile. Six days a week Dad would leave home long before dawn, walk downtown to catch a street car in Carnegie to go to Pittsburgh where he would then walk to the railroad station to catch a train to Aliquippa to arrive at the plant before 8 a.m. This had to be about a two and a half to three hour commute. Fortunately J&L operated on a 24-hour, three-shift, 8-hour a day system. I sometimes think about how tough that commute must have been for Dad in the dead of winter or times of heavy rain. At the end of the work day, Dad caught the train back to Pittsburgh and then the street car back to Carnegie to arrive home usually long after my bed time. On Sundays, Dad would sleep in while Mother, my older brother and I, and later my younger sister went to church and Sunday school.

K: Your father had the same experience my grandfather had during the depression—

they were both employed. My grandmother told me of the ways their little community (a company town) shared food and other items with those that had lost their jobs. Do you remember your father and mother doing this same sort of thing in your community?

T: I remember my dad's proceeding during the depression without communicating with the headquarters of J&L when he would have his workers in the mill load coal into trucks and then have the dump trucks unload the coal in vacant lots just outside the mill. Unemployed workers could then load up baskets and wheel barrows to take the coal home. During the deep depression, militant bitter winter steel mill strikes in the mid 1930s, Dad would have the workers in the mill cut holes in the bottom part of steel barrels, fill them with a few inches of burning coke on the bottom and then fill the balance of the barrel with coke and deliver them to the strikers. These barrels would enable the strikers to get a bit of warmth in the often below freezing weather outside the entrance to the mill. As a result of this, my dad had friends in the union who kept him informed as to when the union intended to pull sudden walkouts shutting down the mill. When the workers of a steel mill suddenly walkout on strike, the furnaces turn cold with the melted steel in them. It would cost thousands upon thousands of dollars to rebuild the facilities at the end of the strike. Since my dad would be warned of the time of the walkouts, he would have the furnaces emptied of the hot metal and banked with coke to keep them hot. J&L was the only mill in the Pittsburgh area that was never caught with cold furnaces during the 1930 strikes. The top gun of J&L invited Dad to lunch one day and told him to maintain that relationship with the CIO union workers but for the top guns' sake, not mention that he agreed with my dad's philosophy of how to communicate with the strikers. Back to my younger years.

During these years I spent most of my time during the day at my granddad Davis's home next door to the duplex my family lived in. Granddad was a carpenter and builder who had built two residences and one duplex on Library Avenue in Carnegie. Dad and Mother rented one of the duplexes he built next door to Granddad's home from Granddad. At Granddad's home, I had lots of adult company with my unmarried Uncle Art and Aunt Harriet who also lived there. But my Grandfather Davis was the main male adult in my life and he and I enjoyed many hours together going to the silent movies, visiting the nearby Carnegie Library and me thinking I was his number one helper with his carpentry work. This might be the reason I have had a life time interest in building properties. My granddad also bought the first radio in our neighborhood and it was a thrill for me when he would coach me adjusting the five different knobs to bring up the new one-and-only Pittsburgh radio station, KDKA. And he would do this for me as my playmates gathered to watch me turn on that mysterious high tech machine. Imagine the excitement we had having a radio station sending speech 20 some miles just through the air all the way from Pittsburgh!

In 1928, when I was six years old, my dad arrived home one night with a 1928 Chevrolet sedan driven by a friend of his. The friend may have been the car salesman.

For a few more days, Dad continued to commute by streetcar and train as he did not yet have a driver's license or know how to properly drive. During that week my older brother, Ray and I, were so proud to show our friends our dad's new car, the first family car in the neighborhood other than my granddad's car.

The first Sunday after the arrival of the Chevrolet I did not go to Sunday school and my dad took me on a short but very, very jerky car ride to the nearby spacious grounds of the Carnegie Library where we met his friend. The friend then commenced teaching Dad how to properly shift gears and drive with me standing at the back of the front seat watching the proceedings. Following these lessons and the departure of the friend in his car, Dad and I went for a much smoother ride about town. Dad practiced parking, backing up and shifting gears and then we visited a few of Dad's friends and Isley's ice cream store.

K: Were drivers' licenses required in Pennsylvania at that time?

Granddad - Thomas G. Davis. I spent a great deal of time with my granddad in my early childhood. He often took me to the silent movies and I remember his laughter as we watched the Oliver and Hardy and other silent movies of the early comedians. Granddad was a carpenter and house builder and let me believe I was his number one helper.

T: I really don't know. I do know that in the state of Ohio, drivers' licenses were not required when I was in my early teens in the mid-1930s as my two teen age cousins, Harold and George, started driving their parents' car in Columbus with no requirement for a license.

Once the Chevrolet became a part of the family, I got to know my father as he would arrive home much earlier from his work. Occasionally Dad and his longtime friend Hassen Fink would take me with them on Sundays to Pittsburgh Pirates baseball games, the circus when it was in town and visiting their mutual friends. And I enjoyed listening to Dad and

Mr. Fink talking about their past team sports, their work in J&L, military service and other events. But I was too young to understand many of their jokes.

One Sunday we went to Forbes Field to see the Pirates play the Brooklyn Dodgers. Prior to the start of the game Mr. Fink and Dad were standing and cheering as one of the coaches of the Dodgers, Babe Ruth, went to the home plate with a bat. The pitcher lobbed balls to the great former home run hitter and the Babe would knock the ball out of the park. Each time the Babe would knock one over the fence, Dad, Hassen and the crowd would cheer and clap as enthusiastically as if it was a real game home run. Even as an older man the Babe could still wallop the ball. I can still remember Mr. Fink telling me as we watched the proceedings that, "Dave, (the name he called me, my middle name is Davis), you have to remember seeing the Babe do this as there will never be another ball player like the Babe."

Two of my brothers and I went to war in WW-II: Ray Jr. in the Marine Corps infantry, Donald served in a destroyer in the Pacific, I served as a carrier fighter pilot, in the Pacific Fleet. The old WW-I Sergeant then never took a day off from work in the steel mill, working 7 days a week, 10 to 12 hours a day until the war ended. He earned the nickname from his co-workers, "the iron man." We were never in the upper income or privileged group of society, but Dad always had a paycheck.

Dave and Davis, (Davis, my middle name), were the names I was called and used until I graduated from high school and entered the Navy. In later life my mother told me they had called me Dave and sometimes Davis because there were so many Tom and Thomas relatives including my grandfather Thomas Davis that it simplified who they were referring to if someone were to ask for example, "Where is Tom?" One of the uncles, grandfather, son, cousins? So using the name Dave or Davis solved that problem.

I was pleased to use the names Dave or Davis which was the name of one of my very favorite uncles, Uncle Dave Davis, my mother's oldest brother. My first favorite uncle, Uncle Art Davis, my mother's youngest brother, died a cruel and painful death during the prohibition years when he and some other young men in Carnegie drank homemade bootleg liquor at a party. Several of them died; some became blind, and others were brain-damaged for life. I was about six or seven years old at the time and remember the headlines in the paper and the grief, sorrow and humiliation of my grandfather, mother and relatives.

Three Great Presidents

In my youth, reading about these three great presidents formulated much of my opinion of my country and how I thought all Americans should try to serve the nation. So I have made their stories a part of my memoir.

My generation of the gay 1920s, the great depression of the 1930s, and WW-II had the opportunity to live, observe and witness the events in the era of one of the three greatest presidents in the history of our country.

We experienced the 1930 depression and WW-II events during the presidency of Franklin D. Roosevelt; 1932 to 1945. In my opinion, the other two greatest American presidents were George Washington and Abraham Lincoln. There is no doubt this new nation experienced great changes from being a group of loosely connected independent states to a firm federal government during Washington's presidential era. It is doubtful whether any other American at that time would have had the prestige and relationship with the population that Washington had to hold the jealous colonies together. Likewise, the nation of states that existed in the year before President Lincoln was elected greatly changed by the time he was assassinated. Before the Lincoln presidency, the citizens of the new nation proudly referred to themselves as Pennsylvanians, New Yorkers, Georgians, etc. After Lincoln's reign, the citizens referred to themselves as, "Americans." It was then a truly united nation, the United States of America, saved through the great leadership of Lincoln.

The changes that came about during the terms of President Roosevelt from 1932 to 1945 were equally, if not more, pronounced than the changes that occurred during the times of presidents Washington and Lincoln.

Few persons born post-WW-II are aware of the fact that in the 1920s, the Civil War in Western Pennsylvania was still very fresh in the minds of Pennsylvanians; very similar to the current feelings of Americans about WW-II. When someone mentioned war, it was assumed they were referring to the "real war" that occurred about 60 years earlier in the 1860s, (more Americans were killed in the Real War than in the total killed in all the other wars from the 1770s to 2006). In the Armistice Day parades of the 1920s, the handful of old Civil War veterans who marched at the front of the veterans were the real heroes of our time. I was 15 years old and the only Pennsylvanian sharing my 6-person tent as a private in the CMTC at Fort Meade with five other young men, before I became aware that many of the soldiers of their states also fought at Gettysburg against the terrible rebel Democrats.

I was raised in a Republican family and in a Republican community. In 1931 at the age of 9, I heard nearly all the anti-Roosevelt statements made by my dad, uncles and neighbors during Roosevelt's first presidential campaign. My opinion of the great president was formulated during that, and his other re-election campaigns. I learned and believed he was a damn socialist, (I didn't know what a socialist was; only that they were bad people in 1931), that he was going to allow people to drink alcohol, whiskey and beer, and all the citizens would become drunks unwilling to work and dangerous to be around. Trains would crash because of drunken engineers and there would be chaos on the roads with drunken drivers. Republicans were strong prohibitionists, even though they drank bootleg liquor. Thousands of people would be killed in drunken driving and train accidents if he was elected. He was also a Democrat, and a friend of the very kind of people we

Brother Ray (in photo at left) attending my first wedding as my best man. My future mother-in-law had the wedding reception located in a hotel in a dry suburb of Chicago so that there would be no drinking at the wedding. Ray was a real prankster and he secretly bribed one of the waitresses to heavily spike the bowls of fruit punch with gin. My mother, future mother in law and my aunts were not drinkers but I must say they were having one hell of a happy time after drinking the fruit punch.

Ray returned from his service in the US Marines in WW-II as a very full of life party guy. A few years later he decided he was drinking too much and joined the AA. After joining the AA in later decades he spent most of his adult life as an AA counselor and attending the AA annual reunions around America.

At one time a bishop of the Catholic Church contacted Ray to counsel a group of over a dozen priests who were having difficulty enjoying too much of the wine they used in services. Ray became fast friends with several of these priests and converted to the Catholic religion.

He was buried in a Marine Corps ceremony and the services were performed by one of his Catholic priest friends. At the funeral, several individuals mentioned to my family that Ray had saved their lives with his AA counseling.

When I was suffering depression as a result of my failed first marriage and divorce, Ray was a life saver for me with his counseling. I never let Ray know how I felt about his Christian religion and its leaders. The bottom picture is Ray in his 70s.

Brother Donald McBride. Top picture taken shortly before 17 year old Don with some six weeks of basic training shipped out of San Francisco to do battle with the Japanese in the Solomon Island Campaign. He was later assigned as an engineer on the DE USS Traw. Don was the first of his three brothers to deploy overseas in WW-II and did not return to the USA until after the peace treaty was signed.

The center photo is of Don in his Army uniform just before he deployed to Pusan, Korea the week after the Korean War started. He did not return until after the armistice was signed.

The bottom picture taken in 2003 with Don on what he called his oxygen leash with my dog Boris. Don took up smoking as a 17 year old in the Solomon Islands and was never able to break the habit. He suffered greatly from the damage to his lungs. In the early 1980s while visiting with Don in Florida, he and I went sailing on his boat and in our conversation about different subjects we both learned we had almost identical views on religion and science. We never broached the subject with our three brothers Ray, John and Ken as we knew they were not of the same opinion. All five of us have maintained a close and warm relationship and Don and I agreed it best to keep our thoughts about religion to ourselves. A few weeks before Don died we were discussing on the phone who we were, why we are here and where we will be going. Don mentioned to me, "We are like all things in the universe, 'star stuff,' elements of the universe, and when we die and are cremated with the 20 to 25 gallons of water in our bodies boiled off, we will be just a small amount of the star stuff to be recycled into other star stuff. Don instructed his family to scatter his elements in the ocean. We also discussed what was in the minds of the ancient Egyptian Pharaohs who built the monstrous tombs and when they died had all of the accoutrements of living (and sometimes members of their court)

buried with them for their travel in the afterlife they believed in. They too will return to the elements of the universe but of course over a much longer time to get there. No star stuff leaves the planet unless it is entombed in a rocketship.

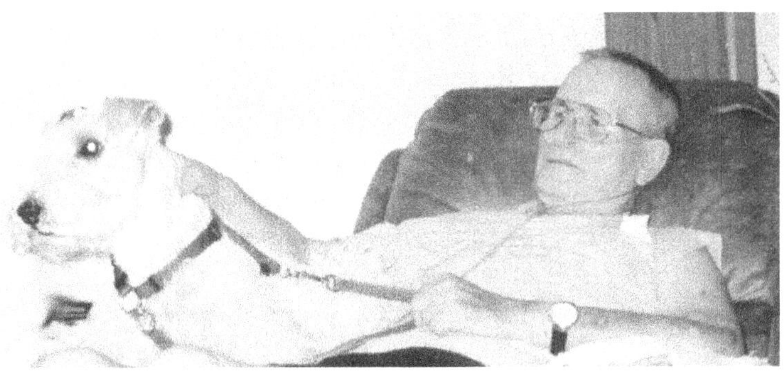

Pennsylvanians had defeated at the battle of Gettysburg.

K: The fear of Roosevelt's ending prohibition would allow Americans to become drunks is really laughable to me. The Women's Christian Temperance Union (WCTU), a Christian organization, got prohibition passed and I've always thought this was fascinating because most Christians believe in "free will"—in other words, that individuals have the will to do the right thing if they want to. So it would seem to me that if you believe in Christian teachings you will follow that doctrine no matter what laws a government passes or does not pass.

T:Kelle, in my opinion, Christians and Muslims believe that you must believe as they believe or else! They have no respect for the laws of the nation unless the laws are in harmony with their beliefs. They consider their dogma superior to all manmade laws. They answer to a higher power! They consider the wall of separation of state and religion a very sinful construction. Back to Roosevelt.

I remember our elementary class holding a classroom secret ballot for the 1932 presidential election exercise. The results startled me when it indicated Republican Hoover being defeated by a huge margin. When I got home, I told my friend Francy about all the secret anti-Americans in my class, and then he told me they had the same result in his Catholic school. We were both amazed that this could be true in the city of Carnegie, Pennsylvania. We were both sure the adults in the real election would vote for Hoover and the country would be safe from drunks and these people called socialists and southern rebel Democrats.

As I grew older and learned more about the nation, I became aware that America in the 1920s and up to about 1936 was in much the same condition as what we see in the current so-called third world nations of 2006. The average worker and citizen in the America of the 1920s and 30s had no rights, no protection against the abuse of the major corporations, no safety regulations or effective pension plans, no social security, no effective banking laws, no oversight of the corrupt stock market, no unemployment work severance benefits or effective government oversight of the corrupt banks. True, we still have much abuse of our American citizens in 2006 by many corrupt corporate CEOs; also the criminal activities of some of the privileged few, and the fund managers, but nothing like what existed prior to the Roosevelt years.

Some of our relatives worked in the coal mines. The corporations owned the mines; they also owned the coal mining towns and the company store. The miners were often paid partly in "company store script" and there was usually only that one company store in the town. The prices for food and goods were never competitive with the prices of products in independent markets. The corporation also owned all the homes in the town, so the miners rented from the same company they worked for. There were little if any real safety precautions, and when miners got injured, they were told they should be more careful. When a miner became disabled or too old to work, he was given a notice to move out of the company-owned home. There was no such thing as severance or unemployment benefits. There were no pensions, unemployment benefits or retirement plans for miners or labor in most all of the major corporations. There were a few exceptions such as the major railroads, which had a weak union.

The steel mill towns and other major manufacturing corporations were often managed in a similar fashion as the mines, but normally not as corrupt or as severe as the mining towns.

In the post-Roosevelt era of the late forties and into the balance of the century, the Roosevelt initiatives of social security, banking regulations, oversight of the stock market activities, worker safety regulations, pension plans, unemployment benefits, minimum wages, overtime pay and citizens' rights in many areas, were continued and expanded.

In the last few years the citizens of America have been shocked by the discovery of the criminal activity of the many corrupt corporate CEOs in America. Once exposed (an example being the corrupt Enron Corporation) they are being pursued and prosecuted by government authorities. They have, of course damaged the financial well being of many hard working Americans. This is a sorry example of the current oversight capability of our government. At least they have been discovered and are being legally pursued. This government action is encouraging many current greedy CEOs and corrupt members of the privileged few to obey the laws of the land. In the pre-Roosevelt era, corrupt activities such as these were considered the normal way business was to be conducted in a survival of the fittest conduct of business.

Roosevelt initiated the oversight of the activities of the banking industry, the investment markets and the treatment of labor by corporations. In the late 1920s, a corrupt individual could establish a make believe corporation (such as the Enron scandal of 2005) or set up a corrupt bank, reap the benefits from bilking the public and walk off with the loot without much worry of prosecution. The American government of that time, like the third-world nations of today, believed in the old saying, "buyer beware," whether selling your own labor or investing; "you're on your own." Survival of the fittest. The law of the jungle.

It was not until the end of WW-II, that I became fully aware of what a great peace and war time leader President Roosevelt was. When we learned in the Pacific fleet that he had died, many of my USS Bennington shipmates were crying on our carrier in the Pacific 38.1 Task Force.

The America of the post-Roosevelt presidency was a vastly different America than the corrupt and cruel pre-Roosevelt American nation. No doubt future historians will rank him as one of the three greatest presidents in the history of America.

K: I have read that the Prohibition years resulted in the deaths of many people drinking homemade liquor that was poisonous. I guess my question is this—did Prohibition work, or was it just a result of religious hysteria on the part of Women's Christian Temperance Unions?

T:I believe the WCTU and the Christian churches were the driving force in the Prohibition movement. Prohibition also resulted in the development of crime syndicates, bootlegging liquor, gang warfare and corruption in the law enforcement and political circles. About the same scenario that exists in 2006 in the failed narcotics war. Historians of the 1920s period have revealed that at least 10 to 15 percent of all law enforcement and elected officials in America were connected with the bootleggers in payoffs. Someday, but far in the future, political leaders and the population will eventually come to grips with the fact that the government cannot effectively control the lifestyle of the citizens with Prohibition-type laws.

In my opinion, the only way to control the use of liquor, tobacco and narcotics is through education, licensing, rehabilitation programs and stiff penalties for unlicensed individuals selling or using any of the products. At this time, our government is spending billions of dollars trying to control the use of narcotics of all kinds with little or no success. If the government spent just a small percent of these billions of dollars on education, licensing pharmacies to sell narcotics to licensed users, the narcotic billionaire kingpins and gang warfare would be eliminated in the same way the bootleggers were eliminated by the government in 1933. A narcotics user would have to obtain a user license in the same manner as we are educated and licensed to drive an automobile or fly an airplane. The purveyor of the substance would be a licensed business answering to the government. The percentage of people resorting to drugs would not increase just as the use of liquor did not increase in 1933. In fact, I am confident that the use of narcotics would decrease because the users would have become well aware of what health problems would come about in their future life in the education they would receive in order to get the license to buy the narcotics. Without an effective government licensing, education and rehabilitation program the narcotic gang warfare and the failed attempts to control the use of narcotics will continue for decades to come.

Thousands more will be killed in narcotics gang warfare and billions in taxpayer funds will continue to be lost in the failed impossible to win drug war.

K: President Roosevelt was a big player in having Prohibition repealed. How did the average American look at President Roosevelt and his ideas during the Depression? Many parts of the National Recovery Act the President got passed were over turned by the Supreme Court. Were Americans on the President's side or the Supreme Court's side in this decision?

T: Kelle, we will discuss much more about President Roosevelt and his programs later. But for now I will just say the citizens were in favor of his moves on their behalf but they were also very much opposed to his actions to try and pack the Supreme Court with six more judges so he could get his programs past the court.

Now back to my Uncle Dave:

Uncle Dave was an engineer on the Pennsylvania railroad and in the 1920s-30s, he was one of the engineers who drove the then famous passenger train, Spirit of St. Louis, on the run between Pittsburgh and Columbus, Ohio. I can remember as a youngster when my mother would occasionally take me shopping with her in Pittsburgh and then visiting with her oldest brother, Uncle Dave, in the railroad station. Occasionally my mother and I would go by street car from Carnegie to Pittsburgh about the time Uncle Dave would be getting the Spirit of St. Louis ready to depart for Columbus and visit with him as he inspected the engine at the station. I remember staring in awe at the huge black steam engine with the hissing steam and listening to the other sounds of the mighty engine. Uncle Dave would sometimes lift me up into the engine cab and let me sit in the engineer's seat and then tell me about the use of the different handles, levers and lanyards around the seat that he used to operate the train. At that time I really dreamed of some day being a railroad engineer like my uncle.

Uncle Dave and Aunt Nora lived in Columbus and had two sons, George and Harold, who became role models for me. They were 5 to 7 years older than me and were in charge of looking after me when I visited Columbus during my school summer vacations. My dad and mother would take me in the Chevrolet to Columbus for some of the summer trips to stay with my uncle, aunt and cousins but some of the years I would go by train as my dad was often too busy at J&L to take time off. When I went by train my mother would take me from Carnegie to Pittsburgh on the street car and then at the railroad station meet with my Uncle Dave who would take me to the conductor who would then take me to my seat in the train. I can remember while traveling on the train and listening to the lickity click of the wheels of the fast-moving Spirit of St. Louis train, how proud I was that my Uncle Dave was up front in the big black powerful steam engine driving the train. On arrival in Columbus, my Aunt Nora and my cousins would meet me as the conductor took me off the train and then we would all drive to their home.

Cousins George and Harold were good athletes and they did their best to teach me how to play tennis and baseball during the few weeks each summer I visited with them. George, the younger of the two, was recruited and signed up at the age of 17 by the St. Louis Cardinals and became a professional baseball player, playing many years with the Columbus Red Birds, the farm team of the St. Louis Cardinals. He moved up to the Cardinals several times when the short stop of the Cardinals was injured but then was sent back to Columbus when the regular player got well. At that time, a player had no right to move to another team in the baseball leagues as there was no baseball players' union in the 1930s. George was quite the man around Columbus giving his autograph to sports fans and also marrying Ms. Columbus, a very beautiful lady. Harold never played in the professional leagues but he earned a scholarship playing as a catcher on the Ohio State University baseball team. My cousins spent a lot of time and effort trying to teach me the game and I really enjoyed playing and living with them each summer vacation. However, unfortunately I never mastered how to consistently hit a curve ball nor gain the fielding ability to quickly catch a grounder and throw the ball accurately in time to get the base runners out.

I was fortunate to have another role model first cousin, Harry (Bud) Bell. Bud was about 12 or so years older than me and he, even more than I, was fascinated with everything about the railroads, steam engines and the reputation of our Uncle Dave as an engineer with the Pennsylvania Railroad operating the famous crack passenger trains. Bud would occasionally visit with my family in Aliquippa and he and I would take the street car down to the railroad station just to see the trains, some stopping and some just roaring by. Bud would tell me what kind and the name of the different steam engines that were pulling the passenger and freight cars. Later after high school, Bud attended the University of Pittsburgh and graduated from the school of business in the field of railroad transportation. Bud was also an ROTC student at the university and became a reserve second lieutenant in the US Army coast artillery branch of the service.

I will never forget the first time he visited our home dressed in his Army officer's uniform and the impression his visit had on me. I was fascinated listening to Bud and my dad discussing the huge 12-inch coast defense cannons of his Army unit protecting our American coastline with the ability to fire shells that weighed as much as our family car for over twenty miles. Unfortunately, when WW-II came, Bud failed his annual Army physical for some reason or another and did not get to serve in WW-II.

When WW-II ended and I was stationed at the Philadelphia Navy Aircraft Factory as a test pilot, Bud was working in the headquarters of the Pennsylvania Railroad in Philadelphia and we shared an apartment together. We became great lifetime friends and were as close as brothers.

In 1946, not many months after the end of WW-II, while sharing our apartment in Philadelphia, Bud and I had an amusing weekend trip indicating what aviation was about to do to (his) the railroad industry. He and I decided to spend the weekend in Columbus with our two cousins Harold and George. So on Friday evening after we finished dinner, I drove Bud down to the Philadelphia railroad station for him to board a Pullman sleeper car bound for Columbus. Of course as a railroad official, Bud traveled free on the Pennsylvania railroad. The next morning I had breakfast in our apartment and then drove down to the Navy Mustin Airfield at the factory and checked out one of our brand new post-WW-II twin engine Grumman F7F "Tiger Cat" airplanes, that had twin 2,100 HP engines, (total 4,200 HP, the fastest propeller-driven fighter plane in the world at that time) and took off for Columbus. Cousins Harold and George picked me up at the Columbus Airport and we then drove down to the Columbus railroad station to wait for the arrival of Bud's train. Bud looked with astonishment at the three of us standing there as he got off the train. As we drove to Harold and George's home, Bud said, "This is hard to believe, I left last night and here you are waiting for me to arrive; I wonder what is going to happen to our railroad passenger business with the development of these new passenger airplanes?"

Now back to my story.

My first years in school were some of the most miserable days of my childhood. Neither of my parents were much interested in education and my mother, married at age 17, was a very busy person with young children, cooking, house cleaning, and home chores long before the many laborsaving devices became available. Because of this and my dad's work schedule, neither of my parents prepared me for school. My dad was working 10 to 12 hours a day, six days a week in the 1920s and 30s.

K: Many people now say that our current educational system is not as good as it was in the past. Do you believe this to be true?

T: No. In my opinion it is better than what we had in the 20s and 30s but since the end of WW-II, many of the foreign nations have developed primary education systems far superior to America's current system. Our problem is we have not continually improved our American educational system over the past six decades while other nations who were not up to our earlier standards have greatly improved theirs since WW-II.

Education was not one of the priority items on either of my parents' minds. My mother did not finish high school and my dad's only college experience was as a football player for Indiana State Teachers College (which is in Pennsylvania) along with his lifetime friend, Hassen Fink. Hassen also worked with Dad his entire career in the J&L firm. In the early 1900s and shortly after the end of WW-I, it was common practice for young men to play on a small college football team but never attend any classes. Some of the players would play for a small college team in Pennsylvania for several years and then travel down to Alabama, Texas, Georgia or some other faraway state and play a few more years. Dad and Hassen played for the Indiana State Teachers College while working at their regular jobs. How they managed to get time off from work for the Saturday games was never explained to me. I did hear them discussing the fact they only practiced on the Saturday mornings before the games.

I well remember the sad day of my older brother Ray walking me to my first grade class and that terrible first day of school. An hour or so after checking in, the teacher of some 30 or so children in the first grade was attempting to learn the background and experience of her students. The kids next to me on both sides of the aisle were making marks on paper that were a mystery to me. They were writing letters of the alphabet! I had never had any instruction with writing, reading or with numbers or ever had a book read to me other than in Sunday school.

During the school year, the teacher had a policy of having all the children use a pencil in penmanship until they reached a certain level of proficiency. Then they earned a pen and an ink container to perform their tasks in writing. Each day the ones selected to get to use pen and ink were indeed proud to be called up to the front of the class, enjoy the class applauding and given their own pen and ink well.

The first day of school, I departed the playground as soon as I could when they had the recess period, causing excitement and a phone call to my home to learn of my whereabouts. I was not at home either. I do not remember where I wandered around during that grim day. I do remember the one event of me helping a lady feed her chickens during that miserable day but I do not remember any other events. I did not get home until the evening dinner time.

By the end of the first month of first grade I was the only student in the class without a pen and ink well. There cannot be many youngsters who detested elementary school more so than me.

In 1936, my dad was promoted to a new position in J&L with responsibilities requiring him to be on rapid call up in case of emergency maintenance repairs in the huge plant. This required my family to move to Aliquippa. Since J&L, similar to the custom of many American corporations of that time, also owned much of the housing near the mill, my mother and Dad acquired a very comfortable home in Aliquippa which they later purchased from the Woodlawn Land Company, a firm owned by J&L, for $5,000. Mother and Dad lived in that home for the rest of their lives.

I disliked school with a passion until entering the 7th grade when for some reason I very much related to the teacher, Mr. Larry Blaney, a former well known college football star, also my first male teacher. I became president of my 7th grade class and an honor student. Before the end of the school year he would occasionally take me aside to discuss a change in my seating position and then sit me next to a dummy student and encouraged me to help him or her by tutoring him/her. Mr. Blaney was not only an excellent teacher, he was also a great counselor for young people in their formative years trying to find their way into adulthood. Many of his former students who entered the service during WW-II, would visit with Mr. Blaney when they would occasionally return home on leave. Mr. Blaney's home was a gathering place for young people and he very much enjoyed exhibiting his extensive antique tobacco pipe collection, swapping stories about his role in the American Irish social activities of Aliquippa and as an enthusiastic alumnus of Edinboro State Teachers College always recruiting students to attend his former college where he had been a star football player.

K: This is not the first time I've had a "Mr. Blaney" story related to me by members of your generation. It seems that most of these events occur during a person's middle or high school years. I've thought back over my school career and realized that the same thing happened to me when I was in middle school. Why do you suppose that students are affected so much by their teachers during that time frame?

T: I think it occurs when an emerging teenager comes into contact with an adult who the youngster learns to admire for one reason or another. In my case it was Mr. Blaney's student body reputation, (like, wow, you get to be in Mr. Blaney's class!), his personality and just something about his presence when he walked into the class room and addressed the students.

My very best childhood friend was Francis Barr, (Francy), a neighborhood devout Catholic boy who was also an alter boy in his church. My mother told me that his mother and she would leave Francy and I together in a play pen for hours at a time while they did their housework as soon as the two of us were able to crawl. Now that I am aware of the disclosure of the Catholic priests sexually abusing young boys in Boston, Los Angeles and many other cities, (Steve Lopez, the prominent Los Angeles Times journalist refers to the brand new $275 million, Catholic Cathedral in downtown Los Angeles as "*Cardinal Mahoney's playpen*"), I hope Francy was not one of the dedicated boys who had been abused in the church. It would be naive to think this abuse of young boys has not been going on for many, many, many years, (more like centuries), in all Christian nations, not just in America. Let's face it: only in recent years in America could journalists initially disclose the abuse. In any of the foreign Catholic-controlled nations, a journalist would suffer not only relentless criticism but also the loss of his career if he were to expose the crimes. The same would have occurred in the pre-WW-II years in America as the church leaders had much greater power in America then than they do today.

K: If Francy had been sexually abused by a priest, do you think he would have told you? Isn't there another reason that makes it possible for journalists to bring forward these events when people are willing to tell others about the abuse they are, or have been, subjected to?

T: I don't think a young victim would ever mention the abuse because of the trauma, shame and his fear of the priests. The stories of adults abused as children pretty well make my observation credible. But that is just my opinion. I think a capable individual working towards a doctor's degree in psychology could earn his/her degree trying to answer that question. In any event, the journalist's revelations could only come about in the freedom of secular America. Continuing my story:

A most memorable event in my childhood occurred at the age of 7 when one of our neighborhood adults built a large replica WW-I French Spad fighter plane for the 1929 Armistice Day parade. I was the smallest kid in the group, so I got to ride in the cockpit while the adult builder of the plane, my older brother Ray, Francy and his older brother, Ed, pushed me along the parade route. The plane had a small gasoline engine making a lot of noise and spinning the propeller. The plane looked and sounded like the real thing and someone provided me with a leather helmet and goggles. The plane was decorated with Army Air Corps insignia with the hat in the ring décor of the famous American fighter squadron in WW-I. At the end of the parade, the adults picked up the plane, ran and released me at the top of a hill about 6 feet in the air and I came to a landing down the hill a short distance away. I was smitten! As a youngster I never got over the thrill of the parade, waving to my school mates along the parade route and the short ride in the air. The next day I was in the nearby Andrew Carnegie Library going through all the picture books of WW-I airplanes. By the age of 12 or so I had read every WW-I aircraft book in the Carnegie Library. Our WW-I enemy, the German great ace, Baron Manfred Von Richthofen, victor in 80 dog fights before he was killed, was my hero. I must have read that "Red Baron Book" a dozen times. I would often quiz my dad about his aviation service in the WW-I signal corps, later the air section of the signal corps would become the Army Air Corps and after WW-II it became the United States Air Force.

K: Had you heard of Eddie Rickenbacker?

T: Yes, of course! He was the great former race car driver who became the number one WW-I fighter pilot ace. Following the war, he established Eastern Airlines with financial partners. My younger brother John followed me into the Navy, served as an F8U Crusader fighter pilot and later elected to leave the Navy to join Eastern Airlines. During his career with Eastern he had several conversations with Rickenbacker. On one occasion, Eddie came up to the cockpit after takeoff and sat in the co-pilot's seat while conversing with my brother. My brother "Captain Jack" was very fond of the old fighter pilot.

So Kelle, now I cannot resist telling you a rather risqué statement attributed to Rickenbacker who was known for making many such statements. As told to my brother by an old long time partner in the airline:

In the early days of the life of the now departed Eastern Airlines, Rickenbacker was in a meeting with a group of the financial partners of the firm when the subject of flight attendants came up. Several in the group mentioned that the policy of Eastern having only male flight attendants was in the opinion of the pilots not as appealing to the male business passengers as the attractive ladies the other airlines were using. The pilots were pressing the management staff to hire attractive female attendants as the competing airlines were doing.

Rickenbacker told the group if the pilots wanted female companionship they could pay for their own nookie. On another occasion in the early 1930s in an Eastern board meeting, one of the members mentioned that competitor airlines were installing the newly developed auto-pilots in their airplanes. The "Captain" (Rickenbacker's nickname) told the board he was paying the pilots to fly the planes and not to be just sitting on their asses daydreaming.

K: Your older brother Ray Jr. , younger brother Donald and you served in WW-II, but what about your brother John?

T: Brother John (Jack) was too young to serve in WW-II or in the Korean conflict and was out of the Navy and flying as a pilot with Eastern Airlines during the Vietnam War.

I have another younger brother, Ken, who was a destroyer officer and who served in the Vietnam War. Ken made a career of serving in the Navy and retired as a Navy commander, the highest military rank of any of his brothers or father had ever held in the military. I should mention both John and Ken live in the Bible belt and are not pleased with my or my late brother Don's thoughts about the fiction of the Christian and Musliim religions. They would have been appreciative if I did not mention their names as my brothers!

At age 16, Donald dropped out of high school, joined the Navy and with just six weeks of boot camp training was the first of the family to deploy overseas in WW-II in 1943. He was the last of the three of us to return to the USA after the war ended. A few years later he was not pleased with civilian life and the Army offered him a good position so he joined the Army. A short time later the Korean War broke out; Don was deployed overseas to Korea in the first week of the conflict and did not return to the USA until the end of that war. That was indeed a great deal of war service. Don then decided civilian life was not all that bad and left the services for good.

Now back to my story. Let's see, where was I? OK, I remember.

Bread, bakery items, ice and dairy products were delivered by horse and wagon in the 1920s and early 30s. Francy and I looked forward to meeting the ice wagon that came down Library Avenue twice a week to deliver the large blocks of ice the ice delivery man put in our parents' ice boxes. Electric refrigerators did not become commonplace in our neighborhood until the mid 1930s. The ice wagon was pulled by two horses and the delivery man would let Francy and me hold the reins while he took the blocks of ice into the homes. The team of two horses was so accustomed to know where to stop and wait for the man to return, they didn't need anyone to hold the reins. Francy and I did not know that and thought we were doing something important. Oftentimes the ice man would let us ride with him while delivering the ice and sometimes he would let Francy and me proudly ride on the backs of the two horses side by side.

A big event in Carnegie in the late 20s and early 30s was the arrival of the carnival each year. Francy and I not only enjoyed the carnival rides and shows, but we also would have fun helping the men set up and take down the carnival. At least the carnival workers let us believe that we were their helpers.

The yearly elementary public school trip to Kenneywood Park, our Pittsburgh area amusement park, was a greatly anticipated event with more exciting and bigger rides than the ones in the carnivals. Many school buses and a train would take the students, plus their parents and teachers, to the park. We left early in the morning for the park and did not return until late in the evening. In Kenneywood Park, we got to ride the big roller coasters, large Ferris wheels, big merry go round and other types of rides considerably larger than the rides in the carnivals that visited Carnegie. Francy's school did not participate in these annual school events, so Francy's mother would give his school teacher a note for his absence for one reason or another and he would go with my mother and me.

The annual arrival of the revival tent shows in the late 1920s and early 30s were also an exciting event. Lots of singing, clapping and shaking by the adults and some would even roll on the tent floor. Our parents didn't go to these shows but Francy, a couple of our chums and I always found a way to sneak in to watch the ceremonies. About a half hour or so after the start of the programs and with the tent organ playing loudly, people in the audience would walk down to the front while the attendees were applauding, weaving to and fro and singing. The preacher would bless them one by one and welcome them into his flock. Some of the people had ailments and he would perform a verbal ritual as they kneeled one person at a time with his hand on their head to help them get well as he spoke some verses in a strange thee and thou tongue.

On one occasion a large red haired lady pushed a wheel chair with a man in it to the front of the audience and the preacher put his hand on the man's head and said some words while the preacher was looking up at the top of the tent. When he finished speaking, the man in the wheel chair stood up and hugged the preacher. Then he and the red haired lady and some other people picked up containers and walked among all the people collecting money while the portable tent organ was playing. The tent congregation was singing, applauding and weaving back and forth. Francy and I were really amazed, seeing how fast the man had regained his health.

K: You can see why adults in the world like to use propaganda on the young. Were there other areas in your youth that you feel you were exposed to propaganda of one kind or another?

T: There is no more truthful saying than, "The first casualty of any war is the truth". War creates the most intense and creative propaganda imaginable. No doubt by the time we finish this conversation you will be convinced that I consider my education in the Sunday school sessions pure fiction, brainwashing the young and propaganda. The Christians have been at both propaganda and often shooting wars with all non-Christian persons on earth for over 2,000 years. Now on to what was one of Francy and my most exciting times as children.

Many of the most enjoyable days for Francy and me were to play in the switching yard of the local railroad and put pennies on the rail to see them flattened by the switch engines. And in those days, long before today's litigation problems, the engineers would occasionally pick us up and let us ride in the locomotive and sometimes also let us blow the train whistle while they were switching the freight cars. The nonstop through freight and passenger line ran nearby the switching yard and we would also stand near the track to feel the wind as the trains went roaring by.

Francy and I were not aware in the years 1928 to about 1935 or so, that we were enjoying our occasional picnics and fishing trips to one of the local fresh water lakes near Carnegie with one of the most famous baseball players of the century. Our neighbor was Honus Wagner, the great Pittsburgh baseball player of the first decade of the 1900s.

Mr. Wagner was a middle aged man at that time and had two daughters, both 8 or 10 years older than Francy and I. He and his younger and then current baseball player friends of the Pittsburgh Pirates baseball team would take us and other boy youngsters with them on their beer and fishing trip get-togethers. I remember three of the players very well; Lloyd and Paul Waner who were brothers on the Pirates 1930s teams and Pie Trayner. They were all then playing for the Pirates. How were we to know that some 60 years later, one of Honus Wagner's chewing gum baseball cards would be worth several hundred thousand dollars in the 1980s! Had we known that, we would have surely saved the baseball cards that came with the very stale chewing gum Honus gave us.

My older brother Ray, younger brother Don and I all got to visit with Honus and meet his baseball friends. Honus had so much old and antique baseball things in his garage that he had to leave his car in the driveway. His garage was full of old baseball uniforms, shoes, gloves, decade old stale chewing gum packages, and other sports related items and equipment, plus copies of many old Pittsburgh Press baseball newspaper stories.

In WW-II, my older brother Ray served in the Marine Corps infantry and my younger brother Don dropped out of high school at age 16 to join the Navy and fight the Japanese. Don ended up leaving San Francisco to serve on a destroyer in the Pacific war after just six weeks of Navy boot camp training. When the war ended, brother Ray returned to our hometown working at J&L and brother Don also returned to work in the mill but ended up quitting the mill work and moving to Florida. I joined the regular Navy and after retirement, settled in San Diego, California. We stayed in touch over the years.

In 1987, when our mother passed away, the family gathered up all of the family's belongings to prepare the house for sale.

K: What was the cause of your mother's death?

T: Mother died of cancer at the age of 87. Fortunately the type of cancer that caused her death was not painful and she had a peaceful passing. My dad, on the other hand, died of a very painful and long lasting illness before he passed away in 1958 at the age of 63.

Following my mother's death some of my old paraphernalia from Mother's home was sent to me in California, I eagerly searched through my old belongings to see if any of ole Honus's items might be in the package. No luck!

So I related the story to my brother Don to see if he had found any of Honus's things in his gear, because I knew Honus had given him one of his old baseball gloves. Don told me a short time after he was given the glove he had traded it to a boyhood friend for a bicycle. We agreed that the bicycle trading transaction ended up as a very expensive bicycle for brother Don! If a Honus Wagner baseball card was worth several hundred thousands of dollars in 1987, what would a signed Honus Wagner glove be worth today? Brother Ray also had none of the Honus stuff in his gear.

My mother, Permillia. I have never met another lady with the name of Permillia! My mother is shown here in the early 1970s in her favorite room of her home - the kitchen. She loved to cook and I found it amusing to try to copy her recipes but never managed to get them right because as I followed the steps as she prepared a dish, homemade bread or whatever, she would say, "Now you add a little of this and then this," but she never used measuring spoons or cups. And I never managed to get the ingredients in the right proportions.

K: Do you think that the people that you encounter during your childhood are just as important, if not more so, to your education as the formal education received at school?

T: I sure do, Kelle. In fact, I believe that old saying that someday each of us crosses the path of someone where an impression or learning experience occurs that will have an effect on us for the rest of our life's goals, ambitions and career choices.

I feel I had a normal childhood: public school, Sunday school, sang in the boys' church choir, played two years on the Southland Dairy soccer team, three years on the junior high football team and three years on the Aliquippa High varsity team but never made the high school first team. The most exciting moment of my high school football career came in a game against Sewickley High School when coach Lippy suddenly grabbed my arm and gave me a play to call when I got into the huddle on the field. It was in the fourth quarter with only a few minutes left to play. The play he called had the right end run straight forward for ten yards and then suddenly turn back and stand still to receive the pass. I was the second team right end. Aliquippa had the ball on the Sewickley 7 or 8 yard line so when I caught the ball we scored a touchdown. Aliquippa won the game 6 to nothing and I earned a new nick name of "TD" on the team. "TD" was also the initials of my first and middle name. Although I was always a reserve player in high school, while serving as a test pilot in the Navy at the Philadelphia Navy Aircraft Factory and Naval base in the post-WW-II years, I was one of only two commissioned Navy officers on the Philadelphia Navy football team and thereby appointed myself to play fullback on the first team.

In the Navy, there is a saying of "RHIP" (rank has its privileges). The most exciting game our Navy team played was with the University of Pennsylvania in 1946 when we played them to a six to six tie. The game ended in a tie because there were no sudden death football periods at that time. In the late 1940s, the University of Pennsylvania was considered the top Ivy League college team. We won more games than we lost in the three years I was on the Navy team. In 1947, we defeated George Washington University six (both in high school and the Navy team we never had a good extra point kicker) to nothing and I am not sure if that school still has a football program. The most exciting event for me of the 1947 game and weekend with the George Washington University team did not occur on the field in the Saturday game in Washington DC even though we won the game and I had a pretty good game on defense backing up the line as the fullback and both running the ball and blocking for the halfbacks and quarterback.

The most exciting event of the weekend occurred Friday evening on the night before the game. Our team arrived in Washington early Friday morning and we had a walk-through practice session on the Naval base athletic field and then the enlisted team members were quartered in the enlisted men's barracks at the Navy Anacostia Air Base. The three officers (only two officer players and one officer coach) were billeted at the bachelor officers' quarters. Our quarterback, Ensign Curry, who was the former quarterback of the Navy Academy the previous year, had academy friends based in the Pentagon he wanted to visit and our Marine Corps captain coach intended to visit with some former Marine friends with whom he had served overseas. So on my own, dressed of course in my Navy aviation corps dark green uniform with my gold wings and WW-II ribbons prominently displayed on my chest, I took off to do some hunting in the night clubs and bars in downtown Washington. At about 9 p.m. or so, having found no interesting targets of opportunity in the singles crowd at the bar in the Willard Hotel, I was walking through the lobby of the hotel just approaching the hotel's double door entrance when the two doors flew open with two tall guys in light tan raincoats entering and followed by President Truman. I was less than 6 or 7 feet from the President as he passed me. The President smiled at me, gave a

1948 Philadelphia Navy Football Team. Tom at fullback position, Ensign Curry at the quarterback position, the only two officers on the team.

A fairly good team capable of taking on many college teams but not the major university teams. Won more games than they lost with a 7 wins and 4 loss season in 1947. Tom is the short guy in the middle of the back row.

short wave of his uplifted left hand and said, "Good evening, lieutenant." I was so shocked to have the President so close and to speak to me that all I managed to do was to finally stammer, "Good evening, Sir." It was all over in a matter of seconds. I should have saluted and said Mr. President instead of sir. Wow, that was an exciting moment I will never forget. President Truman, who in my mind and without question, saved my life and millions of others' lives by ordering the dropping of the atomic bombs in 1945!

K: I have a question about the atomic bomb, do you want me to ask it here or wait until later?

T: I know this is a very controversial subject and I can give you my opinion and answer it quickly. President Truman probably saved at least a million Japanese and American lives as well as the Emperor's life by ordering the dropping of the bomb. The modern revisionists are not aware of the true situation in Japan and in the minds of the Japanese people during WW-II. Even after the dropping of the second bomb, the Emperor's palace was attacked by the diehard military in attempts to stop the peace process. In the Okinawa and Saipan island battles, even the Japanese civilians killed themselves and their children before surrendering. On the islands we captured on the way to Japan, normally the only prisoners captured were the ones who had been wounded and unconscious when they were taken into custody. Usually only a dozen or so live prisoners out of thousands who were killed serving on the islands. Occasionally a Japanese soldier would surrender but it was a rare, very rare occasion. The WW-II Japanese military and civilians preferred to die rather than surrender. No one but the Emperor could change that mindset. The Emperor had to have something as dramatic as the disastrous atomic bomb to save face and permit the surrender. Without this atomic bomb happening, the Emperor would probably have been assassinated by the fanatic military if he tried to surrender. In fact, in the first radio speech of his life to the Japanese people to end the war, he did not use the word surrender; he simply said that in view of recent events he had decided to end the war. He didn't dare to use the word surrender!

The Emperor (even as the representative of their God) could not surrender and bring about peace without some horrible event such as the atomic bomb to give him an excuse to stop the war and to override the fanatic military leaders. We had burned and killed over 80,000 civilians in Tokyo in just a single night B-29 fire bombing raid. The B-29 fire bombing attacks were killing thousands upon thousands of others in the fire bombings of other cities but it made no difference in the minds of the military leaders of Japan. If Truman had not ordered the dropping of the two atomic bombs that ended the war and we had invaded Japan with some additional million or so people killed, what would all of the American mothers, fathers, widows and relatives who lost their sons and relatives think when they learned we could have saved all of their lives with the atomic bombs? I am sure many Americans who would have lost their sons in the futile bloody invasion of Japan would have wanted to assassinate Truman once they learned he could have prevented the massive killings and the needless loss of life. No doubt if any of the presidents we have had other than Roosevelt or Truman in the last century had been in the position to make such a decision they would have had to take a poll first or probably not had the guts to drop the bomb. Truman had seen battlefield killings in WW-I as an up front in combat Army captain so he knew what he had to do. I know I would not be here talking to you some 60 years later if it were not for the decision of President Truman to end the war. Ole Harry didn't have to study polls to make a decision. He often stated, "The buck stops here." He was not a so-called "Teflon president."

There is another reason why President Truman decided to drop the bomb. According to a retired senior officer Navy Academy graduate friend of mine who I greatly respect, British intelligence personnel influenced the decision to drop the atomic bombs. The captain friend spent almost all of WW-II in Naval Intelligence serving in the Pentagon. He told me that in WW-II, both the British and Germans poured a tremendous amount of manpower and research in the study of their opposing military leaders. They believed by knowing a great deal about the backgrounds and psychological profiles of their enemy leaders they could predict what kind of decision the enemy leaders would make in time of stress and military campaigns. The Americans did some of this type of intelligence work but were not as proficient as either the British or the Germans. Churchill made all of the British intelligence available to the Americans. The British profile of Emperor Hirohito was that the Emperor was both an immature adult raised in isolation since boyhood and a personal coward. So with this information, the intelligence advisors to President Truman came up with the plan to drop one bomb on a city, give the war criminal coward a few days to think it over to see if he would stop the war, then drop a second bomb on another city. The idea was to have the Emperor believing the third bomb would be on his palace. In any event, my friend's information true or not, the coward came out of his den and made the first radio address of his life. The thought of an atomic bomb dropping on him was too much for the Emperor to bear.

K: My father was totally against dropping the atomic bomb—but he also felt that we didn't have to invade Japan either, they were isolated, almost out of fuel and food. His choice would have been a blockade of the island, and allowing Russia to do their thing. I'm not sure I'm totally against dropping the bomb, but I do wonder about the use of it on non-military targets. For example I learned recently that there were thirteen Japanese divisions massed on Kyushu to meet an American invasion. Why wasn't the first atomic bomb dropped on these divisions instead of Hiroshima?

T: Kelle, this is a subject that will be argued by historians for years, even centuries. The bombing of civilians in WW-II came about by accident in the air battle between the RAF and the Luftwaffe in 1940. A young German bomber pilot got off course bombing the docks of London at night and dropped his bombs into a residential area. Hitler had ordered the Luftwaffe commanders to make sure no civilian residential areas would be bombed because he was trying to negotiate peace with important British anti-war persons. Hitler knew that bombing civilians would create such hatred in the minds of the British citizens his propaganda of a favorable peace treaty would be doomed. The young German Luftwaffe bomber pilot was severely disciplined and the British government was informed. Rather than accept the apology, Churchill immediately launched a heavy aerial bombardment of German residential areas. Hitler retaliated in kind. Roosevelt condemned both of them for bombing civilian targets. Roosevelt made his opinion clear politely and quietly to his friend Winston but in a heated public manner to Hitler. As the war progressed, the hatred on both sides grew more intense. Both sides hammered the opponents' cities with bombs. By the time we entered the war the bombing of cities was considered the best way to break the will of the enemy and the Americans joined in. Once the war was over, military psychologist strategic planners determined that the bombing of civilians was the worst possible action to try and break the will of the civilians to continue the war. It simply made the civilians ever angrier and determined to fight to the death against the hated enemy.

So back to football:

In that same year we played the Atlantic City Falcons or Hawks. I'm not sure of which name. They were the Atlantic City semi-pro farm team used by the Philadelphia Eagles pro team to keep some of their reserves in shape in case they were needed during the football season. Our Marine Corps captain coach was convinced we could take them on and probably defeat them. Our Philadelphia Navy team then suffered the worst beating imaginable. We not only got beat up, we lost 72 to nothing. I do not remember our team ever making a first down in the game and I think they scored a touchdown every time they got the ball. In the 1940s there was no such thing as a defensive team and an offensive team in football. The same team played the entire game except for the substitution of a few players. As the fullback my position on the defense was as the line backer. I will never forget that game and how I wished the coach would eventually send in the second team fullback and put me on the bench. By the beginning of the fourth quarter the game was so boring for the fans almost all them had left the ball park. Every time we carried the ball we encountered a bone crushing collision! The game was played on a Sunday and I had to report in as being sick until the following Thursday at the Navy Aircraft Factory because of my many aches and pains.

My dad was the Commander of the Aliquippa American Legion in the 1930s which made it possible for me, at the age of 15, to join the CMTC, (Civilian Military Training Corps), a post-WW-I program that the government commenced in 1922. The program continued some 16 years until 1938 when America commenced preparing for WW-II. In 1938, the Army was too busy to have teenage high school boys spending their summer vacation training in their midst.

K: What is the history of the CMTC? When was it created, and why?

T: In the few years following WW-I, there was considerable congressional debate about the failure of isolationist America to properly keep its armed forces in a state of readiness to protect the nation in the event of a war. As occurred in WW-I and again in WW-II, the USA was completely unprepared to go to war as it was in 1917. At the end of WW-I as per usual, the policy of not having a real Army in peace time was mostly limited to congressional debate. But finally, in 1922, the government decided to train a limited number of volunteer youths to augment the small professional Army in the event of any future conflicts. In this CMTC program, (the majority being sons of American Legion fathers), high school boys 15 and older had the opportunity to voluntarily spend a maximum of four summer school vacations training with the US Army. Of course we entered WW-II in even a more deplorable state of readiness for modern warfare than we did in WW-I, but the Army has stated that the thousands of CMTC attendees during the 1930s were a great asset getting the Army ready for combat in 1939 and 1940. The CMTC was a grand and exciting program for teenage boys. The first summer, at age 15, I was stationed in Fort Meade, Maryland with the infantry. We all felt very important being issued our own WW-I infantry rifle and uniforms. We were also paid thirty dollars per month! (One dollar in 1937 would be equal to about ten 2006 dollars.) The second year, I was assigned to serve with the field artillery at Fort Hoyle. In my second year in the field artillery, our battalion was equipped with the famous WW-I horsedrawn French 75mm guns pulled with six horses. Each CMTC private was assigned a specific horse to care for and ride for the summer. Thanks to the influence of my cousin, Homer Davis, (later to serve as a Marine Corps captain dive bomber pilot in WW-II) who was in his third year serving as a corporal with the CMTC, the horse I had assigned to me for the summer was 27 year old Rodney. I was told Rodney was one of the horses returned from France at the end of WW-I. Rodney and I had the front left position of the six horse group pulling my team's cannon. That was indeed a great experience for a teenage city boy to have his own horse for the summer. And of course it was a very, very sad farewell at the end of the summer saying goodbye to Rodney.

Some Called Us 'Cannon Fodder'

1938 Infantry 1939 Field Artillery

But the joke was on them! In the Citizens' Military Training Camps, we were really just a bunch of teen-agers having the time of our lives.

By LCdr Maxwell Hamilton, USNR-Ret.

LATE ON A particularly dreary evening in February 1927, a New York City businessman was on his way home from an office in which virtually nothing had gone right all day. No new orders had come in, he'd had to let another salesman go and the payment on his bank loan was due the next morning. On top of that, he was going home to face a teen-age son who was a chronic runaway, a high school dropout on the verge of being expelled and a failure at almost everything he'd ever tried.

It was at that point that the placard in the store window seemed almost to reach out and grab the man. Featuring an enlarged photo of the great Babe Ruth in the midst of his typical home run swing, the poster carried a quote from The Bambino which said: "If *I* had a son, I'd want him to attend a Citizens' Military Training Camp!"

Citizens' Military Training Camp? What in the world was *that*? More importantly, was it something that could help the businessman with his troublesome son? Come to think of it, wasn't there a line he recalled from somewhere that carried a message very similar to The Babe's: "Send your boy to CMTC camp, and swap him for a man!" If this CMTC camp—if *anything*—could do that with *his* ne'er-do-well. . . .

In the days that followed, the man gathered all the information he could about the CMTC. He learned that the camps were, for the most part, an outgrowth of the preparedness movement preceding World War I. The idea had been shelved until after that war, and the first Citizens' Military Training Camps had finally come into being in the summer of 1921 following passage by Congress of the National Defense

Program cancelled 1941 because of WWII problems.

The first page of a lengthy 1985 story about the CMTC program that was in operation from 1922 to 1938.

The CMTC program was canceled in 1939, a month or so before I was to depart for my third summer of military training. The Army was too busy in 1939 preparing for a possible war to have high school kids in their midst. Regrettably, the CMTC program was not reinstated at the conclusion of WW-II which I am confident has been a major loss for both the American military establishment and today's high school students. Prior to WW-II the Army was white and all male; I imagine it would be a nightmare for the Army commanders to have a co-ed CMTC program in the year 2006. Imagine the number of pregnancies that would be involved!

With the cancellation of the CMTC program for the summer of 1939, I then attempted to enlist in the Civilian Pilot Training program, (CPT), (a new Roosevelt administration program started in 1938), designed to train pilots for the possibility of America becoming involved in the threatening and probable European War.

The CPT program included ground school in aviation subjects and a total of 200 hours of free pilot training. Many of the CPT graduates were immediately hired by the growing airline companies. It was a voluntary program and the trainees were not paid, did not wear uniforms or participate in any kind of military training. Roosevelt was under political attack by the isolationists as a war monger so that was the only way he could set up the program.

The previous two summers while serving in the CMTC program, our battalion would have a parade in front of a senior officer, usually a general, and his staff each Saturday morning. The senior officers would then give us a military inspection which was followed by a meeting with the CMTC troops and one or more regular Army soldiers demonstrating or discussing an Army program, seeing a demonstration of a weapon of one kind or another, such as a WW-I tank, anti-aircraft gun, gas mask demonstration and other types of equipment. Of course in 1938, America was still in the depth of the depression and the Army did not have much, if any, new kinds of military equipment. Following these presentations and demonstrations we were released after our Saturday lunch to go off base to visit in Washington, D.C. until 5 p.m. Sunday.

While at Fort Hoyle, before I would leave the base on Saturday, I would pick up two or three apples at the lunch table and take them to hand feed my horse, Rodney. In fact I took apples to feed Rodney every day during that summer.

On one of the Saturday mornings in 1938, the parade ground was cleared after the parade and a jet black biplane with two machine guns mounted on top of the engine (a plane very similar to the first world war 1918 types of fighter planes) first buzzed the field at low altitude and then landed on the field. We all gathered around the new-looking polished black plane with the impressive red, white and blue American symbols on the tail and both wings after the engine was turned off. We then watched as the pilot, dressed in a smart looking Army Air Corps flight suit, black leather helmet with a white silk scarf around his neck, pilots' goggles pushed up over his forehead and wearing dark black riding boots almost up to his knees, stepped out of the cockpit. He then climbed up on a temporary stand to speak to us about the Army Air Corps. To this day, I can still remember thinking (before he even spoke a word) what a thrill it was for me to see and be so near such an, "icon" of a human.

Then and there at the ripe old age of 16, as I stood in awe looking at him, I decided somehow or other I too would become an American fighter pilot similar to my long time idol, the famous WW-I German fighter pilot, Baron Manfred Von Richthofen. A few weeks after returning from my CMTC summer session, I took my first flight as a student in a 37HP Piper Cub at Conway Airport across the Ohio River from Aliquippa. The cost of $8 in 1938 money would be equal to about $80 dollars of 2006 money.

PIPER AIRCRAFT

William T. Piper is known as the "Henry Ford of Aviation" and the yellow Cub is the acknowledged symbol of personal flight. He was an oilman with no aircraft experience when he joined the Taylor Aircraft Company's board of directors in the early 1920s. The Taylor brothers had developed a small, light monoplane powered by a 20HP Brownbach Tiger Kitten engine. It was in this machine that the Cub took its roots. In 1935, Gilbert Taylor left the company and Bill Piper brought in a new chief engineer. Under his direction, the original Cub was modified to its historic, bright yellow J-3 version. Two years later a fire caused the company to move. It was almost starting over and the company was renamed the Piper Aircraft Corporation. Over the next 47 years, it built 77,000 airplanes.

The first experience I had with airplanes was when I took flight lessons at the private airplane Conway Airport near my home town of Aliquippa. I paid a total of $8 per hour for the plane's rental and the payment to the instructor flying the 37HP Piper Cub. Later as a student in the Navy CPT program at Westminster College, I flew the 65HP Cub (the same model with a 4 cylinder engine) for free.

I remember the instructor at Conway airport telling me the almost new two-cylinder Cub we used cost him almost a thousand dollars. The vast majority of WW-II aviation cadets of both the US Army Air Corps and the Navy flew the Piper Cub in their initial training. Photo credit: National Air and Space Museum.

The CMTC program was canceled the following year as the first American peacetime draftees commenced arriving at the Army bases. The opportunity to join the Civilian Pilot Training (CPT) was made available to the youths of America and I was one of the first in line. But despite my completion of the first two years of CMTC training I was on a long, long waiting list as I had not yet graduated from high school. And I was well aware that at that time a college education was required to become an Army Air Corps aviation cadet. I was not a good enough athlete or top student to get a college scholarship and my parents had never ever mentioned anything about sending any of us to college. I did have hope that if I could get into the CPT I might work my way up to a position as a civilian pilot. I also thought that in the event of a war maybe there would be the possibility of a CPT graduate becoming an Army fighter pilot.

The day after my 16th birthday in 1938, I had reported to Mr. Kelsey, the head of the J&L employment and personnel dept, a long time friend of my dad, at the Jones & Laughlin Steel Company's personnel office to be hired as a tool boy in my dad's general labor department. America was still in much of the depression of the 1930s but my dad had the necessary influence with the firm to have J&L hire me. I had not yet finished high school so thereafter I worked full time in the mill and attended high school part time, (some of the time that is, but not very often), working toward graduation. Mr. Crawford, the principle of the Aliquippa High School, put up with my off and on school program as

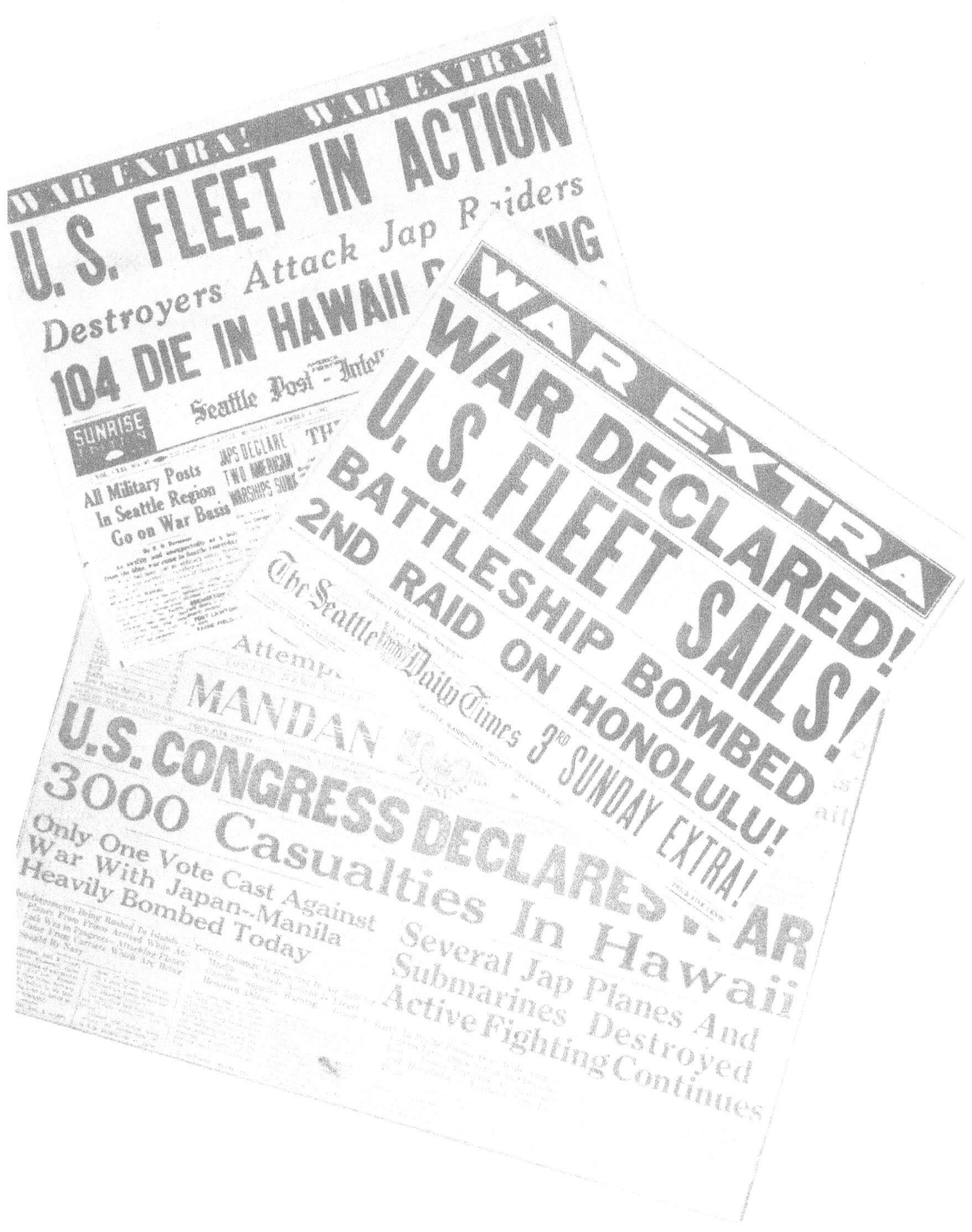

December 7, 1941. WOW! We are in a War!

I slowly worked toward my high school degree. He, as all adults at the time, knew very well that for a young man to get a full time job at J&L during the depression was an important step into the adult world. Although there were war clouds on the horizon in May of 1938, when I had my 16th birthday my mindset was on my intended career as an employee of the Jones and Laughlin Steel Mill with the ambition to get the maximum amount of seniority and work my way up to a position like my dad had accomplished. I could daydream, and often did, of becoming a fighter pilot like the famous German Red Baron or of becoming an officer in the field artillery corps of the Army with the fabulous French 75mm cannons. I thought it would be a great career to ride my own horse like I had Rodney but it was only a dream because in peace time both of these goals were more a daydream than an actual goal. The war in Europe did not start until the next year so jobs were still very hard to come by in 1938.

The War Years

When the Japanese attacked Pearl Harbor on Sunday a.m. on Dec. 7, 1941, I was working on a history term paper in the Aliquippa Laughlin Public Library as a part of finishing up my high school education. I was busily engaged working on my term paper when a significant commotion and loud conversation broke out around the adjoining library tables. I remember shouting back, "Shut the hell up, some of us are trying to get our work done." Then every one commenced excitedly shouting, "We are at war, Pearl Harbor has been bombed." It was the first time I had ever heard the name Pearl Harbor and I didn't learn until later on in the day that Pearl Harbor was in Hawaii.

So I rushed out of the library to go home and listen to the radio news. I remember thinking to myself all the way home, "How did the Germans manage to get all the way over to the Pacific Ocean to bomb our fleet?" Then at home I learned over the radio it was the Japanese.

K: Tom, what made you decide to join the Navy?

T:We will get to my joining the Navy instead of getting into the Army field artillery shortly. I know you will find it an amusing story.

The next day, Monday, I went to see Mr. Crawford in the principle's office with my partially completed term paper and told him about my problem on the Civilian Pilot Training program waiting list because of my need for the high school diploma. I also showed him my CMTC certificates of completing the two summer vacation years of military training. Both the Army and the Navy had commenced recruiting high school graduates as aviation cadets. Mr. Crawford told me to come back Tuesday morning and he would have my high school graduation certificate ready for me as he decided to give me credit for my CMTC service, my "shop like training" in J&L and my nearly finished term paper.

Then I had another problem because after working as a tool boy in Dad's department, I had been transferred to the machinists department. Just a few months after being hired, I had transferred over to the J&L machinist shop. By the time of the Dec. 7th Pearl Harbor attack, I had completed my first two years as a machinist apprentice. My supervisor told me that because of the war emergency, government regulations machinists could not leave their jobs in a critical war plant until a replacement could be hired. I went to see my dad about this situation and a few days later I was released from the machinist program.

Many of my friends rushed to the Pittsburgh post office to sign up and fight the Japanese. Although still young I was already aware that having connections was all important in becoming a part of any organization, military or civilian. I may or may not have been accepted into the CMTC if it were not for my dad being the commander of the Aliquippa American Legion. I probably would not have been picked to have lead horse Rodney assigned to me in the CMTC if it were not for my cousin Homer Davis. No doubt I would not have been hired by J&L the day after my 16th birthday if it was not for my dad's position with J&L. I would not have been able to get into the much sought after position of a machinist apprentice in the machine shop of J&L if my dad and the superintendent of the machine shop were not personal friends. I already knew that once in the Army, a person became just a number whether an eager volunteer or a reluctant draftee. So for a few weeks I plotted and schemed as to how best to use my CMTC background and new high school diploma to best serve my own interests. I was somewhat familiar with the Army and realized I might be able to influence an enlisted recruiter with my CMTC certificates to get into what was termed the "90 day wonder" officers training program.

So after plotting, scheming and picking the minds of friends for a few weeks I took the train from Aliquippa up to Pittsburgh and walked from the station to the recruiting office in the Pittsburgh Post Office to learn what might be available. I could not get into

Three of the six Japanese aircraft carriers manned by highly trained crews and carrying the well trained and combat experienced air groups that participated in the Dec. 7, 1941 attack on Pearl Harbor. Top photo the Hiryu; center photo, the Akagi; bottom, carrier Zuikaku.
Photos: US Navy.

The Sea/Air maturity of the Japanese Navy, 1918 to 1941

At the conclusion of WW-I in 1918, the Great War to save democracy, the only nation with Navy military leaders who took serious notice of the importance of air power coupled with sea power were the leaders of the Japanese Navy. The British had invented the aircraft carrier in 1916 and converted an existing ship into an aircraft carrier during the Great War but following the end of WW-I for financial reasons did not aggressively pursue the building and operational training of sea/Navy air power. The leaders of the US Navy never expressed any serious interest in sea/Navy air power until 1922 when they decided to convert an old coal supply ship (renamed the USS Langley) to an experimental aircraft carrier. In 1922 the US Navy was converting the Navy to all oil fueled ships and had no further use for the old coal supply ship. The Japanese commenced engineering and planning the building of the carrier/seaplane tender Hosho in 1918 immediately after the end of WW-I. This was the first warship in history to be designed, built and launched as an aircraft carrier. Launched in 1921, the Hosho's operations and carrier training gave the Japanese a leg up on all the other world's sea powers in the field of aircraft carrier operations. From 1921 to 1941, the Japanese continued their study of the use of carriers in sea warfare, constructed many first-class carriers, intensely trained the best and most experienced pilots and carrier air groups. The Japanese gained significance experience using their carriers in combat with the Chinese in the late 1930s and in 1940-41. The British and American navies, starved for money to train pilots and operate ships in the 1920s and 30s, were no match to battle the well trained Japanese Navy as of Dec. 7, 1941. The fast learning American Navy commenced intensive training as of Dec. 8, 1941 and six months later in June 1941, were finally able to meet and defeat the Japanese Navy in the first great carrier-to-carrier battle in Navy warfare history near Midway Island.

HIJMS KAGA

The Japanese aircraft carrier Kaga at 38,200 tons, 855ft long with a beam of 103ft, speed of 28 knots and a highly trained crew of 2,019 with several years of combat experience fighting the Chinese from 1939 to 1941 was just one of the deadly aircraft carriers that the inexperienced US Navy had to contend with in the first year of WW-II. The Japanese combat experienced dive bomber and torpedo bomber pilots sank and severely damaged many American and British ships in the first months of the war.

the office before closing time. The line of men trying to get into the recruiting office wound half way around the block. The next day I drove Dad to work early, borrowed his car and arrived early at the post office. I managed to get into the line near the front of the pack and was into the recruiting office in less than an hour.

I met with a tough old Army infantry sergeant, and showed him my CMTC completion of field artillery training papers which very much impressed him; also my brand new high school diploma and requested to become an Army Air Corps cadet. The Army Air Corps was then accepting high school graduates as aviation cadets. The old sarge looked at me and said, "Son, the war will be over before you complete flight training and we need trained people like you on the French 75's right now!" I hinted around about possibly attending officer training before getting into the field artillery but he was not interested. So I told him if I could not be an Air Corps cadet I would wait for the draft or even maybe take the machinist exemption and remain at J&L as a "war emergency machinist employee". Finally he relented and we commenced the paperwork to be an aviation cadet. Then I told him that if I did not qualify as a pilot, I wanted to be sure I would go into the field artillery branch of the Army with the French 75's. At that point he advised me, in no uncertain terms, there was a war on, and if I failed to qualify as a pilot I would damn well serve wherever the Air Corps needed me. We immediately parted company. I had heard the story many times of how the cadets in the Air Corps would be standing in formation at attention during training and the drill master would shout, "Look at the man to your left, look at the man on your right, now look straight ahead. You damn well better do your best, because only one of the three of you has what it takes to earn Air Corps silver wings." I decided to do some more plotting and scheming. My two summers in the CMTC had taught me to be very careful volunteering for anything in the military until you were very, very sure of what you were about.

On the way out of the post office I saw the Navy recruiting office with posters and pictures on the wall; one of which was a Navy fighter pilot in his attractive white uniform and gold wings standing beside an impressive new beautiful blue colored Navy F4U Corsair carrier fighter aircraft. So I thought I may as well talk to the Navy people. The old chief I met with was also very much impressed with my CMTC certificates but made the same statement as the ole Army sarge, that by the time I completed flight training the war would be over and the fleet immediately needed people with cannon gunnery training to man the ships' big guns. Following a short give and take discussion, he finally agreed to let me enlist as a Navy aviation cadet. When I told him if I did not qualify as a Navy pilot I wanted to go back to the Army field artillery with the horses and French 75's, he advised me that when a Navy aviation cadet failed to qualify as a pilot he would be released to civilian life with the option to wait for the draft, volunteer to stay in the Navy or at his option, go into the Marines or whatever service he preferred. That was all I needed to hear and I signed up.

The chief then sent me to the second floor of the post office for my physical exam.

I passed everything but the dental exam. The Navy dentist gave me a slip to take to my dentist as to what had to be corrected for me to pass the dental exam and advised me to come back after the work was completed. I departed and went to a pay phone booth, looked in the Pittsburgh yellow pages and located a dentist office. Since I did not have a Pittsburgh city street map in the car, I took a cab to the dentist's office. I deliberately didn't call first as I was sure his receptionist would insist on a later appointment. On arrival at the office, I showed the Navy paperwork to the receptionist and told her about the problem with my Navy physical. She took it into the dentist and in a few minutes he came out to the reception room and invited me into one of his chairs even though there were several patients waiting in his waiting room. He immediately went to work on the problem and in about a half hour or so I was out of the chair. This was in the years prior to the credit card age so I had to ask him if he would take a personal check for the work. The dentist patted me on the shoulder and told me good luck and to forget about the bill. I went back to the post office and found the same Navy dentist; he checked the dental work and I passed the physical.

The Navy chief had warned me that the Navy had not been prepared for such a sudden war; the service was very short of airplanes, instructors and aviation facilities and that it would be many, many months before I would be called up. And he had advised me that by the time I would be called up the war would be over and I would never get the chance to kill any Japanese.

On my way out of the post office I noticed an important looking Navy commissioned officer with several ribbons on his uniform, standing near the entrance to the office. Because of my CMTC training, I knew how to approach, salute and speak to an officer in an impressive manner. I approached him, smartly saluted, and told him about the CPT pilot program and the waiting list. He reviewed my CMTC papers and high school diploma, took down my name, address and phone number and told me he would be contacting me in a few days. I never heard from the full lieutenant again but less than a week or so later I received a letter from the Navy via the CPT administration that I would be called up to be a trainee in the CPT program as a prospective Navy aviation cadet. I was advised that I would be a candidate in the very next class at Westminster College, located just a short distance from my home. Actually it was a several months wait. The ole Navy chief had that delay information right but the Navy lieutenant had obviously helped me out.

K: How did your mother feel about your persistent efforts to join the military?

T: WW-II was a different kind of war for America. We were not the aggressor. We had been attacked by a very foreign ethnic people who had earned a terrible reputation for in-human conduct in China in the previous months and years. As of 1941, I had never met or even seen a live Japanese person. All I or my family knew about them was from the stories about their cruelty in the slaughter of the civilian women and children in China. When the Germans and Italians declared war on America a few days later we hated them too but nothing like the hatred of the Japanese. And as the war progressed the hatred of the Japanese grew to fever pitch. I think all mothers accepted the fact their sons were duty-bound to join up to kill the Japanese. My mother and father expected my older brother, Ray, who enlisted in the Marine Corps and me to join the military. They tried to discourage our younger brother, Donald, from enlisting when he dropped out of high school and enlisted in the Navy at age 16. As it turned out, Don was the first of the three of us to go overseas and the last one to return to the states after the war.

I was finally called up for the CPT program at Westminster College and commenced ground school in airplane basics, as well as in math, physics and related aviation subjects such as navigation and military aviation tactics. Most of the other 12 CPT students were college men with one to three years of college education, so I had a tough time keeping up with them in the ground school subjects. But we were flying Piper Cub aircraft, and I was the most experienced pilot in the class. I had been taking flying lessons at the local Conway airport near Aliquippa on my own the previous year ($8 per hour in the two-cylinder 37 horsepower Cubs) and so to impress my better educated associates, I wisely kept my mouth shut about that part of my background. I had not soloed at the Conway airport but had completed about six hours of training in the same type Piper planes (the only difference being the CPT Cubs had four cylinders and 65 horsepower) that we were flying in the CPT program. My instructor was amazed when I was ready to solo after just a few training flights and I was the first in the class to solo. My training at Westminster College included about 50 hours of flight time and several months of ground school. On the completion of the training, we all returned home to wait for our call up into the regular military service.

All twelve of our Westminster CPT group successfully finished the program but two of the students experienced some difficulties during the training. One pilot had difficulty with air sickness for most of the first few weeks of the training and was on the verge of dropping out when a doctor practicing at the college came up with some kind of liquid the pilot was able to drink a half hour or so before takeoff that solved the problem. Another of the pilots suffered from severe vertigo problems when practicing stalls and spins in the training but finally overcame the problem.

We (I) experienced some amusing incidents while participating in the CPT training period. One was for me on my first solo flight. After takeoff and climbing straight ahead I eased back on the throttle when I reached about 1,000 feet above the ground but the engine did not respond to reducing the power. While circling the field at full throttle (meaning some 70 or so miles per hour with my 65 horsepower engine) I continued to move the throttle back and forth but there was no response to my attempts to reduce the power. It is amusing for me to think back about the situation now because at the time with so little experience with airplanes I never thought about the fact I might overshoot the runway or fall short of the runway when I completed my solo flight instructions and attempted my landing. I have no remembrance of being overly concerned about the problem with the engine. After completing my 30 minutes of solo flight I made the standard downwind approach, turned off the ignition as I made my left turn to the final approach and landed with the dead engine. My instructor rushed out to the runway as I rolled to a stop and said, "Why did you stop the engine? You can't leave the plane on the runway." I then explained the problem and he said just sit there and I will pull the prop and start the engine. I turned on the ignition and when he pulled the prop through (there was no self starter on these engines) the engine came to life at full power. He started shouting pull the throttle back, pull the throttle back and I kept saying I am pulling it back. Then he said cut the ignition. After further investigation, we learned the bolt on the throttle rod from the throttle handle to the engine had fallen off and the engine was set at full throttle all the time.

Another hilarious incident occurred when we were attending a parachute instruction session on the field on a windy day. In the CPT program we did not wear parachutes flying the Cubs but were taught about the use of parachutes in the program. One of the students, I think it was Jennings, accidentally caused his chute to open and fall to the ground. It was a very windy afternoon and the chute ballooned out and started dragging him across the field. We all chased after him trying to tackle him and bring his journey to a stop. The race went on for about a hundred yards or so before we brought him to a stop. None of us were injured as it all occurred on a smooth grassy field.

While training at Westminster College, we had two amusing phone calls from two different frantic older women living in the nearby city of New Castle. The Piper Cub planes cruised at about 55 to 60 miles per hour and stalled out at about 25 to 30 miles per hour. Much of our training was learning to fly at just slightly above the stalling speed and also how to stall and do a two turn spin and recovery of the aircraft. So on a windy day, one of our pilots practicing flying just about the stalling speed and into the wind would appear to a person on the ground as standing still in the air. On two different occasions, a phone call from two different well meaning ladies came to our airport hanger advising us that one of our airplanes was stuck in the air above their homes! Of course younger people of this day having been born and living in the air age have no idea of how mysterious airplanes were to older people of that time. In 1942, just some 38 years or so after the first flights of the Wright brothers, the vast number of older people had never seen an airplane close up or flown as a passenger in an airplane so aircraft were a very mysterious entity for them.

During the waiting period following the completion of the CPT training I went back to work in the J&L machine shop. It was again a long wait and I thought the ole chief was right about the war ending before I graduated as a pilot. It was also frustrating because I felt I would lose my touch with regards to flying airplanes as it was no longer possible to

The US Navy January 1943 University of North Carolina pre-flight class. Tom is on the left end of the second row. Hard to imagine all these young men if still alive are old men in their mid-80s as of 2006.

US Navy Photo

privately rent or pay for instruction in aircraft because of the war.

This was of course another long wait as the Navy was desperately short of airplanes, instructors and aviation facilities during 1942, the first year of the war.

Finally my first written Navy orders arrived by mail to report to the Navy facility located at the Philadelphia, Pennsylvania railroad station on Christmas Eve, December, 1942. Now wouldn't you think that even in a major war, the clerk who prepared the orders would have thought about delaying the report date for 24 hours? On my arrival at the railroad station I not only checked into the Navy facility but was also immediately taken to a USO Christmas party where I met a few very attractive ladies. Right off the bat I started to think the Navy was one great organization to be a part of. The next day I boarded a train for Chapel Hill, North Carolina to attend the Navy Pre-flight training program at the University of North Carolina.

At that point of the war, all Americans, especially the American Navy senior officers, had learned the Japanese were not just a bunch of physically smaller people who we could defeat in a matter of months. During all of the first year of the war the Japanese had proven to be one tough and aggressive enemy and the U.S. Navy was desperate to acquire carrier-trained pilots and new ships.

K: Were you aware of the rounding up and internment of Japanese-Americans at this time? Are you concerned even today about the way our government uses times of stress and fear to suspend the rights of many of our citizens?

T: Kelle, think about your feelings of anxiety following the attack of the World Trade Center and then try to compare that feeling to the feeling of Americans when they heard about and then saw the pictures of the terrible destruction of our battleship fleet in Pearl Harbor. Also no one was aware that the loss of the battleships was not that important because battleships were already weapons of the last war in 1918, not of much use in the new type of war based on carrier warfare. Not knowing the facts about military logistics or the fact that battleships were no longer important in the new air age, Americans on the West Coast were expecting the Japanese Army to invade California in the same manner as they had invaded China and slaughtered the civilian Chinese. They, and I, thought that without the battleships we had no defense from the coming Japanese attacks. Now think of President Roosevelt's decision to hold the Japanese in camps. The US Navy from 1937 through 1941 had managed to gain intelligence regarding the propaganda being propagated to the Japanese citizens living in California, Oregon and Washington State.

How did they do that? The Navy (big surprise, the pre-war Navy had a few officers on their toes and thinking out of the box! Not very many but a few very bright officers.) One officer came up with the clever idea to plant trained sailor agents (some with Japanese language education) as the civilian employees (jobs like janitors, cleaning personnel, maintenance workers) of theaters and meeting halls on the West Coast and in Hawaii where the propagandists from Japan showed patriotic pro-Japanese programs and movies to Japanese-American only gatherings. These homeland messengers, with their literature and movies from Japan, praised the God-emperor and military leaders concerning the Japanese military operations in China and Manchuria. They were spreading the word of "Asia for the Asians" under Japanese leadership. These gatherings of thousands of enthusiastic Japanese-Americans living in America were monitored and recorded by the US Navy. Taped telephone messages from America to Japan and secretly opened mail from and to Japan of specific individuals revealed to Navy intelligence that pictures of our ships, anchorage locations and the time and departure dates of our warships were being sent to Japan on a daily basis. Identities of the few unpatriotic American-Japanese could not be efficiently nailed down by the Navy.

President Roosevelt was made aware of this Navy intelligence. No doubt it was a mistake to put all the Japanese into the camps but the fear and dislike of ethnic Japanese was understandable at the time. But I fully understand your concern about the use of stressful situations to take away citizens' rights. And I think you and I both will agree there hasn't been any event similar to the 1941 Pearl Harbor attack to justify such drastic actions by our government since that time. In the 1940s, America was regarded by most of the world's populations as the great friendly, isolationist, free nation of the world and millions of people tried to immigrate to America. Of course our current administration's aggressive militant (self-appointed policeman of the world) leadership of America has alienated us from most civilized nations.

K: I thought that 9/11 was a terrible event, but I was not frightened by it—perhaps because I've spent several years living overseas, and have seen the dislike of Americans by foreigners first hand. I felt, and still feel, that 9/11 happened because our government failed to protect our citizens as it has assured us it would.

T: I sure agree our American intelligence services failed big time to protect the American citizens from terrorists prior to 9/11 and I have very little faith in their current operations. I do not believe any of the political appointed individuals holding down home land security positions are qualified to protect us. Our government should send many of the personnel of the FBI and CIA to visit and be trained by the efficient intelligence services of Israel, Great Britain, France, Russia and Germany. We have been generous and helpful to these nations so I think it only fair they now help us train some qualified American security personnel.

K: It seems to me that after 9/11 many Muslims were arrested and are still being detained without trial, just because they are Muslim. Don't you think this qualifies as being very much like the rounding up of Japanese-Americans after Pearl Harbor?

T:Kelle, that is a tough Muslim question that has been intensely debated since the 9/11 attack of the World Trade Center. My personal opinion is that there is no way to differentiate the peaceful Muslim from the terrorist Muslim making the work of our leaders involved with the safety of our nation extremely difficult. Near the end of WW-II, the administration was rapidly becoming aware that the vast majority of the Japanese Americans were fiercely loyal to America with thousands of the young Japanese men volunteering to fight both in the Pacific and in Europe. In Hawaii they were the most dedicated hard workers in repairing our damaged ships. The administration was beginning to release many Japanese Americans from the camps in 1945. I am confident that by 1946, if the war had continued, Eleanor Roosevelt would have convinced Franklin to close down the camps.

Muslims in America are much different than the loyal misunderstood WW-II Japanese Americans in that you rarely hear any Muslims condemning the brutal killing of innocent people by the Muslim fanatics. Occasionally Muslim leaders make weak statements that the Muslim religion really stresses peace. I have read they remain silent about the killings because they are as afraid of the Muslim terrorists as we are. The word is that they know damn well there are a few terrorists among their American Muslim flocks who would kill any Muslim in America who fiercely and publicly condemned the action of the Muslim terrorists. They also know many of the imams in the mosques are teaching hate and recruiting young men to travel to Muslim hate schools in Pakistan. If they were loyal Americans, the imams could easily send anonymous letters to the FBI regarding their suspicions of fanatic members of their flocks. At least a few of the imams know who is financing the hate programs and who is recruiting the young fanatics. But rather than helping the FBI, the vast majority remain silent.

Religious and ethnic hatred of any kind is the most devastating odium that can exist in a society. Since my return from WW-II, I have tried hard to remove the prejudices that were implanted in my mind as a youth by American society of the 1920s and 1930s regarding our dedicated loyal black and Jewish citizens. I will never forget the emotion I experienced a few years ago walking among the many Jewish stars on the tombstones in the American Normandy cemetery in France. In fact, my favorite business partners in my civilian real estate business life have been Jewish business men.

I am sincere and honest when I say that in my opinion, Martin Luther King was one of the greatest of the white or black leaders of the 1900s for the good of the future well-being of all Americans, black and white. I will never forget his emotional speech in Washington, DC, "I have a dream." I can not recall ever hearing my parents making prejudiced statements about blacks (called colored people in those days) or Jews. My mother's black maid, Fanny, was a favorite and much loved by all of our family.

However, derogatory statements about the colored were rampant among my playmates and in Sunday school we were taught the Jews were "Christ killers". I do not remember ever meeting or knowing a Jew until I left home to join the Navy. But if I am to stick to my word of writing only the truth in my memoir, I must admit I detest the sight of the Muslim women and men in America who resist looking, acting and dressing like Americans so I obviously harbor prejudice. I do not believe they have any use for people like me, black Americans or Jewish Americans or our form of democratic government.

Please be sure I strongly believe and support the dictates of my 1776 forefathers, so in my opinion the Muslims living in America must have the right to believe as they do, live the kind of life they prefer and enjoy all the freedoms our 1776 forefathers have made available to all Americans. Nevertheless, it is my personal preference not to associate with any of them. If the majority of the imams of the American Muslim mosques across America were loyal American citizens they would unite in a national coast to coast campaign (in an association similar to the loyal black Americans' NAACP organization) to publicly condemn and help subdue the actions of the Muslim fanatic terrorists. If the American Muslim imams were dedicated loyal Americans, they would recruit loyal American Muslims to infiltrate the fanatic terrorists cults; they would then report back to the imams who could secretly get the information to the FBI. The imams and only the imams have the ability to infiltrate the fanatic hate cells as their recruits would look like and speak the language of the members of the fanatic groups. This type of infiltration activity is/was how the FBI infiltrated the Ku Klux Klan with dedicated educated American southern men who risked their lives infiltrating the clan's groups.

I am so suspicious of the Muslim culture that I doubt if I could ever develop a friendship with a Muslim. I am both suspicious and afraid of them. So now you know that because of my prejudice I cannot truly answer your question about Muslims. At the same time you also know for sure I would never question my 1776 forefathers dictate that all Americans regardless of their authenticity, faith or color are to have both the freedom of and freedom from religion. And I reserve the right for myself to socialize, do business and just hang around with the kind of people I trust and enjoy.

K: But don't you think if the majority of Americans had the same opinion you have that it would be counter-productive in the nation's attempts to assimilate the immigrant Muslims?

T: Kelle, I know this is a prejudiced statement, but I truly believe there are three types of people that cannot be assimilated into a civilized democratic nation unless they give up their teachings: practicing Muslims, fanatic Christians seeking theocracy laws and Gypsies. I know a second generation Gypsy who turned his back on his culture and family and became a true American, military service veteran and business man. He told me many stories as to why a practicing Gypsy can never be assimilated into our culture unless he or she abandons the cult. So be it with the Muslims. Let the American Muslim imams make the first patriotic effort to combat terrorism and embrace the separation of state and religion, then I might reconsider my opinions.

Now I have to tell you another amusing story. Shooting the bull with a security officer at the Los Angeles Airport along with a first officer airline pilot (former Navy pilot) we got on to the subject of profiling passengers. The security officer mentioned it never bothers him to see a bunch of young Anglo, black or Latino guys together heading for the passenger area but when he sees a bunch of Arab or Muslim looking guys together he passes a warning up the line. He is confident his information would result in an anonymous armed marshal being assigned to whatever flight they board. Is this prejudice or common sense? I sure hope there are many alert airport security personnel like this one.

Now back to Navy aviation in 1942. By late 1942, the Navy had lost several carriers in combat in the Pacific, had learned that their battleships were useless against enemy air power and that their carrier air groups were in great need of pilots. Because of the carrier ship losses, at one time in 1942 only three American aircraft battle-ready carriers with fully manned air groups (mostly equipped with inferior aircraft) were in service in the Pacific Fleet and one of them was damaged and under lengthy repair.

Needless to say, once we aviation cadets were called up, we were rushed through flight training in a hurry. Just a week or so past eleven months from the date I departed Aliquippa to report to the Navy facility at the Philadelphia, Pennsylvania railroad station, I was a qualified carrier dive bomber pilot. We had been rushed through the Navy pre-flight school at Chapel Hill University in North Carolina. After that, it was on to primary flight training at the Glenview Naval air station near Chicago, then advanced training at the Corpus Christi Naval air station in Texas and the many other air training fields near Corpus Christi, then back to the Glenview Naval air station for completing simulated carrier landing practice. This carrier landing practice was with a signal officer standing in a grassy pasture with a rectangle of white chalk lines looking similar to both a football field and a carrier's deck near the Glenview Naval Base airfield. This was followed a few days later by flying our SNJ training aircraft out over the lake and making five carrier landings on the Great Lakes training aircraft carrier, the USS Wolverine. The Wolverine was a hastily converted old 1911 side wheel ferry boat made into a Great Lakes aircraft carrier. The Navy simply cut off the entire passenger superstructure and built a flat platform on the old ferry boat. Good thinking on the part of the Navy brass as there sure as hell were no enemy submarines in the Great Lakes.

My Navy basic flight training at the Glenview Naval air station flying the N2S biplanes was a challenge for me. The N2S (nick named the Yellow Peril) was a 1925-designed plane very similar the Boeing PT-17 Stearman that the Army Air Corps used in training their pilots. Apparently during the depression years of the 1930s, the Navy had purchased the license to build the N2S in the Philadelphia Navy aircraft factory to save money. All of the N2Ss were painted bright yellow to help the new pilots see the many other yellow perils milling around in the air in the same vicinity during training flights.

There were several reasons for the challenging problems I and other cadets encountered in the basic training at the Glenview Naval base. The first problem was the terrible weather we experienced when we arrived in the winter months in the Chicago area. Often the temperature in the early mornings was 5 to 10 degrees below zero. The N2S was an open cockpit old fashioned biplane and we were flying in heavy cumbersome flight suits wearing bulky flight boots. Another problem was being rusty because following the completion of the CPT program, we had waited a long time for our call up and then had spent several months in pre-flight training at one of America's universities. The Navy pre-flight program was really copied after the US Marine Corps boot training and was conducted mostly by Marine Corps supervisors with very little ground school training related to aviation. My flight group had trained in comfortable weather at North Carolina University. Another problem was simply the fact the Navy was still having problems with organization, management and a shortage of well trained instructors. The officers responsible for the management of such a massive flight training facility which Glenview NAS had become over a short period of time were obviously in over their heads trying to cope with the demands of the program. The base had about 200 Yellow Peril airplanes, over 500 cadets at any one time and hundreds of mechanics still learning their trade. A few of the flight instructors were excellent but many of them were still learning the fundamentals of being a proficient flight instructor. Each time I went on a training flight I would have a different instructor who would look at my pilot training folder and then give me a brief few minutes' discourse as to what we were to practice on that day's flight. This type of instruction was nowhere near as efficient as the training in the CPT program where each student flew with the same instructor on all training flights making it possible for the student and instructor to develop a sound relationship.

The N2S built by the Boeing Aircraft Company and the N3N built by the Navy Aircraft Factory by civil service workers were identical airplanes, the only difference being the ones built at the Navy Aircraft Factory cost twice as much. They were powered by either Lycoming 215 HP or Continental 220 HP radial air cooled engines. The airplanes did not have any type of radio or electronic gear and with open cockpits it was near impossible to read anything printed or written on paper. It required two people to start the engine, one to crank the engine flywheel and one in the cockpit to work the engine controls. In basic flight training the instructor would sit in the rear cockpit and the cadet would crank the engine. On solo flights, the cadet sat in the cockpit and the mech cranked the engine. The cruising speed was about 85 miles per hour and the top speed about 120 MPH. It was a sturdy aircraft and indestructible in acrobatics and max speed dives with sharp hard pull ups out of the dives. Photo: US Navy

The Navy had a policy of making sure they culled out any cadets that were marginal in the basic phase of the training. This made sense as it was a loss of time and effort and an inefficient use of scarce resources to have a pilot graduate into the advanced training only to be washed out. As I recall the state of affairs of the flight training at the Glenview basic training facility, a cadet faced being eliminated after committing two unsatisfactory aviation incidents. The two incidents could consist of having two consecutive unsatisfactory instructor pilots write ups following check out flights. Another type incident could be damage to an aircraft caused by pilot error or getting lost on a solo flight, landing at some remote field or pasture resulting in lost training productivity. A lost pilot landing in such a place required the use of many man hours to retrieve the plane and pilot. In some cases, the plane would have to be put on a truck to move it to a safe take off field.

Failure of a medical examination which we took on arrival at the base indicating the need for grounding the pilot for several weeks of treatment for any reason was cause for being washed out of the program with an honorable discharge. Failure of a second medical exam about two months after arrival was another cause for immediate honorable discharge. The Navy also conducted extensive information sessions about safe sex and venereal disease. The movies they presented showing the gory effects of the various types of venereal disease to a person's private parts and mouth were tough to sit through. We used to joke after some of these sessions that the next time we went home on leave we wouldn't even shake hands with our own sisters. Nevertheless, we lost a significant number of cadets due to venereal disease. Chicago was a wide open town during WW-II and the attractions on notorious Clark Street in downtown Chicago were tough to pass up on our one day off each week following a grinding tough week of intensive training. A cadet catching a venereal disease at Glenview was given an immediate honorable discharge with no treatment by the Navy for the disease before picking up his railroad or bus ticket home.

Because of the intensity of the program and the significant culling of the cadets in basic training, I remember my months of training at Glenview NAS more clearly than the more unperturbed advanced training that followed at the Corpus Christi NAS in Texas.

I had several incidents at Glenview that came close to sending me back to civilian life. Fortunately, they were not consecutive so I never faced a second incident review board— the normal procedure that ended a cadet's Navy career. In some instances, but not very often, the board would grant a second chance.

My first serious incident that I was able cover up to avoid being eliminated from the program was getting lost on a solo flight. Each day after the training flights departed, any cadet not scheduled to fly in the morning flight could sign up to take off on a solo flight on his own if there were any spare aircraft. I would normally get in the line of cadets to sign up for one of the spare planes in the morning or if I flew in a training morning flight, I would sign up for one of the spare planes in the afternoon. I did this so often that upon graduating from the basic training program, I had logged 55 hours more flight time than the next highest cadet in my class. I have always been close with the buck and a taker of free opportunities (probably as a result of being raised in the 1930s depression era) and I was very conscious of how much it had cost me to rent flight time before I joined the Navy. Now I could fly free!

My N3N flight time combined with the number of hours I had flown in the CPT program approached 200 hours which would be enough to apply for a job somewhere in aviation in the event I failed to qualify as a Navy pilot. We had all heard stories about Navy cadets who had been washed out and then found good jobs as co-pilots in the civilian airlines where the firms were desperately seeking pilots. The notable attraction of the use of the spare planes was not just because it was free, but that I could go on a fun sightseeing joy ride or do a little training on my own.

Chicago was a great city to eyeball. The day I got lost I hadn't been paying attention to my wandering around sightseeing in the northwest part of Illinois. When I realized it was time to get the plane back to the base to be serviced and made ready for the afternoon flights, I realized I was hopelessly lost.

The NSN Yellow Peril had no radio equipment whatsoever and we did not have maps in the planes; all training flights were local and not very far from the base. Besides, being dressed in bulky flight gear and wearing heavy gloves in the windy open cockpit made it nearly impossible to use a map. I decided to land in a smooth green field next to a highway to see if I could learn where in the hell I was because I had to get the plane back to the base on time. I knew I could not stop the engine while I inquired because the N3Ns did not have self starters. To start a N3N engine, it was necessary to have one person in the cockpit and a second person on the left side of the engine to crank the flywheel that enabled the person in the cockpit to engage the clutch and start the engine.

Thanks to a previous experience with the N3N, I was not too concerned about covering up being lost in case I had to stop the engine after I landed. The experience I had was with an instructor a few weeks earlier whereby we had been practicing acrobatics and while upside down in a loop, the carburetor float had stuck and the engine stopped. We made a forced landing in a pasture, went to the farmhouse, called the base and had a mechanic come out to fix the engine. The N3N had a reputation of having the carburetor occasionally sticking in acrobatics during upside down maneuvers.

In that previous incident the field was large enough for the instructor and me to take off safely after the mechanic fixed the carburetor. I made up my mind that if I could not land, learn where I was and take off again, I would call the base and claim engine trouble from practicing acrobatics. I was determined not to have a first incident occur on my record that might lead to the end of my Navy training. So as I made my plans for the landing, my main concern was how I would be able to communicate with someone on the ground with the engine running or whether the plane would stand still while idling as I got out of the plane and contacted someone.

I carefully made my approach to a large pasture to line up parallel to a highway as I saw a few cars traveling on the two way road and figured the driver of any one of them could tell me where I was. When the plane rolled to a stop I sat in it for a few minutes to see if the idling engine would cause the plane to move. The plane sat still with the engine slowly idling. I gingerly got out still wearing my parachute, picked up some debris and put it in front of the right wheel to make sure the plane would not move, got over to the fence, climbed over and walked over to the road. The first car to come by stopped as I waved to him and the middle aged very surprised man found himself talking to a guy dressed in heavy winter flight gear, wearing a parachute, leather helmet and goggles asking him where in the hell he was in the state of Illinois! He was very excited and helpful. He took a road map out of the glove compartment, got out of the car, laid the map across the hood of the car and showed me where I was. He gave me the map to take with me and walked over near my plane as I got back into the cockpit and waved goodbye as I taxied back to the end of the field for my take off. I'll bet that made for a very interesting story to his wife and family when he got home. I got back to Glenview NAS about 45 minutes late but no one questioned me about my late return. I never mentioned the incident to even my closest friends until I graduated with my wings of gold and then it became a hilarious bar and party time story.

Another incident was my first night time solo flight when I ground looped after landing and scraped the lower left wing of the N3N on the ground. The incident occurred following a previous evening of training confusion by the instructors and schedulers of night flying training. What had happened the evening before was the schedulers of the flights had scheduled too many cadets and planes for the number of instructors scheduled to be available for the night familiarization training. As a result, several of the cadets, me being one of them, did not get to fly a familiarization night training flight with an instructor in that exercise. The next evening only the cadets were scheduled. The schedulers did not list any instructors as they mistakenly assumed all of the cadets had been trained the night before. When I saw my name on the schedule I assumed I was supposed to go solo on my first night flight. As luck would have it, there was no moon and it was black as hell around the Glenview NAS that evening. I took off and climbed straight ahead to about 2,000 feet altitude and commenced doing the maneuvers prescribed in the training manual. At the end of the two hour period, I made my approach to the landing and experienced difficulty trying to judge my height above ground as I crossed over the edge of the field. It was a rough touch down and in the melee I over-corrected for the cross wind and ground looped. It was minor damage to the lower wing and when the instructor investigator making the report learned the details of the mismanaged two evenings of night flying training, he told me he was going to terminate the accident report. He said he would just have the mechs patch up the minor damage to the plane.

I also had two negative post-training flight reports by instructors but fortunately they were not consecutive and in the subsequent flights I performed OK. In the second incident, the instructor who gave me the favorable evaluation following the subsequent flight laughed as he was doing the paper work and said, "I see you had a flight with old down check Charlie on your last trip." That was a boost to my morale as I had been pretty depressed about my second poor evaluation report.

I think the most hilarious incident that occurred while based at Glenview NAS was when one of our flight group cadets returned to base and landed without his flight instructor who had departed in the rear cockpit with the student. Here is how this amusing incident came about. In our flight training, the instructors always occupied the rear cockpit and used a communication system consisting of a speaking tube with a mouthpiece on each end of the tube and an extension of the tube into the earpiece of each pilot so that they could communicate with each other. There were no radios or electronics in N2S aircraft. The flight was an acrobatic training flight and for some reason we learned later the instructor had removed his seat belt, possibly to adjust or retrieve something in the cockpit, and then forgot to re-fasten it after he accomplished whatever he was about with the belt not attached. When the student completed a loop he no longer heard any instructions from the rear cockpit, looked back and was shocked that he no longer had the flight instructor aboard. The cadet returned to the field, landed and excitedly rushed into the operations

On our arrival at the Corpus Christi Navy Base we were first introduced to the SNV Valiant and NR-1 Recruit aircraft. I believe both aircraft were built from very similar plans, the SNV Vultee Aircraft Company and the NR-1 by the Ryan Aircraft Company. In any event, when you checked out in either one a pilot would find the other aircraft about the same type airplane. Fixed landing gear, two speed propeller (fast for takeoff and landing and slow for cruise) and the first planes for cadets to fly with landing flaps. The planes were not equipped with electronics or radios. Being the first low wing monoplanes airplanes the cadets flew made us feel like skilled and consummate pilots ready to take on the enemy. Little did we realize how much we were yet to learn before advancing to the fleet as carrier pilots. The aircraft were equipped with Pratt and Whitney air-cooled radial engines of 450 HP. The top speed was about 165 MPH (144 KTS) and they cruised at about 120 MPH. Photo: Fred Bamberger

Once Navy aviation cadets were thoroughly checked out and proficient pilots in the Vultee Valiant and the Ryan Recruit the cadets were introduced to the North American Aircraft Company's SNJ, the most advanced training aircraft used in WW-II. The Army Air Corps called the aircraft an AT-6. Both the Navy and Army used the nickname of "Texan" for the aircraft while the British nicknamed it the "Harvard". Aviation cadets honed many of the skills required for combat on the Texan, including instrument flying, formation flying, navigation, radio communication, gunnery, dive bombing and operation of an aircraft with "complex" features such as variable pitch propellers, retractable landing gear, and flaps. We also made our first five carrier landings with the SNJ. By the time most students began training on the Texan, they had already passed the "weed-out" stage of primary flight training. Navy students would usually have already acquired over 250 hours of flight time on primary trainers such as the Piper Cub, Navy N3N and N2S, SNV and NR-1 before they were checked out in the SNJ. Once a pilot was checked out and proficient flying the SNJ (also nicknamed "the pilot maker") the pilot could easily check himself out in the single seat combat WW-II fighter airplanes with nothing more than a hand book and take off. Most WW-II combat fighters were easier to fly than the SNJ. Powered by a 550HP Pratt and Whitney air-cooled radial engine, the SNJ had a top speed of about 200MPH and cruised at about 150MPH. Of the over 17,000 Navy SNJ, British Harvards and AT-6 (all the same type aircraft) there are about 300 of them still flying around America in 2006.

In this picture I am in the front cockpit of an SNJ. For my 75th birthday gift, my son Robert purchased a one hour acrobatic flight for me with one of the aviation service firms that tour the USA. By coincidence, on the day I flew, a 74 year old WW-II Navy F6F fighter pilot veteran was also enjoying a one-hour flight in the aircraft. So with the consent of our instructor safety pilots in the rear cockpits of both aircraft we decided to have a dog fight with the two camera equipped aircraft. I have to brag here as when the film was developed I had obviously won the dog fight but I must admit my safety pilot in the rear cockpit did much of our maneuvering. Wow, that's a birthday gift I will never forget. I always enjoyed flying the SNJ during my entire Navy career. I would like to fly it some more but it now costs $350 per hour to fly the Texan solo and much more with a instructor pilot. Photo by Robert McBride office to report the loss of his instructor. There was of course great excitement at the base as the loss was a mystery and there had been no communications by phone from any possible witnesses of a man falling to earth from a plane. The flight had departed the base at about 1 p.m. About 5:30 p.m., the very embarrassed flight instructor showed up at the gate of the base with his parachute rolled up in a bundle. He had arrived thanks to the generosity of a citizen who had picked the pilot up thumbing for a ride along a highway some hundred or so miles from the base.

On the completion of the Navy basic flying program, we were put aboard a train for Corpus Christi NAS. Our treatment as aviation cadets on our arrival at Corpus Christi NAS was as different from our treatment at pre-flight and basic flight training as apples and oranges. The respect and treatment from every level of the service from the officers down to the lowest level of rated seaman was very noticeable. We had arrived and were treated as tested and proven capable Navy pilots.

The bulk of our training from that point on for the cadets signing up for single engine, single piloted carrier type aircraft was nearly all solo training. The majority of the flights with two pilots aboard were when one cadet flew with another on instrument flight training with one of the pilots acting as a lookout while the other was training under the hood.

A pilot qualified to fly an SNJ was very comfortable moving up to flying solo in any of the single engine, single cockpit Navy or Army combat aircraft used in WW-II. Very few pilots washed out and discharged from the service during the advanced training in the NR-1, SNV, and the SNJ. The Navy had too much money, training resources and such a great need for fleet pilots that they were reluctant to lose any of the advanced training pilots unless the reason for discharge was of major magnitude. If a pilot at that stage of the game did not seem ready for combat, he would receive orders to be an instructor in one of the basic flight training bases or assigned as a co-pilot or navigator in a multi-engine crew.

Amazingly, I arrived back in my hometown of Aliquippa on ten days leave as a Navy Ensign Officer, with gold wings and me looking just like the poster picture of the Navy pilot I had seen in the Pittsburgh post office just twelve months after departing for flight training. But of course I was not as good looking as the male pilot model. A fully trained carrier pilot in one year of training! Chances are, as just an immature high school graduate, I probably would have taken years to complete the program in the peacetime Navy.

After completing my leave and showing off with my gold wings on my new Navy uniform to as many friends as possible, (especially young ladies), in Aliquippa and my former hometown in Carnegie, I departed by train for the Daytona Beach Naval air station in Florida which was the Douglas SBD Dauntless pre-combat carrier dive bomber operational training base.

In Daytona Beach, I and all the other Navy personnel of that relatively small base

There was no check out with an instructor for our first flight in the SBD. We were given a handbook to study and the next day we flew the SBD. Considered obsolescent when the war started in 1941, the SBD soon proved itself a "slow but deadly" war plane. The two-seat SBD with the pilot in the front cockpit and a gunner, radio man in the rear cockpit, armed with two 50 cal machine guns for the pilot and two 30 cal guns for the gunner, carrying up to a 1,000 lb bomb was the workhorse carrier-based bomber for the US Navy in the first years of the war.

The Dauntless was powered by a 1,200 HP Wright radial air-cooled engine, had a top speed of about 200 MPH (factory claimed it was 250 MPH). It cruised at 125 MPH (not much faster than WW-I fighter planes) but it was built like a tank and could sustain heavy combat damage and still return to the carriers safely. The pilots loved the old bird.

The SBD Dauntless continued as the standard shipborne dive bomber of the US Navy from mid-1940 until November 1943 when the first operational Curtiss Aircraft Company built SB2C arrived to replace it. The official nickname of the SB2C was "Helldiver" but the pilots called it the "Beast." It was pilot unfriendly, difficult and tiring to fly, hard to maintain and much more difficult to accurately bomb targets as well as the SBD. In 1942-43, at the Battle of the Coral Sea, in the early war bitter Guadalcanal campaign and most of all in the crucial Battle of Midway, the Dauntless did more than any other aircraft to turn the tide of the Pacific War. At Midway on 4 June 1942, it wrecked and sank all four Japanese carriers, and later in the battle sank a heavy cruiser and severely damaged another. In the Guadalcanal Campaign the Dauntless–operating from US carriers and from Henderson Field on the island of Guadalcanal itself–took a huge toll of Japanese shipping. SBDs sank the carrier Ryujo in the battle of the Eastern Solomons, and damaged three other carriers in the battles of Eastern Solomons and Santa Cruz. In the decisive Naval Battle of Guadalcanal, 12-15 November 1942, SBDs sank the heavy cruiser Kinugasa and, supported by Douglas Aircraft Company built TBD Devastators, sank nine transports. When the more modern and powerfully-engined 1,700HP Helldiver went into action alongside the SBD it was soon realized–particularly at the Battle of the Philippine Sea–that the new aircraft was faster but inferior to the Dauntless. But the Helldiver was already in large-scale production and despite the anger and demands of the dive bomber pilots, it was too late to reverse the decision that it should supplant the Dauntless in shipboard service. Unfortunately Douglas had already taken down the production lines of the reliable ole Dauntless.

had an experience few men ever get to enjoy and live through. That unusual experience was the over whelming number of attractive young ladies near the base. The Daytona Naval Air Field was located very near one of the largest women's WAC, (Women's Army Corps), training bases of WW-II. When we would go into the city of Daytona Beach there would be at least ten to fifteen young ladies about our age to every male in the city. Sometimes they would whistle at us and in more than one case, I had cute ladies walk up to me and invite me to have a drink with them or to go to a night club where there was dancing and partying. Never again during the war would any of us experience any great liberties such as we enjoyed in Daytona Beach! In California and Hawaii, it was the exact opposite; about ten to fifteen men to any ladies in the cities. The dive bombing training was intense and hard work and the partying in Daytona Beach was also intense.

The SBD Dauntless dive bomber was designed in the mid-1930s and as WW-II started, was an obsolescent 125 knot cruising speed military plane that did not have self sealing fuel tanks, (meaning it caught fire easily in combat), lacked adequate armor protection, modern gun sights or folding wings to save space on the carriers. Even in the worst days of 1940 when the British were desperate for aircraft, they were not interested in the USA sending them any obsolete SBD dive bombers.

The airplane was very stable, pilot friendly and we considered it built as strong as a tank. The SBD was so pilot-friendly that it was much easier to fly than the SNJ we used in our earlier training in Corpus Christi. Surprisingly, during the early years of the war, the SBD was the key aircraft in winning the Battle of Midway, (four Japanese carriers sunk in that attack by SBDs), and several other fleet battles. Needless to say the British RAF experts were amazed, but they never ordered any SBDs.

When WW-II ended, aviation historians noted the Douglas SBD dive bombers had sunk more Japanese war ships than any other type of airplane used by the US Navy, the Army or any aircraft carrier aircraft of the British Navy.

While training in Daytona Beach with the SBD dive bombers, I experienced my first painful trauma of losing my then best Navy friend and roommate, 19 year old Ensign Paul Williams. We had been close friends in training for many months, spent many liberties together and in fact had been partying at a WAC party in Daytona Beach the night before he was killed. Paul and another pilot of our 12 pilot SBD training squadron were both killed in an instrument flying training crash. Paul had been the rear cockpit lookout safety pilot when the crash occurred. Our training squadron was then reduced to just ten pilots.

I was assigned to accompany Paul's body and casket on the train back to his hometown

Lt. William Hall was the instructor pilot for our new 12 pilot fleet operational training SBD group at the Daytona Beach Navy Base. He was an outstanding combat experienced dive bomber pilot, an excellent teacher and leader who taught us how to be skillful dive bomber pilots. Lt. Hall was a veteran of the Coral Sea battle and was serving on the USS Lexington when the carrier was sunk during the battle.

in Mississippi. It was heartbreaking to see the pain and suffering of his family and long time girl friend and fiancée, Patty. Both Paul and I had, of course, been aware of many crash victims during our many months of training, but none of them had been our close friends. I arrived back at the Daytona Beach Naval base a much more sober and safety conscious pilot. Then two days after I returned from Paul's funeral, we lost two more of our group's pilots in a midair collision about 50 miles east of Daytona Beach over the Atlantic ocean in a gunnery exercise. So, of the 12 pilots in our original Daytona Beach training group, we only graduated eight qualified combat ready SBD carrier dive bombing pilots.

K: Do you feel the Navy's assigning you to accompany Paul's body was done for a reason?

T: I had never thought of that. In WW-II, the Navy always tried to send a friend of the deceased pilot killed in the states along with the body by train to the hometown of the deceased. I was shocked when changing trains in Jacksonville, Florida, at the number of flag-draped coffins in the storage room at the depot. There were many Army and Navy air bases in Florida and the training of young pilots in advanced combat type aircraft took its toll. When a Navy TBM torpedo bomber crashed, there would be three flag-draped caskets. When an Army B-25 crashed, there would be six or seven flag-draped caskets.

With the completion of the training in Daytona Beach, I received orders to report to AirPacCommand, (the Pacific Fleet Headquarters in San Diego, California), and had time to return to Aliquippa before heading to the West Coast. In the 1940s, the USA had great and efficient train service from almost any city in America to any other city in America so I was able to arrange my trip home first. At that time the USA railroad service was one of the fastest, most extensive and best in the world.

Following a short visit with my family, I boarded the train in Aliquippa to Pittsburgh, boarded a train to Chicago and then transferred in Chicago and boarded the famous Super

Nineteen year old Paul Williams, on the right, and I in New Orleans on the way to Daytona Beach. My best friend and roommate while based at the Daytona Beach Navy Base was killed in an instrument training flight accident about two months after our arrival to conduct SBD Dauntless training. Paul lived at 187 West Second Street in Clarksdale, Mississippi prior to joining the Navy.

When I packed Paul Williams personal gear following his being killed in a flight accident I kept this plaque that Paul used to joke about and had sitting on his dresser in our room at Daytona Beach. I have kept it for some 65 years or so remembering my old friend.

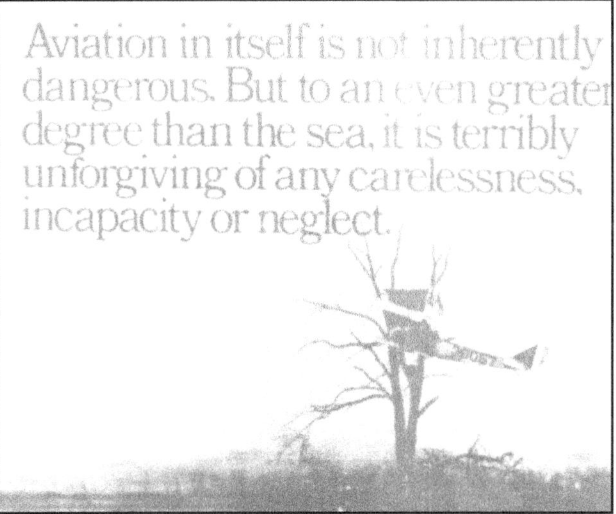

Chief Train for Los Angeles. This was the first trip in my life west of Chicago except for my training in Texas. Few people today are aware of what it was like to travel around America in the pre-WW-II years. There was very little air travel, few decent roads of more than two lanes; meaning a trip to California from Aliquippa or Pittsburgh, Pennsylvania to Los Angeles would take several weeks by car.

The Super Chief Train from Chicago to Los Angeles was the most famous American train to travel on at that time. When I boarded the train and was assigned to my sleeping berth along with the distinguished people who were able to acquire the rationed war time tickets for the train, I was one proud guy. As the only Navy pilot in my new Navy uniform and gold wings on the train I had a great time in the club car. The other passengers in the club car insisted on not letting me pay for any of my drinks or snacks. A few of the folks were professional men and lady actor/actresses who had changed trains from New York City to the Super Chief in Chicago. Imagine the thrill of a young pilot having an attractive actress (but 8 or 10 years older) inviting him to share a table, drink and conversation in the club car on one occasion during the trip with her insisting on paying the bill.

On arrival in Los Angeles, I was checked in at the Navy Los Angeles railroad facility, and then taken by bus to the North Island Naval Air Station in Coronado, across the bay from San Diego, the headquarters at that time for the Pacific Fleet Air Command.

Arriving at about 9:00 p.m., I immediately reported to the duty officer at the headquarters office and met my friend, Ensign McGuire, who I had trained with in Daytona Beach just a few weeks before. Mac walked into the duty officer's office in front of me and was assigned to fill a billet immediately, and to fly out to Hawaii the next day as an SBD carrier replacement pilot. I was next in line and was assigned to report to the Alameda Naval Air Station located on the San Francisco Bay, and to report to SBD Squadron VB-303. As it turned out, I ended up in a very long training period in the states while my friend McGuire was ordered to Hawaii and then immediately deployed just a few days later as a replacement pilot in a carrier air group that had suffered some heavy losses. McGuire's squadron then participated in the famous, "Battle of the Philippine Sea". In that battle, the Navy carrier air groups were launched too late in the day to be able to return to the carriers until late at night. The Navy had not yet trained for night carrier operations and as a result, many Navy aircraft ran out of fuel at night after the attack and were lost at sea.

K: I read about the carrier planes trying to find TF 58 in the dark. Admiral Mitscher ordered the carriers to fully illuminate, and the picket destroyers fired star shells in hopes of guiding the returning pilots in. Mitscher took a big chance there as the Japanese had subs and night-flying aircraft in the area. Doesn't it seem to you that in most tense situations there is someone who puts their butt on the line and does a gutsy thing?

T: You're right about Admiral Mitscher. He was well-liked by Navy personnel and had the reputation of really caring about all levels of servicemen under his command. However, many pilots of that late carrier launch thought he and his staff should have known better than to launch so late in the day. Remember, this was before the Navy had learned how to operate carrier aircraft at night.

The U. S. Navy won the battle as the attacks on the Japanese ships and air groups took place before nightfall, but the recovered Navy pilots were bitter about the fact they could have been launched more efficiently and earlier than they were. The delayed launching was caused by lack of expertise in carrier warfare, indecision, poor communications, in-house staff bureaucracy and turf jealousy among the admiral's staff decision makers. The Navy was still in a "learning how to fight a carrier war stage."

Of course Monday morning quarterbacking is an on-going fact of life in the military.

So about six months later, I was filing a local flight plan at the Alameda Naval base and in walks my friend, McGuire. After a bit of good will ole buddy type of conversation I mentioned, "Boy you sure got into combat in a hurry Mac."

Mac said, "Yep and let me tell you, these bastards have no idea how to fight aerial warfare." He was right about that, as in the early years of the Pacific war the leadership of the senior Navy fleet admirals directing air group tactics was not up to par. Many of the so-called senior Navy pilot staff officers in command of the carriers in the first years of the war were really nothing more than surface big gun ship (battleship and cruiser) officers who went through a brief pilot training program as senior officers, with just enough training to be able to takeoff, land and do a little local flying to earn their flight pay. But they had little knowledge about the actual capabilities, tactics and also the limitations of hard nosed carrier aerial warfare. Actually the senior Navy officers of all kinds had so little training during the decade long depression years of the 1930s they had very little experience to fight any kind of Navy war in the air, on the sea or under the sea. There was a joke among reserve officers about the regular Navy of the pre-WW-II depression years when the ships seldom went to sea and rarely ever fired their guns because the Navy had insufficient money to train.

Kelle, to give you an idea of how tight the Navy budget was in the depression and isolationist years of the 1930s, I have to tell you this story told to me by a retired warrant officer whose daughter I was dating while VF-84 was based on the North Island Naval Air Station in San Diego. He was a WW-I vet who made a career in the Navy and was serving on a heavy cruiser in the 1930s based in San Diego. The ships rarely went to sea and spent long periods of time just anchored in the bay. When they went to sea they seldom, if ever, fired the big guns because of the expense. The Navy would rotate the big ships to tie up at the San Diego civilian pier for what they called visitors days but actually the main purpose was to use the city of San Diego's water system to fill their fresh water tanks so that they would not have to use expensive fuel to manufacture water while anchored in the bay.

K: That was sure a very different era in our history as compared to our colossal lobbyist-inspired military/industrial multifaceted military budgets of today!

T:We would joke, "The pre-war regular US Navy was the only yacht club in the world that had armored ships and guns."

When the war started, they couldn't maneuver at night, couldn't hit targets with the big guns and had no idea of how to launch a coordinated air group attack day or night. This was not the fault of the Navy leaders or the Navy personnel. It was the fault of the isolationist American citizens and political leaders of America who would not financially support either the Navy or the Army during the peace time years between WW-I and WW-II. The military services simply did not have the financial resources to properly train and acquire modern equipment. I was fortunate that due to my long training period, by the time my Air Group One had been reformed from its first tour and deployed again in 1945, the senior fleet officers had more than three years to learn how to efficiently fight air battles and maneuver ships in formation at night. And they had learned under fire very, very well!

A few days after my assignment to VB-303, I departed the North Island Naval Base and boarded the train in San Diego for Los Angeles and then to Oakland. In Los Angeles, Ensigns Miller, Bob Applegate, Oscar Folsom, Charles Moxley and myself, all friends from our Daytona Beach and Corpus Christi training days, decided to stay over in the famous city of Hollywood which none of us had ever seen before. Luckily we ended up at a Hollywood USO party that evening where we got to meet some attractive Hollywood starlets. Miller and I elected to stay over two extra days as we were very lucky in our efforts to meet some new friends at the USO party.

After our arrival at the Alameda Navy Air Base, our squadron picked up our new SBD-5 dive bombers. The Douglas Company was still manufacturing the old SBD birds this late in the war since the new replacement SB2C Curtis Helldiver dive bombers had turned out to be horrible aircraft. The new SBDs had more powerful engines, improved gun sights, self-sealing fuel tanks and had earned the reputation as one of the most reliable carrier planes in the fleet despite their slow 125 knot cruising speed. The SB2Cs required a great many modifications to make them carrier-acceptable for combat. The SB2C aircraft soon earned the nickname of "the Beast."

K: Tom, were Marine pilots flying the Corsair at this time?

T: Yes. In the first real air battle of the Pacific war, the battle for the island of Guadalcanal, both Navy and Marine Corps pilots operated from Henderson Field flying Corsairs. Two of my favorite Navy pilots, my division leader ace, Ike Kepford and my commanding officer LCDR. Roger Hedrick (later a retired admiral) in squadron VF-84 flew Corsairs in that 1943 epic battle.

Our 18-aircraft VB-303 squadron departed Alameda for the Santa Rosa Navy Air Base a few days after we arrived. There we commenced our training in preparation for deployment as an island land-based dive bomber squadron to deploy in the Solomon Islands area of the Pacific.

A few months later, although considered a fully combat-ready squadron (based on our excellent gunnery and dive bombing records), we received word that our squadron was to be decommissioned, our SBD aircraft returned to the Alameda NAS and the squadron personnel to be transferred to the North Island Naval Base to become a part of the newly formed VF-84, F4U Corsair fighter squadron. The BuAer (Bureau of Aeronautics) decision makers in Washington had finally decided to commence carrier dive bombing operations with the 2,000 HP, speed of 400 MPH, six gun and rocket firing F4U Corsair fighter. The Corsair had now been designated as a dual purpose carrier dive bomber and fighter.

The F4U Corsair fighter aircraft was built by the Chance Vought Aircraft Company in Connecticut. Originally test flown in 1939, two years before the USA entered the war, the Corsair, with a speed of 400 MPH, was then the fastest fighter airplane in the world. However, the original design included many operational shortcomings, making it difficult to fly and dangerous for carrier operations. No one has ever been able to explain why the Navy BuAer would not accelerate correcting the problems to quickly get the superior Corsair aircraft into carrier combat. Fortunately the British went to great effort working with the Chance Vought engineers and with the help of the Grumman Aircraft and British aviation engineers, reworked the design of the Corsair making it not only one of the better, fastest and easy to fly Navy carrier aircraft, but also the most deadly combination fighter and dive bomber in the WW-II Pacific theater.

The Army Air Corps had an equally capable fighter bomber in the European theater in the P-47 Thunderbolt with the nickname of "the Jug." The British Navy commenced using the F4U aboard their carriers with great success in early 1943 and a few months later the US Navy decided to start deploying them on its carriers, but did not get around to forming the carrier F4U equipped air groups until late 1944. When used as a dive bomber, it was necessary to lower the landing gear of the Corsair as dive brakes before commencing the dive to prevent the plane reaching uncontrollable speeds.

No other WW-II carrier type aircraft could compete with all of the capabilities of the Corsair. The Navy's F6F Hellcat fighter, the Army's P-51 Mustang fighter and the British Seafire fighter, (British Navy version of the famous Spitfire), were almost as good as fighters, but none of them could dive bomb. The SB2C dive bomber had many short comings and was universally disliked by nearly all the pilots. The Corsair was capable of carrying out all types of air combat. It was a fighter and dive bomber, capable of ground and ship attacks with the new 5-inch rocket shells the same size as the 5-inch guns of the destroyer warships, and delivering devastating napalm fire bomb attacks in support of the marine troops invading and landing on enemy beaches.

While attached to VF-84, I was fortunate to have the opportunity to train and fly as a wing man with two of the Navy's best fighter pilots. LCDR Roger Hedrick, the commanding officer of VF-84, and LTJG Ike Kepford, my division leader. These two Navy aces shot down a total of 28 Japanese aircraft in the Guadalcanal battle before I joined their squadron. A story about their outstanding service at Guadalcanal is on the internet; (see Google, search word, LCDR.Roger Hedrick or Ira (Ike) Kepford). We pilots of VB-303 joined their VF-84 squadron at the North Island Naval Air station after they returned from the Guadalcanal air battles. The training I received in the VF-84 squadron with these experienced great fighter pilots gave me a bit of confidence to face combat when it was my turn to meet the Japanese.

K: I read the Guadalcanal story about Hedrick and Kepford on Google. Kepford was really an ace, only a few Navy pilots surpassed his kills—one was McCampbell with thirty-four. Wasn't it really hard for Navy pilots to rack up a large number of kills? At any rate, more so than land-based planes? Bong had forty, and Boyington had twenty-two, this makes Navy pilots like McCampbell and Kepford really impressive.

Ike Kepford in his battle-scarred F4U while based at Guadalcanal Island in 1943. Victorious in 16 encounters with the Japanese, Ike was at that time one of the top American aces with the 16 kills of Japanese airplanes. The 16 confirmed kills are indicated by the 16 small flags just forward of the number 29 on the aircraft. Ike was an outstanding running back on the Northwestern University football team before the war and a skilled fighter pilot. Ike was my division leader in VF-84, a good friend, patient and thorough instructor teaching SBD dive bomber pilots how to be good F4U fighter pilots. Photo US Navy.

T: Kelle, not to put down or lessen the gunnery skill or courage of our Navy and Army pilots in the Pacific, I have to mention that unlike the fighter pilots flying in Europe against the outstanding German engineered ME-109s and Focke-Wulf-190s, our Navy and Army fighter pilots in the Pacific in the second year of the war had the superior fighter planes. The F6F Hellcat, F4U Corsair and Army Major Bong had the great twin engine Lockheed P-38 Lightning to fight the then inferior Japanese planes that lacked armor and self-sealing fuel tanks. The highly maneuverable Japanese Zero gave our pilots all they could handle in the first year of the Pacific war as we had to fight them with the slow Navy F4F Wildcat and the Army P-40 Tomahawk. It was not until 1945, the last year of the war, when the Japanese came out with a small number of the armored 1,875 HP NIK2-J Shiden-Kai (Americans named it "George") equipped with four heavy 20 millimeter cannons that the Japanese fighter pilots were flying a really first class fighter aircraft. It was a George flown by the Japanese pilots of the crack Japanese 301 Squadron that tore up my USS Bennington cabinmate Apple's Corsair with their 20 MM cannons and forced Apple to bail out of his destroyed Corsair and later be rescued by the American submarine, SS Dragonet, just a few miles from the Japanese coastline. If the George aircraft had had good fuel, they would have been an even greater threat to our American fighters and bombers. Quality fuel is all-important in operating high performance engines, especially at high altitudes. The Japanese were in such desperate shape for lack of oil in 1945 that they were mixing fuel distilled from tree root sap with regular fuel obtained from petroleum.

Many years after WW-II, when both then-retired Admiral Roger Hedrick and I as a retired LCDR/USN/Ret, met in San Diego for lunch, we discussed many subjects including what each of us were doing in our civilian pursuits. I mentioned I was not too pleased owning a real estate firm just selling existing houses. The Admiral suggested I meet his younger brother, John Hedrick, owner of the Hedrick Construction Company as he knew of my interest in construction. A few weeks later his brother John (WW-II Army Air Corps officer) and I met and I then worked with John in the Hedrick/McBride Development Company until my civilian retirement.

Approximately 4 months after we VB-303 pilots joined LCDR Roger Hedrick's large 72-aircraft F4U squadron (that the Navy intended to deploy on an Essex class carrier as the first air group to consist of 72 Corsair fighters plus only two small squadrons of just 12 SB2C Helldivers and another with 12 TBM torpedo bombers), BuAer had a change of policy. I mentioned the Curtis-built SB2C that most pilots considered a beast airplane earlier. The reliable TBM was built by General Motors Corporation and performed well in combat. The top wheels of BuAer decided at a later date to cut the number of Corsairs to 36 planes and to add an F6F Hellcat fighter squadron of 36 aircraft to the ready to deploy Air Group 84. The F6F squadron joining Air Group 84 was already fully trained for combat. No doubt even at this late date in the war, the BuAer desk jockeys in the Pentagon were still leery about using the Corsair as a carrier fighter and wanted to have the reliable ole F6F's along in the air group just in case the Corsairs did not perform as well as they had been performing for the British Navy since early 1943. The Grumman-built F6F Hellcat had the same type engine as the Corsair, was probably the most pilot friendly and forgiving WW-II fighter, very rugged but was a bit slower than the Corsair and could not be used as a dive bomber. The F6F was also less costly than the Chance-Vought-built Corsair in that for the price of three Corsairs, the Navy could buy five Grumman F6F Hellcats.

Since the VB-303 SBD pilots were the last to join the VF-84 Corsair squadron we were all transferred to the re-forming Air Group One which was also based at the North Island NAS. Air Group One also consisted of 36 Corsairs (with the new name of VBF-1, meaning performing as both fighters and dive bombers for our squadron), VF-1 with 36 F6F Hellcat fighters, VT-1 with 12 TBM Avenger torpedo bombers and VB-1 with 12 SB2C Helldivers.

LCDR Roger Hedrick, Ike Kepford and many of the other combat experienced pilots of VF-84 were our role models and heroes so we former SBD VB-303 but new Corsair pilots were very disappointed with this decision of BuAer and AirPac to reduce the number of Corsairs in the air group.

Our new Air Group One commander, Cdr. Harden, was a dedicated, hard-driving leader, who led by example and instilled great enthusiasm into the training programs of all four squadrons of Air Group One. I am sure Cdr. Harden would have eventually become one of the top admirals in the Navy, but unfortunately he was killed in a carrier training accident in 1947 just two years after the end of WW-II.

Although the majority of the VBF-1 pilots were ready to deploy as a result of our extensive training in VF-84 under the leadership of LCDR. Roger Hedrick the other squadrons of the new Air Group One had to have time to organize and train.

While the other three squadrons of the air group remained at the North Island NAS, VBF-1 deployed to the Fallon Naval Air Station in Nevada for extensive 5-inch rocket firing, napalm drops and more dive bombing and gunnery training. The newly developed five-inch rockets had the same devastating power as a destroyer's 5-inch cannons. The Corsair had six rocket launchers installed with three rockets under both the left and right wing. While based in Nevada, the training was intense and we were both thrilled and amazed with the rockets' accuracy and the destruction the 5-inch cannon shells did to the targets. The pilots of VBF-1 were also introduced to the lifestyle of the inhabitants of the various sin cities of Nevada. We enjoyed experiences in Nevada many of us will never forget, the hangovers were tough, sin city life was fun but most of us lost a lot of money in the casinos. One night a senior lieutenant in our squadron lost over a month's salary at a roulette table and as he walked out of the casino, one of the executives of the casino caught up with him just outside of the casino and put two 100 dollar bills in his hand and simply said, "Go get them pal."

K: VB-1 eventually trained at Fallon. Did you ever run into members of that squadron while you were there?

T: We sometimes would enjoy their company at the officers club, having a few beers and I think a few of our pilots and the VB-1 pilots would occasionally go off together to enjoy themselves in the Fallon casinos. I have to admit Applegate, Folsom, Moxley and I were kind of a close knit foursome, having been training together ever since graduating as pilots and we would normally be going about our off base liberties pretty much on our own.

While based in Nevada, several of our pilots with the permission of our skipper, Lt. (and later LCDR Bob Ross), acquired two slot machines, one nickel machine and one dime machine, and these two slot machines traveled with the VBF-1 squadron wherever we were based and returned with the squadron to Alameda at the end of the war. Wherever VBF-1 was located on land or on ships, the slot machines were busy collecting nickels and dimes to support the expense of our squadron parties. Remember, in 1945 a nickel had about the same value as a quarter has in 2006 (maybe more like a half dollar) and a dime had the value of about 50 cents or a dollar in 2006 money. American money was of course worth a great deal more than the American money of 2006. In 1945, a cup of coffee cost a dime, a beer twenty-five cents and a carton of cigarettes a dollar. Our squadron members were not the only players; we promoted their location wherever we were based so every one could contribute to our party fund income. No doubt we were at times operating a gambling operation in violation of local laws in some of the locations where VBF-1 was based. While aboard the USS Bennington there would sometimes be a sign up waiting list for "non-squadron" customers to play the machines. Our squadron slot machine maintenance group knew how to adjust the machines so the payoffs were about the same as in the Reno casinos.

Finally all four fully trained squadrons of Air Group One, (VBF-1, VF-1, VB-1 and VT-1) deployed to the Alameda Naval Air Station across the bay from San Francisco, awaiting transportation to the Pacific Fleet in Hawaii. None of our squadrons had any airplanes at the Alameda Base as we were being taken to Hawaii on a troop ship and were scheduled to get new airplanes in Hawaii. While at the base, the majority of us would check the availability of the airplanes permanently assigned to the Alameda Naval base and when an airplane of any kind was available we would sign it out for a joy ride around California and Nevada, justifying the trip as "a navigational training flight." Our favorite destination in these "training flights" was to the sin city of that time, Reno, Nevada to visit with our much loved friends.

While waiting for our deployment on the troop ship we would sign in each morning between 8:00 and 9:00 a.m., then have breakfast, board the liberty boat for the trip across the bay to San Francisco and return late in the evening or the next morning before the time to sign in on the daily muster report.

One day while we were waiting at Alameda for the deployment, my close friend and roommate, LTjg Moxley, who often flew as my wing man, took me aside and told me he had just received word from his wife in Binghamton, New York that she had given birth to a baby girl. Since we still had no definite date as to when our troop ship would be boarding our air group, Moxy (as we called him) asked my opinion regarding the chance he might be able to get back to New York to see the new little girl and return. I was non-committal in my response, so Moxy then sheepishly asked me if I would sign him in each morning if he tried to make the trip. We both knew it would be a very serious problem for both he and the person signing the false muster if he failed to return in time to board the troop ship. Moxy decided to make the trip and I agreed to sign him in each a.m. muster while he was on the trip. This was a tough trip to make because the Douglas DC-3 airplane transports at that time only cruised at speeds of about 150 MPH, with many refueling stops enroute coast to coast. Every other day at a specified California time, I would wait near the BOQ (Bachelor Officers Quarters) phone to get his call, and brief Moxy about the ship situation and he would tell me his whereabouts. Each morning I would have an early breakfast at the BOQ and then go to the sign up muster desk and sign one of our names. Then I would go for a short walk and return and sign in the other name and then depart on the liberty boat for San Francisco.

Needless to say, while Moxy was on the trip, I suffered by not being able to sign up for overnight fun trips with one of the base's airplanes to Reno. I had to be on the base if not on an authorized Reno trip each day. Moxy made it back loaded with pictures of himself and his new daughter, several days before the troop ship was ready to load, and no one in the squadron ever realized he had departed for the trip as I made sure to sign in for him every day. Moxy carried pictures of the little girl in his flight suit, his uniform shirt pocket and had others mounted in our cabin on the USS Bennington. I believe every pilot in the squadron had, at one time or another, sat through a picture and conversation session with Moxy to be told about his little girl.

K: Tom, of course we both now know it is a different Moxley story than the memoir you are quoting and reading to me now, I refer to the one you wrote prior to our meeting a few months ago.

T: Yep, Kelle, we need to clarify the story as we both know the full story about Moxy's daughter, Katherine Moxley. Actually, it was my story in the USS Bennington history book that resulted in you and I meeting and discussing the ship, Moxley, the Corsair, the VBF-1 squadron, my rough memoir and other WW-II subjects. Kelle, I'll go first.

I was sitting in our living room one evening some months ago and received your

Moxley with wife and baby daughter, Katherine, in Binghamton, New York about a week or so before we deployed from San Francisco to Hawaii.

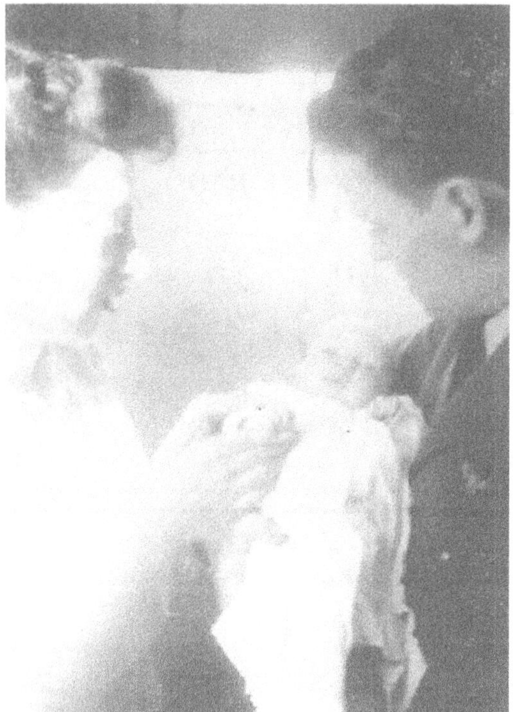

Top: Mox holding Katherine. He of course would never get to see her again.

Bottom: Katherine, husband, son and daughter with their pets. I believe this was a photo taken for their Christmas cards a few years before Katherine's death.

phone call regarding my Moxley story in the USS Bennington history publication. Once we got to know each other and I learned your extensive genealogical research background I requested you try to locate Moxy's daughter as I would like to tell her about her dad and my friend. I did not mention to you or my wife Karen that if you located his daughter I was planning for Karen and I to fly to New York (figuring his daughter would be somewhere in that state) visiting with her and then going to visit the New York library of our past president, Franklin Roosevelt. So now you tell your story.

K: Tom, looking for people sixty years after the fact is hard, but not impossible. Genealogy research requires me to look for people two hundred or three hundred years after the fact. What made finding Katherine Moxley hard to find was her gender. Females in our culture change their names perhaps many times during their lifetime. To complicate this, Katherine's mother was young when her husband, Charles Moxley, died and it was probable that she would have remarried, and that she may be deceased.

The first step was to find Charles Moxley's obituary if possible, so I turned to the library in his hometown of Binghamton, New York. Luckily, in the newspaper account of Moxy's WW-II death, his wife's maiden name, and the name of his in-laws, and the name of his daughter were listed. This is when I first found what Katherine's name was. Now I had two surnames to investigate in case one of them dead-ended. I had a friend who was able to access the 1930 census for the city of Binghamton, and I learned that Charles Moxley was an only child—I could see that the Moxley name was not going to provide many chances for success. I wrote to the Binghamton library for an obituary for Charles' parents—when I received these I was very disappointed to find that Charles' daughter, Katherine was not mentioned as a surviving granddaughter.

It was time to jump to Katherine's maternal grandparents. Since women always seem to maintain family connections with their family no matter what happens, I was sure that I'd have success going down this avenue. From searching the Social Security database, I found the dates of Katherine's maternal grandparents' death. Once more I asked the Binghamton library for the grandparent's obituaries and I finally struck paydirt. Again I asked my friend to look at the 1930 city of Binghamton census, and she found that Katherine's mother had two siblings, one sister and one brother. I contacted a genealogist researching Katherine's mother's family and learned that Katherine's mother had indeed remarried, and was deceased. The genealogist did not know anything about the whereabouts of Katherine's mother's siblings. I was lucky in that the obituaries also listed the places of residence for the surviving children. Now it was time to turn to my old stalwart, the on-line telephone directory. I always look for very unusual names when I go this route, and Katherine's aunt had a very unusual married name—and her husband's first name was listed in the obituary. I looked up every person with that first and last name in the state of New York. The fourth number I called was the correct one, but there was only sad news. Katherine Moxley had passed away about four months earlier. I was devastated—and now it was time to tell you, Tom, what I had found out about your friend Charles Moxley's daughter. I was able to get in touch with Katherine's husband and children, and related to them the story of Charles Moxley and his friend Tom McBride. Katherine's husband was kind enough to send me copies of the pictures that Katherine's father had carried with him into combat—with that this story was complete. And Tom, I gave you Katherine's husband's e-mail address and phone number so you could contact him. The puzzle had been solved, but in a very unsatisfactory way—I filed the details away in my growing file on the USS Bennington and her crew.

T: Kelle, I have difficulty explaining the emotional pain I suffered when I got the story about Katherine's death from my son John. It opened some painful old mental wounds, even though I had never met Katherine or seen any pictures of her since she was a few weeks old. If you remember, my computer was down at the time and you sent the information by e-mail to me with a copy to my son John. John called me on the phone as he knew my machine was out of action (he is the one who fixes it) and told me the bad news. I was shocked still thinking of her as a young lady. Then I started thinking of Moxy's wife, mother, father, grandparents and other relatives. Here was an only beloved son and husband killed strafing an enemy airfield on the last VBF-1 attack mission, on the last attack of the war.

No doubt the entire family celebrated along with the millions of other Americans when President Truman went on the radio to announce the war was over. All of them were thrilled to know Moxy would be home to see his daughter, renew his love affair with his beautiful wife, visit with all of his family and friends. What a joyous homecoming for the returning be-medaled Navy fighter pilot. And then a few days later the arrival of the military team to tell them Moxy had been killed on the last war mission of VBF-1 on the last attack of the war.

What could be more mentally painful and crushing! It had to be a nightmare scenario for the entire community that was so proud of Charles. For several days after hearing the news, I could not get the thought of the pain his wife, mother and father must have suffered with the loss of a dear husband and the parent's only son after celebrating America's victory for several days. Many families and wives suffered the pain and loss of a loved one during the war but this had to be one of the most mentally devastating losses suffered by any American family in WW-II.

To have the military team arrive a few days after the great victory celebration! An unbelievable mentally painful tragedy. A nightmare none of them would ever get over. Then after my reading the sad synopsis of the documentary, "Be Good Smile Pretty", about the life of the lady who lost her father in Vietnam as a one-year old baby and in her lifetime all she had was a photo of her father. Her remarried mother, just like Moxley's wife, did not want to ever discuss the loss of her husband. A very sad story. Then I learned Katherine's mother did not want to talk about Charles so Katherine only had the photos of herself as a few weeks-old baby with her father. And then you told me about how Katherine expended the effort, time and expense to fly to Hawaii just to visit the cemetery to see the memorial headstone of her father, knowing that we never did recover Charles' body from the Japanese. This story still brings tears to the eyes. As General Sherman said in 1865, "War is Hell on earth," or words very similar to that phrase.

K: Any kind of war with people killing each other has to be "hell on earth" for the young people on the front lines.

T:While waiting for deployment in Alameda, our air group was called to a meeting in the base movie theater by ComAirPac. Once we were seated, the admiral took the on-stage podium and stated, all personnel who were not carrier pilots of Air Group One were to leave the theater. Several times he mentioned he had to be sure no one was in the audience, other than Air Group One carrier pilots and himself. Once he was satisfied this had been accomplished, he had Marine guards posted outside the theater's doors and delivered his message.

He advised that his message was to be secret and none of us were to ever to discuss the subject among ourselves or any other persons.

First he reviewed what had occurred with the devastation caused by the Kamikaze attacks on the Pacific fleet in the recent battle for Okinawa. The admiral then delivered a rather long discourse regarding the probable invasion of Japan and his belief the Japanese would ration their Kamikaze attacks with a priority focused on attacking the troop ships rather than the warships of the fleet when we invaded mainland Japan. The message the admiral then delivered was that any Air Group One pilot captured in the pending attacks on mainland Japan in preparation for the invasion of Japan was to tell the Japanese interrogators the names of every ship in the task forces, TF 38.1, TF 38.2 and TF 38.3. That would consist of three separate groups with each group consisting of five carriers, battleships, cruisers and at least two dozen destroyers. This is a total of 15 carriers, plus a British task force of similar size. The purpose of this strategy was to discourage the Japanese about the certain outcome of the war, and encourage them to throw all they had into attacks on the fleet, so by the time the invasion took place, we would have destroyed most of their aircraft, and thus reduce their ability to use Kamikaze attacks on our invasion troop ships, when the later invasion was to take place. He suggested we should even put a rough penciled note in our flight suit showing the makeup of the fleet, so in the event we were killed, the Japanese intelligence officers would have the information to send up the line to the Japanese high command when they recovered a body.

The admiral's strategy was to encourage the Japanese to come out after the fleet so we could destroy them prior to the arrival of the troop ship invasion fleet. The meeting lasted only about an hour and the information we received was completely different than what we had been taught in our previous training, which was to only give name, rank and serial number. But it was easy to understand what and why the admiral was up to in changing the Navy's normal policy in the event of capture. I think he gave this same speech to all air group pilots that deployed in late 1945 for the invasion of Japan.

Our senior officers encouraged all the pilots who had not yet experienced combat to sit down one-on-one with the carrier pilots returning from their tours of combat to learn the latest tactics of their squadrons and what they had observed of the enemy's latest tactics. We learned a great deal of valuable information from these veterans.

The returning vets were mostly interested in the names and phone numbers of ladies in the Bay area, since we were on the way out and would not have any use for them for many months. In return, we learned many things about deployment, other than combat information. One bit of information was the fact that once we were beyond Hawaii, we would find that a bottle of whisky would cost a minimum of a hundred dollars, ($100 in 1945 would be equal to well over $500 in 2006 dollars), if you could even locate a seller.

Since each pilot was limited to two canvas parachute bags to take on the ship when deployed, we were advised to pack a case of whiskey in each bag and then pack what clothes that would fit around the case and board the ship. Once aboard the ship there would be a ship clothing store to purchase new clothes at very reasonable prices. Most, but not all of us, followed this important packing strategy although we were well aware the Navy has strict rules about any personnel taking whiskey aboard a Navy ship. Attention to such peace time Navy regulations by air groups during WW-II were pretty lax in the carrier air group quarters.

The USS Broadwater, an APA, (Navy Attack Transport), took us aboard for our trip to Hawaii. The USS Broadwater was slow, with about a 12 knot cruising speed, single screw steamer with cramped quarters for such a large number of passengers. The weather on the trip was pleasant, the sea smooth, and the ship served excellent meals and snacks. The ship sailed solo with no escorts, and somewhere near the halfway point to Hawaii, the boilers developed a problem; we sat dead in the water for 30 hours or so as the ship's engineers repaired the problem. The sea was as smooth as glass with little if any wind. At the time I did not think about the vulnerability of the situation as we were thousands of miles from any Japanese bases. During the daylight hours, the captain of the ship had large nets hung over the side of the ship and we enjoyed climbing down the nets and swimming in the warm Pacific ocean, occasionally boarding the ship for snacks and soft drinks, (no alcoholic beverages served on a Navy ship!), while waiting for the boiler repairs to be completed. Not much different than a free ride on a cruise ship in peace time.

When we arrived in Honolulu, we learned our former squadron VF-84 serving in the USS Bunker Hill, CV-17, had suffered a very great number of casualties and injured, and many of the survivors were suffering with severe burns. The Bunker Hill was struck by a Kamikaze near the coast of Okinawa. The skipper of the squadron, Roger Hedrick, was not injured, as Roger was positioned in his Corsair on the starboard bow catapult waiting for the launch when the Kamikaze hit the ship amid ship and well behind him.

The Kamikaze hit the flight deck among the Corsairs loaded with bombs and rockets waiting to takeoff on their combat missions and then went through the flight deck and into the VF-84 pilots' ready room below. A group of our VBF-1 squadron's pilots, who had served in VF-84 in San Diego, went to the Navy Hospital in Honolulu and spent the day visiting with our surviving VF-84 F4U Corsair pilot friends.

K: Tom, I'd think that this is where a person serving in a war would begin to believe in fate. Did you ever think about all the "ifs" that had led your path to that point? What if you had stayed in VF-84?

T: Kelle, I am sure the book "What If" would be very interesting for both of us to read. An individual's life, the fate of nations and societies are determined many times by the very slightest of events and timing. In the recent terrorist bombing in London, two men were racing to catch one of the buses that was bombed. One made it just in time and the other just missed it by a few feet as the bus left the stop. The man who made it was killed. A friend of mine told me about a relative who worked in the World Trade Center who missed going to work for the only time in years of employment on one of the top floors of one of the buildings because of a severe hangover from a party. When he got around to waking up and turned on the TV he saw the people escaping the fires, leaping out of the top floors to their deaths and then the building going down.

I often think about my VF-84 friends who were sitting in the pilots' ready room when the Kamikaze hit the Bunker Hill deck then went through the deck and the ready room. What if BuAer had not made the decision to cut VF-84 back to 36 Corsairs from the original 72 planes in the squadron? What if I had gotten to the AirPac assignment desk in front of my friend McQuire? Fate is similar to what the great ancient Greek genius Leucippus of Miletus determined: that there is a random movement of atoms that is beyond the control of any power. Enough philosophy! Back to Hawaii.

A few days after our arrival in Honolulu, we deployed to Maui Island and again commenced pre-combat bombing, rocket attacks and gunnery training. We very much enjoyed our tour on Maui, as the island had not yet changed much from the early 1900s and

Suntans, Beer & Baseball

Watch the hands!

Hula!

Romano Swats One

I Wanted Wings!

Half-Hitch Where's Bettye

Greek & Dutch

Hawaii

El Groupo (Nickname of our Air Group Commander when he was not around to hear it)
Cdr. Harden drops by the athletic field in Kahului to check up on a few of his sometimes wayward pilots.
Left to right: Bob Applegate, Cdr. Harden, Oscar Folsom, Tom.

the population consisted of only a few small villages. The weather was great and the people very friendly. I do not remember any buildings on the island higher than two stories and there were very few of them. During our training time on Maui, we deployed several times to practice both day and night carrier landings aboard the USS Ranger, CV-4; the Navy's first ship designed in 1933 as an aircraft carrier; (all of the three previous Navy carriers, Saratoga, Lexington and Langley, had been modified from some other type of surface ship into aircraft carriers). We then boarded the brand new Essex class carriers, the USS Shangra-La, CV-33 and later the USS Bon Homme Richard, CV-31. Deploying from the Ranger, the old number CV-4 original carrier, and then to number CV-31 and CV-33, we became aware of the great difference in aircraft carrier size and improved technology in less than a decade! In less than three years of war, our Navy had developed from one of the most backward navies in the world in the field of aviation warfare, to become the most powerful air Navy in the world.

During this intensive carrier training, two of our pilots, Ensigns Buckner and Lindquist had a collision and both parachuted to safety, but of course we lost both of the F4Us. Ensign Peterson, who was one of the pilots in my division, was killed in a night carrier landing accident. Night carrier aircraft operations are indeed difficult to become efficient at because with the ship maintaining as few lights as possible, it is black as hell flying over the empty ocean far from land.

In May, we learned Air Group One would be replacing Air Group 82 aboard the USS Bennington, CV-20, and we departed Hawaii for Guam aboard the CVE, USS Breton, one of the escort-type carriers that had been converted from merchant ships during WW-II. These small, cheaply built and mass-produced CVE carriers were humorously nicknamed "Combustible, Vulnerable and Expendable," (CVE), by Navy pilots during the war. The CVEs were deployed, for the most part, in anti-submarine warfare, air support of troops in amphibious landings and as logistic ships backing up the task forces with replacement pilots and aircraft. When the task forces returned from combat actions, they would meet with the logistic fleet of oilers, ammunition ships, supply ships of many types, CVEs and a hospital ship to re-supply for the next operation.

Usually this would take place several hundred miles from the combat areas and the ship-to-ship work of logistics would last one or two days. During these operations, the carrier fighter squadrons would provide continuous combat air patrols over the massed fleet to prevent attacks from long range enemy planes and our destroyers would circle the fleet to ward off submarine attacks.

In Guam, we were based at the Agana Navy Air Field. While waiting for our rendezvous with the USS Bennington, we were able to do a minimum amount of flying using some of the different types of aircraft parked at the field, but there were few F4U type aircraft available at the base.

One day while several of us were walking near the runway at the Agana airfield, we

Top: CVE USS Santee at sea in 1943. The CVE designation stood for a merchant ship converted into a small escort carrier. The crews of the CVEs had a different designation for their ships, "Combustable, Vulnerable Expendable." The CVEs varied in size from about 7,000 tons to about 12,000 tons and from about 510 feet in length to about 590 feet. When used in combat, they normally carried between 28 to 30 aircraft and had a top speed of about 18 kts or so. They were used extensively to hunt for German submarines in the Atlantic Ocean, providing air support in attacks when the Americans were capturing the many Japanese Islands in the Pacific theatre of operations, as supply ships with replacement aircraft and pilots for the major battle carriers of the task forces, for transporting air groups from the states to Hawaii, Hawaii to the front lines of the Pacific theatre and for transporting all types of short range single engine aircraft from the states to England. Over 100 of these ships were constructed and saw service in WW-II.

Bottom: CVE #63 USS St. Lo being shelled and later sunk by Japanese surface ships at Leyte Gulf on 25 Oct. 1944.

Photos: US Navy

saw a damaged Army B-29 bomber returning from an attack on Japan. It was making an emergency landing with one of its engines feathered. The Army B-29 Anderson Airfield base was located only about 20 miles or so south of the Agana Navy field, but this B-29 pilot was obviously experiencing great trouble and was intent on getting on the ground as soon as possible. The huge bomber hit the runway with its landing gear in the up position, skidded down the runway and turned sideways as it slid off the right side of the runway. Then the left wing burst into flames. We all rushed to the scene and two of the crew were rescued, but one of them died a few minutes later. Because of the increased amount of flames and the sound of exploding ammunition, only the two crew men were rescued before the plane was completely destroyed by the fire. This was my first experience seeing the consequences of air combat in WW-II.

K: My mother worked at Boeing on the B-29 in 1942 and 1943. I've read a lot about the aircraft and was surprised at its early safety record. During a test flight in Seattle, a B-29 crashed into a meat packing plant, killing the flight crew and many workers in the building. Male pilots were afraid to fly the B-29, so women pilots were trained to fly the plane safely. Male aircrews were then taken up in the B-29 with a female pilot at the controls—the men decided that if a woman could successfully take off and land the B-29, men certainly could. Had you heard about the B-29 and its early flying history?

T: Yes. The B-29 was rushed into production and the design was the cutting edge of aircraft technology with a large number of new experimental components. So the early models had many bugs to be corrected. Frequent engine fires and severe engine oil leaks were the most dangerous problems. There was no other airplane in WW-II that could compare to the complexity of the B-29. One day in 1944, I was taxiing back to our parking area in my Corsair when a B-29 made an emergency three-engine landing at the North Island Navy airfield. When I got out of my plane I rushed back to the area the B-29 was parked and could hardly believe what I was looking at.

Of course everything about aircraft was secret in WW-II so I had never even heard of the Super Fortress. The plane was parked at our North Island airfield for several days as no Navy mechanic had any idea of how to fix the severe oil leak. A civilian crew was flown in from the Boeing factory to repair the engine. The Army Air Corps used women pilots in a similar manner with the Martin B-26 Marauder too as the young male pilots were more than angst-ridden about the Marauder. As it turned out, the B-26 had the lowest percentage of combat losses of any allied bomber in WW-II because of its speed and rugged 2,000 HP Pratt & Whitney engines and the B-29 proved to be the deadliest piston engine bomber in history.

Many experiences and events during war are not at all pleasant, but occasionally

Without a doubt, the design and production of the B-29 in WW-II was one of the most amazing aeronautical technological achievements of any of the nations engaged in the war. America entered the war with the most backward aviation military of any major country in the world and emerged as the most productive country of advanced war weapons.

The B-29 Superfortress was technologically decades beyond any other heavy bomber of any nation in the war in ability to penetrate an enemy's airspace and destroy the enemy's infrastructure. The huge 141 foot wing span bomber powered by four advanced designed Wright 2,200 HP engines cruised at 290 MPH at a maximum range of 3,200 miles carrying 10,000 pounds of bombs. For many months before dropping the two atomic bombs that resulted in ending WW-II, the B-29s had been fire bombing Japan and had destroyed much of Japan's manufacturing plants and cities. Every objective analysis by military experts regarding the use of the B-29s and the atomic bombs to quickly end the war has indicated the swift ending of the war with the two bombs saved the lives of at least a million American service men and Japanese civilians. Photo USAF.

The B-29 was used to drop the first atomic bomb on Hiroshima on 6 August 1945. I am convinced I and some hundreds of thousands of other American service WW-II men and Japanese civilians would not be here 60 years later if the atomic bombs had not been used to end the war. Photo USAF.

there are humorous events that keep you chuckling each time you think of them or tell the story. Here are few Guam incidents that created some amusement and chuckles, and to this day, when I think of them I have to laugh.

The day before we departed Hawaii aboard the CVE USS Breton for Guam, our Air Group One received several replacement pilots who had been flown over to Hawaii from San Diego a few days before. One of the young ensign replacement bomber pilots was a real eager beaver visiting various compartments of the CVE as he had never been aboard any ship other than his practice landings aboard the Great Lakes USS Wolverine training carrier. Of course, all we pilots did on the Wolverine was fly out to the ship from the Glenview Air Base, make our five qualifying landings, then fly back to the Glenview base, check out and then head for Clark Street in downtown Chicago to party and celebrate. So the young pilot was visiting the bridge of the CVE apparently as the black shoe watch officers, (the nickname of the non-aviation ship officers), were changing watch. The officer being relieved handed his binoculars to the young pilot ensign and casually asked him if he would just keep an eye out helping the other officer of the deck, while he went below for a few minutes. Obviously these two black shoe ensign ship watch officers had conferred with each other before this took place. Of course, on a CVE under normal sailing conditions, only one watch officer was required on the bridge. A few minutes later, as the two ensigns were looking out at the sea, the watch officer mentioned to the ensign pilot, "be sure to keep an eye out ahead with your binoculars for the mail buoy that will have a large orange flag attached". A little while later the watch officer who had been relieved called up to the bridge asking if he could delay his return as he had some details to take care of below. The pilot ensign was asked if he would mind continuing watching for the "mail buoy" and he said he would be glad to accommodate them. The on-duty watch officer then casually carried on a conversation with the pilot ensign about various ship subjects, but emphasized the importance of the two of them not missing the "mail buoy" because of the importance of the morale of the ship's crew to get their letters from home. This went on for about two hours or more before the off-duty officer came back to the bridge, told the pilot about the hoax and the three of them had a big laugh about the joke. However, the next day as the "mail buoy" story spread about the ship, the victimized pilot was pretty pissed off.

A couple of days after we arrived on Guam, Lt. Eason, one of our squadron's senior officers, got up early, went to the latrine with a magazine to read while sitting on the toilet, took his seat among some two dozen other empty seats in the latrine, lit a cigarette and moved his butt over just a bit and dropped the match into the latrine. Swoosh! A large flash! All the solid wood toilet covers in the latrine flew up as if standing at attention and then dropped down. Lt. Eason was swooshed off of his seat too with a very warm butt and a few singed pubic hairs. What had happened was the sanitary latrine crew had sprayed the usual morning fuel into the latrine but had not yet set off the normal short blast of the fumes before Lt. Eason arrived to do his business. The sanitary crew would normally spray the correct amount of fuel into the latrines several mornings each week, then go about some other chores while the fumes built up with all the solid wood toilet covers down and closed and then come back a half hour or so later and throw a match in to set off the fumes. That morning Lt. Eason did their work for them! Our Lt. was not injured, just had a butt that looked like it had a little too much exposure to the sun. Lt. Eason was a real southern gentleman who we all liked but sadly he did not survive the war.

The week we arrived at Guam, a work detail of the Navy brig, (Navy jail), consisting of just minor offense sailors who had been assigned some clean up duty around the air station failed to return to the brig at the required check-in time one evening. The Navy Shore Patrol officers felt they might have skipped over to the outdoor movie on the base which they were not permitted to do. All movies on the island at that time were after dark and outdoors. So the Shore Patrol team went to the movie, had the projector operator turn off the movie and then announced, "Every one stay in your seat, don't move or stand until we inspect the audience." The Shore Patrol team then with the flood lights on commenced walking among the audience looking over the sailors, but did not find any of the sailors wearing Navy brig uniforms. What they did find were two very humble unarmed Japanese soldiers who had been enjoying the movie. At that time, Guam had been captured many, many months before. Later when interrogating the two captured Japanese soldiers, they learned the soldiers had been hiding out in the nearby dense woods and had been off and on attendees at the nightly movies and also had been collecting food from behind the mess hall at night ever since the Americans had taken over the island.

About two weeks after our arrival at Guam, we learned our rendezvous with the USS Bennington would take place at Leyte Gulf in the Philippines. We boarded the CVE, USS White Plains that was loaded with many new F4U aircraft and sailed for Leyte Gulf.

While enroute to Leyte Gulf, I happened to be in the wardroom of the ship enjoying a cup of coffee one evening, when I overheard a prophetic conversation between several of the ship's watch officers discussing the duties and tasks of sailing the unescorted single ship CVE to the Leyte Gulf. Two of the watch officers were questioning the fact that the unescorted USS White Plains was cruising at its normal speed of 15 knots in a straight course making the ship an easy target for a submarine to torpedo. The one officer mentioned the ship should be tacking, (zig zagging), as we cruised to make the ship more difficult for a submarine to torpedo. That made me think about the three ships our air group had traveled on since we had left Alameda; San Francisco to Hawaii, Hawaii to Guam and now Guam to Leyte Gulf, with all three of the ships sailing unescorted, never tacking and so far as I knew, without any other ships anywhere near our ships or the Naval bases knowing where we were located on the trips. I wasn't in on the discussion, and didn't think any more of the conversation until August some three months or so later when I heard the story of the heavy cruiser, USS Indianapolis, CA-35, being torpedoed by a Japanese submarine while the USS Indianapolis was traveling on the same identical route we had taken from Guam to Leyte Gulf, and like our CVE cruising unescorted at a modest speed and on a straight course. The cruiser was sunk in a matter of minutes. As was usually true, during the hectic days of WW-II, the ship was not missed for many days, resulting in hundreds of the crew dying from exposure to the salty ocean, the blistering sun of the tropics and the shark attacks. Someone in the Leyte headquarter base finally became aware the ship was missing but it was too late for most of the ship's crew. The sinking of the USS Indianapolis resulted in the most casualties of American sailors and officers of any one ship sunk in the history of our Navy.

As we neared the Leyte Gulf, about a hundred miles or so away, I was one of the lucky pilots to be catapulted off the ship in a battle weary F4U, landed at the Leyte airfield and waited for the ship to arrive the next day. I knew Donald, my younger brother, was serving in the DE-350, USS Traw, (a destroyer escort), and decided to surprise him with a visit if I could locate his ship among the vast fleet anchored in the Leyte Gulf Bay. So I got into a friendly conversation with a two-man boat crew and with a gift of a bottle of my precious whiskey, arranged for a cruise about the ships in the Leyte Gulf anchorage to search for the USS Traw.

Normally, any Navy ship can be easily located at the headquarters of the operation center of a port by their assigned anchorage location, but the huge fleet had just recently returned from Okinawa and the anchorage records were in chaos. So, the two sailors and I spent a pleasant afternoon cruising about the gulf checking out the numbers and names of all the destroyer escorts we could locate. We finally gave up trying to locate Don's ship and returned to the base boat landing. At a much later date, I learned from my brother that his ship was in the Okinawa area at that time.

The saddest times I experienced during the war were when I would lose a squadron friend, receive a letter or read about a friend being killed in some other theatre of the war. One of the very worst times for me was when my mother wrote me about the loss of my long-time childhood Carnegie friend, Francy, in Europe.

When I received the news about Francy, I remember sitting alone in the wardroom of the Bennington thinking about the last time I had visited with him. He had signed up with the Army Air Corps and I had signed up with the Navy. I had borrowed Dad's car and driven up to visit with Francy in Carnegie. I remembered our parting at the Carnegie Isley's Ice Cream parlor after enjoying chocolate sundaes. He had mentioned we would not see each other again until the end of the war as I would probably fight in the Pacific theater and he in the European theater. Even today, I can remember his smiling face as he wished me good luck making carrier landings. Francy was looking forward to flying off long runways on terra firma. The news I received from Mother, a Pittsburgh newspaper clipping, and later from his brother Ed and family and members of his bomber group, plus my conversations with several other WW-II B-17 Boeing Flying Fortress pilots follows.

Twenty-two year old Francis Barr, (Francy), Lt. United States Army Air Corps, (the

United States Air Force was a part of the Army in WW-II), was flying with a ten-man crew in a Boeing B-17 Flying Fortress on a bombing mission over France when all ten of them were killed by a German ME-109 fighter colliding with the B-17 in a head on collision.

All American bombing crews were blessed and comforted by a chaplain before departing from England on their missions. The Christian chaplains, of course, prayed with them as did our chaplains aboard the Navy carriers in the Pacific, for God to help the airmen to complete their missions killing the enemy and to return safely.

The German ME-109 fighter pilot, probably about the same age as Francy, no doubt received the same blessing and comfort from his German Christian chaplain prior to taking off and climbing up to kill the enemy B-17 airmen.

One of the German fighter pilots' favorite tactics in shooting down B-17s, was to fly head-on at the bomber, shooting at its nose. The reason they preferred this approach was the fact the B-17s had two manned powerful 50 caliber machine guns located in the tail of the bombers. Since the bomber was normally flying at a speed of about 250 MPH, and the fighter overtaking the bomber would be flying at approximately 300 to 350 MPH, the closing speed from the rear was about 100 MPH or so. This gave the tail gunner of the bomber considerable time to shoot at the fighter with his heavy twin 50 caliber guns. The head on approach was the preferred German fighter pilot approach because the closing speed of the two planes would be approximately 550 to 600 MPH giving the nose gunner of the bomber much less time to shoot at the fighter.

The danger of this head-on type of approach was that the German fighter pilot had to be very precise and prompt to "split S" and dive under the bomber or pull up sharply in a timely manner to go over the bomber after firing his guns at the nose of the B-17. This young German fighter pilot misjudged the timing or possibly was killed by the nose gunner of the B-17 and all 11 on the two aircraft perished in a split second by the head-on collision of the two planes.

So the Christian chaplain's prayers and blessings on both the German and American sides were not effective to protect any of the warriors in the American bomber or the German fighter plane. They used the same Christian Bibles, one in English, one in German.

K: In your opinion Tom, what role does religion play in war?

T: For people like me at that time in WW-II, the fictitious stories of the chaplains provided a calming effect and without realizing it, I got the feeling that some guy, like a Santa Claus, was out there somewhere and would try to protect me. It never occurred to me to question any of the fiction. The truth is that facing combat alone in a fighter cockpit was

The B-17, designed in the early 1930s and first flown in July 1935, was like the Navy's SBD dive bomber—an obsolescent, vulnerable, very slow flying bomber when we entered the war in 1941. The ten crew members of the thousands of B-17s built by Boeing and the many other associated aircraft firms performed heroic deeds bombing enemy targets all over the European and Pacific theatres of the war.

Flying at high altitudes in extremely low temperatures, the exposed 50 caliber machine gun gunners suffered great hurt and hardship. Powered by four 1,200 HP engines, the slow-flying B-17s were especially easy targets for the nearly 400 MPH German fighters. My first inspection and look at the venerable old Flying Fortress was as a test pilot in the months following the end of the war when the Navy was evaluating the B-17 at the Patuxent Navy Test Center as a possible patrol and anti-submarine aircraft.

Later on, I flew the B-17 (Navy designation PB-1W) as an aircraft commander in squadron VW-1 in the Pacific fleet. I surely have the utmost empathy and respect for all of the pilots and air crews who flew and fought in WW-II flying the highly vulnerable Flying Fortress bombing our enemies. In the European Theatre of operations, the B-17 Army Air Corps crews were limited to 25 missions before being relieved and transferred to other duties.

Since their casualty rate was usually a loss of about 5% per mission (on some missions they would lose as many as 50 B-17s taking 500 airman to their death or prison camp) it did not take a very bright person to realize very few would live through 25 missions. I do not think any branch of the American military suffered anywhere near the catastrophic percent of losses that the bomber crews of the Eighth Army Air Corps suffered in WW-II. The only comparable WW-II catastrophic casualty rate I can think of is the crews of the German submarines in the Atlantic.

My friend Francy Barr was one of the brave B-17 warriors who paid the ultimate price.

very tense and even though I was suspicious about the counseling of the chaplains about God looking after us, I was in need of any kind of crutch available to face the challenges when the word over the intercom ordered, "Pilots man your planes." At the time I never thought about the fact that if he didn't look after the safety of my friends who I had lost, why would he look after me? Now that is just a personal observation.

Of course history indicates there is no question that religion has been the major cause of wars, especially for the past 2000 years. Kelle, the answer to that question needs the input of highly educated philosophy majors preparing documents on their way to doctoral degrees. My personal belief is that it would be very difficult for the leadership of a completely secular society to get the population to support a war of any kind except in self defense. Historically, religion has been used as propaganda-spreading hatred of supposed enemies. To tell you the truth, I had not thought about the importance religion has played in aggressive nations that start wars. I think if some learned philosopher tackled that subject he/she would be involved in many months of research answering that question.

Of course, any person who has an interest in history and is familiar with the religious wars in Europe from about 1600 to the early 1700s as the northern nations of Europe commenced breaking away from the dictatorship in Rome, is well aware of the millions of Protestants and Catholics killed in that century in the name of their specific sect of Christianity. Then in the 1700s, the Protestant sects commenced persecuting each other. Even in 2006, we keep reading about the splitting up of the different Protestant main line religions as the different sects' flocks cannot tolerate each other.

One thing is for certain, Christians of all denominations cannot put up with anyone who believes differently even in the slightest way than they do. Until the later part of the 1900s, the Catholic faith was able to hold all factions of the Catholic faith together, but in the last few decades as the supreme power of the popes has diminished in the literate and educated nations, we have observed growing dissension with priests dropping out and the formerly faithful disregarding the dictates of Rome. I predict in the next few decades we will see the rise of new Catholic groups that practice the true Catholic doctrines of past centuries but recognize the fact that science has proven that gays and lesbians are just normal people like the rest of us but were born attracted to the same sex. They will also recognize it is best for couples who hate each other to divorce, that remarriage is not a sin, that birth control makes sense for many at different stages of their lives and that women are capable of becoming excellent priests. A good name for the first breakaway group would be The American Catholic Church. What's your take on the role religion plays in war?

K: Like you, I think religion is used as a rallying cry to get men and women to fight for their country. In your story about Francy's death, you related the fact that chaplains on both sides of the conflict gave blessings to the individuals who would eventually meet each other on the battlefield that day. It reminded me of a line in a movie I saw. The movie was set in WW-II and a young boy had taken some German war souvenirs to school to show his class. On the belt worn by the German, the belt buckle had an inscription which translated to "for God." One of the boys in the group of spectators said, "you mean God is on their side too!" I also think that there are people in the world that need a reason for doing things— they are the ones which can be manipulated by the idea of a higher force.

I am one who has a talk with myself when it comes to hurdles in my path, and I get over the hurdle because I have the ability to motivate myself to get on with clearing the path ahead. I know that there are people in the world who don't have self-motivation and need an outside force to create their ability to go out there and get on with it. War needs lots of reasons—governments use any and every excuse that works to recruit warriors and to get them to go into battle—and if they have to fall back on religion, they do that too. Let's face it, the U.S. had several reasons to enter WW-II, but for some reason the events that could have persuaded the American people to enter the war were not strong enough until Pearl Harbor was attacked—then the flood gates opened.

Once you have the populace, you have to continually motivate them to carry on— religion is just one way to do that. My father's motivation throughout the war was his family, my mother and me, not religion or country.

T: I really appreciate your input and it answers a lot of questions in my mind about the role religion plays in war. Recently I was in Las Vegas and read a story in the Las Vegas paper about the death of a 22 year-old Marine while serving his third tour of duty in Iraq. In the story it mentioned he had spent his 20th, 21st and 22nd birthdays in Iraq during his three different tours. The story also mentioned his devotion, patriotism and comments about his past statements to friends regarding his philosophy about the war. While reading the very emotional story I was wondering what part the fiction his military chaplain was feeding him had to do with his philosophy about the war. Like the little boys said in your comments, "You mean God is on their side too!"

I am sure the Muslim nut cake suicide bombers go to their deaths in the belief they are doing their God's work. And please believe me when I tell you your father was not the only WW-II vet who was primarily concerned about his family, siblings and parents. And many WW-II vets are still pissed off about the Christian fanatics putting "under God" in the pledge of allegiance shortly after we came back from combat in 1946. For over 200 years, patriotic Americans have answered the bell when the country had to defend itself and then after WW-II, the worst war in the history of civilization, we were made to believe we were fighting for some fictitious invisible God's nation! Now I'll try to cool down and get back to the Bennington.

So we boarded the USS Bennington, the flagship of Task Force 38.1 with the admiral of the task force and his staff aboard in early June. As you would expect with each of us carrying our two permitted parachute bags of clothes and the valuable "personal" gear carefully packed in the bags with our clothes. Once assigned to our accommodations, unpacked and ready to cruise, we were called to our VBF-1 ready room and briefed on information regarding the ship's routine, general quarters assignments when not flying, abandon ship drill information and other general helpful information about the ship. After the briefing we were like a bunch of tourists visiting the ship's engine room, bridge, gun installations and other sections of the carrier.

K: Ah, now we are entering territory that I am familiar with. The Bennington had her flight deck damaged in a typhoon on 5 June 1945 and was in Leyte for repairs. The powers that be decided to cut off the damaged portion of the ship's flight deck, thus shortening it quite a bit. Was this a concern to you and your squadron?

T: Yes, it was of concern when we became aware of the situation. The deck wasn't cut short, it was just bent down. But once we saw the first Corsairs takeoff and then after each of us experienced a takeoff ourselves we were no longer concerned. The Corsair's Pratt & Whitney 2,000 HP engines had more than enough power to get us off the deck. But I know the bomber VB-1 squadron with the SB2Cs had plenty of trouble getting the "beasts" off of the deck with not much leeway.

My first assignment was to return with five other pilots to the Leyte Airfield by boat and wait for the ship to get underway to Japan the next day. We were instructed that when notified by radio the next morning to fly our new Corsairs out to the ship. My number one concern with the assignment was the safety of my valuable personal belongings aboard the ship while I was at the Leyte Airfield. I was worried about the fact that if my new Corsair developed any kind of trouble, I would miss the cruise and all of my valuable personal gear would be lost (consumed that is). As it turned out, the new plane was in perfect condition and my two cabin mates, Bob Applegate and Oscar Folsom, took good care of my precious bottled belongings while I was on the beach.

While leaving the Leyte Gulf for our attacks on Japan we stood on the flight deck of the Bennington watching the mighty Task Force 38.1 of several dozen ships maneuvering. My roommate LTjg. Oscar Folsom, (nicknamed Chief, as he was one of the descendents of an Oklahoma Indian family), and I joked about the statements we both

A few inquisitive crew members looking over the typhoon-damaged bow of the USS Bennington while anchored in Leyte Gulf in the Phillipines. Photo US Navy.

had received in our respective 1942 recruiting experience as aviation cadets, "The war will be over before you complete your flight training." Here we were deploying for the greatest battle of the Pacific War, the invasion of mainland Japan. A battle our senior officers were telling us that would make the European Normandy invasion appear to come across like a minor beach landing.

Once at sea and on the way to Japan, Task Forces 38.1, 38.2, 38.3 (including a total of 15 carriers) commenced intensive drills, firing anti-aircraft guns at towed targets and fleet maneuvers of some three dozen warships in each task force. Our air group commenced practice gunnery, dive bombing, rocket and dog fighting missions preparing for our attacks on the airfields in and around Tokyo.

We, of course were saddened anytime our squadron lost a pilot, but every once in a while we would lose a pilot who made a very big difference in the atmosphere of our quiet private parties in the squadron living quarters aboard ship.

This was the case when we lost Ensign Peter Parthemouse, nicknamed, "Greek," who was always the life of our drinking parties with his singing, amusing antics and jokes. In a practice dive bombing exercise on the way to Japan, I was following Greek down in a dive bombing run from an altitude of about 15 thousand feet on one of our maneuvering destroyer escorts when I saw Greek's plane simply disintegrate as he pulled out of his dive about 2,000 feet above the destroyer. As I recovered from my dive about 300 yards behind Pete, I saw one of his wings and other smaller parts of his plane flying by my Corsair. Neither Pete nor any parts of his Corsair were recovered. That was a shock for all of us and it was a long time before our party atmosphere recovered after losing Pete.

K: Tom, what could possibly cause such an accident? I've read about a lot of pilot deaths during WW-II where the same description was given—"the plane disintegrated."

T:I don't know why these kinds of accidents happen. It could be the fatigue of a critical part of the plane as a result of heavy use. Pete may have pulled out of the dive too sharply resulting in a G force that was too high. In the many years I flew the Corsair during the war and in later years, I never witnessed any other Corsair failures similar to Pete's accident.

In the last months of WW-II, my VBF-1 squadron's primary activity and the Navy's Task Force 38.1 missions were mostly concentrated on destroying airfields in Japan. This destruction of the runways and wrecking their airplanes was making it difficult for the Japanese to use their night fighters to combat the Army B-29s night fire bombing their cities with incendiary bombs. These B-29 attacks were gradually burning and destroying all the major cities in Japan in preparation for our expected October invasion. In many of the nightly attacks, the B-29s would destroy more property and kill more people in a single attack than the atomic bombs later did at Hiroshima and Nagasaki. In one night raid on Tokyo, they killed over 80,000 people.

My first combat mission was, without a doubt, one of the most exciting and scary missions of my combat experiences. With my landing gear extended (to slow the Corsair in the dive) and diving on the Japanese Atsugi airfield some 20 or 30 miles west of Tokyo, I felt a jolt just before I released my 1,000 lb. bomb. Then when at a low altitude after my recovery from the dive, I heard my wing man call on the radio, "Mac, you're on fire." Actually my airplane was not on fire; the Japanese anti-aircraft shell had struck my left landing gear and broke my hydraulic system. The stream of hydraulic fluid pouring out of the broken landing gear briefly looked like smoke from a fire. With part of my left gear and right gear both hanging and with no hydraulic fluid to retract the gear my Corsair was reduced to a very slow speed and I was unable to catch up with my squadron returning to the fleet.

I knew being alone, and at such a slow speed, my best opportunity to get to the ocean safely was to fly as low as possible to avoid detection by enemy planes. So it was a very slow,

Returning from Tokyo with the left landing gear shot off and with no hydraulic fluid to lower the landing flaps.

Any landing you can walk away from is a satisfactory landing!

very low level altitude, terribly lonely, and anxious flight over the suburbs of Tokyo in broad daylight to get to the coast, out to sea and out of sight of the Japanese. In training flights, it's enjoyable to occasionally fly "flat hat" just a couple hundred feet above the ground, but not so much fun when flying over enemy territory. Once over the ocean and reaching a position approximately 100 miles or so from the task force, I knew the air control radar operators on the carriers, (we had five carriers in Task Force 38.1), could see me on radar as I had climbed to a higher altitude and they would have fighters protect me from any Japanese aircraft. They would know my location from my IFF, (identification, friend or foe equipment), in case my Corsair had to be ditched in the sea. To put it mildly, the thought of knowing that the carrier radar operators could surely see me on their scopes created a nice warm comfortable feeling as I homed in on the fleet!

Since I was the last and very late airplane to return from the Tokyo mission to the fleet, I had a few minutes of feeling very, very important; seeing the mighty fleet of five carriers, two huge battleships, many cruisers and two dozen destroyers all turning into the wind for this (to me) very important junior officer to land his airplane with no landing flaps and only one landing gear completely extended on the USS Bennington, the flagship of the fleet. The admiral of the fleet and his staff would be on the bridge of the USS Bennington watching the landing. Unable to use my landing flaps to slow the Corsair, I missed the first approach. It was getting pretty dark and late in the day. No doubt this was of great concern to the admiral as the wind was from the west. The fleet had to continue to head toward Japan at high speed for me to make another approach. I got it aboard trapping the third landing wire on my second approach. The landing was not much different from a normal carrier landing, but of course my plane was beyond repair and had to be pushed overboard into the sea. A few days later I was transported by a destroyer to a CVE carrier, (a small logistic carrier with replacement planes and pilots), since helicopters were not yet operational in the fleet in WW-II, to pick up my new plane and then flew it back to the USS Bennington.

Needless to say, for the balance of the war I had great respect for the ability of the well-trained anti-aircraft gunners of the Japanese Army.

Attacking airfields and destroying aircraft on the ground was tough on our thin aluminum-skinned Chance Vought Corsairs. In many ways, you could compare the hobby of peacetime skeet shooters firing at clay pigeons to what the Japanese airfield anti-aircraft gunners had in shooting at our Corsairs as we strafed, fired rockets and bombed their parked airplanes, buildings and runways. From June through July and August, our Corsairs took such a anti-aircraft beating that we only had about a dozen of the original F4Us still in service aboard the USS Bennington that we had deployed with from the Leyte Gulf. The rest of the Corsairs were new replacement aircraft. When we would return from these airfield attacks, the planes that were damaged but still flyable would be flown to one of the

CVE carriers and traded in for a new Corsair; however, the planes severely damaged and not judged as safe for another carrier landing would be just pushed over the side into the ocean. WW-II was indeed a very, very expensive war!

My cabin mate Indian, Ltjg. Oscar Folsom, "Our Indian Chief" had a very exciting experience on one of our airfield strafing missions. The Chief became so engrossed in strafing a Japanese airplane partially hidden among some trees at the perimeter of the airfield that he continued firing while flying about fifty to a hundred feet above the ground and pulled up late as he approached the trees. Oscar flew through the tops of the trees and returned to the carrier with small bits of branches, twigs and leaves stuck in the cowling of his engine, around the pitot tube and in his oil cooler inlet. So for several days we called our Chief the ship's gardener. Although the plane did not appear to be damaged, the skipper was concerned about the engine and after the mechs carefully checked it out, Oscar flew it over to a CVE and picked up a new Corsair. The Chief and I gathered a few of the small green branches from his plane, put them in a container of water and set it in our cabin as a decoration.

Ltjg. Oscar Folsom USN, my USS Bennington roommate and long time Indian friend from Oklahoma. "The Chief", our nickname for Oscar, was one very proud Indian. He came from a family of leaders of Indian societies in Oklahoma. "The Chief" was a booster and fan of any team that used an Indian name or symbol that referred to the past history of the American Indians. The use of names such as the then Stanford University Indians and the many other athletic teams in America using names such as the Chiefs, Warriors, Braves, etc., very much appealed to Oscar. He once told me he could not understand why no one was using the impressive name of "The Tomahawks." As a result of this friendship with Oscar and learning his pride in the American Indian culture, I have been criticized for my lack of empathy for the American Indians who protest teams and institutions using the names of symbols of the American Indian society. I cannot understand why they aren't proud of their heritage like Oscar was.

We had great pride and faith

in our F4U Corsairs and knew it was one of the best fighter aircraft in the world. We also knew we had been well trained under the enthusiastic command of Cdr. Harden, (CAG ONE). CAG ONE was the designation, meaning Commander Air Group One. Air Group One had one of the longest and most intensive training periods of any air group deployed to the Pacific Fleet during the war. Regrettably, a great number of Navy personnel, both aviators and ship personnel, were lost in the first three years of the war because of the lack of training during the 1930s and the lack of up-to-date aircraft and equipment. It was late in the war when we arrived at Leyte Gulf and the Navy had matured to a very high point of carrier warfare professionalism in the last months of the conflict. Our outstanding practice gunnery, bombing, rocket firing, torpedo launching and napalm use records indicated the high state of readiness for combat of Air Group One. So we were deploying aboard the flagship of the Pacific Fleet, Task Force 38.1, from Leyte Gulf to attack the airfields around the Japanese islands full of confidence we would accomplish our missions with great efficiency.

However, we were not mentally prepared for the unexpected fierceness and great preparation with the heavy concentration of anti-aircraft guns the Japanese had installed around their airfields. The veteran pilots of VBF-1 who were on their second tours were amazed at the difference we encountered attacking the Japanese homeland airfields compared to what they had experienced in their earlier tour of combat attacking the airfields on the remote Pacific islands.

We knew the planned invasion of the homeland of Japan would take place in late October or early November. We also knew we were scheduled to be relieved by the next air group in November. But by the end of July, just four or five weeks after we deployed, we had lost so many pilots and Corsairs that we were convinced that by the end of October, VBF-1 would probably consist of nearly all replacement pilots and replacement F4U Corsair airplanes.

The F4U Corsair was one of the fastest and best air to air fighter combat and dive bombing airplanes of the war but it had not been designed as a ground attack strafing airplane in the face of heavy low level ground attack anti-aircraft fire. The BuAer department of the Navy was well aware of the Corsair's structural limitations for ground attack and had rushed the production of the heavy rugged and armored Douglas AD-1 Skyraider for deployment to take over the ground attack role of the airfields but it was not yet in the fleet.

The surviving VBF-1 pilots had no doubt that President Truman most certainly saved us when he made the decision to end the war with the atomic bombs. The Japanese were hell bent and determined to fight to the last man to save their homeland as they had done in Okinawa and the other Pacific islands. The word surrender was not in their vocabulary. This was to be a war to the death of every Japanese soldier. This was to be a kill or be killed savage invasion. For over 2,600 years, Japan had never lost a war and the military leaders intended for all of them to die honorably rather than surrender.

Two of my more interesting missions were the ones attacking a military base on

The Corsair was designed as light as possible to enhance the dog fight capability with enemy fighters. It was originally not designed to be a dive bomber or a ground attack aircraft. Nevertheless, it proved to be the best airplane the Navy had to perform the ground attack and dive bomber missions. As a result of the light fighter plane type of construction the planes took a terrible beating from the Japanese airfield anti aircraft gunfire.

Photos by permission from
Genda's Blade

Hokkaido island where I came upon a very large oil or fuel storage tank and hit it with six of my 5-inch rockets. The tank blew up in a huge explosion several hundred feet high. The other interesting, but scary mission for me was with eight aircraft (four TBM torpedo bombers and four Corsairs), led by our air group commander, Cdr. Harden, that flew completely across Japan and attacked a small oil tanker in the Sea of Japan between Korea and Japan. While the TBMs were dropping bombs on the ship, I was firing my six 5-inch rockets (each with a 5-inch diameter shell attached) and my six 50-caliber machine guns at the pilot house. We sank the ship and in our mission of more than 5 hours over and back from the other side of Japan, we never lost any of our eight aircraft.

On the 17th of July, we attacked the battleship Nagato and several cruisers gathered together in port as the Japanese were out of oil and could not put them to sea. Nevertheless, their anti-aircraft guns had plenty of ammunition and the gunners had a great deal of experience from the early combat years of the war. Our task force did not sink the ships but severely damaged all of them. We were disappointed with the results of the attack but the admiral sent his congratulations to all the air groups for putting the ships out of any kind of military service. Air Group One lost nearly a dozen aircraft in two days of the attacks and my roommate and long time friend throughout my squadron service and cadet years, LTjg. Bob Applegate, did not return from the missions.

Our squadron skipper, LCDR. Bob Ross, told me he would write a letter to Bob's parents and suggested I also write them, since we were cabin mates and longtime friends. I wrote a letter to his mother and told her the truth, as I knew the facts. I told her that she would receive notice from the Navy that Bob was missing in action, but I had spoken to the fighter pilots who saw his plane go down and that there was no parachute, so Bob did not survive. I then put all of Bob's personal gear together for storage in the ship until we got back to port. Fortunately, the day Mrs. Applegate received my letter, she also received a letter from Bob who advised that he had had some combat trouble but had been rescued by an American submarine and he was OK. Mrs. Applegate took the two letters to the local Navy office in Oregon who then contacted the Pentagon and confirmed the fact that Bob was OK and to disregard my letter.

About three weeks or so after the atomic bombs had ended the war, I was sitting on the edge of the flight deck watching the fleet's activities when a destroyer came alongside and commenced sending gear and persons over to the Bennington. One of the men in the transfer caught my eye and I thought to myself, "If I didn't know my friend Bob was dead, I would for sure think that was Bob." I didn't think any more about it and about 15 minutes or so later, I had a tap on my shoulder and Bob said, "where is my damned whiskey?"

I said, "Hell, Bob, I thought you were dead and passed it around the squadron." He wasn't too happy about this, but understood there wasn't much else I could do with it. Bob became the longtime City Manager of El Cajon, (a city near San Diego) after the war and we were lifetime friends until he passed away in 1998.

In the early morning the day the B-29 dropped the first atomic bomb, Air Group

Shiden.

On July 24 just a few weeks before the end of the war, several of our VBF-1 Corsairs and a group of F6F Hellcats from another carrier got into a dogfight near the Japanese Kure Navy base. The Japanese pilots were flying the latest and deadliest Japanese fighter planes nick named "George" by the allies. The George was a N1K2-J Shiden that was equal to any of the allies' aircraft with respect to speed, armor, durable construction and heavy fire power with four 20mm cannons. Powered by an 18 cylinder 1,850HP two row air-cooled radial engine, the George could hold its own with the best of allied fighters in WW-II.

Late in the war (too late for Japan with limited resources) General Staff Officer Minoru Genda (the Navy staff officer who designed the 1941 Pearl harbor attack to start the war with America) was given permission to form a squadron consisting of only the best surviving top gun pilots and aces of Japan to confront the growing number of American air attacks on the mainland of Japan. The squadron of aces was named the 343 Kokutai and was equipped with the N1K2-J Shiden (George) fighters. In the dogfight, my roommate Ltjg. Robert Applegate shot down two of the Georges but one of the Japanese pilots tore Apple's plane up with his 20mm cannons and Bob bailed out. He was rescued by a US submarine but we were never advised of the rescue. Two other pilots of our squadron, Ensign Speckmann and senior Lt.Tabler were shot down and killed in the engagement.

Apple's two kills of the Japanese were confirmed by the F6F pilots by message from their carrier with the additional information that Bob had not survived when his plane went into the sea. They did not see his parachute after Bob bailed out. Much of the information about the formidable N1K2-J Shiden (George), the 343 Kokutai squadron of Japanese aces and the 24 July dogfight I have divulged from the contents of the English version of the Japanese book *Genda's Blade* by Sakaida and Takaki. Anyone interested in the Japanese side of the final desperate months of the war will find the book very interesting.

Photo by permission from *Genda's Blade*

Left: Lt. (jg) Robert M. Applegate. Center: ENS Robert J. Speckman. Right: Lt. Rodney Tabler.

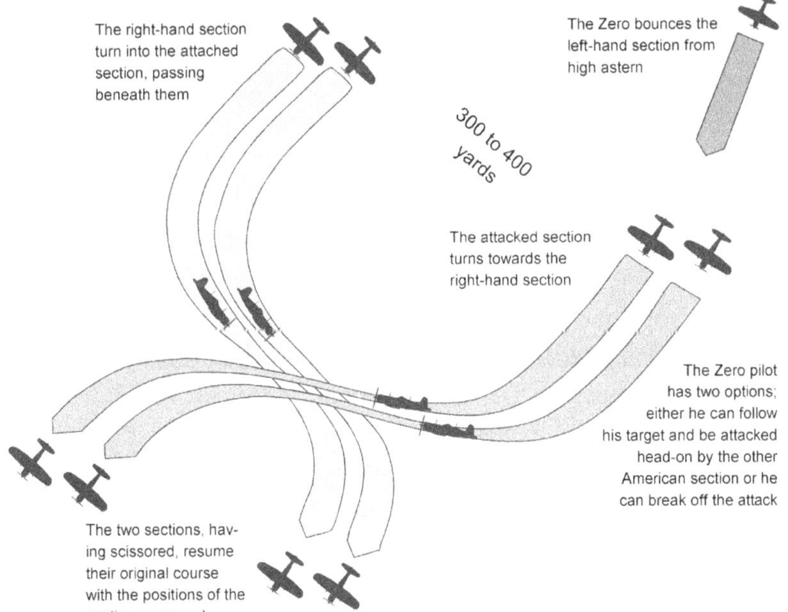

The reason we lost the three Corsairs on July 24 (Applegate was rescued by an American submarine the next day and Speckman and Tabler were killed) to the George type fighter aircraft of the crack Japanese 343 Kokutai squadron was that when making dive bombing attacks on the ships, the Corsairs were temporarily separated and it required sufficient time for the pilots recovering from the dive bombing to reorganize and set up the fighter weave. The 343 Kokutai squadron hit our VBF-1 squadron just as they were recovering and trying to get reorganized following the dive bombing attack. Before they tore Applegate's Corsair apart with their 20 mm cannons, Bob had shot down two of the Georges but we had no record of what Speckman and Tabler may have accomplished in the dog fight before they were killed.

Illustration by Robert McBride based on info in *Genda's Blade*.

One had launched its first wave of aircraft to attack airfields near Tokyo. I was the wing man flying next to Cdr. Hardin about five hundred feet above the bombers when we received a message from the task force to drop all ordinance and return to the ship. This resulted in a near tragedy for our TBM torpedo bombers, since the SB2C dive bombers flying above the TBMs dropped their bombs through the TBM formation. Luckily none of the bombs hit any of the TBMs, but we did hear a great deal of radio cursing of the SB2C pilots by the TBM pilots.

When we returned to the ship, we could not get any information as to why we had been ordered to abort the mission. We knew the war had not ended but there had been a major occurrence somewhere in Japan. Apparently no one in the fleet, including the admiral, all the intelligence personnel or any of the pilots had ever heard of an atomic bomb. A few hours later in the day we learned of the existence of a great atomic bomb that made it not only impossible for Japan's continuing the war, but also impossible to have any future wars between nations. We had no idea what an atomic bomb was.

K: Did you know that the Bennington was ordered away from the area by Admiral Nimitz before the bomb was released? My father told his sister that the ship made a sharp turn and it shook when the bomb exploded. A good shipboard friend of my father's confirmed the details my father related about the explosion.

T: It could be things were going on in the fleet following our pre-dawn departure and that the Army Air Corps had advised the Navy the bomb was dropped. Since we were in the air and about half way to Japan when we were told to abort and return, the message from Nimitz must have arrived after we had taken off. Nimitz could not have known about the bomb until the Army Air Corps released the information when the crew of the B-29 radioed to home base that the drop had been successful. Surely our admiral would not have launched us if he had known of the message prior to our departure. In the air, we never experienced any kind of air disturbance that would indicate a bomb of such magnitude had been dropped as we were many hundreds of miles from the detonation.

One thing is for sure…no senior officer of any of the services, including Nimitz, or even Vice President Truman until the day after the death of President Roosevelt, knew of the existence of the atomic bomb. The development of the atomic bomb was the best kept secret in America of WW-II, only the people actually working on the bomb and Stalin in Moscow (because he had spies in Los Alamos) knew about the bomb. The crew of the B-29 (except for the aircraft commander Col. Tibbits and the atomic arming person) did not know what they had been training to do until days before the take off with the bomb. Even in the pre-take off briefing, all the crew knew was that it was a big bomb that had the capacity to destroy a city. The words "atomic bomb" were never used in the briefing. That is what I have been told by Air Force friends about the crew and the dropping of the bomb.

That evening all discipline concealing our whiskey and private parties ended in our squadron ready room party that I don't think any of VBF-1's pilots will ever forget. We really believed the war was over and we would be going home in a few weeks. (See p. xxii.)

The question has to be asked; "how could it be the pilots of Air Group One could have a party with alcohol in their ready room aboard ship to celebrate the end of the war when alcohol is forbidden aboard American Navy ships?" The answer is simply that during WW-II, the Secretary of the Navy had three separate major commands in his service. The regular Navy surface ship and submarine command, (nicknamed the black shoes), the US Marine Corps and the Navy Air Corps. The Marine Corps and Navy Air Corps had very little to do with the "black shoe" branch of the Navy service. The surface ships, (including the aircraft carriers), had officers operating the ships which transported the Marines and the Navy Air Corps to the battles; in many ways you could compare the condition of the WW-II relationship among the three Navy branches to that of a peace time cruise ship that has the workers of the cruise ships doing their thing and the cruise passengers enjoying there cruise. The Navy Air Corps officers had their own dark green officer dress uniforms, similar to the Marine Corps uniforms and the black shoe officers wore the traditional blue Navy uniforms. Aboard the carriers, the air group pilots lived in quarters as separate from the ships officers as the passengers aboard a peace time cruise ship live separately from the cruise ship officers. The pilots ate at the wardroom's tables separate from the ships officers, and often at different times. There was very little social or working contact between the three different branches of the Navy aboard carriers in WW-II. This would all change for the Navy Air Corps shortly after the end of WW-II when the black shoe element of the Navy became alarmed about the Army Air Corps breaking loose from the Army to set up the separate United States Air Force, completely independent of the Army.

In the late 1950s, against my and many other regular Navy pilot officers feelings, the black shoes stripped us of our forest green uniforms that were similar to the Marines, then had us wear the same blue dress uniforms as they had and commenced assigning many of the Navy pilots (including me) to non-aviation Navy duties from time to time. That answers the questions as to how the VBF-1 pilots could hold such an "end of the war" party in our ready room at the end of WW-II. Much like the Marines, we considered ourselves an independent Navy Air Corps with our own rules and regulations.

K: The pilots weren't the only Navy personnel who had booze on the ship. Sailors in ordnance drank "torpedo juice," and the V-2-E Unit (engineering maintenance division) had a still which cranked out wine made from fruit from ship's stores. The men in V-2-E had their little party way before the war ended, in fact they had their party before you were even assigned to the ship, their party took place while the June 5, 1945 typhoon was raging. These guys decided that the ship was not going to survive the typhoon and the only thing for them to do was to drink all the wine they had on hand. The combination of the wine, violently pitching seas, and decks covered with hydraulic fluid made for quite a party. Of course the ship did survive the typhoon, but the next day V-2-E sailors had a heck of a hangover. Tell me something about the "medicinal shots" of booze air crews were sometimes given after returning from combat.

T: On our return to the ship from actual combat (not just air patrols) the pilots could report to sick bay and receive a two ounce shot of bourbon or scotch whiskey if they so desired. The flight surgeon on the Bennington was more than accommodating so if you took the first shot and went back to the end of the line and came through again he would let you have another shot as he gave you a wink as he served it. Sometimes he would draw the line after the third trip through the line. I must say that was one of the good ideas the Navy came up with during the war.

The next day we learned the war was not over yet and a few days later we commenced our attacks on the airfields again. Later when the second atomic bomb was dropped the fleet went into a defensive mode, not launching strikes but with extensive CAP air cover to protect against the last ditch Kamikaze fanatics.

K: I was surprised to find out that the primary target for the second atomic bomb was Kokura, a place that housed a POW camp filled with allied prisoners. The only reason these poor souls were spared the horrors of an atomic bomb was because the weather was socked in over Kokura, and after several passes, the B-29 bombardier could not get a visual on Kokura, so the plane moved on to the secondary target, Nagasaki. As it turned out, Nagasaki was also socked in and a visual of the target could not be made. The personnel in the B-29 decided to disobey the order to drop the bomb only with visual sighting of the target and not with radar. The crew was skeptical of returning to their base with the bomb, as it had been armed before takeoff—and they were running low on fuel. They decided to use radar to see the target and dropped Fat Man on the people of Nagasaki. I also found it amazing that the selection of targets for both atomic bombs was based on the lack of bomb damage by previous bombing missions. Our government and the people in charge of the Manhattan Project wanted a target that was intact in order to see the kind of damage the bomb would do to a metropolitan area. Therefore, the targets were picked because they were not considered military targets by the Army or Navy. It has also been revealed that Truman's Secretary of State wanted to use the bombs for the benefit of the Russians. He wanted to keep the "bulldozer" Russian forces from reaching Japan before the Allied forces, and he wanted Stalin to see just what an atomic bomb could do and that we had the technology. The invasion of Japan by American forces wasn't scheduled to take place until November so don't you think that the line put forth that the bomb was used merely to end the war and save American lives was basically propaganda?

T: Much of what you mention has been reported with some degree of accuracy by journalists, but there has been much second guessing and Monday morning quarterbacking involved. Any time there is a great event or assassination of an important person, the cottage industry of imaginative journalists seeking something to write about and sell takes off. In my opinion, Truman was greatly influenced by British intelligence advising him the emperor would be assassinated if he attempted to surrender without some great reason such as that the diehard fanatic war leaders were determined to fight to the death of all Japanese.

In their 2,600 years of known history, Japan had never lost a war. The idea of surrendering rather than dying with honor was inbred in the minds of all Japanese soldiers. For years the fanatics had been chanting it was preferable and honorable that 100 million dedicated Japanese die rather than suffer the disgrace of surrender. There was no such thing as honorable surrender in their culture.

The British intelligence had carefully studied the emperor and was convinced if Hirohito thought the third bomb would be dropped over the imperial palace that the immature, cowardly adult raised in seclusion would overrule the fanatic militarists and decide to end the war. No doubt the fact the Russians would soon be attacking and taking over much of the area as they had done in Europe was a major incentive to end the war before they came in to help us. And of course since Truman saved my life with the decision to drop the bomb, I have feelings different from many people about his decision. Had the war continued until a late October or November invasion, I sincerely doubt whether many if any of the VBF-1 pilots would have survived. The Corsair was a great air-to-air fighter plane, but a very easy and vulnerable target for the anti-aircraft gunners protecting the airfields we were strafing. We were the equivalent of ducks flying by duck hunters during hunting season.

I do believe the thought of the Russians taking over Japan also had much to do with the dropping of the bomb. In fact, I relate the same thought to the June 1944 Normandy landing in France. In June 1944, well before the Normandy landings, the Russian military on the ground and in the air had already defeated the German Army and Luftwaffe. The Soviet's great Army was rapidly rolling west toward Berlin. If the Americans and British did not land an Army in France, the Russians would have rolled all the way through Germany and France to the Atlantic and up through Denmark and Norway. If the Russians also invaded and occupied Japan, all of Europe would also have been in the hands of the Soviet Union except for Italy which the Americans and British had occupied.

I will always believe that the Normandy invasion was the first battle of the Cold

War of the late 1900s. Churchill, Roosevelt and General George Marshall must have had nightmares thinking about the Soviet Union occupying and controlling all of Europe and Japan. Imagine the Soviet Union controlling all of Euro Asia from the beaches of France on the Atlantic to the eastern beaches of Japan on the Pacific!

The second day after the second atomic bomb was dropped; we had one last all out air group attack of Japanese airfields before the war ended. Unfortunately, I lost my friend and new roommate who had replaced Applegate in my cabin in this last VBF-1 attack of WW-II. LTjg. Moxley had moved in with Oscar Folsom and I after Bob Applegate had been shot down. That was really a very sad task of gathering Moxy's personal belongings together and seeing the pictures he so treasured of his new daughter and wife and himself among his personal gear. As I packed his personal gear I was so happy I had falsely signed the muster sheets at the Alameda NAS while he snuck back to NYC to see his baby daughter.

K: I guess I have to ask you something about luck and rituals here. Since Robert Applegate and Charles Moxley, Jr. used the same bunk, didn't you start to think that bunk might be jinxed? Many sailors on the USS Franklin believed she was jinxed because she was designated CV-13. Was it just that Moxley was pre-ordained to not return, and Applegate to squeeze through? Did you have a ritual you went through before you took off—a lucky charm you carried with you or wore—you know much like professional athletes do? I read that many pilots in AG-82 had garments they wore for luck, one wore his wife's pajama bottoms as a scarf for instance.

T: It seems all people have these kinds of feelings, but I do not recall having any personal ritual other than saying prayers. At the time I was at least a semi-true believer and looking for any kind of crutch that would help me survive. I remember going to the rest room just before "pilots man your planes" so as to be alone in one of the stalls before we attacked the Kure naval base the second time and saying a prayer and promising God that if saved I would contribute 10% of all that I ever owned to him if I survived. In the first Kure attack, the anti-aircraft fire was so intense you felt like you were flying through a gigantic fourth of July fireworks display and I had already been hit once before. I will say (and I can't say who as his widow may still be alive and he was not one of my cabin mates) one of my best friends always slept with the panties on his pillow of the lady he slept with prior to our deployment from Maui in Hawaii. I don't know if that was for luck or for some other reason. About Moxy getting killed and Apple squeezing through, all I can say is that I am now a firm believer in the philosophy of the great Greek genius, Leucippus of Miletus, who in 490 BCE was the first to declare the movement of atoms is random with no power in charge of them and the same is true of all other happenings in life. He taught that since no power is in charge in the random action of atoms or events…there is no power guiding the course of events…therefore thoughts or prayers for some supernatural power to become involved are foolish.

Kelle, I would like to make it clear neither I nor my brother Don, a couple of old vets, have ever said we do not believe there is something out there beyond the Big Bang. How could a couple of ordinary citizens be smarter than Albert Einstein who could not be sure? At the same time, I am sure the Christian rain dancers of all the different Christian sects and faiths are going to have one hell of time trying to get old vet adults to believe in their six-day God constructing our tiny planet, a guy being swallowed by a big fish (the ancient story tellers didn't know the difference between a whale mammal and a fish) and setting up housekeeping for a few days inside the fish before being coughed up on the beach or some guy building a big ship with his sons that carried two of every living animal, insect and apparently worms on the ocean for an extended period of time. No one knows what is out there beyond the Big Bang. We and I am sure the brilliant Professor Van Doren of Columbia University hope "SHE" is out there in some kind of form or cosmic force as Einstein stated. What's your take on this subject?

K: Of course I think all humans, including atheists, would be pleased if eventually the scientists of the universe could reach beyond the Big Bang and truly learn that there is some kind of cosmic power or supernatural icon responsible for the birth of the universe. In the meantime we can only hope "SHE" is out there.

T: I honestly believe the majority of literate American adults do not believe the fiction of the Christian six-day God and the other fiction of the early creative, sci-fi and imaginative ancient story tellers but are too timid to admit their true thoughts.

Now I have to tell you about a conversation between me and one of the elders of the church I was attending at the time. While in a business meeting, ole Bob (now passed away), one of the most influential businessmen in San Diego, mentioned to me that although we were not Catholics, it would be good if he and I would call our mutual friend Elmer who was a Catholic to go with him to light a candle in his church helping to influence God to help save a young couple who were in intensive care in the local hospital. What had happened was that the couple who were friends of Elmer had departed the church after being wed and got in a terrible automobile accident about an hour following the church ceremony and on their way to their first night of their honeymoon. I replied to Bob, "Why would lighting a candle do any good? Why would God help them now after having them crash before their first night in bed together?" Bob said, "For Christ's sake, you can't talk like that Tom!" I had never heard Bob swear or curse at any time before or later in our long time business and social friendship. He was really very upset with me. Bob and I were good friends and business associates even in later years when he became well aware I no longer wanted anything to do with our or any other Christian church. The last time I visited with Bob he was 100 years old and he made a statement I will never forget. He said, "You know Tom there is something awful about living too long." He had lost his wife and both of his sons; was in good health but very sad and all alone.

I still cannot understand the scenario whereby every time there is a national disaster of some kind our political leaders come on the TV and request a national day of prayer. What the hell are we to be praying about?…Please don't do it to us again?…Help us repair the damage?…Or in the case of Elmer's young friends, light candles to urge Him to put them back together after He smashed them?…This scenario of prayer and lighting candles really amazes me.

Back to the war.

Immediately after the ceasefire was declared, our fleet intelligence officers outlined the post-war missions for the air groups of Task Force 38.1. The Japanese were to park all their aircraft out in the open on all their airfields with the propellers of all the aircraft removed and laid on the ground in front of each aircraft. We then flew airfield inspection missions at low speed, about a hundred feet or so above the airports, inspecting the compliance of the Japanese with this agreement. The Japanese complied with the arrangement and our airfield inspection missions were terminated a few days later.

When we were briefed on the details of the airfield inspection missions, there were some humorous comments made, regarding the idea of who would be the first American to land and visit in Japan following the end of the war. We were warned that this was serious business and we would be disciplined if any of us made a landing on any of the Japanese fields. Nevertheless, I must admit, a couple of VBF-1 F4U Corsairs were known to make touch-and-go landings, (the planes would just touchdown on the field and then apply full power and take off again), on the fields while we were inspecting the Japanese aircraft. No one ever mentioned these landings on our return to the USS Bennington.

Once the airfield inspection flights were completed, we simply flew CAP missions, (air patrols over the fleet), and commenced flights seeking out and inspecting prisoner of war camps in Japan. It was a thrill to see the prisoners wave to us as we flew low over the camps. The second day of these missions someone came up with the idea of dropping candy bars and cigarettes to the prisoners. So we went to the ship's snack bar and purchased candy bars and cigarettes and wrote our names and home addresses on a note attached to the gifts with a rubber band. For many years after WW-II, I would occasionally receive letters and Christmas cards from former prisoners of war thanking me for the morale-building gifts. Naturally the TBM carrier bombers did a better job at this than the fighter pilots as they had a crew man to throw out the goodies while the fighter pilots had to both fly their aircraft and throw out the candy and cigarette packages at low altitude. In later missions, the TBM bombers dropped large bundles of packaged food and medicine into the camps.

I was concerned about the fact that some of the candy bars might hit and injure one of the prisoners, but later learned no one was ever injured with the candy bar drops.

One of the TBM bombers had an engine failure while engaged in dropping the gifts and ended up landing on a Japanese road just outside the prisoner of war camp. The pilot and his two crew men spent the next couple of weeks in the camp with the prisoners. Later on I learned that the pilot had been so wrapped up in his gift mission activities that he forgot to switch gas tanks and made the forced emergency landing because he ran out of fuel from his selected tank. I am still not sure if it was a VT-1 TBM or one of our other task force carriers TBMs because we often flew in mixed formations on the prison of war flights.

A PLEASANT EXPERIENCE

Last year, almost 60 years since we flew these prisoner of war inspection flights, my wife and I were attending a fund raising dinner at the nearby California State University Long Beach, (CSULB), and as I took my seat at the table, the lady sitting next to my seat noticed my miniature gold Navy wings on the lapel of my coat. She asked, "were you a Navy pilot?" I told her that yes, I was a retired Navy aviator. Then she said, "I have to tell you an interesting story about the American Navy WW-II pilots."

She continued: "My father served in the New Zealand Army and was captured by the Japanese in Hong Kong in 1941. He was sent to Japan as a slave laborer in a prisoner of war camp until the war ended. A few days after the war ended, American Navy carrier airplanes would fly low over his camp and drop candy bars and cigarettes to the prisoners. He told this story so many, many times to our family and friends until he passed away a few years ago."

I told her I was a retired WW-II carrier pilot who had participated in flying those missions, but I didn't know if one of my candy bars had been picked up by her father. She was so thrilled to hear that, and at the end of the dinner as we stood up to depart, she grabbed me and gave me a big hug. It was a thrill for both me and my wife. Imagine some 60 years after the event.

A TBM3 Avenger from the Bennington drops food to one of the POW camps. Photo US Navy

ANOTHER THRILLING EVENT FOR AN 83 YEAR-OLD RETIREE

On Tuesday February 2, 2005, I opened my e-mail and right out of the blue the following message arrived in my in-box. Needless to say I was surprised and thrilled to get this message from the son of one of the prisoners of war we dropped candy bars to some 60 years ago. From Jim Nelson Jr., son of the late WW-II former prisoner of war, Jim Nelson Sr. His father, who was captured in the Philippines by the Japanese in 1942; survived the brutal Philippine death march and was then sent to Japan as a slave laborer until the end of the war. His son, Jim Nelson, Jr., recently came upon this information through research as he was writing a memorial about his late father and reading some of the war diary in his father's belongings and other sources. Obviously his father was one of the recipients of one of our candy bars.

Pertinent Part of Jim Jr's Email Message

Large red "P" "W" letters were painted on top of the compound's buildings in anticipation that American aircraft would locate the camp, and on August 27th they did. It was on the 27th that one of the pilots from Search Patrol One off the Carrier USS Bennington, probably LTjg. Tom McBride flying his F4U Corsair POW PAT 1, spotted the camp and over flew low and slow to drop a message telling the POWs to be prepared for a food drop. The package with the message almost hit Dan Holder on the head as he was walking across the compound to get Tillman, who wasn't sure what was going on when he heard the plane buzzing low over the camp. It wasn't long after the single fighter dropped the message that the Bennington's Air Group One consisting of Grumman TBM3 Avengers with a fighter escort of Corsairs flown by McBride, LTjg. Oscar Folsom and Commander Harden dropped food, medicine, magazines and clothing to the starving POWs below. In addition to the food drops made at Hanawa and the near by camps at Kosaka and Hanaoka on the 27th of August, altogether the Bennington made 28 food drops to POW camps on the Japanese islands in Hokkaido and northern Honshu, easing the suffering of many POWs, and probably saving the lives of some of badly malnourished and sick prisoners. Ironically, some of the prisoners they helped may have been part of a contingent of ten men from the Bennington who were shot down and captured by the Japanese earlier in the war.

K: I recently read an interesting article about the cause of the Japanese cruelty to the allied prisoners they held in POW camps. The writer said that the Japanese treated the prisoners of war they held during the Russo Japanese War and WW-I very well, much as we treated the prisoners of war held in the US during WW-II. The change in the treatment of POWs during WW-II by the Japanese was attributed to the conservative military leaders who took charge during WW-II. Liberal military leaders were against the atrocities committed against POWs (this makes me wonder if our seemingly poor treatment of prisoners of the war on terror is spurred on by our current conservative leaders). The Japanese loved to have submariners and pilots as prisoners because it was hard to prove that they had survived the sinking of their ship or the downing of their plane. Supposedly General Doolittle said, when asked about the possibility of him being taken prisoner during the raid on Tokyo, that he wasn't prisoner material and that if his plane were damaged he would crash his plane into one of the targets to avoid capture. Pappy Boyington had an evenhanded version of his captivity saying that there are good and bad in all cultures and that some of the Japanese treated him cruelly, while others treated him very well. The main question I want to ask you is if you ever thought about the possibility of being taken prisoner?

T: Of course we all thought about the fact we might be shot down and captured. We were well aware of the Japanese belief that a military man who would surrender rather than die was beyond their understanding and should be tortured and killed. Proof of this belief was well documented from intelligence gathered in the islands invaded and captured in the earlier years of the war and intelligence information acquired in China. I vividly remember one of the pictures found on one of the islands after our invasion, of a Japanese officer swinging a sword, cutting off the head of a captured kneeling blindfolded Australian pilot. There were numerous pictures of them killing thousands of Chinese children, women and men. If I had gone down alive I would have taken my chances of being captured rather than killing myself or trying to end it all shooting at them with my 38 caliber pistol.

I was awarded two air medals for my service in VBF-1. My victory participation included flying my F4U Corsair in the "air parade flyover" (as one of over 1,000 Navy, Army and British aircraft) over the Battleship USS Missouri anchored in Tokyo Bay as the peace treaty between the United States and Japan was signed on the battleship. I later learned that there had been a light overcast during the early morning as just the first of the 1,000 aircraft in the parade approached Tokyo Bay, the sun broke through to a beautiful sunny day with all of the aircraft making a very impressive show.

K: I can see that we are about to leave WW-II, but before we do there are a few questions I want to ask about plane operations on a carrier.

T: Wow, you are sure into this carrier scenario! I'll take it one subject at a time and do my best. Most of these questions regard ship deck personnel, but I was a pilot not closely associated with the command of the decks.

K: What were "plane captains" and what were they responsible for?

T: Plane captains were mechanics assigned to each airplane so that one mechanic would know all the information about the specific plane's quirks and maintenance history. This plane captain could then coordinate all the information he had with all the different maintenance and ordnance personnel involved in military operations. Each plane was also assigned to an individual pilot. In our VBF-1 squadron, we did not normally fly our own plane. Of course the squadron had more pilots than planes so surprisingly the most junior pilots were assigned a plane because that required them to stay in touch with the plane captain and also be available to him if he needed assistance. My plane was number 12. After I got hit by anti-aircraft fire and it was pushed over the side I had number 12 on my new Corsair too. The squadrons spotted the planes for take off in a manner that sometimes resulted in the pilots flying their own planes.

K: In a book I read, it said that the plane captain would start the plane engine and leave the cockpit when the pilot was told to man his plane—was this how it worked in your experience?

T: No. In our squadron, the plane's captain would stand on the right wing and assist the pilot getting ready to fly the plane. Once the pilot was set to go, the plane captain would jump off the wing and stand in the front clear of the prop and signal the pilot to start the engine when the bull horn of the air officer of the carrier announced "start engines." Often times there would be a delay waiting for the bullhorn announcement for pilots to start their engines.

K: When were the planes armed?

T: It seems to me that once a decision was made by higher command, the number of planes for the mission would be spotted and then the right kind of ordnance for the mission would be mounted on the planes.

K: How many planes were kept ready for launch and on the flight deck?

T: The number of planes spotted (meaning ready for the next mission) depended on the type of mission to be launched. Strafing, bombing airfields would of course require different ordnance than missions to attack ships. One thing for sure—during daylight hours there would always be a Corsair on both of the catapults ready to start engines and immediately launch in case of a surprise attack in the event an enemy had gotten through the radar searches undetected.

K: What does the term "spotting a plane" mean?

T: This term means how the planes were positioned on the deck. For instance, a deck responsible officer would refer to different planes by their position spotted on the flight deck. He could then for example give orders like, "Arm spots 6 through 12 with both rockets and 500 pound bombs." The responsible deck officer had a miniature deck layout in his compartment with small model planes so that he could quickly review the actual spot of all aircraft on the deck.

K: Did all pilots carry revolvers and survival knives?

T:Yes.

K: Where was the life raft stored in the cockpit?

T: The pilot's small inflatable raft was a part of the parachute assembly. If a pilot bailed out, the raft went with him.

K: How long did a pilot and aircrew have to exit their plane after a water landing?

T: Surprisingly, it took a WW-II carrier type aircraft a considerable amount of time to sink if it made an undamaged water landing. I guess about three to five minutes to sink. I lost my Piper Comanche airplane when I lost power after taking off from the Catalina Island airport some years ago and similar to the planes that made water landings in WW-II, it did not sink for several minutes. I had plenty of time to get out of the plane.

K: In my research of the Bennington, I found that there were only three deaths onboard the ship, and all three took place during the period of your assignment to the ship. Did you ever attend a burial at sea ceremony? Two of the deaths on board were a result of men walking into propellers—one was an airdale, the other a pilot of VF-1. Would there have been a burial at sea in incidents like these?

T: I remember the events. The burials were conducted similar to what you see in the movies. The sermon is conducted, the Marines fire a salute and the body slides out from under an American flag and sinks into the sea.

Walking into propellers was a very dangerous problem in dark predawn launches. While training in Hawaii on the carrier USS Kearsarge CV-33, a tractor driver ran too close to the stern of the ship. As he made a sharp turn at the end of the deck, he and the tractor tumbled into the sea so there was no sermon for him.

K: I've been told a story about the hospital ships. It's about one transfer of injured personnel from the Bennington to the hospital ship, USS Rescue. This also happened during your assignment to the ship. Do you remember this event? Almost everyone on the ship lined the rail in order to get a glimpse of the Navy nurses on the Rescue (some said it was a wonder the Benny didn't capsize). Lt. Ray Morgan of your squadron was transferred to the hospital ship along with ACRM Lovelace Boussard of VB-1. The tension of seeing Morgan leave the ship was broken when the Bennington crew noticed a sailor on the Rescue waving a pair of pink panties from a porthole. Did the transfer of sick or injured sailors to a hospital ship take place often?

T: You bet I was watching the operation. Ray Morgan was a personal friend and had suffered a fractured skull when he hit the barrier and his damaged Corsair flipped upside down after landing. I saw that crash and was amazed he lived through it. He was as limp as a wet towel when they got him out of the wreck. I did not see the pink panties but I sure did eyeball the nurses and was emotionally stirred when a few of them waved and blew kisses to us. We were of course just a very short distance from them; about 40 to 50 feet. We had been at sea for a very long time and they were more than appealing. I believe we had more than one meeting with a hospital ship but the one you mention is the only one I witnessed. Many times when we joined up with the logistic fleet I would be assigned to CAP (combat air patrol) many miles away from the carrier doing slow cruise figure eight patrol between the fleet and Japan so I may have missed other hospital and logistic ship missions.

K: When did your squadron leave the ship and how did you get back to the states?

T: A short time after we flew our Corsairs as a part of the over 1,000 plane victory parade over the USS Missouri as the peace treaty was signed, we departed for Guam and then boarded the transport USS Hawajalien back to the USA. We passed under the Golden Gate and arrived in San Francisco on 24 October. A few hours later I was knocking on the apartment door of my girl friend and great pen pal, Rene Reid, nickname, "Dennie." There were very few mail calls during my overseas deployment that I did not receive one or more letters from Dennie. If she is still around, that beautiful young lady is now 84 years old. Dennie was a year older than me. Since my first peace time assignment was being based 3,000 miles away from San Francisco at the Navy Aircraft Factory in Philadelphia, all Dennie and I could do was to continue to communicate as pen pals in peace time plus phone calls just as we had communicated while I was overseas. I got caught up with the excitement of testing the new post war aircraft and the parties in Philadelphia and so eventually received the so called warm and friendly, "Dear John," type letter advising me someone had taken my place in Dennie's life.

Both before and during the deployment of Air Group One, I had fortunately been assigned to occasionally fly as the wing man of Cdr. Hardin, the air group commander. Sometimes I would have conversation and coffee in the wardroom with him. He and I had a secret to share about a training flight when we were based in San Diego. Occasionally over a cup of coffee and when just the two of us were there we would joke and laugh about the flight. Just the two of us had been flying with me as his wing man and practicing a maneuver named "Thatch fighter weave" whereby each plane turns and weaves past the other head on making it possible for each to shoot at any enemy aircraft on the tail of the other. We were practicing the weave and acrobatics above the clouds for an hour or so. When we descended below the clouds, we were lost with nothing but unfamiliar land

Transfer of wounded to hospital ship. USS Rescue.

in sight. Cdr. Harden finally became aware that we must be a considerable distance south of the border in Mexico, so we flew westward until we got to the isthmus between the mainland of Mexico and the Baja peninsula and then north along the Baja coast to the USA and San Diego. We arrived very, very low in fuel in both planes and the commander's plane's engine stopped out of fuel as we entered the parking area.

A few days after we had flown in the victory parade over the battleship in Tokyo Bay and the city of Tokyo, Cdr. Harden and I were having coffee in the wardroom and he asked me, "Tom, what are you going to do when we get back to the states?" "Would you consider applying to be a career regular Navy officer?"

I told him I was only a high school graduate; he then advised me that he was aware that the Navy would accept high school graduate veteran combat pilots as regular Navy officers and then send them to college with their current rank and also on flight status with flight pay.

As a teenager with the experience of the 1930s depression behind me and still very fresh in my mind, wondering if there was another depression ahead of me and the thought of a career as a Navy aviator, I jumped at the opportunity. Cdr. Harden sent a letter to Washington recommending me to be a regular Navy officer, with the suggestion I be assigned to the Philadelphia Navy Aircraft Factory, near my home, as a test pilot. Upon our arrival in the United States at the Alameda Naval base, I received a letter from the Navy regarding my commission in the regular Navy and my orders to the Philadelphia Navy Aircraft Factory.

Thanks to Cdr. Harden and the Navy, I attended and graduated from the US Navy Postgraduate School in Monterey, California and the University of Mississippi with a BA degree.

Cdr. Hubert B. Harden USN

Commander, Air Group One

As recorded in Cdr. Harden's log book.

In the Navy the pilot's log books were

maintained by a yeoman.

USS Bennington 1945: (War just ended)

8-21: FG-1D #92267 3.1 hrs "DCAP"

8-22: FG-1D #92091 3.8 hrs "PHOTO"

8-25: FG-1D #88336 4.5 hrs "SEARCH PATROL"

8-26: FG-1D #92091 4.5 hrs "SEARCH PATROL"

8-27: FG-1D #92091 5.1 hrs "SEARCH PATROL"

8-28: FG-1D #92091 4.5 hrs "SEARCH PATROL"

8-29: FG-1D #92091 4.5 hrs "ESCORT"

8-30: FG-1D #92091 4.5 hrs "ATSUGI PATROL"

9-02: FG-1D #92091 4.0 hrs "TINTYPE" Tokyo Victory Parade

Air parade over the BB USS Missouri as the WW-II peace

documents were signed. Cdr. Harden was the lead pilot of Air Group One which led

the over 1,000 mass of aircraft over the Missouri and across Tokyo.

Post WW-II

Last flight Jan 31,1947 USS SAIPAN CVL 48

1-31: F6F-5 #72676 0.5 hrs "FG" Plane crashed at

sea Lat 30:11 N Long 87:22.5 W

Pilot Harden did not survive.

K: Tom, when did you start college?

T: I attended Westminster College in 1942 and then Temple College at evening courses in Philadelphia in 1946 and 1947 while based at the Navy Aircraft Factory. I also took college correspondence courses during my Navy career. Later I was assigned to the Navy ROTC command at the University of Mississippi in 1956 and graduated with a BA in business in 1958 as I had completed many prior semesters of college work, college correspondence courses and Navy schools before attending Ole Miss. The Ole Miss staff thankfully gave me credit for all of the completed prior courses which entitled me to attend graduate school in economics the last six months I was based at the university.

When the Navy sent me to college attending the University of Mississippi following the end of WW-II, I fell in love with the City of Oxford and the southern hospitality of my neighbors. But I had to keep my mouth shut about my feeling about the treatment of the blacks in the south. The only black persons on the campus were the janitors. At the Frosty Freeze store at the end of our street they had a separate takeout window for blacks and whites, the black one being at the back of the store. Wherever there were water fountains or rest rooms there would be two sitting side by side with one marked for whites and one marked for blacks.

Kelle, I have to tell you this amusing story. While attending the University of Mississippi as a Navy pilot, I earned my flight pay using the Navy aircraft based at the Memphis Naval air station. On one of the flights I took (for navigation training of course) to attend our Ole Miss Rebels football game against the University of Tennessee in Chattanooga, I checked out a Douglas Navy R4D (Civilian version being the DC-3) and invited a couple dozen Ole Miss Navy ROTC cadets to enjoy the game with me and my co-pilot. Ole Miss lost the game but we still ended up in the Sugar Bowl that year. At the end of the game I was walking across the field gathering the cadets together when I noticed one of my classmates standing near the goal posts in her cheerleader dress crying. I walked over and said, "Don't worry about it Mary Ann we can't win them all." Mary Ann said, "That's not the problem. The bus has left without me, my suitcase is in the bus, I don't have money to call my folks and I don't have a change of clothes."

In the military it is of course very illegal for both legal and insurance reasons to give civilians rides in military planes without Navy superiors' approval. Of course, at that time to take a beautiful lady cheerleader for a ride was even more of no-no than if it was a male passenger. In any event, I figured we would be arriving late at the Memphis Naval air station and only a couple of ground crew would see us arrive, deplane and depart the base. So I told Mary Ann to come along with me and I would get her back to Ole Miss. On our approach at Memphis to the air station my co-pilot gave the wrong code (in the Navy when a transport is on the approach the commanding officer of the base wants to be called in the event a senior officer is aboard) but I did not pay any attention to the message. After touching down and taxing back to the parking area, the tower operator advised me to park at the turntable in front of the tower. The turntable permits the pilot to taxi one wheel on to the turntable and then use one of the engines on either side to turn the aircraft placing the passenger door facing the tower office. Then the tower operator turns on the search lights as the VIP guests step out of the aircraft. This of course is the method to greet senior officers. I looked at co-pilot Chuck and asked what code did you give? He told me he now realized he had made a mistake in the transmission. So here I was unloading a couple dozen ROTC cadets in uniforms (there were no lady cadets at that time in the Navy) along with me and Mary Ann in her very sexy cheerleader dress. The captain of the base gave me a very unsmiling steely stare, never said a word, did not return my salute, turned on his heels and walked over and got in his car. It was of course late at night and no doubt this was not an enjoyable interruption of whatever he was about that evening. His driver also gave me a less than pleasant look. The ground crew meeting us were of course very pleased to eyeball and have Mary Ann in the arriving party.

K: Tom, that must have been a very embarrassing event for you!

T:More than embarrassing Kelle, all the way back the hundred or so miles to Oxford, Mississippi, I was wondering what the phone call would be like from the captain of the air station to the captain of the Ole Miss NROTC the next morning.

The next morning I was in the commanding officer's office at Ole Miss first thing and told him about the previous day's events. The captain of the Ole Miss NROTC was a great guy, nearing retirement, with a distinguished WW-II combat record and he just laughed about it. He told me not to worry, that he and the captain of the base were good friends and he would take care of it. I never heard any more about the trip from the Navy.

Kelle, that's the story my NROTC Captain discussed with the commanding officer of the Memphis Naval Air Station. After I told him the real story that morning he said, "Tom, I sure as hell can't tell my friend you just happened to meet Mary Ann as you were walking across the field and invited our cute "Ms. NROTC" (Navy Reserve Officer Training Corps) Mary Ann to fly back to Memphis with you rather than to ride the bus home." A few years later when the captain was retired and he and his wife were living in Hawaii I happened to be spending some time at the Barbers Point Naval Air Station in Hawaii having some work done on my Super-Connie. I invited the captain and his wife to dinner at the very best Chinese restaurant in Honolulu to talk about our enjoyable tours of duty at Ole Miss U. Our Mary Ann airplane ride recollections were a humorous part of our conversation.

The next year, Mary Ann Mobley won the Miss America contest and today is an actress living in Beverly Hills. She recently sent me an 8x10 photo signed, "To Tom, my favorite Navy pilot." Mary Ann told me the R4D ride back to Ole Miss was the first time she had ever been in an airplane.

After WW-II, my first peace time Navy assignment as a test pilot at the Philadelphia Navy Aircraft Factory and the Patuxent Naval Air Station from 1945 to 1948 was without question, the most enjoyable three years of my post-WW-II Navy career.

During these three years, the Navy was bringing online a great number of cutting edge new carrier type aircraft that had been in the design and manufacturing phases as WW-II ended, and it was a thrill to have the opportunity to fly and test them. I especially enjoyed the opportunity to fly the first Navy jet airplanes. I had the opportunity to fly over two dozen different types of the newest Navy and Army (and the new USAF) post war cutting edge aircraft while serving as a test pilot at the Philadelphia Navy Aircraft Factory and at the Patuxent Test Center. I must admit the old WW-II Army North American P-51 Mustang was my favorite really fun airplane to fly, I loved the old bird.

I was fortunate during my training in WW-II to fly with two of the Navy's finest fighter pilots, both top Navy aces: LCDR. Hedrick (credited with 12 kills) (later Admiral Hedrick) and Lt. Kepford with a record of 16 kills. While a test pilot at the Navy aircraft factory in 1947, I had the opportunity to meet with one of the top fighter pilots of the USAF at the Wright-Patterson AFB in Ohio; Capt. Chuck Yeager (later General Yeager). A short

Mary Ann Mobley, in 1958/59, the University of Mississippi's prettiest cheer leader, Ms. Navy ROTC of the university and the 1959 Ms. America. Later a movie actress. Married to the same man, lived in the same house and has had the same phone number for over 60 years!

time after checking me out to fly the Lockheed Shooting Star F-80 jet fighter, Chuck became the first test pilot to fly a plane that broke the speed of sound flying above Edwards AFB in California. I had been sent to Wright-Patterson AFB from the Patuxent Naval base to pick up the first combat capable Navy jet fighter from the USAF; the Lockheed F-80 Shooting Star. After being checked out in the airplane by Capt. Yeager, I delivered the jet to the Navy Aircraft Factory where a carrier type hook was installed. In later tests aboard the carrier USS Roosevelt with the F-80, we learned that our existing Navy carriers were not suited for jet aircraft operations. Fortunately the British Navy invented the "canted flight deck" type carriers and the steam catapults for jet operations. The Navy hydraulic catapults could not get the jets up to sufficient speed to launch from the carriers. The US Navy immediately copied the British Navy's invention and converted our carriers into canted deck types making our Navy jet equipped carriers a much more efficient and deadly war weapon than we had in WW-II. Canted deck means the approximately first half of the carriers deck has an angled deck pointed to the left of the straight deck so that a jet aircraft missing a wire on landing can take off like a touch and go landing and make a new approach. On a straight deck WW-II carrier if you missed a wire you would end up in the barrier with a much damaged aircraft. We had a saying, "There are the pilots who have been in the barrier and there are the pilots who will eventually be in the barrier." Fortunately over my 22-year career, I never once ended up in the barrier.

K: In my research work with the Bennington I noticed the different look of the flight deck from the pictures of the ship during WW-II and in the later years of the ship's history and wondered what the significance was to have the angle deck added to the original straight deck. Weren't different types of aircraft added to the ship?

T: The canted deck makes the flight deck look much different and is a very important addition because a jet aircraft cannot respond quickly enough to a last minute wave off by the signal officer. Actually the spin up to full acceleration when you apply full power to a jet engine is so slow that when a jet hits the deck, the pilots add full power as soon as the landing gear touches down so the plane can take off if the hook fails to catch a cable to stop the plane on the deck. All of today's combat carrier aircraft are much different than our old propeller driven planes that possessed the instantaneous response to full throttle wave offs. Thanks to the British Navy's inventions, our carriers can now handle the most advanced supersonic jets.

Top photo: USS Franklin with the WW-II straight deck.

Lower photo: USS Bennington with modified canted deck.

The USS Bennington CV-20 and the USS Franklin CV-13 were two of the 26 Essex class straight deck aircraft carriers built by the United States during WW-II. The American shipyards working 24 hours a day with never a day off during the war amazed both the Navy leaders of America and the world with their productivity.

Essex class carriers are considered by military historians as the best and most efficient aircraft carriers of any nation engaged in the war. The ships were of 27,100 tons, 872 feet overall in length, 147 feet overall wide, had a top speed of 33 knots and carried approximately 100 airplanes. The one great weakness of the Essex class carriers was that the un-armored, wooden flight decks made them vulnerable to bombs. As a result thousands of Navy personnel were killed from dive bombing and kamikaze (suicide) attacks by the Japanese. However, no Essex class carrier was sunk by the Japanese in WW-II.

With the end of WW-II, the straight deck Essex class carriers were found to be unsuitable to operate jet type aircraft because of the poor acceleration of jet engines resulting in the jet planes ending up in barrier crashes when trying to perform a "wave off" (meaning the necessity to go around again for a new approach to the carrier) or when the arresting hook of the jet missed the arresting cable on the ship. The British-designed canted flight deck modification of the 26 Essex class carriers solved this problem and the Essex class carriers then served as front line battle, jet-equipped carriers of the US Navy for nearly 40 additional years.

Canted Deck Modification

The bottom photo shows the USS Bennington sporting its post-WW-II modified canted flight deck making the operation of jet and large twin engine aircraft possible. With this modification of the deck, if an approaching aircraft's hook missed the arresting cable after touching down on the deck, the pilot would simply pour the power on and go around again for a new approach. Also in the event of a last minute wave off, the pilot would simply go to full throttle and go around again. Because of the poor acceleration of jet engines, the plane might touch down on the deck while performing the go around but this was not a problem.

Patuxent Catamaran Carrier Concept

This is a drawing of a catamaran carrier concept similar to the design the Patuxent River test pilots submitted to BuAer at the Pentagon in 1947. We could understand the Navy adopting and using the British concept of a canted deck to solve the problem of the new jet aircraft being unable to take wave offs on approaches on existing WW-II type straight deck carriers and also when the arresting hook of the jet occasionally missing the arresting cable and destroying the jet in the barrier cables. Of course it would be financially impossible to junk all of the almost new WW-II carriers and build all new catamaran carriers. All of our American carriers were less than 4 years old in 1947. But we could not understand why the Navy would continue to build new carriers with canted decks rather than to use our Patuxent concept of a twin hull catamaran type carrier. Our catamaran concept and the British canted deck concept both solved the jet landing problems but our concept also provided a much larger deck area for parking aircraft. Adequate deck space is a very critical consideration on all carriers. The more deck space available, the greater the efficiency in combat operations. A catamaran type design would also improve the sea worthiness of an aircraft carrier as the heavy armored flight deck causing top heaviness problems on single hull vessels would not be a problem for catamaran vessels. As of 2006, one thing is for sure. That is the fact the occasional police actions the United States gets involved in as the self-appointed world policeman confronting small militarily ill equipped rogue nations indicates no need for the United States to spend billions of dollars for new aircraft carriers. Our present state of the art nuclear powered carriers are adequate to serve in these police actions for at least the next 50 to 75 years, possibly a hundred years. Drawing by Robert McBride.

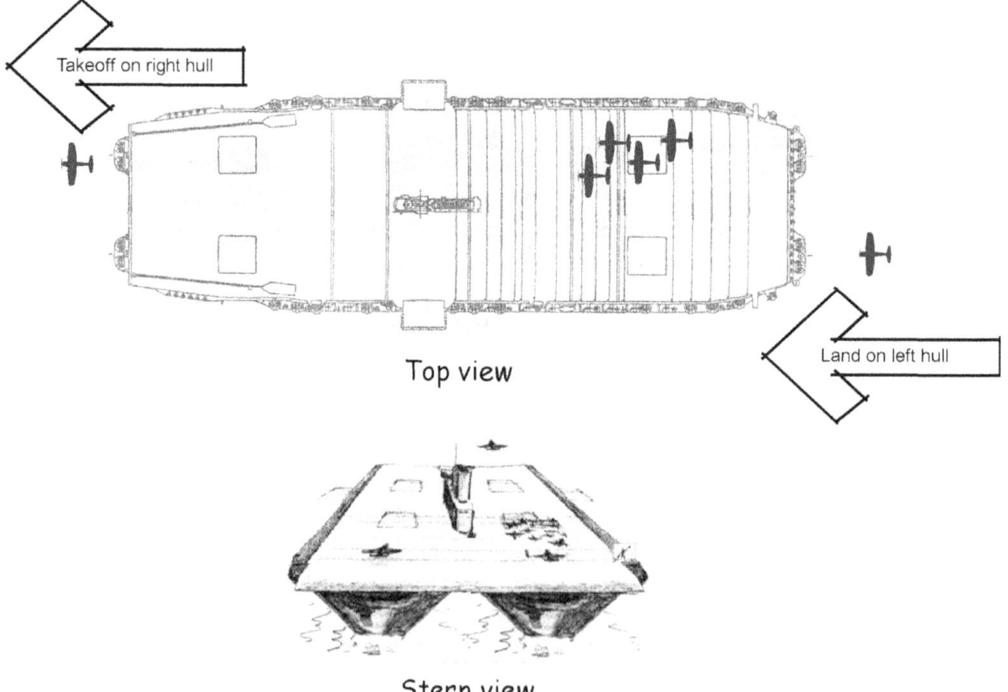

Conceptual Drawing of Catamaran Carrier

K: You seem to have a very high opinion of the engineering skills of the British Navy. You mentioned that the Corsair was not initially suitable for carrier operations until the British re-engineered the plane and now you mention their invention of the modification of carriers to handle jet aircraft.

T: You're right, I do admire the engineering, scientific and problem solving skills of the British Navy leaders. They seem to be able to "think out of the box" in developing weapons and problem solving in Navy and military fields. Let's review some of their aircraft carrier accomplishments: first they invented the idea of aircraft carriers in the first World War. The US Navy copied the idea converting an old coal supply ship into the carrier Langley CV-1 in 1922.

The British developed the first effective hydraulic catapults and efficient hook and cable carrier landing systems. They invented the use of radar to solve the problem of carrier pilots finding the ship after flying off on long patrols...there are no road maps to help a carrier pilot find the ship, especially on low visibility days in the great wide ocean. When both the British and we learned our straight deck carriers could not handle the new jet aircraft in 1945, the navies of both nations tried to solve the problem. At the time I was a test pilot at the Navy Aircraft Factory in Philadelphia and also worked from time to time at the Patuxent Navy Test Center. I remember our commanding officer at Patuxent, Col. Marion Carl USMC, calling us to meetings to try and come up with ideas of how to land jets on carriers and also launch jets because the hydraulic catapults were not powerful enough to get the jets catapulted. I remember one pilot mentioning he had recently been doing some landings on a CVE (the small converted merchant ships converted into small carriers in WW-II) and that they left the barrier down and kept the deck clear of aircraft and equipment so that he and a couple of other pilots practicing landings could keep their hooks up and just keep circling the carrier making touch and go landings, very similar to what most of us had experienced qualifying aboard the old converted ferry deck in the Great Lakes with our SNJ airplanes. Of course we trapped and stopped in training but there were no barriers in the event we failed to hook a wire. So he mentioned why not take two of these CVEs side by side and connect them so that they would be in effect a catamaran using the ship on the starboard as the launch deck and the ship on the port the landing deck. All of us became enthusiastic believers in the idea. A rough layout was prepared and two of us flew over to the Washington, D.C. Anacostia Naval base and took the van over to the Pentagon. We presented the idea to several senior officers and civilians in BuAer. We could tell from their expressions they were not very much interested. We left the meeting leaving the information with them but we never heard from anyone in BuAer about our ideas.

Later on the British invented the canted flight deck and the powerful steam catapult to launch jets. To this day I still believe small fast 600 foot catamaran carriers with the two decks would make the best and most efficient carriers to handle modern supersonic aircraft.

In WW-II both the Japanese and American navies suffered terrible damage and loss of thousands of personnel lives when our wooden flight deck carriers were hit by bombs or in the American case Kamikazes or bombs. The British on the other hand built their modern carriers with armored flight decks so when they got hit by a bomb or Kamikaze they just swept up the trash. Finally, the US Navy started to build the Midway class carriers with armored flight decks but these ships did not reach the fleet until 1945 after the war had ended.

Now that the British are not financially capable of building giant multi-billion dollar nuclear powered carriers, they invented the Harrier Jet fighters that can take off and land on small ships in the same manner as helicopters. Yes, I think we have to admire the British Navy's know how when it comes to naval warfare. They have had a lot of practice with Navy warfare having been at it for about 400 years or so. But the British with all of their capabilities, just like the Japanese and American Navy leaders, did not realize even many months into the war that heavy gun warships such as battleships and heavy cruisers were not capable of competing with sea air power. All three of the nations continued to waste billions of dollars, yen and pounds and vast amounts of manpower and material building these kinds of ships during the war. It was not until the last year of WW-II that the US Navy finally cancelled the construction of all planned battleships and concentrated on huge armored aircraft carriers like the USS Roosevelt, Coral Sea and Midway carriers; all three completed too late to serve in WW-II.

Although I served in the Navy during the Korean War and the Vietnam War, I did not get to fly in combat in either of these wars. During the Korean War, I was an aircraft command pilot in a radar search patrol squadron in the Pacific fleet flying former WW-II Army B-17 Boeing Flying Fortress aircraft that had been converted into radar equipped anti-submarine aircraft. Having qualified to fly the old four-engine B-17s, I had been retrained from a fighter pilot to be a qualified aircraft commander of Navy patrol airplanes in my last years of Navy service. The old B-17s had the former bomb bay section of the aircraft converted into a large radar search equipment with a rotating antenna plus room for a crew of three radar operators. Since the North Koreans didn't have any ships or submarines, about all we accomplished was a great deal of training, experimenting with the sophisticated radar of the time and boring expensive holes in the sky. However, the converted radar-equipped B-17s were the forerunner experimental radar/electronic mission aircraft that led to the development of the later Lockheed civilian Super Constellations the Navy converted into the top secret Navy Constellation WV-2 air early warning, air control patrol planes and typhoon/hurricane trackers.

In 1958, I was serving in patrol squadron VW-2 equipped with 12 WV-2

Constellations home-based on Guam. The closest I got to Vietnam was much later in 1959, when my "air early warning radar crew" and I, in our super-advanced, radar-equipped air early warning Lockheed WV-2 Constellation escorted USAF jet fighter planes flying from Clark AFB in the Philippines to their new bases in Vietnam.

The WV-2s were the first very successful sophisticated air early warning aircraft used for locating hurricanes, typhoons, radar search for enemy planes and ships and the radar air control of friendly fighters.

Flying the 2,000 horsepower F4U Corsair as a young man in WW-II was exciting and I never thought flying a big four-engine airplane could ever compare to the enjoyment of being alone and in complete control of my own airplane. I did enjoy flying the old four-engine B-17 Flying Fortress planes the Navy had converted into experimental radar search aircraft and the companionship with the crew members. But it was a come down from being a Corsair fighter pilot and at times it was very monotonous boring holes in the sky flying on auto-pilot patrol flights.

My attitude about flying four-engine planes changed with my introduction to the Navy Super Constellation WV-2 aircraft. The WV-2 had a wing span of 126 feet, was powered by four Wright-built R-3350 engines of 3,400HP and carried 20 hours of fuel. The top secret electronics packed into the airplane cost more than three times as much as the airplane. In my mind, flying the WV-2 on missions as the air command pilot near the unfriendly borders of nations and being responsible for all sudden decisions when events occurred was an exciting challenge. Following my preliminary squadron familiarization and training flights with the WV-2, I was sent to the Lockheed factory to pick up my assigned brand new WV-2. At the factory, I met the famous Lockheed test pilot, Tony LeVier, who instructed me with reference to all the nuances and capabilities of the WV-2.

I was amazed in the confidence Tony had in me as a newly qualified WV-2 air command pilot. We took off on our first flight with me flying as the command pilot and Tony in the co-pilot's seat. After the takeoff, we circled the field a few times, did an engine stop and prop feathering exercise and then made three touch-and-go landings. Following the fourth landing, we taxied back to the takeoff spot. Tony got out of the co-pilot seat and my young ensign co-pilot got into the seat while Tony took his position in the flight engineer's seat behind the co-pilot. He told me to take off again. As we roared down the runway and just as I raised the nose to lift off, Tony in the flight engineer's position, cut and stopped my number four outboard engine. Wow, what a surprise! My co-pilot and I conducted the proper emergency engine failure routine and climbed straight ahead. Tony then told me to make a final approach to the field and make a three–engine, no-flap landing. After parking the plane and as we were leaving the WV-2, I mentioned to Tony, "Thanks for the confidence in me." Tony said, "Let's have a beer and call it a day." The next day my crew and I took off from California for Guam via Hawaii and Midway Island.

In my last overseas career years, I served for nearly three years as an Aircraft

The Lockheed Constellation (Navy named the WV-2 Warning Star) was designed at the cutting edge of aeronautical engineering in the early 1940s and was modified in the military as an "air early warning aircraft." Powered with four 3400HP Wright R-3350 turbo-compound radial engines, the WV-2 could cruise for over 4,000 miles at about 250 MPH.

With a crew of 28 to 30, the WV-2 was capable of providing radar control of fighters intercepting hostile aircraft, radar search and patrol of great areas of the oceans, providing accurate locations of hurricanes and typhoons to protect the surface ships of the fleet and finger printing (meaning high tech analysis of all frequencies of both communication and radar facilities broadcast by potential hostile nations).

The high tech top secret electronics in the WV-2 cost more than three times the cost of the aircraft. The accommodations for the air crews in the quiet air conditioned plane were equivalent to first class travel in commercial aircraft.

Although it was not as exciting to fly as a Corsair fighter, the experience of being alone just off the coast of hostile nations and thousands of miles away from the top brass in the Pentagon with the responsibility for all decisions made in emergencies made the position of aircraft commander very interesting. I really loved the great old bird. Photo US Navy.

Command Pilot of the Navy air early warning radar equipped Constellation WV-2s, tracking typhoons for the Pacific Fleet, flying the radar barrier flights from Midway Island to and from Alaska, and later flying in cooperation with the Taiwan Air Force in the then secret, "Snowball Operation." The Snowball Operation with the Taiwan Air Force was my last personnel involvement serving as best I could in gunfire wars opposing enemies overseas.

The Constellation WV-2s were the most luxurious military aircraft of the time. In the passenger section of the plane they were equipped with the type of seats now found in the first class sections of civilian aircraft for the off-duty crew members. The airplane was completely pressurized and air conditioned for crew comfort, a few comfortable bunks and a quality galley equal to the galleys in submarines was also included. We usually flew 16 to 18 hour missions along the coast of China from Vietnam to North Korea so we had to have relief crew members and to have the aircraft equipped for off duty crew members' rest and relaxation. The Lockheed Corp. went overboard in creating the WV-2 as one of the finest airplanes possible for the missions the plane was designed for. Although we were homebased on Guam, we flew most of our operational missions from bases in Japan, Okinawa and the Philippines. Occasionally we operated from the Midway and Wake Islands.

At that time, (1958-1960) the Taiwan fighter squadrons equipped with the North American Corp. built F-86 Sabre fighters were engaged in aerial combat with the People's Republic of China Russian-built Mig fighter aircraft for the air control of the Taiwan Straights. The narrow sea between mainland China and Taiwan, Taiwan Straights, was the name given the undeclared war. The situation was similar to the Germans' problem in WW-II whereby they could not invade England until they got control of the air over the English Channel. Like the Germans' failure to control the air over the channel, the People's Republic of China could not gain the control of the air over the Taiwan Straights so they could not invade Taiwan.

The American Navy and Taiwan Air Force secret "Snowball Operation" used the cutting edge of military electronic technology of that time to battle the Chinese mainland air force. Our air early warning Constellation WV-2 aircraft were equipped with the latest and most powerful radar, plus the then top secret "Red Cap" electronic equipment that was capable of transmitting radar displays for long distances. With this equipment, the air controllers could determine which radar targets were friends or foe, their speeds, altitude and could maneuver the friendly aircraft fighters into the side winder rocket (an air-to-air rocket designed to shoot down aircraft) kill position behind the enemy fighters. The sidewinder was equipped with heat sensitive homing equipment making it possible for the rocket to seek out and home in on the heat from the tail of a jet fighter.

With this advanced equipment, the radar crews of the WV-2 aircraft had radar capable of picking up aircraft over 100 miles away, tracking them and noting their speed, altitude and course. The red cap equipment would then transmit the radar display to our

Navy carriers off of the east coast of Taiwan and also to the top of a mountain near Taipei on Taiwan code named "Snowball" during the operation. Our WV-2 air controllers were not bilingual, so they could not direct the Chinese pilots of the Taiwan F-86 fighter equipped air force. With the red cap equipment, the Taiwan Chinese air controllers on top of Snowball mountain and the air controllers aboard our carriers were receiving the same identical radar display picture via red cap on their radar screens as on our radar display in the WV-2 Constellations.

The Chinese air controllers in the station on top of the Taiwan mountain then directed the F-86 Taiwan fighter pilots over the Taiwan Straits engaging the Migs. The American carrier air controllers would launch and direct their American carrier pilots into a back up location over Taiwan. With this electronic radar advantage and the use of the Taiwan American-built F-86 Sabre jet fighters equipped with the sidewinder heat seeking rockets, the Taiwan Air Force maintained a 20 to 1 kill ratio over the Migs. We flew our Constellation WV-2s in an oval pattern about 50 miles from the Chinese coast so that our radar operators could pick up the Migs after they took off in China and well before they departed the coastline of China. The Republic of China Taiwan F-86 fighter pilots had to protect our Constellation WV-2s as we carried no armament and were equipped only with the sophisticated radar, red cap equipment and some other types of secret electronic gear. Since the carriers of the Pacific fleet were on the east side of Taiwan several hundred miles away we had to rely on the Taiwan F-86 pilots to protect our vulnerable, slow, unarmed WV-2s from the Migs. I found the Taiwan Straights War one of the most exciting tours of my career even though I did not get to fire any guns, do any strafing, bombing or rocket firing. Oftentimes I would turn the aircraft over to two of my younger pilot officers and go back into the radar section of the plane and watch the action on radar of the F-86s maneuvering in behind the Migs to make the kill with their heat seeking sidewinder missiles.

For diplomatic reasons, we never flew into or operated out of any airport bases in Taiwan. In the event of mechanical trouble, we had permission to fly into Taiwan and land for repairs. We operated out of Subic Bay Naval Base in the Philippines, Okinawa and Atsugi Naval base in Japan. The operational plan we used in the Snowball Operation was to have one WV-2 at a specific time leave one of the two southern bases either Subic Bay or Okinawa with a flight plan to fly to Japan. A similar flight would leave Japan to fly south to one of the southern bases so as to relieve the on duty aircraft that had left one of the southern bases at a specified time. As we approached the Taiwan Straights, we would set up an oval flight pattern about 50 miles long and two miles wide back and forth along the Chinese coast some fifty miles or so east of their coastline. In the event we were shot down or crashed, the USA could claim the Chinese had shot down an unarmed aircraft on a flight plan from say Subic Bay in the Philippines to Japan or vice versa. So likewise, if a WV-2 was shot down flying south from Japan to one of the bases in the south, the same diplomatic claim could be made. There were no crew briefings concerning these missions.

In the event any of the crew was ever captured, they would be unable to tell the enemy interrogators about the operation. Only the WV-2 aircraft commanders of the crews knew what was being accomplished flying the missions with no one else in the aircraft knowing that the red cap transmissions to the fleet were also going to the Taiwan air controllers on Mount Snowball.

In fact it was not until I attended an Operation Queen conference (a conference outlining the first 24 hours of squadron tactics as soon as we were aware a war of any kind broke out and before any orders from superiors arrived) that I learned that we were sending red cap transmissions to the Taiwan air controllers on Snowball. Since no Operation Queen attendees could ever mention the conference or who attended the conference I am not even sure if many of the patrol air aircraft commanders of the WV-2s were aware of the full details of Operation Snowball. All plans and operation details were based on verbal instructions, limited to what an individual needed to know to perform his specific duty.

Every aspect of the WV-2 aircraft and the operations they performed was top secret in the late 1950s and early 1960s. No unauthorized person was permitted to visit the electronic operation section of the airplane. As a WV-2 aircraft commander, I was briefed that in the event a foreign nation's fighter aircraft was to ever intercept me on patrol, I was to turn and go as directed by the intercepting fighters but then cut all four of the engines off, feather the props and drop into the ocean and wait for rescue. Our Navy patrol aircraft are equipped with the finest ocean survival gear money can buy. I am sure if any WV-2 air commander permitted his top secret aircraft to fall into the hands of a foreign nation, he would have been court marshaled. So a great many other former WV-2 aircraft commanders and I were shocked and disbelieving when a few years ago an aircraft commander of one of the US Navy's latest top secret air early warning aircraft flying pretty much on one of the same routes we flew some four decades ago voluntarily turned his top secret air early warning aircraft over to the Chinese following his aircraft being damaged in a collision with a Chinese fighter aircraft. The modern Navy plane cost over a hundred million dollars and the development of the top secret equipment in the aircraft had cost the USA billions of dollars and millions of man hours of the top engineers in America and Great Britain over the past fifty years or so. The Chinese acquired all of the codes and hardware to study and copy for free! Why the aircraft commander failed to ditch the top secret aircraft into the beautiful, warm, blue Pacific Ocean and use the aircraft survival gear is beyond my imagination.

The only close call emergency I had during the Snowball operations occurred in the Philippines as I took off on a Taiwan Snowball mission from the Subic Bay Naval Base. Although we knew it was illegal and against regulations to depart on missions with the aircraft over the weight limits, many plane commanders often did it because the 16 to 18 hour missions required lots of fuel. When operating out of Subic Bay, the distances of the operations off of the coast of China were a problem. Depending on the wind direction, the takeoffs from Subic Bay were very comfortable or very touchy. Taking off in one direction, you lifted off the runway and out over the bay, but in the other direction you were headed for the nearby mountains and had to make an uncomfortable turn just after take off to head back toward the bay. On this one occasion with a night take off and over weight, we were taking off toward the mountains. Just as I lifted the nose wheel off the runway and commenced to climb, my number 3 engine failed. Thanks to my alert and efficient co-pilot and flight engineer we handled the emergency feathering the prop quickly. Then the problem was to gradually make a 180 degree turn with the overloaded plane before we got close to the mountain without stalling and spinning into the ground. We barely made the turn not more than 500 feet above the ground and just above stalling speed but we finally got back over the bay, out to sea and dumped fuel until we were light enough to return to the base and make a three engine landing. There is no question in my mind that if we had taken off in the middle of a hot day we would never have made it as in hot weather the engines and wings are not as efficient as when flying in the cool night air.

Thoughts on the Roosevelt Administration, Pearl Harbor, and More

K: Tom, I have to interrupt you as I have some thoughts I have to address before they slip my mind about the leadership of our nation during WW-II. Could we address this leadership and then come back to the Super Connie WV-2 story?

T: Sure, we can skip around in this conversation.

K: OK, I can understand why many of your generation are so impressed with the leadership of President Roosevelt and later President Truman in winning the war, but I have had to grit my teeth not to interrupt as you were discussing the leadership of President Roosevelt because of a few questions I have in my mind about the conduct of the leadership of his administration during those trying times. For instance:

If it was okay at the time to round-up the Japanese after the Pearl Harbor attack, why weren't the German and Italian Americans sent to interment camps after Germany declared war on the U.S.? After all, German saboteurs landed on the east coast of America, planning to do harm to the U.S. and her citizens. Why weren't Lindbergh and others in the America First movement incarcerated as German sympathizers? Since the Navy had conducted maneuvers in the late 1930s which proved that Pearl Harbor was a disaster just waiting for an enemy attack, why didn't the U.S. government make sure that they didn't have too many of their eggs in one basket? Or was it to Roosevelt's advantage if the Japanese attacked American territory? Why did the American people wait so long to get into the war with Germany—especially since England was on the verge of being invaded? Weren't we the same then, when it came to our view of the world, as we are now? With our leadership's attitude of we're the only good guys and the rest of the world is far below us!

T: Wow! That's a load of questions. Let me take them on one at a time. (All of my answers are of course just my own personal opinions.)

K: If it was okay at the time to round-up the Japanese after the Pearl Harbor attack why weren't the German and Italian Americans sent to interment camps after Germany declared war on the U.S.? After all, there were German saboteurs that landed on the east coast of America, planning to do harm to the U.S. and her citizens.

T: The German/Italian-Americans question first. Both of these types of Americans had proven in WW-I that they had become dedicated loyal Americans. Of course there are always a few exceptions. Both the German and Italian-Americans had for the most part blended into the American culture. They were neighbors, friends, currently many of them were military personnel in our armed forces of 1941 and some were our political leaders such as Italian Mayor La Guardia. He was a nationally wellknown popular American politician. The Germans and Italians had not attacked us; Japan attacked us without warning or a declaration of war. The German saboteurs you mention did not live in the USA. They arrived after the start of the war and all but one (the one who turned himself in and squealed on the others) were executed about six months after they were caught.

Now consider the average black and white American citizen's relationship with the Japanese-Americans. Kelle, first put yourself in the shoes of President Roosevelt who was personally responsible for the safety of the American population. The Oriental exclusion laws of most of the states since the mid 1800s had isolated the Orientals from the general American population similar to the Jewish situation in the ghettos of Europe. In many states they could not become citizens, own land or marry non-Oriental Americans. The vast majority of Americans living east of the Rocky Mountains had never seen a live Japanese person and had no knowledge of their culture. In the late 1930s, thanks to an ingenious Navy intelligence operation, the President had been briefed in past months about the visiting of individuals from Japan showing glorious propaganda movies and delivering nationalistic Japanese speeches promoting the military actions of Japan in Manchuria and

China. They emphasized the establishment of Asia for Asians, under Japanese leadership and the withdrawal of all European nations and American influence in the Far East. These gatherings of thousands of enthusiastic "Japanese-Americans only" congregations were held in rented movie theaters, lodges, and convention centers on the West Coast and in Hawaii.

Surprisingly, there was an enterprising Navy intelligence officer in the peace time late 30s and 1940/41 years who conceived the idea of secretly training Navy enlisted men as janitors, maintenance men and security personnel for such buildings and making arrangements for them to appear as employees of the establishments. Navy intelligence had also managed to intercept Japanese communications between America and Tokyo that revealed Japanese operatives were reporting the anchorage sites, departure and arriving times of Navy warships. As a past Assistant Secretary of the Navy in WW-I and with little if any knowledge about the fact battleships were no longer the important war weapon they once were, you have to make life and death decisions about the safety of the citizens on the West Coast. We now know in post-WW-II that putting them in camps was a wrong call but in my mind an understandable one. I truly believe only American and Japanese WW-II Pacific war veterans have a true picture in their minds of how great the hate and prejudice was between all things Japanese for the Americans and all things American to the Japanese.

When the RAF and the Luftwaffe battled over the English Channel after the fall of France and the pilot of either side was not killed and parachuted from a damaged plane it would not be unusual for the victor of a dogfight to report the position of the enemy pilot in the water. The pilots of both the RAF and the Luftwaffe would radio the position to enhance the rescue attempts. In the Pacific area, the winning pilot, Japanese or American, would, if possible, shoot and kill the pilot in the parachute and if he could locate him in the ocean he would strafe him. In the Atlantic, when a young (usually a young late twenties or early thirties German) skipper of a submarine sank an allied ship it was not unusual for the sub skipper to have his radio man send an SOS location on international frequency so that the survivors might be rescued. This was not permitted by the German high command but the skippers most often did it anyway.

In the Pacific, when an American submarine sank a Japanese ship, it was not unusual for the sub's crew to then machine gun the lifeboats of the survivors. Downed American airmen picked up by Japanese ships were usually cruelly de-briefed and then thrown over board with weights attached. The hatred between the Japanese and Americans was so intense that if an intelligence officer had come into our VBF-1 ready room and said, "Do you realize within a month of the end of the war, our American occupation military personnel will be very fond of the Japanese and they very fond of the Americans?" he would have been laughed out of the room and accused of being out of his mind. But that is exactly what came about. If someone had told prejudiced me at age 20 that at age 83 I would have two Chinese daughters-in-law and six beloved Chinese-American grandchildren, I would have found the statement unbelievable! If a black soldier in WW-II was told that if he survived the war he would live to see a black General Powell as the commander in chief of the armed forces; later the US Secretary of State, he would have had a great belly laugh. It's a different country now. People who did not experience the various prejudices that existed in the late 1930s and 1940s in America have difficulty understanding many of the events of WW-II.

K: Why weren't Lindbergh and others in the America First Movement incarcerated as German sympathizers?

T: First we have free speech rights and the isolationists in America were anti-British more than they were pro-German.

The majority of the America First Movement members were dedicated isolationists who wanted nothing to do with Germany or the British and French. In the late 30s and 1940/41, many Americans were bitter about the way the British and French treated President Wilson and put down Wilson's appeals for a fair and just treaty to end WW-I. This was a treaty which Americans believed may have accomplished Wilson's pledge to all Americans. He said that our sacrificed military losses in WW-I were made in the belief they were sacrificed to ensure the WW-I victory. It was a war that would guarantee against the possibility of any future major wars. Many Americans sincerely believed if President Wilson's advice had been followed, there would not have been a second world war with Germany. It was common adult conversation that our terrible depression of the 1930s was caused by the British and French not repaying the massive WW-I war loans America gave them to finance WW-I. It wasn't true but many believed it.

P.S.: After Pearl Harbor, Lindbergh voluntarily performed many heroic acts in the Pacific war. Roosevelt was suspicious of Lindbergh's German feelings and would not permit him to have a military commission. In fact, in the 1942 Guadalcanal battle, Lindbergh was many times an unpaid civilian volunteer flying F4U Corsair fighters in combat in the early months of the war.

K: Since the Navy had conducted maneuvers in the late 30s which proved that Pearl Harbor was a disaster just waiting for an enemy attack, why didn't the U.S. government make sure that they didn't have too many of their eggs in one basket?

T: The US Army has a history of sometimes having leaders with strong personalities and the guts to speak out. Good examples of such men would be General Sherman in the Civil War and famous Army pilot General Billy Mitchell in the post WW-I area preaching about the coming age of aerial warfare. In 1941, the Army had General Marshal as the commanding general, one of the greatest military leaders of the 1900s. In the 1900s, the US Navy rarely had a strongly opinionated admiral who had the guts to put his career on the line to argue his opinion as to what or how the Navy should accomplish strategic defense policies and tactics to protect the nation.

Admiral Rickover, who forced the defense department to develop the nuclear submarine, was a rare Navy exception. Many of the top Navy admirals had written communications and conversations among themselves about the fact that basing all the battleships in Pearl Harbor was dangerous and that they should have been scattered among several different bases on the West Coast. But none of them had the guts to publicly take on the politicians in Washington. If one of them had made an issue of the president's decision, it may have cost him his career advancement as it did General Billy Mitchell when he tried to wake up America about the coming importance of aerial warfare. But Mitchell did wake up many important decision makers. No Navy admiral publicly made an issue of the administration's decision to put all the Pacific battleships in Pearl Harbor.

K: Was it to Roosevelt's advantage if the Japanese attacked American territory?

T:The two most powerful leaders of WW-II, President Roosevelt and Chancellor Adolph Hitler constantly demanded absolute discipline at all levels under their respective military commands. Regardless of the actions of the other nation, their military was not to make the first attack. Any deviation of these orders would be dealt with in the most severe manner. Roosevelt's orders to the military also applied the same procedures to Japan. In the US, Roosevelt was under tremendous pressure from the isolationists, America First members, American communists and a large percentage of just plain everyday Americans not to get involved in another European or Pacific war. The Chicago newspapers were especially editorially and vociferously accusing Roosevelt of being a war hungry aggressive leader trying to send the young men of America to fight Europe's wars again. Roosevelt did manage to semi-prepare for the war by getting the draft approved by a "one vote" majority in the House of Representatives. If the Japanese had not attacked Pearl Harbor, there is no way Roosevelt could take the nation to war to save Britain and the free world. If the Japanese had stuck to invasions of French, Dutch and British colonies in Asia, I sincerely doubt if Roosevelt could have pushed a war declaration through Congress. Once we were at war with Japan, most people of my generation well knew Roosevelt would have had to only fight the Japanese because of the mood of the American population. But Hitler then made his greatest mistake of WW-II (he made many military mistakes but this was the worst) by getting Roosevelt off of the hook by having Germany declare war on the US just a few days after the Pearl Harbor attack. If presidents like Roosevelt had been in office over the past five decades, the only war we would have fought would have been the Afghanistan War. Their Taliban inhouse friends hit us first, we gave them a chance to cough their friends up, they declined the offer, we bombed good and hard. That was the simple international Roosevelt program; never strike first, it was never his intention for the USA to be the world policeman. Roosevelt was the driving force to establish the United Nations to be the post-WW-II world policeman.

K: Why did the American people wait so long to get into the war with Germany—especially since England was on the verge of being invaded?

T: America had never been an aggressive strike-first nation in all of its history up until that time, except for attacking the American Indians. Always the other nation had to strike or commit an act of violence against America first. The current Iraq war is the first time in our history where we have become an aggressive strike first nation and the civilized nations of the world condemn our aggression.

K: Weren't we the same then, when it came to our view of the world, as we are now?

T: No! No! No! America was a much different nation prior to WW-II. America was admired by the majority of the people in the world as the most peaceful and least aggressive major nation in the world. America was one of the very few nations in the world that never set up any type of military defenses with our neighboring nations of Canada and Mexico. In 1940, our Army was ranked about seventh or eighth of the size of the armies of the other nations in the world and was equipped with few if any modern weapons. Our Navy was more like a yacht club than a military Navy. As of the appointment of post WW-II dumb ass Secretary of State John Foster Dulles under President Eisenhower, America's leaders for the first time commenced sliding down the slippery slope of seeing the American nation as the world policeman. Dulles's nut cake idea referred to as the "Domino Theory" set the nation on the way into the Vietnam War, bailing out the French in their illegal effort to deny the Vietnamese their right to self rule.

In 1945, immediately following the signing of the WW-II peace treaty, the leader of the Vietnam nation, Ho Chi Min, made one of the most pro-American speeches ever made by a foreign leader. The speech to thousands upon thousands of his citizens in the last week of August 1945 praised the US for its great constitution, bill of rights, citizen's freedoms and the American nation's pledge to stop the subjugation of smaller nations by the powerful European nations. He visualized himself as the Asian great communist leader similar to the pro-British communist Yugoslavian leader, Marshall Tito, the long time ally of the British in Europe.

This is a true fact: there were a few Americans in Vietnam who heard the speech and the speech was recorded. So instead of promoting the United Nations as the world policeman as Presidents Roosevelt and Truman intended, American leaders since Truman have decided to have America take on that responsibility.

There is no possibility of an international political vacuum. Some force will develop to fill it. If the US would simply take its seat in the United Nations, support the United Nations and absolutely refuse to unilaterally cure any international problems with North Korea, Iran or whoever and let the problem simmer, the other nations would eventually step up, commit to action and the UN would take on the world policeman role with a united front. It may mean we will be in a war as a member of the UN but we would be in the war with all the allied United Nations armed forces along with us. Of course, if ever we are struck first, then like Roosevelt's program, we immediately and unmercifully commence massive bombs away and destroy the attackers.

*K:	With our current political leadership, the attitude seems to be "we're the only good guys and the rest of the world is far below us!"*

T: You got it. That is the attitude of all of the leaders since President Truman and General Marshall retired from the scene. Truman and Marshall saved the free world with the "Marshall Plan." The two of them with Winston Churchill are responsible for the strategic plan to isolate and contain the Soviet Union behind the iron curtain rather than engaging in combat. They are the three leaders who should be remembered as the men who won the cold war. The leaders whose long range plan was to isolate, contain and wait it out to what they knew would be the eventual collapse due to the stupid actions of the misguided leaders of the Soviet Union. Once the Marshall, Truman and Churchill plan was set up, none of the later American leaders changed it. If leaders like Truman, Roosevelt and Marshall had been in office since the 1950s, there would not have been any of the police actions the US has suffered through over the last 55 years.

Truman of course took the USA into the Korean War as the lead nation of the United Nations. Truman also knew once the North Koreans were driven out of South Korea, the United Nations wanted the war to end. With the help of the government leaders of India, Truman did his best to end the war quickly. However the less than brilliant military leader, General ("Dug out Doug") Mac Arthur, and his "super patriot" political allies in Congress screwed up Truman's efforts to end that war quickly and diplomatically with the assistance of the United Nations and the government of India.

My now departed younger brother Don, who I mentioned was a Navy veteran of WW-II and an Army veteran of the Korean War, suggested to me some time ago that if any of the American leaders since 1960 had instigated a major Truman/Marshall type plan for

Palestine (America could have made Israel permit the establishment of a Palestinian nation) we would now have peace in the Middle East. Such a Truman/Marshall type plan to contain and isolate Iraq and the regime would have collapsed with no loss of American lives. It would have cost about 2 or 3 percent of the cost of the 2006 Iraq War. With a Palestinian population not as large as the City of Chicago the low cost of a Palestinian Truman/Marshall Plan to build factories, provide employment for every Palestinian who wanted a job, plus give the Palestinian nation such advantages trade arrangements (similar to what we gave to Japan and Taiwan while engaged in the cold war) this small Muslim nation experiencing prosperity and friendship would have also become one of the most pro-American nations. They would have been too busy enjoying life to bother making bombs to kill the Jews.

Brother Don, like many veterans of real combat, thought differently than the leaders we have had since the Truman/Marshall reign. Truman was the only president in Don's or my lifetime who had been involved in actual bloody ground war combat, witnessed hostile gunfire, saw shells fall near him and saw comrades killed in WW-I. With the Truman/Marshall type plan for the Palestinians, the other Middle East nations would then have been more inclined to get along peacefully with the US.

A Military Theocracy Incident

T: Back to the WV-2 Super Connie. Kelle, I only had this one additional incident that occurred while I was serving as a WV-2 aircraft commander on Guam. It's going to take a while to paint the total picture but I think you will find this story very absorbing. The crew of a WV-2 aircraft ranged from 26 to 32 depending on the mission assigned. Our squadron's home base was in Guam and all of the married personnel had their families living on Guam during their tour of duty. For some strange reason when a WV-2 Connie (the plane's nickname) destination was Atsugi Naval Base near Tokyo or Hong Kong, the crew would swell to over 40 members. Whatever the number of seat belts the plane was equipped with would hold a crew member on those flights departing Guam. Of course, once we arrived at the destination only the normal-sized crew would fly the missions. The others would enjoy the pleasures of the visited country. Guam island was a great place for the families to enjoy but not very exciting for the single men assigned to the squadron. On the other hand, Hong Kong and Japan offered fantastic and very enjoyable liberty opportunities. We also operated missions out of Okinawa and Subic Bay in the Philippines which the service men also enjoyed.

During the Snowball operations, when we deployed from Guam to Japan, Okinawa or the Philippines, we would normally deploy for a period of three to four weeks before returning to Guam for aircraft overhaul and maintenance. Then about a month later we would deploy again to one of the three operational bases. On one occasion when I returned from Subic Bay after a three week tour, the squadron commander called me into his office and told me it would be necessary for me to get my crew together immediately and prepare to redeploy to Okinawa with a different aircraft while my aircraft was turned over to the maintenance crew. He mentioned the crew that was scheduled to deploy needed some additional training. This seemed strange to me as that crew had performed well on its previous deployment. In the Navy you do not question your commander's decisions unless you are sure of what you are talking about. Besides, I always enjoyed my tours on Okinawa so I was pleased to go again.

I contacted all of my crew and gave them the word. The single crew members were of course delighted and the married crew members were of course disappointed. The next morning we deployed for Okinawa.

We were busy operating out of Okinawa flying to and from Atsugi in Japan in operation Snowball for the next two weeks when I received an emergency message from the skipper in Guam that my youngest son Robert had been injured in an accident. Our neighbor hit him with her automobile. The skipper also said in the message to return to Guam immediately and a replacement aircraft commander would be sent to take over my crew.

The message arrived in Okinawa at about 7 a.m. when the crew of one of the WV-2 planes was preparing to depart for Guam and I and my crew were filing our flight plan to proceed to the Taiwan Straits and then on to Japan. Ron, the aircraft commander of the flight departing for Guam gave me his flight plan, scratched off his name and took my flight plan and replaced my name with his name and said, "Get going." I never questioned the change or what might be said when I arrived with my crew in Guam. My crew took over his plane and his crew took over our aircraft to fly the mission and we both departed. On my arrival in Guam late that afternoon, the skipper greeted me as I rushed off of the plane, took me to his car and drove me to the hospital to see my son and wife who was with him. His injury was painful but not serious and he was released from the hospital a few days later.

As the skipper was driving his car to the hospital, I was expecting some comment about my and the other aircraft commander's decisions to swap our missions and me rushing back to Guam. As the skipper was driving he started to laugh and made me promise not to ever mention the story he was about to tell me about my immediate redeployment to Okinawa following my return from the Subic Bay deployment.

This is the story he told me. Several officers had come to the skipper and told him their wives were very concerned about the condition of the four year old son of one of the radar officers in my crew while he was with my crew at the Subic Bay Philippine base. The youngster had been playing with a cigarette lighter and the fluid had leaked onto his clothes and caught fire. He had suffered burns on his arms and legs. In Guam because of the tropical humid climate the fungus infection that developed was getting ever more serious with each passing day. But the mother and father belonged to a religious sect that believed that only God heals and they refused to take the child to the Navy hospital. They constantly prayed to God for their son's recovery and would not pay attention to the comments of their friends. So the wives who were friends of the mother encouraged their husbands to seek help for the youngster from the skipper of the squadron. Once my crew and I, including the father of the youngster, deployed for Okinawa, the wives of the officers who had gone to the skipper worked on the wife to get her to relent and at least just let the doctor at the hospital look at the child's fungus infection. In the hospital, the well-meaning wives who were good friends of the mother, the doctor and the hospital Navy chaplain finally managed to get the mother to relent and let the doctor treat the child. The following day the mother saw the improvement in the child's condition and was pleased to let him remain in the hospital to continue the treatment. He was still in the hospital when I returned with my crew along with the father who with much reluctance and in a dire mood permitted the Navy to keep the child in the hospital until he was in first-rate condition. Nevertheless the father was never convinced that the doctor and the treatment had played any part in the child being cured of the fungus, claiming that his prayers to God had really cured the infection. I wanted to ask the father why in the hell would praying do any good if God had permitted his son to be burned in the first place but I kept my mouth shut as the skipper told me to never discuss the subject with the father. The skipper's only concern was not to be ever charged with interfering with freedom of religion so he simply deployed me and my entire crew for his own reasons! One of the best men I ever served under in the Navy. I later heard from several former squadron friends that when the skipper retired he attended a religious school and became a minister.

On to Retirement 1961

Following my retirement from the military in 1961, my family and I settled in San Diego. I entered business as a one man real estate office and eventually owned three real estate offices. One on Point Loma, one in Pacific Beach and one in La Jolla, each staffed with about ten agents. Later on I settled in San Gabriel and Long Beach, California in a real estate career with John Hedrick, the younger brother of one of my former Navy commanding officers, (in squadron VF-84) Admiral Roger Hedrick.

K: Tom, before we leave your military career I would like to hear about the F-80 accident you had while attending the University of Mississippi as a Navy officer. I forget when I heard that you had an accident flying the F-80 jet, it may have been a statement you made in one of your e-mails or it might have been in one of my communications with your son John. When and where did it happen?

T: Yes, I crashed an F-80 at the Memphis air base in 1958. I was flying above a thunderstorm on my return to the Memphis Naval Air Station from New Orleans when I lost all electric power and therefore lost the ability to transfer fuel from one tank to another. I realized my electric instrument flying gauges would be going out in a matter of minutes. So I did a rapid dive from 30,000 feet out from the Memphis radio beacon and at 15,000 feet rolled over in a "split S" and headed back 180 degrees until I broke out underneath...I was in one hell of a hurry to get down while my instruments were working and land so I dove the F-80 at the maximum permissible speed in the dive. Luckily I ended up right near the radio beacon as I broke out...then headed for the Memphis Navy field. With my failed electric system, I had no idea how much fuel remained in the tank I was using and also knew I could not transfer to another tank without electrical power. I have retained the pilots' handbook for many of the planes I flew in the service but I do not have an F-80 pilots' hand book to recheck what happens to an F-80 when the generator fails in flight.

The approach end of the Memphis Air station field had a steep bluff just before the start of the runway so I knew if I ran out of fuel and was low on the approach I would no doubt slam head on into the bluff. I also remembered that was what happened to the great ace of the Army Air Corps, Major Bong, who had an engine failure in the F-80 he was flying and had been killed crashing into a bluff he could not clear. So I made a higher than normal approach to the runway with the engine idling. I could not lower my landing flaps to slow the approach, probably because of the lack of electrical power (as mentioned I no longer have a copy of the pilots' hand book so the landing flap problem may have been a failure in addition to the electrical failure). Making the approach higher than normal, landing fast with no landing flaps about one third of the way down the runway and with lots of water on the runway, my brakes could not slow the jet down by the end of the runway. The jet skidded and careened off the end of the runway, slammed through the end of the runway barrier, crashed through the Navy base security fence, then across the highway (luckily through a break in the highway traffic so no cars or trucks were hit) and then several hundred feet into the woods. The sturdy wings of the F-80 cut down trees with trunks as much as 3 to 4 inches in diameter as easily as a sharp sickle cuts through wheat. Lockheed surely builds tough birds. No injury to me but the F-80 was totaled. Amusing footnote, I had tried to eject when I broke out under the clouds as I did not think I had enough fuel remaining in the selected tank to make the approach but the canopy failed to blow off. The F-80 did not have the type of ejection seat of late model jets that ejected both the pilot and the canopy. So unable to open the canopy I had to stick with the plane and make the approach. When the plane finally came to a stop in the woods, I could not open the canopy. When the crash rescue trucks arrived, they saw me banging my hands against the canopy trying to get out and of course came to my aid. Fortunately the plane did not catch on fire.

When the first rescue guy jumped up on the wing with his ax, the shaking of the plane triggered something and the canopy blew off high in the air. Both he and I simultaneously shouted, "Oh shit" because the two of us thought the dammed canopy would come down on top of us. Fortunately it came down 10 to 15 yards behind the plane and clear of the crash rescue trucks.

Several members of the accident investigation board made some derogatory remarks about my handling of some of the emergency procedures but in the final report sent to Navy headquarters in the Pentagon the accident was declared due to be a mechanical failure plus weather related, not pilot error. No doubt I could have saved the plane if the weather had been clear.

So now at the age of 84, still a licensed pilot with 68 years of experience having been a pilot since age 16, I have been responsible for the destruction of three airplanes: the one -wheel landing on the Bennington after having my left landing gear shot off with the damaged Corsair pushed off the ship into the sea, the crash and destruction of the F-80 and the loss of my Twin Comanche at Catalina Island after having engine failure following take off, then landing in Avalon Bay and with me having the painful memory of watching my lovable ole Comanche sink to the bottom of the bay after I got out of the cockpit. Hopefully under the watchful attention of co-pilot Karen, I will not experience the loss of any more airplanes.

Peace Time

K: Did you miss the airplanes you flew after you left the service?

T: Yes, very much to put it mildly. Immediately after retirement from the military I would occasionally rent the small two passenger Cessna 150 trainer aircraft just to keep myself current as a licensed civilian pilot. Later in my business career I was always adept in convincing clients and the decision maker top executive of the firms I worked with regarding the importance of having the use of a business plane to enhance the growth of the business or the efficiency of completing projects we were involved with. Since I was the only pilot in the business organizations, I considered the planes involved as my personal aircraft.

K: Tom it is obvious you enjoyed your real estate career using the airplanes to investigate the potential buildable sites and the many you refer to as "navigation and instrument training flights."

T: That's true. All airplane costs were a tax-deductible expense! Now in retirement, I surely do miss the airplanes but I do not miss the tension and worry about holding sites in escrow until the feasibility studies were completed, investors could be found, environmental details cleared up and construction financing could be arranged. Some sellers were cooperative but some could really be pains in the butt. I will have to relate one very sad flight and experience with my Comanche 250.

Excuse me if I tear up a bit as I tell you this story.

A Sad Comanche Flight

In the mid 70s, about two or three years before I met Karen, I was sitting at my desk in our San Gabriel Hedrick McBride office building when Bonnie, our secretary receptionist, informed me a real estate agent was on the phone who had a buildable site not far from the city of Fresno in the San Joaquin Valley. I took the call and made arrangements

Tom McBride
Developer

Tom McBride has a B.S. in Business Administration from the University of Mississippi, is a graduate of Management Administration from the Navy Post Graduate School in Monterey, California, and has earned a Certificate of Real Estate and Finance from the University of California at San Diego. He was President of McBride Realtors (later Key Realtors) in San Diego. Since 1965, he has been involved with various major California builders in the site acquisition, financial structuring and development of over $100,000,000 of commercial and residential properties. These developments have spanned the field of real estate construction including single family homes, high-rise hotels, motels, restaurants, apartment complexes and neighborhood shopping centers.

In the hotel-motel field, Tom has had experience in site acquisition through ground leasing and land purchases, feasibility analysis, conceptual preliminary planning, building consultation, recruiting and staffing, handling of furniture, fixture and equipment procedures and pre-opening programs for "turn key" delivery of major hotel-motel developments.

John Hedrick was the younger brother of my former commanding officer, Roger Hedrick, a Navy fighter pilot ace (Roger shot down 12 Japanese aircraft) in the Pacific theatre of the war. Roger remained in the Navy and retired with the rank of admiral. John Hedrick following his return from the war serving as an officer in the Army Air Corps first worked with the City of Los Angeles building department and later opened his business in the construction industry. I very much enjoyed working with John on many real estate projects. Now approaching the nineties, John is retired from the business.

A Hedrick Construction Project

These are my two favorite airplanes that I flew in my civilian career:

My only personal airplane was this single engine Piper Comanche 250 which was really a fun airplane to fly around the Southwest. It was the number one love of my life until I met Karen. This is the airplane I took Karen in to visit her brothers in Albuquerque. Later after we were living together and then married, Karen participated in the Aircraft Owners and Pilots Association "Pinch hitters" courses whereby the wives of pilots are taught how to take over and land the airplane in the event the husband pilot passes out or dies in the air. The instructors were very much impressed with Karen's ability to land and take off the Comanche.

Our Twin Comanche flying over our Long Beach Belmont Shore neighborhood on a bright sunny Southern California afternoon. These are the kind of days I like to remember!

Mother age 80 and the Comanche just before our flight from Conway Airport (across the Ohio River from her home in Aliquippa) to eyeball Niagara Falls from the air. Mother flew as the co-pilot. This was the first time she had seen the Falls since her honeymoon with Dad about 60 some years earlier.

for me to fly into the nearest airport to the site in my single engine Comanche 250 and for him to pick me up to drive to and inspect the site. At that time I had not traded in the ole single engine Comanche 250 for the twin Comanche.

Skip, the agent, I think his name was Mike McKensie or McKenna, I am not sure and I did not get to know him as we did not make the deal on that property. It was a suitable flat lot but the later rent survey did not indicate its potential income would support the construction financing. After inspecting the property and gathering up the plat maps and demographic information surrounding the site, Skip (his nickname) and I went to lunch at a Denny's restaurant on the way back to the airport. While at lunch I learned Skip was also a vet of WW-II and a bit younger than me. In our discussion about our service in the war I learned Skip had entered the Army at age 18 and at age 19 having never had any combat experience he had landed on the beach at Normandy a few days after the battle and after much of the terrible carnage and dead bodies had been cleared away.

Later he had been involved in the Battle of the Bulge but not on the front lines as he was serving in a mobile field artillery company. But he was engaged in doing a lot of firing the big 105mm cannon his squad was assigned to. At a much later date his Army group was one of the first units to come across one of the Holocaust death camps. Skip mentioned that up to that incident he had never seen any dead soldiers or dead civilians in the war or in civilian life. He mentioned he was horrified at the sight of the dead bodies and the gapping mouths of the dying persons with their mouths hanging open and the terrible look in their hollow looking eyes. He mentioned the stench was beyond belief or description and he could hardly breathe. He had arrived at the camp about two hours after having breakfast and with the stench and sight of the dying and dead he commenced vomiting. After he had thrown up all in his stomach he had the dry heaves so bad his older platoon sergeant took him aside and had another soldier escort him out of the area to recuperate.

The next morning he returned to the camp and had the same experience so his scrgeant had him sent to another unit away from the camp to recover. Skip mentioned he could not sleep at night and the memory of the victims and stench memory kept coming back into his mind day and night.

When Skip returned to the states and to his hometown, he married his high school girlfriend but the marriage was short lived with his wife telling him she had to have the separation because of his problems at night waking up sobbing and his moodiness.

After the divorce he sought psychiatric help and told me he thought he had overcome his problems. I noticed he had tears in his eyes as he told me the story and he said, "I'm sorry Tom, this is the first time I have talked about this in many years. I'm going to the rest room for a few minutes and will be right back." Skip mentioned the psychiatrist he worked with in civilian life told him his problem was probably similar to what people who get shell shocked in combat suffer. If he had been more mature or if he at least had seen a dead person in a funeral parlor before he left home at age 18 he could have most likely handled the situation much better.

While he was gone I finished my desert and drank my second cup of coffee but Skip had not returned. Finally I went to the rest room and did not see him at first and then thought I could hear a sobbing sound in one of the stalls. I tapped on the door and then opened it and saw Skip sitting on the stool quietly sobbing. He said, "I guess I have to go seek some help again."

On my return to San Gabriel, Bonnie asked me how my day had gone and I told her the story. Then of all things we both started to cry. Prejudice is such a horrible element of any society. Christ, here I am decades later with tears in my eyes again!

K: That was indeed a very sad day of work for any person. You mentioned you have not seen him since; let's hope all has gone well for him since that meeting.

T: I haven't seen Skip since that time but I think of him and hope he is OK when I occasionally walk past the memorial on the wall of the local Jewish community center. They have a bench there that you can sit on while you read and try to comprehend the message of the memorial, which states:

REMEMBER THE HOLOCAUST
In their deaths they commanded us to life.
Never forget the millions of men, women and children who died and suffered at the hands of tyrants, may we always hold them in our minds and hearts.

Kelle, six million Jews were murdered simply because they were Jewish. Over one million five hundred thousand of these Jews were innocent babies, youngsters and young pregnant mothers. I sometimes wonder how the minds of the tyrants were programmed to such intense hate to participate and to watch babies being slaughtered and incinerated.

K: It surely is hard to believe they could find enough twisted minds to man and operate the death camps.

T: Well it's best we get off of this gruesome chronicle. We can only hope it never happens again; there is nothing that can be done now about the terrible past proceedings of the misguided tyrants. Back to our conversation.

Divorced from my first wife after 22 years, I later remarried and now have a wonderful love of my life, great companion and best friend wife, Karen, for the past 28 years. Wow, 22 plus 28, that's a total of 50 years in the harness!

Karen is hopeful this memoir of mine will never be published for fear her Christian friends will immediately become former friends and never speak to her again, because many Christians and Muslims have no tolerance for anyone, or anyone associated with anyone questioning their beliefs.

K: How did you meet Karen?

T:Here's the story of how I came about meeting and marrying Karen. Brainwashed as children, we were taught to believe God is in control of all things so this means he (it is a he for sure in both the Muslim and Christian religions—men wrote the stories) determines each and every incident that occurs in our lives. I know Karen will give me hell for telling the story and it will curl the hair of Baptist and Protestant ministers, TV Bible pounder ministers and "celibate" Catholic priests, bishops and cardinals (if there really are any celibates among them) as well as imams and ayatollahs. Here goes!

After my first wife asked me to move out after 22 years of marriage because she believed her drinking problem was caused by her ever-growing dislike of me, I moved into a condominium in the Point Loma Tennis Club (PLTC) in San Diego. This is a complex of some 388 condos in a parklike setting including a giant pool, club house, tennis courts, fitness workout rooms, Jacuzzi and many other amenities to enjoy. The complex is very similar to a private country club. Once a month and sometimes on special occasions the PLTC association would have an owners' party in the clubhouse that overlooked the pool. At one of the parties I noticed this attractive young lady I guessed at the time about twenty something (actually she was 31) attending the party. I was in my mid-fifties and as I eyeballed her laughing and talking to the younger men in the crowd I remember thinking how nice it would be if I was a young buck again.

As the hours went by and people started to depart I noticed Karen standing alone looking out over the swimming pool and the park and so I decided to approach and just say hello. We had a pleasant conversation, events of the day, which condo she owned, which one I owned, about the PLTC and so forth. Finally most of the people had departed and I asked Karen if she would like to join me at the nearby San Diego Yacht Club for a drink before we both called it an evening. She accepted the invitation. While at the club we discussed the upcoming Christmas holidays and I learned Karen was a member of the San Diego Ski Club. She mentioned the club had chartered a bus to take the club members to Lake Tahoe for the holiday period and she and her boyfriend were going on the trip.

When she asked me my plans I mentioned I intended to fly over to Albuquerque in my Comanche to visit some pseudo relatives for Christmas. She excitedly and immediately said, "My two brothers live in Albuquerque. What's the chance of me sitting in the co-pilot's seat?" She had no idea of how much this old man would like to have her as a co-pilot on the flight. My pseudo relatives were Elaine, sister to my youngest brother's wife and Captain Harold USNR who had served with my youngest brother on a destroyer in Vietnam. Being a bit of an egotist and show off I thought this would be enjoyable to fly in with this attractive young lady and have the captain see her as my PLTC friend when he and Elaine picked us up at the airport. So I called Elaine on the phone (no e-mail in those days) and told her a PLTC lady friend of mine would be coming over with me to visit with her brothers.

Karen and I set a time for our meeting and take off at the San Diego Montgomery private plane airport. I arrived at the airport, checked the Comanche over and prepared the flight plan but Karen did not show up. I figured she and her boyfriend had talked about the trip and that she had changed her mind but I decided to wait awhile to see if she did arrive. About a half hour later Karen showed up looking like the party she had attended the night before must have been a real wing dinger. Obviously Karen had a bit of a hangover. So we took off and had an enjoyable flight with one refueling and lunch stop on the way. On our arrival Elaine and the captain met us with their station wagon and off we went to their ranch home on the outskirts of Albuquerque.

On our arrival at their home, Karen called her brother and learned there was going to be a delay for them to pick her up as one brother would not get back to town for a few days and the other brother already had his home full of guests. With this news Elaine took charge, picked up our luggage and we followed her down the hall as she deposited our bags in one of the bedrooms and said to Karen, "You can stay here until your brother comes to pick you up" and off she went. So Karen and I stood there in the room looking at each other and wondering what we were going to say or do about the situation.

Finally I said, "Look, we are both adults, lets not say anything just put the pillows between us and you sleep on one side of the king sized bed and me on the other." So we agreed we would do that. The next few days all went as we discussed the situation but following a great party at an enjoyable nightclub spot with Elaine and Captain Harold with a bit of drinking and merriment somehow during that night the separation pillows were no longer there.

On our return flight the weather was god-awful and I overextended my fuel reserve trying to make it into the Lindbergh Airport, the commercial San Diego airport. I had business appointments scheduled early the next morning and was concerned about canceling them if I had to land at the alternate airport, Palm Springs, on my flight plan. Since the San Diego field was closed because of heavy rain and below minimums for instrument landings, when we arrived at San Diego I had to tell the flight controllers I had made a mistake with my fuel management and lacked sufficient fuel to reach the alternate airport in Palm Springs which was very true.

When I intentionally over extended my fuel reserves I felt comfortable because who could imagine the weather turning so bad in beautiful San Diego. The flight control person turned me over to the tower operator who gave me permission to make the instrument approach and land. We experienced very heavy rain and low minimums and did not see the runway until we were about 400 feet above the ground and about 500 yards from the beginning of the runway. The landing was uneventful with the Comanche coming to a quick stop because of the deep water on the field. So now we were at the San Diego Lindbergh Municipal Airport some 15 miles from the private aircraft Montgomery Airport (Montgomery Field did not have instrument approach facilities) where our cars were parked. It was after 11 p.m. by the time we had secured the Comanche; we called a cab to take us to the PLTC with the intention to go and pick up our cars the next morning at the Montgomery airport. When we got out of the cab at the PLTC, I picked up my bag and wondered what Karen would do when she picked up her bag as our two condos were not very far apart. Wow, imagine my excitement and delight ...what do you think happened?...Karen walked with me to my condo and we have been together ever since.

In October of the next year, we celebrated our first meeting at the SDYC by having our marriage on the club's patio. So following this, I had to think about the occurrence and sequence of these events. Since I've been a pretty good guy (most of the time) could it be the six-day God was sending me a message like: "Look Tom, I know you have strayed from my flock, you no longer usher at the church, you no longer put money in the plate and you have been a rather lonely bachelor in recent years and always on the hunt. Now I have placed this attractive lady in your life with all this love, companionship and happiness. Don't you think you should think it over and rejoin my flock? What if she had immediately gone to stay with one of her brothers? What if the weather had been good on your return and you had landed at the Montgomery Airport and each driven home in your separate cars? If she had driven home in her car and gone to her condo no doubt there would have been a message on the answering machine from her boyfriend. If you had not been a pretty good guy most of the time I would not have arranged all these events and circumstances." Did God really make these things happen? Was he sending me a message? Should I rejoin the flock, put money in the plate and thank God for making my dreams come true? Or was it as Leucippus of Miletus taught that there is no supernatural power calling the shots and that all events are simply random occurrences?

Next I will address the greatest tragedy and trauma of my life.

The Greatest Trauma and Suffering of My Life

As a military officer and also on several occasions in my civilian life, I have witnessed the death of friends, close relatives and military associates. I have experienced the painful work of removing the bodies of close friends from crashed airplanes. Like many older adults, I have lived through the pain and grief of losing both my father and my mother.

None of that personal trauma, pain and grief in my life approaches the suffering I experienced when I lost my beloved oldest son, Tom Jr., when he was 40. The evening before he died by his own hand, I had experienced an engine failure in our Volvo on Interstate 5, as Karen and I were on our way from Long Beach to San Diego. It was late in the evening so I had the AAA tow the car to the nearest service station in the nearby city of San Clemente.

I called my son Tom in Anaheim for help and as usual he cheerfully said, "Dad, I'll be there in about a half hour or so." Once he arrived, he, Karen and I had a warm conversation and discussed our plans to solve the car situation.

We decided we wanted a long time trusted Volvo mechanic in San Diego to repair the car. To accomplish this, we decided Tom would drive me back to Long Beach to pick up our second car and Karen would stay with the broken car until I returned. Then both Karen and I would go on to San Diego and Tom would go back to his home in Anaheim after dropping me off at my home in Long Beach to pick

Tom McBride Jr. Portrait of him on his wedding day. Every day of my life I ask, WHY?

up our second car. When Tom and I arrived at my home in Long Beach, I thanked him for the help and Tom gave me a warm hug and said, "glad to help, good bye Dad." I got out of his car, and as he made a u-turn on our street on his way home, he gave me a wave good-bye.

After that I took our second car back to San Clemente, picked up Karen, made arrangements with the service station to let us park our Volvo there overnight, and we drove on to San Diego.

The next morning I met with our mechanic and we made arrangements for me to go with his tow truck driver to the San Clemente station to pick up the Volvo and take it back to his San Diego garage for the repairs. This was about a 150 mile round trip to San Clemente and then back to San Diego, a pretty long day in a tow truck.

When the tow truck driver and I arrived at the San Diego garage with the Volvo, my youngest son John, along with Karen met me and I told them, "Boy, it's been a long tough day." My youngest son John hugged me and said, "Dad, it's a lot worse, Tom is dead."

I couldn't believe it. I nearly collapsed. The three of us immediately departed for

Anaheim with John driving as I was in a state of near collapse in the back seat of the car. I couldn't believe it was for real. I didn't want to live through this pain and suffering.

Later at the funeral, as the minister went through his ritual and rain dance, it was of no comfort for me as I had already lost all belief in the Christian religion and knew full well this minister, a literate college graduate, also knew as well as I the fiction and fairy tales of the Christian religion.

What made it worse for me was that I had not yet reached the understanding of who we are, why we are here and where we all will be going when our time on earth is over and we return as elements, "star stuff," of the universe to the universe.

Parents should never have to bury a son or daughter. I truly believe, regardless whether an individual is a believer in fiction, myth and fairy tales or a realist, the loss of a child has to be the most painful experience a human being can possibly suffer.

K: Tom, I certainly sympathize with your loss. Several of my friends have lost children, and it is the worst experience of a parent's life. My family also experienced a suicide. My grandmother's brother ended his life, and I remember reading the entry in her diary written on the day she was notified of his death. All she could write over and over was "why?"—I believe that was the question she wanted answered the most.

T: There is no answer. It is a catastrophe and for realists the fiction and BS of the practitioners of fiction-based religion just made me feel worse. To me, the practitioners of the fiction have the same credibility as ancient Indian rain dancers during the droughts in America.

Our 1776 Forefathers

K: *Why do you think these men were so important to the well being of not just America but as a political role model for the world?*

T: Good question, Kelle. Let's refresh our minds about the achievements of this handful of educated, aggressive, imaginative and daring men. Remember, their lives were on the line. If the revolution failed, they would all be hanged as traitors.

It is indeed regrettable we Americans receive so little historical education about our 1776 forefathers. In 1776, all large nations of the Western World were ruled by emperors, kings, dictators, ayatollahs, the pope or politicians blessed, controlled and directed by the pope. The citizens of the Western World's nations in 1776 (with the exception of the majority of the citizens living in the colonies of North America) lived in conditions of fear, myth, superstition, and fictitious beliefs not much different than what the citizens of the pope-led Dark Ages of the past centuries.

In 1776, China was the most civilized nation in the world while the citizens of most of the nations of the Western World were living in theocracy-controlled nations suffering poverty, corruption and slavery very similar to the Dark Ages. Once the 1776 forefathers established this first great secular nation with all of the citizen benefits of the American Constitution and Bill of Rights this nation became the ideal nation in the world attracting immigrants from all over the planet desiring to enjoy life with freedom of and freedom from religion, kings, emperors and dictators.

The great men of any generation often stand on the shoulders of the great men who preceded them. Let's review the significant events of northern Europe in the few decades before the 1776 forefathers created this nation.

K: *I've also read that the French Revolution was a result of a series of events put into motion by the prominent forefather George Washington in the Ohio Valley when he unknowingly started the French and Indian War—this resulted in higher taxes on both the British and French populations. Do you believe in fate as a factor in the creation of our nation? At the time of the French Revolution, many of the founders you speak of were upset with the way the French were conducting their revolution. Why do you suppose our founders disliked the French people's methods?*

T: That's a series of tough questions! I am not an academic historian to debate the subject so there may have been some aspects of the French and Indian war I am not aware of. I do believe the war in North America occurred about 1756 and was merely an extension of the larger war between the British and French in Europe. I have read much of the English side of the arguments regarding the cause of the American's 1776 revolution indicating the English Parliament only insisted the colonies in North America were to simply pay their share of the cost of the French and Indian War. In the peace treaty between the French and England powers in Europe, England gained the ownership of Canada from the French. Prior to the start of the war I believe George Washington was just a young man sent by the governor of Virginia on a mission to what is now the city of Pittsburgh, Pennsylvania either as a scout or messenger to the French regarding the ownership of the territory. Surely this young man just carrying out the duties he was charged with cannot be responsible for starting a war. The only French revolution I am aware of is the one that started to rumble about 1789 and reached full-blown crises about 1800 when the revolutionary victors commenced using the guillotine cutting off the heads of the Royalists.

With regard to fate being involved in history; it is almost scary to read how just a simple incident that breaks one way or the other can affect the course of history. There is a book I have not yet read titled *What If* in which the author tells how the world would be so much different if fate had changed just very small incidents of what actually occurred versus what did occur in history. In my opinion, fate and luck have been all-important in shaping the course of world history. Now back to the subject of fate and luck that brought together our great 1776 forefathers.

They created the greatest secular nation in the modern world and they also set in motion the political changes for the benefit of billions of people in the majority of all the other nations who have copied the American form of democratic government since 1776.

Recently a great scientist/engineer died, Mr. Jack Kilby, the inventor of the integrated circuit that changed the way people live in the world from microwave ovens, to computers and the internet, cell phones, automated devices of all kinds in the homes of people around the world. It was his invention of the "chip" that spawned a multi-trillion dollar worldwide industry. In the story about his death it was mentioned how just one individual person's lifetime work can change the world.

The story mentioned that Thomas Edison lit up the world, Henry Ford put the citizens of the world on wheels, the Wright brothers invention eventually put a man on the moon and today at any given hour, well over a 100,000 (that's right, over one hundred thousand people) are sitting in airplanes around the world. (Over 30,000 passengers are sitting in airplanes over the Atlantic and Mediterranean Oceans as you read this.) This is surprising and almost beyond belief how one or several individuals working together can invent, discover information or start a movement that will change the lives of billions upon billions of people who live in later years. But none of the accomplishments mentioned above made as great a change in the world as impressive or as beneficial for humans as compared to what the 1776 forefathers accomplished. They changed the form of governments and the lifestyle of freedom for the billions of people around the world over the last two centuries. This change from theocracy-influenced laws to laws designed by the citizens in less than 200 years tops all other accomplishments mentioned. In fact, few if any of these fantastic inventions could have been accomplished in a theocracy-governed society.

Robert Greenberg Explains History through Music

Robert Greenberg, professor at the San Francisco Conservatory of Music explains political changes through changes in music. Professor Greenberg teaches the history of opera from the time of the ancient Greeks to the present time in a program titled, "How to Listen to and Understand Opera." In one of the sessions of the course, he teaches about the sudden changes that took place in the themes of opera in Europe from about the 1720s to about the 1780s. Until the early 1700s, operas entertained with themes and scenarios related to royalty, cleric hierarchy and nobles.

Suddenly in just a couple generations beginning in the early 1700s and in less than 50 years, the vast number of opera themes and scenarios changed to topics related to common citizens. The sudden change in opera themes was due to what Greenberg referred to as the period of enlightenment (universal humanist movement) in the nations of northern Europe. Because of the efforts of Martin Luther (1483-1546), the populations of these nations had begun to realize common people were not just peons and serfs as they were in the Dark Ages but human beings (the origination of the "middle class") entitled to live normal lives. The transition had moved slowly for a century or so following Martin Luther's actions but then gathered speed in the late 1600s and exploded in the mid 1700s. Martin Luther dealt the symbolic blow that commenced the breaking of the iron fist dictatorship of the Dark Ages when he nailed his Ninety-Five Theses to the door of the Wittenberg Church. It would not be necessary to include any further information about the brave Martin because any person living in the Western World has to be aware that this is the man whose activism brought about the freeing of the nations of northern Europe.

This period of enlightenment was not limited to just the opera, but was evident throughout the societies and nations of northern Europe with the citizen's freedom to speak out, own businesses, make scientific discoveries and expound philosophical thoughts. The American colonies were a land of common folk immigrants from these nations. Separated from Europe by about a two-month voyage of thousands of miles across the Atlantic Ocean, the colonies were inhabited by common people who learned to govern themselves. So as much as many Americans give credit to the brilliant minds of our 1776 forefathers for our democratic government, we must admit their concept of a nation governed by and for the citizens themselves was very much rooted in the period of enlightenment in northern Europe. Fortunately (thanks also to the publicity of the works of Thomas Paine) the 1776 forefathers were well versed in history and were very much aware that a state-sponsored religion would doom the future of the nation. They wisely constructed the wall of separation of state and religion with the freedom of and freedom from religion.

Since 1776 (a period of only 228 years), the vast majority of the citizens of the nations of the Western World have either forcibly or peacefully caused their nations to adopt the same or similar types of government that we enjoy in America. Our 1776 forefathers were the role models who opened the door to worldwide democracy.

The citizens of France were the first of hundreds of small and large nations of the world over the past 200 years to adopt our form of government, beginning less than a decade after our forefathers founded this secular nation. Citizens electing their leaders! Common citizens all over the world began adopting a revolutionary new kind of government whereby the citizens themselves became the leaders of their nations.

But before we move on, let's not forget the greatest of the illustrious forefathers, Benjamin Franklin.

Benjamin Franklin

Although Ben was too old to be a president in the late 1770s he must surely be regarded as important (if not more so) for his contribution to the documentary construction of the United States of America as any of our presidents! Unfortunately America has never had another diplomat to equal his abilities.

I have read at least one of the biographies or autobiographies of every one of the most prominent 1776 forefathers. Not so, Ole Ben. With the first book I read of him in my late teens, I became so interested in Franklin and the tour de force of his lifetime ventures and achievements, I took to reading every book I could find about him. In my opinion all young Americans should be familiar with the life of Ben. I believe, after reading many books over the years about his life as a scientist, publisher, diplomat, inventor, experiments with lightning and electricity, spin master, revolutionary activists, humorist, the discoverer and mapping of the gulf stream, writer and promoter of all types of organizations from the first Pennsylvania volunteer fire department, first colonial free library, our colonial (now national) postal system, starting the University of Pennsylvania and many other unrelated ventures that with the exception of George Washington, Ben is really the most important forefather of our nation. His most important achievements were bringing the troops, fleet, supplies and financial loans from France to win the war and convincing his friend Thomas Jefferson to remove the word "sacred" from the contents of our constitution.

Ben's many failed experiments, offbeat medical cure concepts and various other interesting ideas, such as trying to find an herb or substance that could be taken with meals to make farts smell like perfume, were sometimes amusing and always interesting reading. His brief treatise, setting forth the many advantages of having intimate relations with older mature ladies, versus young inexperienced beauties, is a riot of humor. Ben had one of the most active and searching minds imaginable. He was the most prominent combination scientist, business man, inventor, publisher, writer, spin master, humorist and diplomat of the 1700s. A few could equal him in any one of the specific fields, but no one could touch him as a master in all of the diverse fields.

Without question, it is my opinion there would not be a United States of America if Benjamin Franklin had not accomplished the diplomatic tasks he performed in France during the Revolutionary War and in the immediate months following the war.

No one but Ole Ben of the 1776 forefathers, including John Adams and Thomas Jefferson, had the "spin master diplomatic skills" necessary to get into the minds of the French King and Royalists of France to acquire France's aid for the commoner revolutionist Colonists to fight and defeat the English. Without France's loans, supplies, troops and fleet the Colonists would have been defeated.

None of the royal kings of Europe were about to give revolutionary commoner low class trash people access to the chambers and court of the royal offices, even though the different kings in Europe fought each other. It would be impossible at that time in history for a commoner revolutionary type person to get an immediate appointment in the royal court of any European king; however imaginative spin master Ben found a way to get into the minds and thoughts of the French Royalists.

As a young man Ben was a superior athlete, kept himself in good shape and had strong sexual desires. He had great charm with the ladies and possessed both charisma and leadership qualities with males. He had the unique ability as a spin master to meet with groups of people attempting to accomplish something and having the other individuals proceeding in the venture thinking they were the ones who had the ideas of how to accomplish the task even though it was Ben the "spin master" who planted the ideas in their heads.

All of these early life Franklin experiences, leadership abilities to get groups of people to focus on projects and opportunities were necessary for Ben to get the help of France to defeat the English.

It was not easy for a commoner, a revolutionary anti-king Colonist to get into the minds of the Royalists in France. The more books you read about Franklin, the more you feel as if you personally knew the ingenious man. Ben had a reputation of charming and bedding ladies from his formative years. Don't let this information color your opinion of Ben. In our American history, we have had many important leaders, who like Franklin enjoyed intimate relations with other than their wives, such as Presidents Roosevelt,

Eisenhower, Kennedy, Johnson, Clinton, as well as important Senators and Congressmen. As Jackie Kennedy said when asked how she felt about the conduct of her late husband she said, "boys will be boys." Of course it is not socially accepted for great leaders to have these affairs, but in no way should it be considered detrimental to what they accomplished in their careers. On his arrival in France, Ben with his inventive mind, master spin ability, and charmer of ladies knew how to adapt his past lifetime experiences and techniques to get into the minds of the decision makers of the French realm.

I realize my analysis of how Ben accomplished his mission in France will make the Baptist ministers, born again evangelists and Catholic priests, cardinals and bishops cringe in horror. Nevertheless, I am sure Ben sized up the situation on his arrival in France and with his prodigious imaginative mind, charisma and past cozy and intimate lifetime female friendship experiences, immediately knew how to successfully get the important undertaking of influencing the minds of the French king and Royalist rulers underway. Spin master Ben would in a short time have the royal consultants to the King thinking it was their own inspiration and initiative to aid the radical commoner, anti-king, anti-royalist Colonist revolutionaries fight the king of England. Imagine the immensity of the task to influence a king (who believed kings were made kings by an act of God) to back trashy commoners to fight another king!

In France, the spin master got his message into the minds of the French king and royalty circles through friendship, flirtation and intimacy with the mistresses and wives of the French rulers. He got the message to go from whispering his message in the ladies ears and minds, into the ears and minds of the king's male court consultants and ministers in France. The spin masters story of, "Look you got your butts kicked by the English and lost Canada in the French and Indian War of the last decade, you have been fighting the English for centuries, and now is the time to join with us and get back at the English." His whispers in the ears of the ladies ended up in whispers in the ears of the key decision makers of French foreign policy resulting in meetings and friendships between Ben (the diplomat spin master charmer) and the Royal court policy makers. Without a doubt, thanks to Ole Ben, the advisors to the French king truly believed it was their own idea to help the commoner anti-royalist-king radicals in the New World fight the English king.

Washington had lost every battle he led in the war, except the small surprise attack at Princeton, and the final battle at Yorktown, where he won with the help of French money, troops and fleet.

Franklin was singularly responsible for the French money, supplies, troops and fleet that arrived in America during the war to make the victory possible. Victory would have been impossible without the aid of the French.

I know Ben would have been very sad about the happenings in France a few years after Franklin's death.

Following the formation of the United States of America with the 1776 forefathers' Constitution and Bill of Rights the activist radical anti-royalists revolutionaries in France became aware of our 1776 forefathers documentation, and then demanded the same rights from their rulers as was granted to the American citizens.

The rights of the French commoners were refused by the Royalists. The ensuing French revolution of the late 1790s resulted in the revolutionary front arresting the pope supported Royalists, guillotining over 2,000 of them and their court members, confiscating all of the assets, cathedrals and land of the pope and the Catholic church, as well as the property of the Royalists and turning the property and assets over to the new secular government of France. Many of the guillotine beheaded male and female French Royalists had been close and intimate friends of Franklin.

Franklin's final great stroke of genius for America was when he advised his good friend Thomas Jefferson to remove the words "sacred" from the rough of the constitution before the document was presented for the vote of the forefather members.

In a recent respected poll of European nations it was learned France, the first nation to follow in the footsteps of our 1776 forefathers, is now the most secular nation in Europe, South or North America being ahead of both of the two former secular leader nations, Holland and Sweden.

Kelle, I believe if I had not been so taken reading about the two great presidents, George and Abe, plus Ben and then living through the Roosevelt years I would never had the interest, inspiration or motivation to write my memoir. It occurred to me that even as just a plain ordinary citizen my memoir may trigger some ideas in at least a few individual's minds on how to support the ideals and goals of the 1776 forefathers.

See Google: search words "Benjamin Franklin." Follow the links to some very interesting and celebrated Benjamin Franklin information and books!

K: I've read several books on Franklin, and I feel that he was very much like Lindbergh (I must tell you here that Lindbergh is not one of my personal heroes) when it came to changing times changing his philosophy. At first Franklin was a Loyalist, and he urged the colonists to not rebel against England. He used his connections with the English hierarchy to secure a position for his illegitimate son (later to become the governor of New Jersey). After Franklin saw that the Revolution was inevitable he switched sides and even cut his ties with his son, Governor William Franklin, and took William's illegitimate son, Templeton, away from him—never allowing Templeton to see his father again. Franklin was quick to speak his mind, but usually under the guise of a pen name. To me Franklin was a lot like the other founding fathers, in that he was hypocritical and fond of living the axiom, "do as I say, not as I do." He rejected his son because he did not agree with his political views, and was very vengeful in his repayment of William's democratic right to speak one's own mind.

T: Kelle, you are breaking my heart making derogatory statements about one of my greatest heroes. True, he was an on the ball clued-in politician and had to dodge and scramble to accomplish his goals and objectives. In many ways he maneuvered in a manner similar to FDR to get the job done. With this comparison to FDR, I mean he was well aware that to be a leader he had to determine which direction the parade was going in order to position himself at the head of the parade. Whatever the "Franklin warts" please remember there would not be a United States of America if Benjamin Franklin had failed in his efforts to acquire French help for the colonists. With regards to his son William we have to remember that in the Revolutionary War families split up with some members of the same family fighting on the different sides of the conflict in the same state of affairs and hatred that existed in the later Civil War. I do believe he gave William his best efforts and advice to come over to the side of the colonists. The 1776 forefathers had to make many unfair compromises to entice the jealous and greedy colonist's leaders to come together as one nation but in the end they did construct the greatest democracy in history. Several of them spoke openly about the horrible compromise regarding slavery and knew full well they were obscuring a deadly fault that was a time bomb that would explode at a later date; but they had to do it to form a Union.

Thomas Paine is another great American we need to know more about.

Thomas Paine

It is a great shame that many of the important American 1776 intellectuals are not remembered for the great impact their works caused for the benefit of all mankind, not just Americans. The documentation of our 1776 forefathers has been spreading across the entire planet for the past two hundred years.

Mr. Paine made a tremendous contribution to the welfare of all Americans born from 1776 to this day, and the welfare of billions of other people throughout the world

Thomas Paine suffered great humiliation at the hands of the American Christian leaders and their followers following his publication of the pamphlet "The Age of Reason" just prior to the meetings of our 1776 forefathers creating our Constitution and Bill of Rights. In this publication, Paine caught the attention of the 1776 forefathers and many historians credit its contents for much of what is included in our Constitution and Bill of Rights. In later years, other nations have improved the lifestyles of their citizens by adopting much of the contents of our Constitution and Bill of Rights.

The 1776 forefathers were brilliant scholars and we can be sure the majority of them took to heart the facts Mr. Paine set forth in his publication concerning the evilness, cruelty, corruption, and bloodiness committed in the name of all of the fictitious manmade religions. Paine was plain spoken, stating that the many religious orders themselves were morally flawed and administrating incoherent dictates based on fictitious stories.

It has to be seriously questioned whether the 1776 forefathers would have arrived at the foundation of the greatest secular nation since the Roman Empire if Mr. Paine had not made it clear to all literate persons of that age that, if in the event any religious sect could get the control of the new American government and set up a theocracy controlled government, the nation would be plunged into an age similar to the pope dictator directed Dark Ages. If it were not for Thomas Paine's work, the citizens of the United States of America today may very well be living in the same lifestyle as the average citizens of South America.

Every American needs to keep in mind that at the time the 1776 forefathers were setting up this great secular nation, all other nations in the western world were ruled by dictator kings, emperors, the iron fist of the pope, ayatollahs or followers and believers of these corrupt leaders. The citizens of those nations were not enjoying the freedom of thought, freedom of speech and prosperity that the future American citizens would be enjoying. America would be much safer from the enemies from within our borders if every high school student prior to graduation was required to quote the following words of Thomas Paine from memory in the same manner as students quote poetry:

"I put the following work under your protection. It contains my opinion upon religion. You will do me the justice to remember that I have always strenuously supported the right of every man (should be stated in this century as person, not man) however different that opinion might be to mine. He who denies to another this right to his opinion, makes a slave of himself to his present opinion, because he precludes himself the right of changing it. The most formidable weapon against errors of every kind is reason. I have never used any other, and I trust I never shall."

One of the great thrills of my life would be to witness some very wealthy individual or energetic younger person who would by chance read your book and take it upon him/her self to have a large bronze statue of Thomas Paine erected at a prominent location in Washington, D.C., accompanied by a complete presentation of what his intellectual contribution was in the development of this great nation. Erected right on the mall near the Lincoln Memorial!

"THIS MAN SHOULD NOT BE LOST IN HISTORY!"

The following material is from www.thomaspaine.org.

"The Thomas Paine National Historical Association, founded January 29, 1884 in New York City, is among the oldest historical associations in the United States. Our mission, to educate the world about the life, times and works of Thomas Paine, is designed to ensure Paine's rightful place in history as the preeminent founder of the United States of America. He was, in fact, the first person to coin the following words: THE UNITED

STATES OF AMERICA. In the course of his lifetime, Paine was an outstanding political and social influence upon the entire world."

To honor and remember your 1776 forefathers I encouraged every American to become a member of this group.

Statecraft

Like the Christian leaders of the ages, our less intelligent American leaders now insist that the nations they consider inferior or with different types of government than ours must change and act, think, be like us or else suffer the consequences. Our current administration's foreign policy is similar to the Christian leaders' historic programs where they killed many millions of people over the past 2,000 years to set the non-Christian believers straight with their Christian God. The current American leaders seem to be of a similar opinion of we will bomb your ass into being like us. Democracy cannot come about from the top down by an invading aggressor power; democracy has to come up from the grass roots of a society. Future leaders of this nation have to eventually come to terms with reality in their foreign policy decisions.

In the 1600s, Holland and Spain were the number one economic and military powers in the Western World. In the 1700s, France became the number one power with all the nations of Europe using the French language as the diplomatic and international language. In the 1800s, England and the British Empire became the superpower of the world with English becoming the business language of the world. In the late 1800s and into the 1900s, the United States became the number one superpower in the world. Where are we going to be in the year 3,000 ACE?

If the United States of America is to continue as the greatest nation in the world, its citizens have to be aware of any enemy overseas and any evil doers within our borders that could slow or even bring to a halt the continued success of our nation. I intend to continue addressing the very real danger to our American lifestyle that exists within our borders.

All of the nations of the new world in South America and North America have been fortunate in possessing vast natural resources with in their borders. But only two of these nations, America (along with Canada) in the Western hemisphere have developed into nations with the most freedoms, enjoyable lifestyles and economic wellbeing of all of the new world's nations. Why? No one has to have the mind of a brain surgeon to know why all the nations from the Mexican border to the southern tip of Argentina have lived in poverty and corruption for the past several centuries. The answer is that all of the nations south of the American/Mexican border were ruled with theocracy-controlled leaders until the early 1900s. Since the beginning of the 1900s, the citizens of many of these nations have broken free of the iron fist theocracy control of their lives and are beginning to enjoy more freedoms, economic well being and better lifestyles. It makes no difference what type of religion is controlling the government, Muslim or Christian, the resulting poverty, corruption and economic deprivation will be the same.

So I feel I did my duty as best I could in my younger years in the shooting wars to help my nation and now I am contributing what I can to verbally combat the forces attempting to change America into a theocracy-controlled government.

We have a major threat from theocracy within our borders. In the last few decades, I have witnessed the Christian coalition taking control of a few school boards and then forcing the teachers to teach only the science they approve, taking the control of a few local governments and recently attempting to even take over the legislature of one of our states, South Dakota. As a life-long registered Republican I have witnessed their successful efforts to take over the leadership of the Grand Old Party. Friends have mentioned that with my thoughts I should drop out of the party but in my opinion, it is best I stay in the party and attack them from within.

I see the danger to America in the following scenario. The advocates of theocracy control of our government have concentrated on attempting to first take over the management and control of the Republican Party. Wealthy persons unrelated to the Christian coalition; meaning the one percent of the American population, who own one third of the economic wealth of America, also support the Republican Party. The other 99% of Americans share the other two-thirds of the wealth. So even though the majority of this wealthy privileged one percent of our citizens are loyal Americans, no doubt very intelligent, mostly secular and strongly believe in the form of government established by our 1776 forefathers, they are unknowingly supporting the Christian coalition's efforts to change America into a theocracy-controlled government. The one percent privileged class are heavily financially supporting the Republican party because the party is pro-business and fights for the tax write-offs and the corporate welfare the wealthy citizens are seeking. Although the Christian coalition is not related in any way to the privileged wealthy loyal Americans, they are enjoying the financial support of the candidates they select with the contributions of the wealthy 1%. The wealthy one 1% are seeking tax benefits and corporate welfare; the Christian coalition is seeking theocracy control of our government.

K: Why do you think fictitious religions are so dangerous to America?

T: Because they teach that they have the answers to all questions about life and government and that all citizens must believe as they dictate in their "dogma of certainty" which is all based on ancient fictitious and very imaginative sci-fi stories. They do not tolerate any questioning of their dogma. They demand all citizens must obey their theocracy designed rules and laws. They believe all citizens must comply to their invisible fictional higher power rather than with the manmade laws of America. Fictitious religion dictator controlled nations cannot grow and survive unless they have imagined or real enemies to verbally attack which binds their members or citizens into their flock. Over the past 2,000 years the Christians have used the Jews (the so called Christ killers), gays, lesbians as their imagined enemies. Since the Holocaust of WW-II they have moderated a good bit on the attacks on the Jews but intensified their attacks on the 8 to 10% of the population born homosexual and the so far secular judicial branch of our American government. And of course they have had the Muslims as a real enemy and the Muslims have had the Christians as their real enemy for the past 1,600 years to energize their respective flocks. I firmly believe they have every right to believe in whatever they choose. America must always protect the freedom of religion of all kinds. America must also guarantee freedom from religion. I personally wish the good Christians the best but I insist they stay the hell out of our government with their theocratic "dogma of certainty."

The objective of this memoir is not to question the existence of a higher power or of the existence of a god or supernatural force creating the vast universe. Nor is it my intention to show disdain or disrespect for the millions of Christian believers in any one of the many Christian sects who daily volunteer to do good and beneficial work of all kinds for their communities and country. The vast majority of these hard working volunteers are to be admired and thanked for their efforts.

It is my goal to bring to the attention of as many people as I can in these last years of my life about the danger to America from the "Trojan horse (Greek scenario) and Fifth Column (WW-II scenario)" activities of the evil Christian coalition leaders attempting to install theocracy into our secular American government. They are not content to have the freedom of religion provided to all Americans by our 1776 forefathers. Their agenda is to install theocratic laws which force all citizens to believe as they do or suffer the consequences. If an individual politician, educator, professional person, or important corporate leader fails to comply with their views, the Christian coalition leaders will diligently smear and verbally marginalize the individual. They will encourage a boycott of any firm sponsoring a TV program they do not agree with. The members of Congress which they have sponsored in elections are counseled to consider the grades and character of young people they give appointments to the military academies and also to make sure the candidates have acceptable religious views. They will confront and smear any individual eligible to be appointed to a justice position on any level of the judiciary system unless the individual has a legal resume acceptable to their beliefs. They work diligently to get control of school boards so that they can eliminate the teaching of any science that debunks their stories. In their minds, a women has no right to control or manage her body. They believe that they and they alone have God's word and advice on how a woman should conduct all affairs of her life. The American Supreme Court decision that women are equal and free citizens who are permitted to make their own choices with regards to having children is a cause of outrage to the leaders of the evil coalition leaders. In their minds, they and they alone know what any individual should believe. Please be sure if these religious coalition leaders ever succeed in inserting theocratic laws into our government, we Americans will descend to the economic level and lifestyle of the citizens of South American nations. We will be descending at the same time as many of these long suffering nations are finally breaking loose from their failed theocratic dictatorships and ascending to more enjoyable lifestyles of freedom.

K: I sure agree. To live in a society led by leaders who govern with ideas based on the "dogma of certainty" based on ancient stories would be less than enjoyable.

T: You could experience such a society by simply visiting nations currently governed by Muslim leaders which you will find are ruled similarly to how the Christian nations were ruled before Martin Luther arrived.

Kelle, on my 83rd birthday, the thought came to my mind that this nation is about 220 years old. So at the age of 83, I had lived and observed the history of America for about one-third of the age of the United States of America. Thinking back to my earliest memories in the 1920s, and comparing the America of that age as I saw it to the America of today is like comparing apples to oranges. In the early 1900s, the United States had developed from just one of many more or less equal major nations of the 1920s to the most powerful economic and military nation in history. Observing this evolution since the age of 8 or so has been a most exciting 75 years to witness. Many people state they miss the good old days. In my opinion there never were good old days in America as compared to the greatness of our America as of this new century. And much of this great improvement in America, especially for women, blacks, Jews, Orientals and homosexuals, is due to the weakening power of the Christian religious leaders influence on the judicial branch of America's government.

America in the early years of the last century was a great nation compared to the rest of the world but our nation also had some very ugly warts in its make up. When I was an Anglo youngster I was not aware of the many prejudices that existed in our nation to the detriment of the happiness and well being of many of the people "not just like me." Although I lived in Pennsylvania I was not aware that black people would not dare to be visiting in the area of my town in which I lived after dark or even in the daytime unless they were on the way to or from employment in the area. The situation was never discussed and there never were any incidents in Aliquippa to cause me to think about the subject. With no exceptions all major professional athletic teams were white. The white professional baseball players with non-Anglo sounding names that ended in "ski" or similar endings found it necessary to change their names to advance to the big leagues. It was not until after WW-II that Jackie Robinson broke the color barrier in major league baseball. As a youth I never knew a Jew and only knew from my Sunday school teachings that the Jews were bad people because they were responsible for the killing of Jesus. During WW-II it has been stated from many sources the German and Italian prisoners of war were treated with much more dignity than our loyal black American soldiers.

The black sailors and soldiers in WW-II were assigned to the most menial types of duty. If anyone had ever had a conversation with a WW-II black service man and said, "You know if you survive the war and live a normal life you will see the day there will be black major city mayors, congressmen, senior military black officers, black captains of Navy ships and even a black chief of staff of the armed forces, black secretary of state and a vast number of black multi-millionaire athletes and business men," he might have questioned your sanity.

My first business associate following my retirement from the military was a big six foot two about 210 pound ex heavyweight Jewish boxer. My associate was Abe 'Babe' Siener, who introduced me to the civilian business world. If it were not for what Babe taught me I would no doubt be living on nothing more than my Navy pension money now. As I often fumbled around trying to learn the real estate business Babe would sometimes joke, "Hell Tom, even if the frustration of teaching you business puts me in the grave I'm going to teach you how to put these deals together." My association with Babe and the many other business Jewish men I later became involved with in business, the Jewish weddings, parties and the bar mitzvahs I attended introduced me to the colorful and interesting Jewish culture. Sometimes while attending these events I would look out across the attendees and think, "Are these people really the bad people, the Christ killers, I was taught in Sunday school to dislike?" Sometimes while attending Jewish events I also would look across the room and think, "Was it people like these who were gassed, murdered and thrown into furnaces by the millions in WW-II?" Religious and color prejudice are terrible detriments and road blocks to the development of a successful civilized society.

Let me give you an example. Some years ago before Karen and I met, she was traveling in the South, stopped for fuel and when going to the restroom, the white one was occupied so she used the one marked for blacks. When she exited, she encountered scowls and a few insulting comments from the white people in the service station. Seeing what blacks are accomplishing in America now as compared to those days some fifty years ago makes me think about all the lost talent that was available to our society because of prejudice. There is still prejudice today but nothing like it was back in those very mean days. Last year while visiting in Paris, France, I noticed the much better relationship between the French blacks and whites as compared to what exists in America. Based on what I have witnessed in the continuing change of the black and white relationship in America, over the past five decades, I think in another two or three generations the American society will catch up to the French society's much better relationship of the blacks and whites. Of course, the horrendous problems with the fanatic Muslims in France has helped to bring the black and white French together as friends.

Let's take a moment and discuss political "statecraft" decisions.

K: What do you mean by statecraft decisions?

T: Here is my take on the subject. Some decisions of the past great empires were referred to as "suicidal statecraft."

America's Cataclysmic Suicide Actions

Many distinguished historians, too many to name them all, have devoted their lives to the study of the course of events regarding the rise and fall of past great empires and nations. Why did specific nations become so prominent and why did they eventually collapse? One of the most revered historians, Arnold Joseph Toynbee, 1889-1975, stated that the ultimate cause for the collapse of past great superpowers was "suicide statecraft."

My opinion is that, because of the wisdom of our founding 1776 forefathers, America has become the most important, most powerful nation, with the finest wellbeing of its citizens economically and the freedom of its citizens in the world over the past 225+ years. This tremendous rise from a modest group of 13 separate and jealous colonies into a unified great nation in such a short time was the result of great leadership from 1776 to 1948 by competent dedicated American leaders who have not been equaled in ability by the leaders elected to high office since 1948.

Since 1948 for the most part under less than brilliant leadership, America has been gradually changing from a great model of government in the eyes of the world to an arrogant, aggressive, self-styled, self-appointed world policeman and despised nation in the eyes of the leaders and citizens of a vast number of the world's nations. Having made this derogatory statement about the leadership of America for the past 57 years by the leaders of both the Democratic and Republican parties let, me explain what I have truly observed in America's less than intelligent foreign policy "suicidal statecraft" decisions over this past half century.

The free world's great leaders of the 1940s, Roosevelt, Churchill, Truman and General Marshall of the Marshall Plan, had promoted the development of the United Nations as a world policeman to prevent wars and invasions of nations by evil leaders. They had also developed the concept of isolating evil nations until they collapsed from within. Obviously these were correct and intelligent statecraft decisions.

One of the first major military situations to develop following the end of WW-II was the invasion of South Korea by communist North Korea in 1950. Working closely with the United Nations, President Truman formed a coalition of free nations that attacked the North Korean forces and drove them out of South Korea.

The next administration, led by President Eisenhower who had the misfortune of selecting John Foster Dulles as his Secretary of State, the US began to slide down the slippery slope of becoming an aggressive, self-appointed world police state. Dumbass Dulles, his staff, the CIA and leaders of our military forces first laid plans to oust Cuban leader Castro from Cuba and handed this stupid operation off to the next elected president, President Kennedy. The operation commenced just weeks after Kennedy took office. Kennedy, a true combat war veteran, realized it was a stupid invasion, took full responsibility for the debacle even though Dulles was the individual who had commenced the planning of the operation in the prior administration. The operation was cancelled by Kennedy following a brief failed flurry of combat.

Dumbass Dulles had also convinced President Eisenhower it was America's responsibility to bail the French out of their difficulties in Vietnam by supporting the troops of the pro French South Vietnam government against the communist North Vietnamese. Dulles had conceived a so-called domino effect that if one nation fell to the communists the dominos (meaning nations) would keep falling one after the other. This was a horrible statecraft concept and decision by the administration.

The true facts of the Vietnam situation were that the loyal, dedicated Vietnamese with a mindset similar to the American Colonists of 1776 throwing off the yoke of the British Empire were attempting to end the cruel rule of the French government over their nation. They were seeking independence and self government. The fact they were led by communist leader Ho Chi Min was really none of America's business. Ho Chi Min had been a staunch and valuable alley of the United States during WW-II having been assured that once the war was won, Vietnam would be free of the French rule. The Vietnamese were not attacking America, hated the Chinese and were not aligned with the Soviet Union. Of course, once America committed to fight the North Vietnamese, the Soviet Union commenced helping the forces of Ho Chi Min. President Kennedy also inherited this fiasco from the Eisenhower administration.

Nearly all of the important persons close to President Kennedy and his administration have claimed Kennedy was about to withdraw from the support of the French associated South Vietnamese government in the weeks before he was assassinated in Dallas, Texas. Vice President Johnson became president and did not have the political courage to withdraw from the fiasco fearing the political consequences of being declared soft on communism and the first president to lose a war. So the Vietnam fiasco became the first exercise of America declaring our nation unilaterally as the world policeman with no regard or adherence to the dictates of the United Nations. When the Vietnam monks began to pour gasoline on themselves and burn themselves to death in South Vietnam during the police action, the American people were never told the truth as to why the monks were killing themselves. Only years after the conflict and the loss of some 58,000 innocent, dedicated young American men and over two million Vietnamese, was it learned the monks were incinerating and killing themselves in protest of the French friendly and many converted Catholic South Vietnamese leaders fighting the Viet Cong Buddhists of the north seeking independence from French rule. No American in any political or military position or any journalist dared question why the monks were incinerating themselves and suffering a painful death in the religious controversy.

In my opinion the word "war" can only be used when two fairly equal powers or nations become engaged in conflict. Nearly all of the conflicts America has been unilaterally involved in since WW-II are really police actions of a self-appointed world policeman superpower fighting poor third world nations possessing very few military capabilities. We have been involved in three very legitimate United Nations backed and supported major military actions which were Korea, the first Gulf War and the Balkans/Serbia clean up. The United Nations approved and supported America's attack on the Taliban and their associated terrorists in Afghanistan following the 9/11 destruction of the World Trade towers in New York. Why? The UN supported America's decision to attack because the terrorists had attacked us first.

All of the American presidents since Truman have been of the opinion they have the authority to bypass and ignore the dictates of the post-WW-II United Nations and the World Court that was promoted by Roosevelt, Churchill and Truman.

What the American people need is an ironclad declaration that no president can commit American forces into a unilateral police action attacking any nation or society without the consent of both the United States Congress and the approval of the United Nations unless we are attacked first. Powerful anti-United Nations political forces in America have taken it upon themselves to cripple the United Nations and the World Court since the passing of Roosevelt, Churchill, Truman, and Secretary of State General George Marshall.

Unless America's leaders correct this militant aggressive self-appointed scenario of the United States being the "World Policeman," America will pass from the scene as the world's greatest superpower. America must abandon this past half century of "suicidal statecraft" and return to the Teddy Roosevelt scenario of speaking softly, being peaceful but carrying one hell of a big club just in case. The United Nations will always support America or any other nation that is attacked by an evil power.

America's leaders are making another great mistake in that they are spending billions of dollars building expensive high tech weaponry to fight the next war that they envision will be similar to and won in the same manner as we won WW-II.

What they fail to understand is that WW-II was the last worldwide gunfight war in the civilized world between major nations. Whether the United States eventually becomes a solid member of the United Nations or not, the other major nations of the world will prevail in making the UN the eventual policeman of the world with America standing alone as an isolated nation. Future conflicts will be more like the police actions that have occurred since the Korean War with small rogue dictator-ruled third world nations.

In this century, the greatest powers in the world by the year 3,000 ACE will be determined by which nations have the finest education system developing outstanding engineers, business minds and scientists; not by gunfire, colonialism and invasions and occupations of other nations. Colonialism is just as dead in this century as old fashioned pirates and government encouraged privateers of the early 1800s. In the unlikely event another cold war situation develops with a superpower similar to the United States, the war will be fought by intercontinental rockets making all ships on the surface of the ocean and advanced land-based armaments as obsolete as the battleships were in WW-II. Throughout history, military and political leaders have always prepared for future wars based on the same mindset of the last war. Instead of spending money for a single multi-billion dollar super nuclear-powered aircraft carrier and its air group, the money could be spent on the education of the next generation of Americans. It would be the greatest investment for the future of our nation.

I wonder if any of our current American leaders are thinking about the longterm future of America, not just their next election campaign, and what kind of "statecraft" decisions they will be making in this century. Let's discuss possible future wars.

Preparing For Future Wars

K: OK, now I know what the term "strategic decisions" means when related to so-called suicide statecraft. But before you discuss future wars, let me hear your thoughts about "thinking out of the box" to prepare a nation for future major wars. So now I would like to challenge you to make a few suggestions as to what you would attempt to implement preparing a nation to defend itself in a future war if you were in a position to make such decisions for the good of America.

T: Good challenge, because so far in our discussions I have been like a Monday morning quarterback criticizing many of our past leaders' decisions. Here are a few suggestions I would try to implement:

1. Commence a brain drain of the world. America is still the one nation many intelligent people around the world want to immigrate to. I would have our embassies around

the world make a list of all of the world's best universities in all of the foreign lands and then set up a program whereby top students in the fields of science, physics, mathematics, chemistry, engineering and other "hard core subjects" graduating in the top per of their class (regardless of race, color or gender) would have the automatic right (following a security check of their backgrounds, especially of Muslims) to come and live in America with their spouse and parents if they desire to come with the brilliant student.

2. Make sure our ambassador to the United Nations is pro-United Nations and does all in his/her power to attempt to make friends with every nation's ambassadors in the UN. Support the UN in every way possible and make the UN body truly believe America will never again appoint itself as the world policeman. When the UN body and leadership makes a decision not favorable to the USA, abide by the decision unless the decision would endanger America to an attack.

3. Develop unquestionably the very finest public education system (including free college scholarships to the top 5% of all American high school graduates who elect to study the hard sciences, physics, mathematics, chemistry and engineering courses).

4. Maintain a powerful military in case of need. As the great Republican President Teddy proclaimed, "Speak softly but carry a big club" or something to that effect.

In a matter of just a few generations, America would have the most intelligent population in the world and these citizens would have the intelligence to elect top quality leaders to direct America in future years. With just those four steps, America would remain the number one nation and also the most admired nation in the world. America would then be fully prepared to combat the tactics of the non-gunfire and non-bombing types of future modern economic warfare. I sincerely believe if the US possessed the brightest and most innovative minds in the world, we would continue to be a superpower in both productivity and militarily.

Here is just one example of why I believe the possession of the brightest innovative minds in the world will result in America remaining the superpower of the world. We now have a major problem competing with low wage third world nations that build equipment and make products at such low cost. I predict that acquiring the most brilliant and innovative minds in the world will in a relatively short time result in the development of robots with the ability to produce nearly any kind of product from shoes and toys to complicated machinery and electronic products at prices no human labor can compete against.

Regardless of what our current leaders think of the United Nations, it will become ever more significant in binding the world's nations into a unified global society, much like the weak federal government of 1776 America finally joined the 13 colonies into a single great nation. Naturally, America must always maintain a strong military to combat any rogue nation that threatens it. But the small, poorly trained and equipped rogue nations are not the greatest threat to the future of America. Our greatest threat is the economic consequences of possible "Future Major Nation Wars" with the major economically powerful nations. I hope I have answered your challenge. Now about my concept of how future major nations will conduct wars to become the world's leading nation.

Future Major Nation Wars

Nations have always prepared for new future wars with the idea they would fight the next war the same way they fought the last war. Prior to WW-II there were a few individuals "thinking out of the box" envisioning new methods to win wars such as air power minded individuals in Germany, our American General Billy Mitchell (disgraced and forced out of the Army for his declarations), Genda of Japan (designer of the Pearl Harbor attack) and the developers of the tank and blitzkrieg Army of Germany in the late 1930s. And as we now know WW-II was a very much different war than WW-I. We must always maintain a strong military to defend our nation but our American military and political leaders are now focused on thinking the next major war will be fought in the same manner as we fought WW-II. In my opinion, the world may now become engaged in a new war whereby thinking out of the box nations abandons all ideas of how WW-II was fought and won. True the American self-appointed police actions against small rogue third world nations such as Iraq can be fought with high tech, upgraded weapons similar to those used in WW-II. In the new type of major nation warfare, high tech gunfire and nuclear bombs will not be used and are of no defense for the nation or nations being attacked. The next war between major first world powers will be a very long "step by step" non-lethal economic war probably with the winning nation becoming the economic superpower of the world in the last few decades of this century without firing a shot or dropping a bomb.

I am addressing my anger at who in my opinion is really the internal enemy of our great nation and my grandchildren's future lifestyle. We are not in a shooting war with this enemy but we are engaged in a battle for the minds of the American citizens.

The question is, "Will America become a theocracy-controlled nation whereby all citizens must believe the dogma as the religious leaders dictate or will the nation continue as the original major secular nation in the history of modern civilization with freedom of thought for all citizens?" Will our grandchildren and great grandchildren have the same freedom we have of "freedom of and freedom from" religion?

Throughout history, nations have always prepared to defend their nation in the next war with the same weapons and tactics as the last war. Invariably this has proven to be a major mistake. This has been especially true in all wars of the past two hundred years.

In the late 1930s the impressive pictures of the mighty battleships of all of the navies of the leading nations of the world convinced people, political leaders and military personnel of all ranks that the nation with the biggest and most powerful battleships would be the major military sea power of the world in the next looming war. Churchill, Hitler, Adm. Yamamoto in Japan, Roosevelt and all of American's admirals believed this to be true. Little did they know that for the most part, the battleships of the world would be proven to be nothing more than a minor supporting weapon in WW-II. In fact, the American Navy leaders continued to pour vast amounts of manpower, money and scarce materials into the building of battleships and heavy big gun cruisers until late 1944 in WW-II; over two years after it was as clear as crystal that the big gun ships were of little use in modern sea/air Navy warfare. Aircraft carriers protected by a screen of destroyers and equipped with deadly modern aircraft had replaced the big gun ships as the major weapon of modern sea battles.

Unrestricted Warfare

Unrestricted Warfare is the title of a "thinking out of the box" book written by Qiao Liang and Wang Xiangsui, both Colonels and graduates of the top senior military strategy staff colleges in China. The information presented here is my paraphrasing the contents of their book and other information I have read by bloggers on the internet as I understand their and the bloggers thinking. The book is published in Beijing by PLA Literature and Arts Publishing House, February 1999.

I suggest every American leader should get a copy and study the book, and also study the many bloggers statements about modern economic war on the internet. In my opinion the weapons and tactics of the next major nation war (not a police action shooting war with a small rogue ill equipped nation such as Iraq) but will be a war that will be a long non shooting economic war between major nations.

The Strategy (Studied and Revised by Tom)

1. Develop the most advanced education system in the world concentrating on graduating overwhelmingly the most number of engineers, scientists, chemists and Ph.D.s in important strategic fields of any nation in the world. Send students to many of the most prestigious universities of the most advanced foreign nations in the world to bring home and teach in their nations top universities and manage the major manufacturing and scientific firms in the nation.

2. Take every advantage of the new globalization of the world economy. Become the greatest producer of goods of all kinds from the most mundane to the most sophisticated products for export and national profits.

3. Acquire massive amounts of profits and cash in a debt free nation to finance the acquisition of the world's oil, energy and strategic materials reserves. Eventually be in command of the worldwide distribution of all of these products. Finance the debt of any major nation demonstrating out of financial control spending making the targeted nation of less economic importance in the United Nations and world diplomatic negotiations.

4. Become the foremost economic power member of the United Nations. Be in a position to economically influence the voting of the majority of the other member nations of the UN and if necessary using financial incentives to gain their support.

There is no question our powerful American modern nuclear powered aircraft carriers present an awesome military presence to any potential hostile nation. Our aircraft carriers are indeed of major importance in America's continued efforts to perform the duties as the world's policeman rather than the United Nations having that role. In the event the United States changes its policy and supports the United Nations to be the world policeman, our aircraft carriers will continue to be the front line primary weapon in police actions in cooperation with the United Nations.

However, if ever another superpower similar to the United States and similar to the past and now defunct Soviet Union should appear, the aircraft carriers of any future conflict will be as obsolescent as the battleships were in WW-II. The reason being both the hostile superpower and the United States will both have satellite technology and know the exact position of all the hostile nations' surface ships and will destroy them with inter-continental missiles within minutes after the war starts. With this knowledge, the United States should realize the existing fleet of powerful aircraft carriers is all America needs to continue as the world policeman. The superpowers of the future will be armed with the best education system, the greatest number of the best educated citizens in the world and will have the most productive and technological work force on the planet...it will not be a gunfire war. Rather than pour some $3 billion to build each new nuclear-powered aircraft carrier, America should spend billions of dollars building the finest education system of any nation in the world. The prospect of a future gunfire war between two major nations similar to the United States is no more probable than to have pirate warships similar to the early 1800s roaming the ocean.

5. Once a target nation is designated:

A.   Recognize the "information age," globalization, growing power of the United Nations, World Court and instant communications around the world have made WW-II type shooting wars between major first world nations obsolete. Use the tools of the information age to create propaganda and misinformation to confuse and break or lower the morale of the targeted nation's population. Influence the population of the target nation that they are a declining nation.

B.Clandestinely as possible using superior economic wealth create economic chaos in the targeted nation toying with their national debt you have financed and also their financial markets.

C.   Clandestinely use highly trained hackers to repeatedly disrupt and create chaos in the business and financial sectors of the targeted nation.

D.   Clandestinely as possible support the drug and narcotic barons around the world to infiltrate the targeted nation with low cost easy to acquire narcotics used by the population of the targeted nation.

E.   Similar to past American CIA clandestine operations, be in a position to always deny any involvement in any and all of the above tactics when charged with misconduct in the United Nations or World Court. Of course America should not engage in these tactics unless the American leaders become aware a hostile nation is attacking America with these tactics.

6. Slowly but surely, the continued periodic use of all or some of the above tactics (non-gunfire weapons) over several decades will eventually bring down to second class status any first world targeted nation in the world. In my opinion the United Nations and World Court will gradually become the most important bureaucracy in the world in this century and the nation with the greatest economic influence, best educated population, and the most productive work force in the UN will then be the number one nation in the world.

K: Do you think such a war is now in progress?

T: I have no idea if such a war is contemplated by any world leaders. But if the internet bloggers of the world have been thinking about it and an over the hill senior like me has been thinking about the subject, it may be a few world leaders are also thinking about these tactics.

Again, over the past few centuries the mantle of being the leading nation of the world has changed rapidly. In the late 1500s, the Dutch were the economic leaders of the Western World. About 75 years later the Spanish Empire was the leading nation and in the 1700s the French became the leaders with all the nations in Europe conducting diplomatic relations in the French language. By the early 1800s England and the British Empire became the world's leading nation with the British in the 1850s having control of 50 percent of the world's economic wealth with only two percent of the worlds population. Just 40 years later in the 1890s America had become the foremost economic power in the world; then 80 years later America also became the only super military power in the world. America having spent over $250 billion in Iraq as of 2005 in the capacity of being the self-appointed world policeman in this century, now spending $6 billion a week in Iraq with no end in sight and facing an estimated $250 to 300 billion to repair our infrastructure in the gulf area with all of this debt piled on top of a very historically high massive existing debt, where will America be in the year 2050 if America fails to develop the most intelligent population in the world? The American leaders in the coming decades cannot sit on their status quo butts.

K: *I think you have answered my challenge. Will it be possible for America to come up with any new leaders with the common sense, intelligence, guts and ability of Lincoln, Teddy Roosevelt, Franklin Roosevelt, Truman and General George Marshall in the next critical decades?*

T: That's another good question. For the past 55 years or so all we have had for leaders for the most part have been spin masters, poll studiers and photo opportunity leaders. The one and only exception of genuine American world leadership since Truman being the WW-II Navy carrier TBM bomber pilot, the first President Bush. He was a master intelligent world leader equivalent to the likes of General George Marshall putting together the United Nations coalition forces in the first Gulf War. Since the first President Bush, America has never again been a great coalition leader in the United Nations.

In 1981, actor Ronald Reagan added the Hollywood production scenario to the spin master and photo opportunity entertainment in Washington. Oh well, at least it was as entertaining as the foolishness of the Royals in Britain.

Fictitious Religion

In Sunday school, I heard all the typical fictitious stories exposed to Christian children. As I matured, by middle age, I began to ask questions, and received unsatisfactory answers.

K: *Tom, in your mind, who is God?*

T:I am sure that the brilliant minds of free scientists and philosophers over the past two centuries have proven whatever supernatural power or icon is out there that power is not the fictitious Christian six-day God. If there is a god, "SHE" is too busy attending to this vast universe we now know of and the possibly many other vast universes yet to be discovered for Her to give individual attention to just one of us on this tiny planet, so we must find in ourselves the inner conviction and strength to meet life, to grapple with it, to make do with the cards we are dealt by the random action of the atoms, to subdue it and to enjoy our lives on this, one of the tiniest planets in "Her" vast universe.

Knowing this and realizing life will have many ups and downs, hills and valleys, if we sometimes mentally descend into a valley, we will not pitch a tent down there in long time despair or believe some Santa Claus-like figure is going to take the time to hear us cry and come to our rescue.

I am sure "SHE" (remember men wrote the Bible; I will keep repeating that statement) has no interest in humans lighting candles, waving scented lanterns, dressing in fancy colorful robes, ringing bells, fasting, not eating beef on Friday, not consuming bacon and pork, or denying themselves beer and cocktails, dancing, coffee or sex. "SHE" has no interest in the building of great palaces and monasteries for her because "SHE" has no need for such lavish buildings.

Of course we all hope "SHE" is out there somewhere and looks like former Ms. America Mary Ann Mobley or Marilyn Monroe and not like my old Jewish boxer partner Babe Siener.

Let's keep in mind that the TV Bible thumpers, Jerry Falwell, Pat Robertson, the Pope, all the Protestant ministers in both the small storefront operations and the wealthy ones in their crystal palaces, all the Cardinals dressed in their Halloween costumes, priests and religious fathers have no better idea than you or I whether She/It/He may be out there. We all hope so. But no one knows what is out beyond the Big Bang. The atheists may be right or a superpower of some kind may be there. Let's hope "SHE" is really out there and continues doing good work. None of us know.

Our 1776 forefathers were not atheists, they simply would only believe in what could be proven. The leading forefathers responsible for documenting the wall of separation between state and religion considered themselves Deists (prove it or forget it).

As of 2006, we know we are not the big important planet created in six days; we know our planet earth is a very tiny speck in one vast galaxy of the many millions of other galaxies; each holding billions of stars, planets and countless meteors in just this one universe. As of the discovery of new astronomical knowledge in 1995, we have become aware that this universe may very well be just one vast universe of possibly many (possibly of uncounted of millions of other vast universes) which astronomers claim may be connected by what they call "worm holes." Some scientists are now questioning whether the atom (cosmic material of the Big Bang particle) dropped out from the bottom of a "Black Hole" of one of the older universes. Most all of this science was discovered in just one person's lifetime, mine since 1922!

K: Before you proceed, Tom, why do you refer to the possibility of a supernatural being as "SHE"?

T: One reason for sure is because of my Navy background. In the Navy, our ships were always referred to as "She" and in fact often times we even referred to our aircraft as "She"; like when talking to one of the mechanics after a flight, other pilots and I would often mention a discrepancy such as a brake problem like this: "I think she might need a fix on the right brake, etc."

But also it is obvious that the Christian Bible is the work of imaginative and creative male writers who repeatedly wrote in a fashion indicating the lesser status of females and often discounting their worth. Of course, anything I can say to irritate any male Christian coalition religious leader preaching fiction is intentional on my part. Since I've been a pretty good guy (most of the time) I hope "SHE" is a pretty cute gal when I get to set up housekeeping in her domain way out there beyond the Big Bang. Damn, I sure hope "SHE" is out there.

K: However, Christians can certainly publish books and articles criticizing those that do not follow their ideology! Doesn't this seem rather undemocratic on their part?

T: I cannot think of any ideology more undemocratic than the ideology of the Christian and Muslim dogma. Believe as we believe or else! Don't rule the nation under man-made laws but by theocracy dictates from a book of fiction. Both of these faiths are a danger to the future of the wellbeing of the country our 1776 forefathers envisioned for America. In my opinion, they should enjoy the freedom we all enjoy in America and stay the hell out of our government. As of 2006, many dedicated Americans are fearful of what is going to come about with regards to our freedoms, equal rights for women, separation of state and religion, the attacks on our secular judicial branch of government and the rights of citizens regardless of their legal sexual orientation. I am optimistic this is a short term threat to our form of government that will be overcome in the decades to come as the education level of our citizens continues to improve.

Well Kelle, I think I'll let you guess as to what I believe. For the life of me I cannot comprehend how Christian and Muslim believers resort to prayers to their God following any kind of event good or bad. After any kind of good event or great tragedy like earthquakes, floods, hurricanes, accidents, whatever; they pray to God for help or if it was a good event thanks. OK, in the event of some good event I can understand saying thanks but if it's a bad event and he is going to take charge and help why did he have the tragedy happen in the first place? The next time America suffers a major tragedy the first thing that happens is that leading neocon Christian politicians call for a national day of prayer. What for? Is it to ask God to please not strike again? It is beyond my understanding.

Let's think about how all this fiction came about and why. Let's start in Egypt, the birthplace of the one and only God belief.

Early Religions

The Many Egyptian Gods

As Professor Van Doran taught at Columbia University, hundreds of Egyptian gods of the past thousands of years "now lay nameless in the compost of civilization." More on Van Doren later.

Each of these Egyptian gods was and had to be created in the dream, hallucination, fit, imagination, or simply an act of self promotion by a person or a group of individuals selecting an individual of the human species as a god or representative of a god. It could have come about as an animal or an entity representative of an animal or an entity, body or thing such as a distant mountain, an animal, or in Egypt the Nile River communicating with the individual. Such a god communication as a burning bush speaking to an individual on a mountain that came about in a much later century was not a new idea, thought, scheme, inspiration, brainstorm or approach for a human to transmit his communicating with a god. The invention of a son of god in heaven living in and among the persons on earth was not a new idea of the Christians, it was invented some many thousands of years before in Egypt.

From the earliest days of known history and thousands of years before the Christian popes took down the emperors of Rome and ruled the Western World with an iron fist, religion has been used to govern and control societies and nations. Whether it was a god- related leader such as the ruler of the Inca and Aztec civilizations in the unknown other side of the world or in Egypt and the Middle East, an individual who possessed the aptitude and skill to convince the multitudes he was god-related had the facility to control the society.

However, the Egyptian individual created the god, the originator had to then have the ability and charisma to attract a following of believers who, some in turn would become priests and disciples promoting the god. Thus each of the gods mentioned below became a major longterm Egyptian religious industry consisting of a bureaucracy with thousands of practitioners promoting, selling and creating a career earning a living in the business as that specific god's rep (priests). Following are just the names of a couple of dozen of the many Egyptian gods with each god having been created by an Egyptian human or a group of humans:

Gods Khnoum, Meen, Khonsu, Set (one of the oldest gods in Egypt), Hapi, Soker, Aton (the sun god of Pharaoh Akhenaton: give the Pharaoh credit for coming up with the new idea of being the son of god Aton), Neith, Isis, Osiris, Ra, Mat, Nwphtees, Atum, Khepri, Sobek, Geb, Sekhmet, Tefnout, Shu, Nefertem, Amun, Tweret, Ptah, Moot, Horus, Anubis, Nut, Monto and Hathour. These are just a couple of dozen or so of the hundreds of gods who were worshipped at one time or another in the thousands of years of Egyptian history.

Many of these gods were held in the highest esteem by countless millions of Egyptians over hundreds of years with the believers looking to them for help, protection from disease and catastrophic events and also hopefully for the receiving of some benefit or gift from the god in return for something in the plate of the practitioner, financially supporting the (priest) and also burning incense, sometimes beating themselves with chains, wearing some kind of ornament, tattoo or whatever suggested by the god's representative.

Just for the fun of it look up some of the Egyptian gods on Google. Check out the prominent Egyptian god Horus to start, as he is one of the more interesting gods.

K: The Egyptians surely did have a great number of gods. I intend to Google and learn more about the Egyptian gods.

T:I think it might be best to start with the professor at the University of Arizona who is an expert in the field of Egyptian history and address the very beginning of the one and only god concept that led first to the peaceful Jewish god and then branched off into the two militant Christian and Muslim religions with each having their one and only militant God.

Professor Richard H. Wilkinson

Director Egyptian Studies, University Of Arizona

Professor Wilkinson is considered one of the foremost American scholars of Egyptian studies, having spent many years in Egyptian expeditions and researching the history of Egypt. He is the author of many Egyptian history books including, *The Complete Gods and Goddesses of Ancient Egypt*. Pages 42 to 64 of that book describe the history of religion in ancient Egypt.

Nearly all literate persons are well aware that the Jewish religion was the original European Middle Eastern area religion with both the Christian and Muslim religions being branches of the Jewish religion. Fewer persons are aware of how the Jews initiated their "One and Only One God" concept that originated in Egypt.

The Jews initiated their religion by adopting the concept of just one God from the ancient Egyptian Pharaoh Akhenaton. The ancient history of Egypt is sketchy, since fanatic Christians destroyed the great Egyptian historic library and nearly all of the literature in the Alexandria library many centuries ago. The archaeologists' expeditions researching ancient Egyptian culture and history have verified that it was this ancient pharaoh who conceived the idea that the sun was the one and only God and that he was the son of that God. Needless to say, the priests and reps of the other pagan gods were not pleased with the Pharaoh's invention. Many historians believe the pharaoh who really came up with this idea, either from a dream, or a political power play was Pharaoh Akhenaton of the 18th Dynasty. The chaos which erupted in Egypt following his invention was led by the pagan priests of all of the other gods of such things as the moon, tigers, cats, the Nile and so forth and was overcome by later pharaohs who then simply negotiated a position with the pagan practitioners as a layer of bureaucracy between them and the many gods of the pagan priests. The sun god was still an all important god, but no longer the one and only god in Egypt.

So the Egyptians did not accept the "one and only one God" invention of the Pharaoh Akhenaton. During the rein of Pharaoh Remises the 2nd (about 1290 BCE), the idea of there being just one and only one God traveled by boat along with trade goods to the Jews in the middle east. Many prominent Jewish historians now dispute, even ridicule, the story that there was a mass exodus of Jews from Egypt with the one god idea for two reasons: one, the primitive logistics of that time would make such a mass exodus impossible, and two, it's a fictitious fairy tale that the ocean temporarily split and permitted the Jews to walk across the dry sea bed to the other side. The current Moses, (Charles Heston), who now lives in Beverly Hills and the past president of the NRA (National Rifle Association) truly believes the story of God rolling back the ocean for the Jews to walk on the dry sea bed to the other side of the ocean because he has viewed his movie many times.

In any event, the Jews liked the "one and only one God" idea and declared themselves his favorite people. Good idea! Too damn bad they also took up the chant that they were waiting for the one and only God to send down his son to visit them. How did they know the Jewish god up there only had one son? This innovative and creative idea resulted in many young men either promoting themselves as the son of God or having a following promoting him as the son of God. In my mind, I continue to question how did the Jews know it was to be a son and not a daughter? Then I had to keep reminding myself to always remember the Bible was written by men.

The Jews lived in peace with the believers of the pagan gods and made no effort to convert the pagans to believe in their God. When the Christians adopted their God, they commenced the chant, "convert to our belief and God or we will kill you in the name of our God". Six hundred and thirty two years ACE, (after the Christian era commenced), the Muslims adopted and commenced the same militant chant as the Christians, and in 2006 are still killing the infidels and non-believers in the name of their one and only God, Allah. Allah is also a descendent of the old Pharaoh's one and only God invention. Ole Akhenaton's God has a very complicated Jewish, Muslim, Christian dysfunctional family! To put it mildly, the Jewish, Christian, Muslim original God is obviously the father of the most dysfunctional family in the history of civilization! Without question, this God's family represents the ultimate in sibling and hate rivalry!

WARNING: Don't write a secular book or make a secular or agnostic statement while in a Muslim country. As of 2006, no Muslim has made a move similar to the 1500 ACE acts of the brave Christian priest Martin Luther to break loose free nations in the Muslim world.

The ayatollahs have no intention of having a free thinker, agnostic, atheist or skeptic break their iron fist dictator control and create free Muslin nations from those ruled by deadly dictators. The ayatollahs have observed what happened to the control of the popes, when they permitted Martin Luther to live and are not about to make the same mistake.

No doubt the boys in Rome, the American Baptists ministers and TV evangelical Bible thumpers look with envy at the dictator control the ayatollahs currently possess in the Muslim world. I am sure in Rome in their daily Latin mumbo jumbo sessions the boys have Latin phrases that mean something like, "If it were not for that rotten turncoat Martin Luther, we too would still have absolute control of the Western World as the ayatollahs enjoy in their world. By god, if we had maintained the control we once had we would not have these damn problems with these crazy feminists and sinful gays and lesbians. If it were not for that turncoat Martin Luther, the possibility of a group of the so-called 1776 forefathers in the new world setting up that terrible sinful secular government would never have come to fruition! Damn it, now that secular American stuff, democracy and freedom of and freedom from religion have spread all over the world in the last 200 years!"

The information I have written on these pages is my own interpretation I arrived at from reading Mr. Wilkinson's impressive history book, along with much other information about the history of Egypt on Google. None of the statements are direct quotes from his book.

See Google, search words "Richard H. Wilkinson" and "Egypt" and then follow the links.

Mr. Akhenaton's God

Almost all religious rituals and symbols of the Western World cults and sects in existence today have been inherited from the Egyptian religions of 4000 BCE to 2006 ACE, a period spanning over 6,000 years.

When Pharaoh Akhenaton of the 18th Dynasty of Egypt declared there was only one God of the earth, (the Sun God) and that he was the son of this one and only God, he immediately knew he had created great chaos in his nation. No one was powerful enough to put all the Egyptian pagan priests out of business. Without contributions in the plate how could they survive? They would have to seek employment. There was no way the ole pharaoh could pull this caper off.

Pharaoh Akhenaton of course had no inkling that his invention, idea, hallucination, dream, political power play or whatever that brought about his one God declaration and invention would have such an impact on the future of the Western World. There is no way he could have known his declaration would set the Western World off on a future path of the cruelest, bloodiest and mass killings in the name of one God in the history of mankind.

Actually his declaration had created the future "Curse of the Western World." Millions of innocent people would be killed in the name of this one and only God from "0001" ACE to 2006 ACE. A span of over 2,000 years of unbelievable mass killings in the name of Mr. Akhenaton's "One and Only God" with the pharaoh being his son idea. A God in heaven with his son on earth was not a new idea when Jesus was born.

History has proven that when one religious belief or sect overtakes and replaces an existing cult or religion, the new religion adopts much of the ritual and symbolism of the sect or religion it replaces. This is necessary since the converts to a new religion or sect will not be comfortable unless the familiar practices and rituals of their old religion are a part of the new overtaking sect or religion. They have to have this bridge to the new sect or religion if the new religion is to be successful and grow.

The Jews, Christians and Muslims have adopted many of the rituals, symbolism and practices of the ancient Egyptian practices developing their new religions. One of the best Christian examples is of the pope changing the time of Jesus' birth to be December 25th instead of his actual birth in March. It was important to the Christian converts for his birthday to be at the same day as the many thousands of years of the pagan believers' greatest holiday; the end of the year winter solstice with each day of the year thereafter the holiday being longer.

The Christians of all sects have copied a great deal of the ancient Egyptian's practices such as having specific, very grand holy places to meet with God. Their six-day Christian God who looks like you (that is if you are a male and Jewish) resting on the seventh day, of course is out there someplace looking after his tiny planet. This means the Christian practitioners who are enjoying all the luxury and lifestyle of comfort in God's crystal palaces and cathedrals here on earth are just his hard working representatives. God, for one reason or another, never gets to use the facilities, limousines, jet aircraft, great Halloween-like costumes, other luxuries of the privileged or enjoy the lifestyle of his self-appointed representatives. God's reps will assure you that all of this grandiose enterprise is not theirs. They will also convince you of the need for contributions to support these costly enterprises and lifestyles because the grand facilities all belong to God.

They have also adopted many of the same holiday dates as the pagan sects and much of the symbolism of the pagans. This was necessary to give comfort to the converts from the pagan beliefs. The pagan practitioners filled their coffers for the most part selling favors and good treatment from their god of the distant mountain or whatever. They could not compete with the three great products of the new Christian religion (favors form God, forgiveness of their sins, and to live with God when they die). Truly a fantastic bargain for a bit of change in the coffer.

Of course the most important Christian-adopted item was Egyptian Pharaoh Akhenaton's idea that a person on earth is the son of the one and only God. The Christian storytellers adopted this concept when promoting Jesus, starting some four or so decades after his death. Other religious leaders have also been promoted for having had a one-on-one communication with the one and only God. Our American Pat Robertson TV Bible thumper frequently advises his followers about his discussions with God. As in ancient Egypt, the promoted one had established contact through messengers or some form of personal contact with a supernatural power related to God. Much of the virgin birth myth about Mary came straight from the many tales in Greek mythology about the promiscuity of the Greek God Zeus with young maidens on earth. Credible historians have documented the fact most all of these religious ideas and tactical approaches to recruit converts to a new sect, belief or religion were practiced by energetic entrepreneurial individuals in ancient Egypt thousands of years ago.

It is doubtful whether the promoters of Christianity have actually initiated any new ideas in the procedures and steps to establish a new religion since the time of Pharaoh Akhenaton in the 18th Dynasty of Egypt and the great Greek god, Zeus. Thanks to Mr. Akhenaton, we now have three huge religious organizations worshiping his "One and Only God" and killing each other in this one and only God's name: the Christians, the Jews and the Muslims.

The Jews for the most part throughout their history have only killed in self defense.

But the same cannot be said for the Christians and Muslims. They are killing each other in the name of the original Mr. Akhenaton's God. Thanks Mr. Akhenaton, we are all thrilled with your very ingenious and creative invention and idea.

The Bible

Let's take a look at the book that is the basis, instructions and what we might consider as the long range strategic plan for all of these Christian invasions of other cultures, societies and nations following the Christian takeover of the Roman Empire.

Do you believe the Christian God's reps have really voluntarily renounced the "Koran-like" dictates in the Bible? Are you willing to accept the fact that they have elected to ignore these inhumane, insane and ugly punishments depicted in the Bible only because of the past three centuries of activism of the secularists, agnostics, atheists, skeptics, and free thinkers? This activism was of course made possible as the result of the brave Martin Luther taking the steps resulting in setting the northern nations of Europe free in the 1500s. The activism of the skeptics would not have been possible without the northern nations of Europe gaining their freedom from the dictatorship in Rome.

There can be no question that if the northern nations of Europe had not been set free through the actions of Martin Luther, the iron fist of the dictators in Rome would still be performing exactly as the ayatollahs are performing in 2006. To take history a little further down the line, it becomes obvious that the existence of a group of free men such as the 1776 forefathers could not have come about if it were not for the actions of Martin Luther some two centuries earlier.

So let's get the most widely distributed book in the world and note some of its "Koran-like" dictates:

The Bible clearly states the policy to be followed and the required punishment in the same manner as the Koran. A few examples:

"Witches should not be permitted to live." Remember the New England witch killings? Just three normal lifetimes ago!

"Slavery is to be condoned." Only 145 years ago! A time less than twice my age.

"Women must never be permitted to speak in a church." Want to be excommunicated?
"Those who violate the Sabbath should be killed." Better not be late either!

It's all in the book. That is enough, the point is certainly made. So the comments of many believers are that the times have changed. In the modern age they would not do those terrible things. But it's in their book! The ayatollahs are doing the things that are specified in their book in this modern age. They have not mellowed.

Has any cruel dictator ever voluntarily mellowed? Dictators never voluntarily give up their control of a nation or an organization. Try to recall any dictator in history who ever voluntarily gave up control. Why have the ayatollahs not made a similar change in the cruel treatment of their subjects? Answer: they kill questioners or dissenters.

The Christians, (except for a small number of fanatics in Ireland, the Balkans and some killers of physicians, gays and lesbians in America), ignore these absurd, ugly and inhumane Bible dictates only because of the past 400 years of activism of the secularists, agnostics, atheists, skeptics, and free thinkers in the free nations who have made the Christian leaders reform. Without this past 400 years of political pressure pursued in the free world on the Christian leaders, gays and lesbians would still be hung upside down by ropes tied to their ankles and sawed in half. That is about as tough a death as being nailed to a cross. The trials of the Inquisition would have continued until this day if it were not for the actions of the activists in the free nations.

Please be sure your brilliant 1776 forefathers were well aware of the cruelty, bloodiness and evilness that existed in the Christian's theocracy dictator-controlled history when they documented the foundation of our secular nation.

If you feel a need to worship, worship your 1776 forefathers and also the possible great God of the universe. If inclined to do so take a walk this evening and have a free private chat with the great God of the universe as "SHE" may very well be somewhere out there. The conversation is free. But realistically, a literate person capable of reading the works of the great brains of the scientists of the past several hundred years has to admit that if there is a supernatural power out there, it has to be some kind of cosmic force similar to what Einstein mentioned. It can't possibly be a she/he/it image of a human keeping notes on individuals being bad or good like Santa Claus.

There is no risk, but commonsense should dictate that you are not an image of her/him/it or whatever is busy as hell taking care of the vast number of Carl Sagan's billions and billions of stars and planets in the vast universe.

I admire the genius, earliest sci-fi imagination and creativity of the many writers of the Bible. Long before any person in the world had any inkling or knowledge about the universe, that the world was round, Darwinian evolution, the dinosaurs, the Big Bang and all the other great scientific discoveries of recent times, they produced a book that can to this day prove anything a person wants to authenticate. Give me a topic addressing a controversial subject such as slavery, marriage, military service; just any subject that comes to your mind and with a few hours of study with the Bible, I can prove to be correct whatever side of the controversy you want me to prove. With the Bible's dictates, I can prove slavery is the will of God or I can prove it is sinful in the eyes of God. I can prove a man should only have one wife and is sinful if he has more than one wife. I can also prove a man should have three or more wives to be in good standing with the Christian God. I can prove a man should fight for his country or be a conscientious objector in case of war.

Here in America we have a high and mighty TV Bible thumper, Pat Robertson, who proclaims to his TV followers to occasionally have conversations with God. Pat thinks he is a very exclusive individual to have God come to him with messages. I didn't want to hurt Pat's feelings but I sent him a letter (with no monetary contribution enclosed) and advised him that his God has communicated with a great number of persons over the past 2,000 years. I told Pat he should not do so much bragging and exalting about his conversations with God. God enjoys communicating with the people inhabiting the little planet he set up with his six-days of hard work. For instance in my letter to Pat I noted just a few instances of God's many chats with earthlings:

Genesis 3:11. He spoke to Eve: "Who told you, etc, etc and so on."

Jonah 1:2. "Jonah, arise and go forth, etc, etc and so on." (Poor Jonah ended up three days in the big fish.)

Jonah 2:10 God speaking to the big fish: "Vomit Jonah onto dry land…etc…" And the big fish obeyed!

My Sunday school teacher told me the big fish was a whale. Of course when this story was written, whales and dinosaurs were unknown to the imaginative story tellers so they used the term big fish. We now know a whale is not a big fish but is a mammal that once roamed on land and through the evolutionary process moved into the ocean.

Matthew 1:18-22. It was in this series of gospel that the lord had his messenger tell Joseph not to be concerned about Mary's loss of virginity prior to their marriage as he, God, was responsible for her pregnancy. Ole Joe went along with the story. It would be very embarrassing not to go along with the story because Mary was already showing a bit of a bulge.

Genesis 6:3-20: Whereby God gives Noah instructions to build that really big ship with no modern tools to work with and with the help of no one other than his three sons, Shem, Ham and Japheth. Let me tell you that was one hell of a tough project!

Genesis 12:1-2. In this conversation God told Abraham to get off his butt and get out of the country.

Exodus 3:2. In his conversation with Moses, God masquerades for some reason as a burning bush and the conversation goes on and on. Moses listened carefully and from time to time was chipping away on the big rock with his hammer and chisel all the way through many pages to Exodus 40:38. These conversations with Moses were without a doubt the most all-embracing conversation God has had with any one individual in the known history of civilization.

Judges 1:2. In this conversation with Judah, God gives Judah instructions regarding combat with the evil Canaanites.

Chronicles 1:7. In this conversation, God for the first time asks someone what he can do for him. He said to Solomon, "Ask; What shall I give you?" And the interesting conversation continues through the balance of the Chronicles. If God should ever ask me that question I think I would ask him to free and clear my real estate properties and do away with my damn taxes.

Amos 1:2-15. In this conversation with Amos the lord is really pissed off and makes it clear he intends to wreak havoc because of the transgressions of the people of Damascus. This guy really has a very bad temper so you better not offend him! Jerry Falwell is right; if you piss the guy off, he will knock down your buildings.

Amos 8:2. In this conversation with Amos, the lord is in a better mood and they have a pleasant conversation about a basket of fruit.

Mark 9:7. This was not so much a conversation with God but simply an announcement by God while either hiding in a cloud or masquerading as a cloud. In this declaration, God advised Peter, James and John who were visiting with Jesus on the mountain that Jesus was really his son.

Luke 1:13. In this encounter, God sent a messenger to advise Zacharias that he shouldn't be concerned as his prayers had been heard and that his wife Elizabeth would bear him a son. I don't know why God didn't take care of this himself as he did with Mary because Zacharias's wife was reported to be a very sexy lady.

Luke 17:6. In this conversation, God speaks to all of the apostles. This conversation goes on through chapter and verse until Jesus also speaks from above in Luke 17:17 about the cleansing issue.

John 20:12-17: In this conversation, God sent a couple angels down to visit and give his message to Mary. Then in John 20:18, Mary passes the word on to the disciples. No doubt God and Mary were well acquainted because he had impregnated her some 30 years or so earlier. It seems strange he would send messengers rather than to visit himself with his former intimate friend. I guess they had some kind of falling out in their relationship.

In my letter to Pat, I also suggested that the reason he failed in his recent bid to become our herd leader (president of the US) may have been God's notice of him exalting himself; Luke 14.11: "For every one who exalts himself will be humbled." Pat never wrote back to thank me for my helpful suggestions.

But Kelle, you don't want to close the book until you read Revelation 12:1-17. This sci-fi story about the fiery dragon with the seven heads and ten horns will hold its own with the best sci-fi fiction of 2006. A very exciting Bible story, don't miss it.

*K:	While you were discussing the Bible the thought crossed my mind about the training of children. True, what you and some others might refer to as "closet secular, agnostics, non-believers and even atheists" feel they themselves have the maturity and reasoning ability to deal with true facts. However, I am sure many parents are of the opinion the Bible and Sunday school are very important to teach children right from wrong. How do you address that situation?*

T:I think I can address the situation relating to children and how I arrived at the belief I now have about who we are, why we are here and where we will be going after our journey on earth. I was still a believer when my first wife and I were raising our four sons. At that time I thought Sunday school was one of the best methods to help teach children right from wrong. Surprisingly, I still think Sunday school is of great help in raising and training children. The stories are no different from fairy tales and very entertaining for the children.

If I was raising children now, here's how I would address the task. First, I suggest the parent think about and truly answer to themselves, "What am I with relation to religion?" Am I an agnostic, skeptic, atheist, free thinker, deist, believer, secularist, closet secularist?"

With regards to religion, maybe the following will help you evaluate who and what you are as you relate to these terms: (this is my amateurish understanding of the terms). You may or may not concur with my understanding. I am not a philosopher or scientist, just an ole Navy fighter pilot throttle jockey and real estate promoter and developer.

Agnostic: One who holds that the ultimate cause (of existence) is unknown and can never be proven. There may be a god but it cannot be proven or disproven.

Atheist: One who denies the existence of any god. Usually, also believes in the random chaos of atoms with no supreme power control whatsoever by any power or god over the atoms' random activity. An atheist philosophy first expressed in the 575 BCE to

475 BCE, (before Christian era), period by the great Greek genius, Leucippus of Miletus. He has often been considered by historians to be the first true atheist based on science and learning. Einstein wasn't sure if there was some kind of supernatural cosmic power beyond the Big Bang so are atheists egotists to be so sure of themselves? And what about my Physics 101 professor's teaching that nothing can come about unless there is some thing causing it?

Deist: A term often associated with the thinking of many of America's 1776 forefathers. They stated they would believe in only what could be proven. No belief whatsoever in any unproven supernatural happenings. Deism is a belief in God based on reason rather than faith.

Believer: One who, based on faith alone, believes the truth of a body of writing and teaching on doctrine without any positive knowledge or proof. Example: God in the form of a burning bush speaks to a human. A human walks on water; feeds multitudes of people from a handheld pitcher that never needs to be refilled; a sea opens up so that a multitude of people can cross to the far shore on the dry sea bed; a man places his hand on the head of a kneeling sick, handicapped person or blind person and they are immediately made well and cured of their problems; a human body raises up and departs to somewhere in the universe without the use of a rocket or a space vehicle. All believed without question or any investigation.

Secularist: Not belonging to any religious order. A person not questioning the right and freedom of others to believe or not to believe in whatever their choice may be so long as their activities are lawful in the American society in which they live. Such a person is, of course, following in the footsteps of many of his/her American 1776 forefathers who established this great secular nation giving us the freedom to believe or not to believe that all Americans now enjoy.

Closet Secularist: My personal term for the educated adult individual, who as a child, (similar to my life experiences), lived through the enjoyment of the tooth fairy stories, the bunny rabbit with the attractive eggs, Santa Claus and then the disappointment of later learning the truth. Now either not attending religious services or just going through the motions by quietly sometimes attending religious services with the family; enjoying the proceedings but looking past the beautiful music, the ringing of bells, the waving of scented smoking canisters and the colorful Halloween type costumes of the cult leader. Very aware and knowing full well the practitioners' tales are based on fiction. All of these goings-on frivolities being every bit as enjoyable as many of the plays on Broadway. And of course also enjoying the social aspect of the experience. But thinking: "Why should I say anything about this fiction and get myself alienated from the many uneducated believers? How can I be sure of my closest friends' loyalty in keeping my true feelings and thoughts confidential between ourselves if I openly state my true belief and convictions? Better not rock the boat! The cult leaders have spent centuries of tremendous energy and resources in brainwashing their followers that an agnostic, atheist, skeptic, free thinker or non-believer is a heretic and terrible, sinful individual. I have a career and social life to consider. After all, history has shown that when one manmade fictitious cult or religion slowly replaces an existing cult, the new order adopts many of the entertaining and colorful activities of the older cult it is replacing. For example, the colorful pagan end of the year celebrations that have existed for thousands of years have been continued by the current Christian, Muslin and Jewish religions. The Christian popes in 400 ACE even changed the birthday of Jesus from the spring to the end of the year to coincide and carry on with the former pagan end of the year entertaining and colorful celebrations. My family, (myself as a child), and my children enjoy the tooth fairy, bunny rabbit and colorful eggs, Santa Claus stories and celebrations. In my opinion, it would not be fair to my children to deprive them of these enjoyable and entertaining events, beautiful music, pageantry and stories. I'll be sure my children will be educated and encouraged to learn the history and importance of the acts of our 1776 forefathers and the scientific discoveries of the recent past two centuries at the proper age. Then they can decide on their own future belief and conduct. This will be a maturing learning experience very much similar to the erudition about the truth on the subject of Santa Claus and the Easter Bunny at an earlier age.

Many adults feel this is the practical and sensible stance. If the closet secularist of whatever type has a political career, an executive position in a major corporation or teaching position to consider, this stance makes sense. The financial welfare of the family must always come first. The Christian leaders have made sure with great emphasis that any non-believer will be ridiculed, considered an immoral person and an undesirable individual to be associated with. You must believe as they believe, PERIOD! You must not question!

Once the parents have made peace of who they really are in the field of religious beliefs, I suggest they need to give serious thought about Sunday school for their young children.

Kelle, before we address the subject of Sunday School as related to the education of youngsters, I would like to have you take what I call a "Bible Readers Test." Is that OK with you?

K: *OK, lets get to it.*

READERS' TEST

T: Kelle, I think we should take this reader's test to determine whether you or our readers are interested in one of the important things that influenced me to engage in a communications assault on the people I consider a danger to America. Many people are only interested in exciting gunfire conflicts, but I do believe many people are interested in the works, scientific discoveries and philosophies of some of history's great men and women challenging the Christian Empire.

K: *I think that is something we should do as I am sure some of the readers are only going to be interested in the part related to WW-II, the Corsair and the WV-2 Super-Constellation stories.*

T:I think it advisable for our readers to first read the opening five pages of the Christian Bible, Genesis 1:2 to Genesis 5:32 before continuing to read further. This is only five pages which can be read in just a few minutes. Then take the easy test below.

Having read these pages you will have a much better understanding of the contents of the balance of my memoir and how I came about asking questions about what I was taught in Sunday school; about religion in my youth and then later in life doing research, reading about the works and discoveries of scientists, educators and philosophers to try and learn what is truthful and what is fiction in many religions, primarily Christianity.

Take the Test

Assuming you have read the first five pages of the Bible, truthfully answer the following questions:

Do you truly believe how the planet earth came about in six days?

Do you truly believe a woman was made from a man's rib while the man was sleeping?

Do you truly believe all the animals on the earth were created at that time and that evolution never took place?

Do you truly believe the woman and the serpent are the originators of sin?

Do you truly believe Mr. Lamech, the father of Noah, (the ship builder) lived to the age of 777 years (that's seven hundred and seventy seven years)?

Your answers to these questions are sufficient to qualify you or any reader of the Bible as a legitimate open minded person or a closed-minded person who really should just drop this book in the nearest trash can and be on their way.

If your answer to any of the above questions is "Yes," start looking for a trash can to deposit this memoir of mine. If your answer is "No" to all of the questions, I assume you have a mind set similar to mine...questioning your religious teachings...the obvious fiction in the religious teachings we were taught...lived through the tooth fairy tales...the Easter bunny proceedings...then the Santa Claus phase of childhood...and now trying to learn what is the truth about who we are...where did we come from...where are we going to go following our journey on earth...seeking peace of mind.

K: OK, I read the pages assigned and I for sure passed the test, but again, what about Bible stories and holidays as related to children?

T:As a result of my friendly spiel (seeking friendly clarification and help) regarding the understanding of the first five pages of the Bible with adults, I have had many conversations with parents on the subject of Sunday school and children in relation to their own beliefs. I think it is important for the parent to know who he/she is and how they intend to live their lives as related to religion.

When my wife and I were raising our four sons, this was not a problem for me because I was still a questioning, feeble Christian believer more or less in the closet at that time. I knew full well at the time that it was all false, but was afraid to let go of the crutch just as a child learning to swim is afraid to let go of his/her water wings.

For some years I dedicated each Sunday morning to work as an usher in the church while the children attended Sunday school. My sons were raised as I was; through the Sunday school programs and we celebrated and enjoyed the various Christian holidays. We still celebrate the Christian holidays with my sons and my grandchildren!

Now I am sure of my beliefs and I am very frank about them with my adult college-educated sons. I have no intention of attempting to influence them one way or another with regards to what I consider manmade fictitious religions. Common sense would indicate it is important they find their own way in religious matters.

It is comforting for many to use faith as a crutch for comfort when facing the hardships, disappointments, deaths, sicknesses, injuries of friends and family and other unpleasant happenings that occur in their lifetime. Some people may have a very great psychological need to light a candle and seek supreme help.

But my comments above were 'then' in the mid 1900s and you are addressing the 'now' in 2006 about my feelings of how I would address the Sunday School concern of today's parents with youngsters. So here is my opinion if I were today a young parent with children of Sunday School age.

In my opinion, any atheist, free thinker, secular, closet secularist or Deist parent who brainwashes his children to think and believe as he/she believes is every bit as guilty of evil as Pat Robinson, Jerry Falwell, priests, cardinals, the pope or any of the many evangelical Bible thumpers brainwashing children.

In my opinion, children should be taught to live a moral life in accordance with the Bill of Rights and Constitution conceived by our 1776 forefathers and to obey all of the laws of the land. They must be taught this is a nation of law and order and frequently be told stories about their 1776 forefathers.

I also believe it is cruel to deprive a child of the enjoyment of the tooth fairy stories, the bunny rabbit, Easter egg hunts, and the joy of looking forward to the visit from Santa Clause. Why should an innocent child be put into the position of defending his/her parents' beliefs with their playmates?

I feel a child should be taught as mentioned above and engage with his/her friends in all of the enjoyments of childhood fantasies and stories. If the child questions why he/she does not go to Sunday school like their friends do, I believe the secular or atheist parent should simply ask, "Which one of your friends would you like to go to Sunday school with?

As the child approaches 16 or so, I suggest the parent (if a secular or atheist person) advise the child several book reports are going to be required before the driving license instruction or similar great event the teenager is expecting or seeking will take place. About five or so book reports during the child's 15th and 16th year such as: the works of Dr. Charles Darwin, Ben Franklin, Thomas Jefferson, Dr. Carl Sagan, Thomas Paine, Thomas Jefferson, Professor Bronowski and similar great men's lives and teachings. No less than five or so book reports of this type. The parents should then review the book reports and discuss the child's rejoinder to the books.

Once the youngster has completed the book reports, I suggest the parent should then hand the teenager a Bible and request a book report on only the first 25 pages of the Bible with the simple statement, that upon the completion of this report the sought after event will be made available. In my opinion, common sense should dictate the parent make no effort to influence the youngster's thoughts regarding the contents of this last Bible book report.

Once the child is an adult of about voting age he/she is for sure eventually going to question the parents about their beliefs. In my opinion, that would be the time to level with the offspring.

As young adults, if your offspring needs the comfort of a manmade fictitious religious faith as a crutch to face the rigors of life, why not accept it? They may have a psychological need to enjoy life with the help of one of the Christian or Muslim faiths. Hopefully they will not fall into the clutches of one of the many dangerous offbeat Christian cults. Agree with them that all Americans have the right to believe or not to believe thanks to the great 1776 forefathers citations.

Also, this would be the time to emphasize, without question, the parents' firm belief that all Americans have the right to believe or not to believe as dictated by our 1776 forefathers.

What are your thoughts about children and Sunday school?

K: I think you and I have pretty much the same ideas. I agree innocent children should never be placed in a position of defending the beliefs of their parents. I also feel they should have the opportunity to enjoy the great holiday stories.

K: So does that make you an atheist?

T:In discussion groups when I am asked my opinion concerning bringing the facts of religion to children, I first advise the person or group of my opinion of Christianity and the many other fictitious religions. I also mention that because of what Mr. Hartley taught me in Physics 101, that there is no such thing as perpetual motion or any reaction from zilch (meaning nothing), and later I read Einstein's biography and about his work and learned he believed there might be something supernatural out behind the Big Bang that brought about the birth of the universe and even Billy Graham on the Larry King CNN show mentioned there has to be something out there (he did not say it to be the six-day God constructing tiny planet earth). So how can I, just as an old throttle jockey say there is nothing out there? No matter how many bits and pieces on the subject I review or read the substance of professionals in the field to the subject the only thing I can be sure of is that all the things I learned in Sunday school and from Christian leaders is fiction. Christ, maybe I should study the Buddhist stuff! Some one must have the non-fiction answers. I cannot consider myself a true atheist although I have made small financial contributions to Ellen Johnson, the president of the Atheist Organization.

I occasionally attend atheist social meetings and sometimes joke with them about the possibility of a she/he/it or something supernatural behind or beyond the Big Bang. They just shrug it off as just some scientific discovery yet to be found and for sure there won't be any she/he/it or supernatural power in charge. I find discussing the subject with atheists an enjoyable exchange of ideas as they never get uptight or belligerent because I do not quite accept their belief. In fact, I admire their web opening page information on the internet.

www.atheists.org

"AMERICAN ATHEISTS has been the premier organization laboring for the civil liberties of atheists, and the total, absolute separation of government and religion. It was born out of a court case, begun in 1959 by the Murray family which challenged prayer recitation in the public schools. That case—Murray v. Curlett—was a landmark in American jurisprudence on behalf of our First Amendment rights. It began:

"Your petitioners are atheists, and they define their lifestyle as follows. An atheist loves himself and his fellow man instead of a god. An atheist accepts that heaven is something for which we should work now— here on earth—for all men together to enjoy. An atheist accepts that he can get no help through prayer, but that he must find in himself, the inner conviction and strength to meet life, to grapple with it, to subdue it and to enjoy it. An atheist accepts that only in a knowledge of himself and a knowledge of his fellow man can he find the understanding that will lead to a life of fulfillment."

This type of conversation with an atheist, of course results in a much different reaction than if in conversation you question a true Christian hardcore believer. To address such a subject as questioning the Christian belief with such a Christian believer will many times result in scowls, insults and sometimes heated arguments because of their demand that you must believe as they believe. Or else. The Christian leaders have spent great energy and billions of all kinds of currency in all western nations to brainwash society that any non-believer or free thinker is an immoral, low life individual. You must not question their teachings! Period.

K: But what about some of the restrictions religions place on people?

T: Over the centuries, leaders of religions based on fictitious stories have been well aware of the four key aspects of comfortable survival: food, water, security and intercourse for the survival of the species. Religious leaders have pounced with a vengeance on three of these: food in using wafers as a symbol of flesh, wine as a symbol of blood, restricting specific foods such as beef on Fridays and fasting for specific periods of time; water as droplets or in some cases immersing the entire body and of course the Christians' longtime cahoots with any topic related to sex or the female body. They have added the waving of smoking canisters, colorful costumes, music and the ringing of bells for effect, fire in the form of lighting candles, ambience and engrossment in many of the sect's beliefs. (Seriously, do you think SHE really cares about all this fuss on this ever so tiny grain of sand-sized planet?)

K: I agree; I don't think SHE has any interest in all that ceremony.

T: In my opinion I think SHE would be very angry to see all these self appointed representatives of the fictional six-day God carrying on and controlling people's lives with their fictional stories.

Kelle, picture this panorama of a beautiful wedding I attended with a WW-II marine veteran some years ago of a young couple in their late 20s which would be amusing, if not so stupid a scenario. Picture this scene:

The bride was a trim, beautiful, blond, sexy former college cheerleader and the groom was a tall athletic, obviously full of testosterone, male. The performance of the official dressed in his colorful Halloween-looking costume was impressive. The cathedral was spectacular. The music was as enjoyable as a concert. It would not take much imagination to what these two energetic newly married individuals had on their minds in the upcoming honeymoon as soon as they could get away from the guests. They were of course carrying the inherited human genes that we all have. But the man in the Halloween costume who performed the ceremony had insisted that any sex not for the purpose of having a baby is sinful. Of course they were also taught they were born sinners. Only church attendance and money in the coffers could cure that problem.

Later in the day I was visiting in the Point Loma Navy Officers Club and discussing the wedding over a couple of gin and tonics with my WW-II vet Catholic friend with whom I had attended the wedding. When we joked about the vagaries of the state of affairs regarding sex and what the church considers sinful sex as related to the so-called rhythm cycle as he called it, Planned Parenthood, the pill and use of condoms, he was as perplexed as I was about his church's centuries old sex dogma. Many of the mainline Protestant Churches and the Catholic Church are obsessed with the micro management and control of the females' body and their lives rather than to just possibly counsel as they do the males but then let the individual lady make the decisions. This obsession of the different church's getting involved with the lifestyle of females and the conduct of married couples in the privacy of their own bedrooms has to be attributed to the fact that ancient very bright but nevertheless uneducated in science men wrote the Bible. They could not conceive the fact the females of society were not the property of the male members of the society and that only males were capable of dictating the official church dogma.

We also talked about some of the heated discussions that are going on in his church. He mentioned that he attends church on Easter, Christmas Eve, weddings and funerals. He also mentioned he did not believe Jonah was swallowed by a big fish (whale) and set up housekeeping in the big guy for several days, that God ever masqueraded as a burning bush and held a conversation with a guy holding a hammer and chisel wandering around on a mountain, that Joshua ever made the sun stand still, that some guy named Noah ever built a ship about ten times the size of Columbus's Pinta and welcomed aboard two of every kind of the earth's animals and insects for a long voyage or that messengers from

God visited a lonely camel herder under a hot sun in a desert. Then he said, "Hell, Tom, if the church should ever sanction priests to marry, congregations to select their own priests, women priests, birth control, women's right to choose the care of their own body, divorce, stem cell research and the Supreme Court's legal abortion provisions, our church will have become just another kind of a new Protestant religion. All this stuff was passed down to us for many centuries and I just have to keep my mouth shut and pretend to believe it."

I truly believe my friend spoke for many millions of educated American citizens of diverse religions, who, for the good of their social life, have the same thoughts and remain in the closet. And of course Muslims would be in great personal danger if they publicly expressed their true beliefs. My friend's statement about the Protestant sects is correct because many of them believe as the Catholics do and are different only in that they will not answer to Rome. Christian Fundamentalists believe every sentence in the Bible is the absolute unquestionable word of God. Catholics believe that every statement of the pope is the infallible word of God and he interprets the Bible for them; so there is little difference between the two religions. There is no room for questions of authenticity or accepting the facts of scientific discoveries in either of the organizations. You believe as we believe or else!

Of course if you are a Protestant and have a different belief or interpretation of something in the Bible than the belief of the others in your flock, you just form a new church that agrees with your take on the subject. Or just find and join another existing Protestant sect that agrees with you.

K: I doubt if many Catholics and Protestants will accept your opinion that their beliefs are pretty much the same. It seems to me there is a real difference in the one group interpreting the Bible word for word and the other accepting the statements of the pope as infallible gospel.

T: Could be. When I was single between marriages, I would sometimes go to church with whoever I was trying to make out with and of course always kept my mouth shut about my own beliefs. For some reason many single women seem to enjoy taking their male friends to church services. I never noticed much difference from the services of the Catholic, different Protestant churches or the Mormon services other than the décor of the buildings and the costumes or lack of costumes of the persons performing the service. I found the Jewish services the most interesting because the rabbis had very entertaining voices when performing. The most painful services to sit through were the Christian fundamentalist sessions. Kelle, Christian fundamentalists give people like me nausea and a headache and we know Muslim fundamentalists want to chop our heads off. I have never attended a Muslim service and for sure will never attend one.

Religions and Business

In the Navy while training to become commissioned officers, we were taught never to discuss religion, politics or sex in the wardroom of a ship. In fact, we were not to ever talk about these subjects in any military or social environment. Aboard the carriers and other ships both during the war and later in peace time I can vouch for the fact I never heard any officers discussing politics or religion in a wardroom during my military career. Conversation about sex is another matter. Especially during the war aboard the Bennington, it seemed to me sex was often on the minds and in the conversation of pretty much every one aboard the ship. Each evening after the evening meal, junior officers had to each censor several dozen letters being mailed home by the crew of the ship. Since the Bennington had about 2,500 men manning the ship, this was a tremendous amount of mail. We were provided scissors to cut out any confidential or secret statements. WW-II was a real war, not a minor police action, and secrecy was a top priority at all times. Some of the mail to girl friends and wives was about as sexy as any pornography you can imagine. Often the contents of a letter would be so outlandish and sexy the officer reading it would say to the others at the table, "Hey guys you got to read this one, this letter will really turn her on!" But I some times wondered if the writer ever wondered what the woman would do once she was turned on while the writer was so far away? Anyway after an hour or so of reading and censoring these letters you can imagine what was on our minds (average age of the junior officers assigned to do the censoring of the mail being 19 to about 22 years of age) and then what we talked about in the wardroom while enjoying a cup of coffee after all the mail was picked up for delivery to the ship's post office.

In later civilian life with business associates, I followed the same procedures about never discussing religion and politics but once I knew a business associate and was on friendly terms, often sex and sexy jokes were no longer verboten.

I have to relate one exception when I engaged in a conversation with a close friend and business associate about religion. Ernie, a mortgage broker, and I had been working together on many different real estate developments for several years and had become close friends. At the time he was a widower and had no relatives in Southern California. I never heard him ever mention any family members so I assume he and his wife never had children. Ernie was at least a decade older than me and passed away over two decades ago. I was involved with a Hedrick/McBride Co. motel project that was to be built at the Ontario airport about 40 miles or so east of Los Angeles. I had a Canadian investor with the financial wherewithal to qualify for the construction and permanent loan so all we needed was for Ernie to locate the financing for the project. In the 1980s, motel loans were very tough to come by.

Ernie and I normally had lunch together once a week at the San Diego Yacht Club to discuss social and business matters as well as to enjoy each other's company. We had been struggling to locate a source of loan money to commence construction for several months and I was having difficulty holding the landowner to the escrow until we could negotiate a satisfactory loan. During one of our lunch dates, Ernie made a comment right out of the blue, "Tom, I have a good feeling about the motel construction loan. Last Sunday in church I really prayed to get this loan and I just feel that we are going to hear from the lender with good news in the next few days." Without thinking, my exact words were, "For Christ sake Ernie, you're a war veteran, a college graduate with a masters degree and you're telling me your praying in church for some fictional god to help us get the damn loan!"

Then as longtime friends we got into a discussion regarding religion and our beliefs. Once he heard me out about my opinion of the six-day God, the women being made from the rib of a sleeping man, the guy with his three sons building the huge ship, boarding all the animals and the man setting up housekeeping in a big fish for several days Ernie said, "Tom, think about what all is involved in religion." Ernie then elaborated on his views as to why he was sure God was aware of our need for the loan and that God was going to help us acquire the loan. The reason I can recall this conversation so well despite my poor memory is that following our luncheon discussion and Ernie's departure from the club I jotted down some of his comments in my business manual with the intent of countering some of his statements in our next get-together. Of course if we acquired the loan before our next meeting I would have thanked Ernie for recruiting God to be a member of our developing team.

When we had our next meeting we still had not acquired the necessary construction loan. I took out my manual of notes and as best I could reviewed each of Ernie's prior statements in a manner similar to how a pilot and a co-pilot review an aircraft pre-takeoff check off list:

Ernie's (E:) statement: "Without God how can we have morality?"

Tom (T:) "Millions of years of evolution have developed an animal (us) with the ability to know right from wrong in the herd. If an individual lives his/her life in compliance with the 1776 forefathers documentation of our Constitution, Bill of Rights and the laws of our society, that person will be a moral person."

E: "Without God, who can we turn to for help in a crisis?"

T:"We each have to attempt to rid ourselves of superstition, belief in myths and fiction and learn to grapple with reality and learn to cope with the ups and hostile downs we encounter in life. Accept the hostile downs as a painful part of your journey on earth and if necessary seek true professional help to ease the grief when encountering traumatic events.

Some of the pain will be overwhelming and professional help may be of real assistance to overcome or cope with the grief; but psychic readers and fictional beliefs are not going to help."

E: "What is the purpose of life if there is no God?"

T: "The answer to that is that we were all brainwashed as children in Sunday school to believe we are a part of a herd or flock with the purpose of our lives to be submissive peons following self-appointed messengers of a fictional god. This is a very similar scenario to the peasants of earlier times believing that their royal kings and emperors owned them and all the land and assets of their surroundings."

E: "Without an afterlife with God, how can there be reward for virtue and punishment for misdeeds?"

T:"This is a concept closely related to the scenario of my opinion of the purpose of life."

E: "Without God, how can a society or nation resist the onslaught of atheistic communism?"

T:"This is a modern belief based on the ridiculous rantings of McCarthyism and related to the cold war with the Soviet Union. The fact the Soviet Union was (is at the time of this conversation) a communist nation and also promoting atheism are two very different unrelated particulars. America is fortunately a nation of freedom of and freedom from religion. So long as the American population continues to support the 1776 forefathers' documentation of the structure of our government, the population will enjoy all the freedoms we now enjoy."

E: "If there is no God, how can a person achieve happiness?"

T:"This goes back to the fact that we were brainwashed as children in Sunday school to believe that we were born sinners and only the self-appointed messengers of the man conceived fictional god can bring about happiness in our lives. We all have to get over our immaturity and learn to confront the so-called hostile world on our own. We should really enjoy our one and only journey on the planet and seek true professional help in time of need."

As we were leaving the club that day Ernie said, "Tom, I know all those stories in the Bible are fiction but I just can't let go of the crutch. I'm so suspicious I never walk under a ladder, step on a crack in the side walk, cross the path of a black cat and eagerly look forward to the statement in my fortune cookie in the Chinese restaurants. I guess I'll never get over the need for a mental crutch."

Ernie and I had both made our beliefs clear to each other and got on to other subjects of the day in subsequent meetings. I do not recall either of us ever discussing the subjects again in our long running friendship and business relationship.

K: Did you, Ernie and the investor finally acquire the loan?

T: Nope, it was a difficult period in the American economy and we never built the project. The provisions of the escrow stipulated that if we did not successfully comply with all of the terms of purchase of the land that all of our engineering and architectural construction plans would become the property of the land owner upon the cancellation of the escrow. About eight or ten years later, I saw our proposed motel built by others at the airport. If some day you happen to visit the Ontario Airport take a look at what I believe is the third or fourth motel on the west side and that is the exact building our engineers and AIA architect M. Pisciotta of San Diego designed for the site. These things occasionally happen in the real estate development business; you make some and you lose some!

Ernie and I were involved in many successful projects and enjoyed each other's company. While I was a divorced bachelor and he a widower, we frequently double-dated at parties and social events. One day Ernie advised me he was retiring due to his diabetes condition and intended to live in an assisted living retirement facility in Alabama. Ernie was a financial conservative and in his research of such facilities across America he had learned he could retire in the south for about one-half the costs of living in a similar facility in Southern California. After he departed, we occasionally exchanged cards and letters with each other. A few years later, I received a phone call from a lady in the facility in which Ernie was residing advising me that Ernie had died. She told me my name was on a list of names Ernie had left in his belongings for the facility to call regarding his passing. She said, "Beside your name is a notation for us to tell you that Ernie said to tell Tom that he tried but was never able to give up the crutch. But Ernie never had any crutches here." Knowing the pleasant and caring lady was a citizen in the Bible belt, I just told her the statement was related to a joke Ernie and I had between us.

I was thinking about Ernie and our long ago conversation when I recently crossed paths with 93 year old Professor Walter Goldschmidt of UCLA (University of California Los Angeles) who was giving a lecture at CalTech (California Institute of Technology) discussing his book, *The Bridge to Humanity*. Following the meeting, I had a discussion with the professor regarding one page in his book that would have answered all of Ernie's questions and would have made him comfortable with spirituality without his crutch based on fiction and uneasiness about living without the spirituality he was comfortable with in his religion. Ernie really knew Christianity was based on fictitious stories but had that strong want to cling to the crutch. I have since learned there is more than one way to have spiritual feelings and experiences in life. Professor Goldschmidt gave me permission to quote him and the passage in his book along with a statement Dr. Michael Shermer, founder of the CalTech Skeptics Society, had made to put in my memoir. That is:

"Spirituality is a way of being in the world, a sense of one's place in the cosmos, a relationship to that which extends beyond us. Religion is only one of the many ways to experience spirituality."

The proven science of evolution to the professor as he explained it to me was the cornerstone of spirituality. He said, "I have read in the vast mythic literature on the subject, (meaning evolution) and it is to me even more beautiful and soul-satisfying. Just the thought that we are one with all other beings now living in the world or that who have ever lived over the billions of years since life emerged on the planet and that we share DNA and the whole machinery of inheritance with the mushroom and the butterfly, the elephant and the amoeba is to me a grand (meaning spiritual) realization." I wish I had had that information to pass on to Ernie years ago. While driving home from the Pasadena CalTech campus, I had a warm feeling knowing that I also share the same relationship with all living things, not only the animals but also with the giant thousands of years old redwood trees as well as with the huge multi-ton whales I sometimes observe swimming along our California coast. When I got home, I gave my dog Boris a big hug and told him we are really distant relatives.

K: Two interesting experiences, Tom!

The "Evil Theocracy" Coalition

K: Tom, who in your opinion, are the members of what you refer to as the evil theocracy coalition leaders?

T:I'm going to give you some background about my opinions regarding the danger from within American's borders from members of the Christian coalition. I will get around to naming a few of their leaders shortly. There are many, probably the majority of Christian ministers, who respect America's manmade laws and look favorably upon the 1776 forefathers' wall of separating religion from the state. However, there are a very significant number of Christian leaders working diligently to tear down the wall and have our laws based on their theocracy rather than on the laws constructed by our judicial brench of government. This significant number are the "enemy within" our borders who I am addressing in my memoir.

The Following was Recently Published by Jerry Falwell, One of the Most Prominent TV Evangelists

"I told the President last week in the Oval Office," I said, "Sir, there are 80 million of us evangelicals in this country and we've come to look upon you not only as our President, but as a man of God."

He said, "Jerry I'll do my best. You put great pressure on me. I'll do my best not to disappoint you."
Jerry Falwell, 2003.

"I trust God speaks through me. Without that I couldn't do my job."
President George W. Bush, July, 2004.

PS: I was a very active supporter of the President's father in both of his runs for the presidency. He was also a Navy WW-II carrier pilot. But unlike his son he did not bend to the wishes of the religious coalition and without their bloc of votes and support he was not re-elected to a second term.

Falwell Again in 2005

"We (most likely he meant 'I') will not adopt 'inclusive' policies to accept other religious teachings". OK Jerry, all must think and believe as you do. I better write a letter to Jerry to make sure he realizes he is going to piss off the pope and a few ayatollahs because I am sure they have the same idea about their beliefs.

Some Interesting Coalition Participants

When I refer to "The Coalition Participants" I am not meaning they actually all meet together in conferences. That would be impossible because many of them cannot stand each other, even hate each other, but they do have a common purpose, goal and greater hate. That number one hate is the 1776 forefathers' wall of separation of church and state. In fact, they remind me of my generation's experience in WW-II when we Americans and British hated the Soviet Union and the Soviet Union hated us but we were allies because we both had a greater hate, Nazi Germany.

Jerry Falwell: The "intellectual?" Bible thumper TV evangelist who proclaimed the 9/11 attack and destruction of the New York World Trade Center and the killing of the workers was God's punishment of America because of our nation's citizen's sinful ways of life. No doubt Jerry got this information from his friend Pat Robertson who frequently has conversations with God. He made it clear that permitting freedom of choice to women, our nation's permission for gays and lesbians to enjoy their lives without persecution and our secular Supreme Court laws were God's reason to punish America. God punished Rome and now he is punishing America.

When I heard that announcement, it seemed strange to me that the agents Jerry's God had selected to carry out the punishment of America in New York were crazy fanatic hijacking terrorist Muslims.

I took the liberty to send a postcard to Jerry's Lynchburg address and wrote, "Damn it, Jerry; what kind of God do you have who commissions agents such as these fanatic nut cake Muslims to do his holy work on our tiny planet? As you know your close friend and fellow TV Bible thumper Pat Robertson has told us of his many conversations with God. I sincerely request you have Pat ask God the next time he and God have their conversations to explain why God picked these nutty fanatic Muslim hijackers to carry out his undertaking."

I sent a postcard to Jerry rather than a letter because it cost less and I was still pissed off about the boys at the Vatican not replying to my earlier expensive snail mail letter.

Pat Robertson: The TV Bible thumper multi-millionaire repeatedly charged by the IRS for using tax-free religious funds in his own personal non-religious business ventures to the tune of several hundred millions of dollars. Pat also advises his followers and financial supporters of the comments and advice God personally delivers to him about world and political affairs. Pat is indeed proud to be the one and only individual God enjoys speaking to in this country. No doubt many people sincerely hope the IRS will finally nail Robertson for his alleged illegal private investment use of his tax-free TV-solicited funds.

Cardinal Mahoney of Los Angeles (just one of the many American cardinals): Nicknamed "Stonewall Mahoney" by the police department and county prosecutors of Los Angeles for his stonewalling all the legal efforts of the county and state legal authorities to acquire information regarding the abuse of children by the priests under his jurisdiction. Mahoney and many other American cardinals are threatening that any Catholic politicians or church followers will be sent to hell if they oppose the church's teachings and dogma. (Where is hell?) The cardinals have no use for the 1776 forefathers' wall of separation of state and religion and support the efforts of the coalition to teach religion in both private and the public schools. They have been fighting the government for over a hundred years to acquire taxpayer money to teach religion. Thanks to the brilliance of political genius Karl Rove, many billionaires support the coalition.

Richard Mellon Scaife is an example of one of the most notorious fanatic billionaires, who are funding the workings of the coalition's efforts to make sure the coalition's leaders have the financial backing to support their selected politicians in winning elections. Richard's only other claim to fame happens to be that he is the great grandchild of the famous and successful banker, Mr. Mellon, of the last century. Richard is a real gentleman who the coalition can be proud of. In a 1981, Pittsburgh, PA., media event, the prominent journalist, Ms. Karen Rothmyer of the Columbia Journalism Review, asked him about his known contributions of about some $200 million to his favorite fanatic neocon organizations and received the following reply: "You fucking communist cunt get out of here!" Richard is really a person whom the very dignified and righteous religious leaders can be proud of. Of course, Richard is most interested in the tax benefits he would obtain with Republican victories rather than the religious goals of the coalition. Richard and the many other billionaires, many of whom are for sure secular, but financially supporting the coalition's neocon religious politicians to secure tax benefits and corporate welfare are therefore also supporting the coalition's efforts to take down the forefather's wall so they too are unknowingly a part of the evil coalition.

Alan Sears, president of the ADF (Alliance Defense Fund) who always proudly announces at their coalition association meetings and conventions that they are successfully removing the bricks of the wall of our 1776 forefathers, "one brick at a time." Proudly proclaiming and firing up the coalition attendees with his fists in the air, "One by one, more and more bricks that make up the wall of separation of state and religion are being removed."

Ralph Reed, former Coalition Executive Director, often referred to by his detractors as the "little sissy boy" is anything but a little sissy boy in his never-ending battle with the believers of the 1776 forefathers' wall. Reed maintains secure day-to-day contact with express precedence with the White House office of Karl Rove, the strategic mastermind of the Christian coalition's political activities. He is the number one operative managerial official coordinating the attacks by the neocons and Christians of all the various sects attacks on the 1776 forefathers wall. He is also the coordinator of the diverse Christian groups' attacks on women's rights, gays and lesbians' civil liberties. A high priority item on his agenda is opposing the public schools' secularist education stance (and demanding government taxpayer money to support private Christian schools) using the taxpayer funds that should be used to support the public schools.

Currently Reed is under investigation by various federal and state authorities probing his alleged illegal political activities with his associate, the notorious criminal lobbyist Jack Abramoff, whereby authorities allege he and his friend Jack have been involved in political illegal lobbying activity earning hundreds of thousands of dollars supporting the goals of existing Indian tribe casinos battling other Indian tribes trying to open new gambling casinos. Robin Vanderwall, recently deposed head of Reed's Faith and Family Alliance

Association, is also a prominent member of the coalition but at this time is in prison, having been caught by authorities for soliciting sex with minors over the internet. These are indeed two outstanding members the religious coalition can be proud of.

Karl Rove, who has devoted his career to the implementation of Christian theocracy into the American government. I am not a White House historian and do not have the research capabilities of career historians, but I do believe the appointment of a Christian strategic political activist operations planner to a private White House office with day-to-day communications with the President is the first such appointment in the 229 year history of America. His White House title is "Political Strategist" (Karl is good at that, too) but any individual who takes the time to Google Karl Rove and follows the links to learn of Rove's inclusive background, knows better what he is really up to. Many evil con men are also brilliant organizers and strategic planners.

I rate Karl Rove as one of the most brilliant political organizers of recent decades. Over his political career he has molded two very dissimilar groups into a major political power. He has the wealthy top 1% of the population interested in tax write-offs and corporate welfare benefits on one hand and the Christian coalition fanatics on the other hand. These two very different groups have little in common but Karl has both of them working together in politics. The Christian coalition seeks the candidates who will do their bidding to destroy the American judiciary and the wall of the separation of state and religion. The top 1% privileged group support the same candidates to acquire the tax benefits and corporate welfare they seek. Karl has demonstrated his brilliance in making it possible for the pro-theocracy government evil doers to gain the financial support of the wealthy top 1% of the population and the corporations of America.

In 2002, a White House source revealed to a journalist that the wife of Joseph Wilson, an ambassador who had written a report contrary to the desires of the administration, was a CIA agent in a foreign country. It is a federal crime for a government official to reveal the names of undercover CIA agents. Special prosecutor Patrick Fitzgerald was assigned to locate the criminal source of the anonymous White House leak. It took prosecutor Fitzgerald many months of expensive diligent research to locate the source. Finally on July 10, 2005, Karl Rove knew that Fitzgerald had located the source and admitted it was he who leaked the information to the journalist. Karl considers himself a very patriotic American proudly wearing the American flag pin on the lapel of his coat each and every day. He will continue to be the key strategist of the Christian Coalition's political activities and handling the financial support of the billionaires and major corporate supporters of the neocons. For political reasons, a minor official on the vice president's staff was selected to take the blame for the leak on lesser but related charges.

K: Tom, you refer to these people as coalition evil doers. Who in your opinion are the good Americans?

T: Good Americans are the people who hold the same beliefs of our 1776 forefathers. My favorite assemblage of citizens being the United Americans "UA", Americans for Separation of State and Religion. So naturally when TV Bible thumper Pat Robertson made the following statement, "Americans United for Separation of Church and State —they are enemies of the state….And they're enemies of good, decency and order" my blood pressure zoomed with anger. I think ole Pat and I are about the same age and I daydream about what pleasure I would get to meet him someday and give him a hard bare knuckle fist smack into his asinine anti-American mouth. That would make news, two old cranky guys in their 80s in a fisticuff! But of course being a gentleman, I would really never do that. I would just say, "Pat you sure are a stupid bumbling idiot with a case of diarrhea of the mouth."

I think another great assembly of dedicated loyal Americans is "The People for the American Way." Google "PFAWF." This is an organization of dedicated and loyal Americans (many of them very religious) who believe in America's government, the separation of church and state and believe our leaders should govern with manmade humane laws and not govern in accordance with or answer to a higher unknown invisible theocracy power. And of course there are the many other patriotic organizations to name just a few who have become powerful pro American organizations established in the last century, most since the end of WW-II in 1945; such as The American Humanists, The American Civil Liberties Union, the American Atheists and many other smaller pro-American groups. And remember Kelle, professional accurate polls prove secular Americans are the fastest growing percentage of the American population. Surely in just a couple more decades America will be 'secularly even' with the most secular nations of Northern Europe.

Well Kelle, here I am in the last years of my journey on earth internet blogging, using "friendly' conversation to develop some doubters and writing this memoir as a token of my respect for my 1776 forefathers to at least make a small step confronting the evil coalition neocons. So I was pleased to learn an important celebrity, Walter Cronkite, is also concerned about the onslaught of the neocons on America. Walter is promoting the financial support of the pro-American Interfaith Alliance of religious persons who are also concerned about the evil of the neocons. So you see even millions of Christian religious persons are also concerned about the importance of separation of church and state. Let's review the first half of the first page of Walter's letter to me. It's a three-page letter but the first half of the first page is the meat of it.

K: You correspond with Mr. Cronkite?

T: No Kelle, I am just one of probably millions of people who received a copy of Walter's letter. My name is probably on the "contact him" list of individuals known to be anti neocon and of anti Christian Coalition groups. So here is a scan of the first page of Walter's letter promoting me to make a contribution to the Interfaith Alliance; which I did.

K: Tom, did you really send that reply to Walter Cronkite? Incidentally I have always admired Mr. Cronkite as a level headed and dedicated American.

T: Yes. I made a copy and snail mailed it to The Interfaith Alliance along with a modest donation. I am sure they would forward my copy to Walter wherever his "retired office" is. Probably on that beautiful yacht he owns.
But Kelle, Pat Robinson and Jerry Falwell are just a couple of country boy, Bible thumping clowns who the vast majority of Americans look upon with amusement. The real danger to the future wellbeing of America is the quiet high placed Christian members of the dangerous "Christian Coalition." They are determined to take down the wall of separation of state and religion and commence their standard operating procedure of insuring that all citizens think and act in accordance with their theocracy beliefs. They are determined to limit the rights of women to be in charge of their own bodies, the rights of gay men and lesbians to live normal lives, to install judges in the judicial branch of our government who will sanction laws in accordance with their theocracy teachings.

K: Mr. Cronkite is a well known celebrity who commands a great deal of respect and attention. What can an ordinary citizen do to help curb the attacks on our manmade government of commonsense law?

T: I sincerely believe an ordinary non-celebrity citizen can at least feel good about themselves by supporting one or more of the loyal pro-American organizations that have come into existence in America over the last 75 years confronting the fanatic Christian leaders who are working tirelessly to undermine the America we love. Remember in total darkness the lighting of a single candle (meaning a modest donation) by a citizen brings about a little light but becomes a great bonfire of light and support if a great number of us join up and make modest donations to these pro-American groups.

From the Desk of

WALTER CRONKITE

Dear Friend,

When I anchored the evening news, I kept my opinions to myself. But now, more than ever, I feel I must speak out.

That's because I am deeply disturbed by the dangerous and growing influence of people like Pat Robertson and Jerry Falwell on our nation's political leaders.

Especially after Robertson and Falwell both shamefully blamed America's courts and the highest levels of our government for the horrific September 11 attacks on our nation. They said it happened because we "insulted God." Falwell went on to blame feminists, pro-choice Americans and other groups he despises.

Like you, I understand that freedom of speech is a founding principle of our nation, and I respect people with the courage to speak their minds.

As a concerned person of faith, however, I have watched with increasing alarm as the Christian Coalition and other Religious Right groups manipulate religion to further their intolerant, political agendas.

Over the years, Robertson and Falwell have gained considerable influence on local school boards, in the administration, and in Congress. They have shrewdly twisted the traditional healing role of religion into an intolerant, political platform.

Dear Walter,
We all know the vast majority of the Christian Americans are good loyal patriotic citizens. We also know many of their leaders are fanatic haters of our secular government. We common folks will fight them in the press, in the polls, in conversations and as bloggers on the internet. America will survive as a government of man made laws as envisioned by our genius 1776 Forefathers. Sincerely,
Tom McBride

Here is a short list of pro-American organizations that are growing and deserve the support of loyal pro-Americans:

- The Interfaith Alliance: www.interfaithalliance.org

- Americans United: www.au.org

- Stanford Humanists Organization: www.stanford.edu/group/Humanists/ or go to the American Humanist Society at www.americanhumanist.org.

- American Atheists: www.atheists.org. OK, so many of us do not agree with the atheists that there is nothing out there beyond the Big Bang. Nevertheless, if you read their home page and what they stand for, there is no organization more pro-American than the American Atheist Organization.

- American Civil Liberties Union: (ACLU) www.aclu.org No organization in America has fought the Christian Coalition's efforts to inundate our public buildings and public schools with Christian propaganda more successfully than the ACLU.

- The Skeptics Society: www.skeptic.com. This organization, true to its name, intellectually attacks any unproven proclamations or claims of any kind.

- Universism: To reach this "Freethinkers Society," just Google "Universism."

There are many other pro-American organizations combating the Christian Coalition; the ones mentioned here are the ones I try to support with my limited financial capability. I intend to send a copy of your book to wealthy Ted Turner to encourage him to financially support these organizations. I will also try to find some other wealthy secular pro-Americans to encourage them to step up and join the team. It of course costs a great deal of money to successfully battle the wealthy and fanatic Christian Coalition.

A Major Modern Christian Defeat

As of 1900, the Christian militant religious leaders had experienced one victory after another throughout the world, invading nations and islands and one by one destroying the culture and religions of millions upon millions, (actually billions), of people. From North America to South America, to Hawaii, the many other islands of the Pacific and Atlantic and parts of Africa they invaded, took over and destroyed both the cultures and the religions of the many civilizations. They are still experiencing success in Africa but in the years 1898-1902 they ran into a powerful nation capable of taking them on and suffered repercussions leading to their first major defeat, in China!

Few Americans are familiar with the Boxer Rebellion of 1900 in China. This was a religious rebellion of the Chinese attempting to crush the Christian invasion and to rid China of the coalition of Christian nations taking control of the major coastal cities of China. The dedicated loyal patriotic Chinese leaders were intent on ending the practice of the Christian missionaries throughout the nation taking control of the minds of the young. In 1900 both Catholic and Protestant Christian missionaries were widespread and with growing numbers throughout China intent on taking control of the minds of the young Chinese. The Chinese leaders of the Boxer Rebellion and their followers were finally defeated by the coalition of European Christian nations who were assisted by Japan. Eleven years later in 1911, the Chinese resentment of the Boxer Rebellion defeat was boiling in the minds of the Chinese patriots. The great Chinese leader, Sun Yat-Sen, gathered together a force of sufficient strength to oust the corrupt ruling Empress, who had been a weak and reluctant collaborator with the Christian powers. Sun Yat-Sen then set up the new Chinese Republic in 1911.

The history of China from 1911 to 1945 and on to 2006 is beyond the scope of my memoir, but let it be said that regardless of what any one thinks of the current government of China, never again will Christian nations take control of Chinese coastal cities, or will the Christian missionaries of any sect proliferate the Chinese nation and invade and undermine their culture. Buddhist and Taoist beliefs of the Chinese people are booming in China at this time. During my trips to Guangzhou and Beijing in 2002 and 2003, I visited the temples and they were crowded shoulder to shoulder every day of the week. As of 2006, all Chinese have the freedom to teach and practice Buddhism and all the other ancient Chinese religions and beliefs. The shouting and shrill of the Christian leaders that the current Chinese government does not permit the practice of religion is just so much propaganda. The government of China is determined to protect their nation from the disastrous consequences of the Christian invasions of the new world, Hawaii, the many other islands of the world and areas of Africa. The Boxer Rebellion may not be familiar history for western citizens but in my recent visit to Beijing I learned first hand that the patriotic 1900 Boxer Rebellion is taught in the schools and very well remembered in the current Chinese society. Please be sure the leaders of the Boxer Rebellion are historical heroes to the current generation of Chinese and I am sure will remain so in future generations.

Now I would like to address one of the more recent Christian empire's crimes: The Spanish Revolution of the late 1930s.

The 1936-39 Fascists/Christian "White Wash"

Prior to WW-II, even in America, any publisher or journalist who made derogatory statements about any Christian sect would be taking significant financial risks on the part of the publishers or the loss of his/her job for the journalists. For this reason the recent exposure of child abuse in the Catholic hierarchy could not have been exposed in the 1930s or earlier in America. In 1938-39, the first truly post WW-I major killings of innocent Western World citizens in the 1900s took place in Spain. The shaky and struggling Spanish Republican government, fighting the same worldwide depression America had been facing in the 1930s, was along with many other reforms attempting to document a policy similar to the American separation of state and religion in their government.

The pope in Rome and the religious hierarchy in Spain were not about to have any of that nonsense as a part of the Spanish government. With the support of the Catholic hierarchy, the fascists' dictator Franco commenced a revolution that was backed by both Mussolini and Hitler to bring down the Spanish Republican government. On August 19th in 1936 three of the first persons executed in the city of Grenada were the secular liberal world famous poet Federico Garcia Lorca along with a well known liberal bull fighter and a teacher both of whom had expressed liberal and secular views in support of the Spanish Republican government. Hundreds upon hundreds of other Granada citizens were executed in the following months which were followed by the execution of republican government supporters throughout all of Spain in the following two years.

As a 15 to 17 year old teenager I was well aware of the revolution over the two years listening to the radio news broadcasts and also reading the front page of the Pittsburgh Post newspaper. I cannot recall a single story or news broadcast mentioning the non-military atrocities in Spain or why it was occurring. The full historical truth of the revolution atrocities and the dictator Franco-Rome relationship never came to light until late in the 1900s.

I often wonder if the Spanish revolution was just the first time the pope would remain so silent about the Spanish atrocities and the Franco, church and pope relationship. Later during WW-II, the same papal secrecy would be followed by the pope keeping secret all of the details the brave German priests were mailing to Rome about the 1941-45 Holocaust. To this day in 2006, the pope will not permit the release of any of the documentation or letters received in Rome from the German priests in 1941 to 1945 denouncing the Holocaust.

A Few Recent Theocracy Incidents

The most dangerous aspect of the Christian coalition's attacks on the 1776 forefathers' America is their interminably ferocious attacks of the important secular American judicial branch of our government. Here are just three recent incidents.

In a legal case in the courtroom of a dedicated judge of the Catholic faith involving whether the feeding tube of a brain dead lady should or should not be removed, the judge ruled in favor of the doctors, husband and expert witnesses' statements despite his Catholic beliefs. The tube was removed and the comatose brain dead lady passed on. He stated that he had followed the guidelines of the Supreme Court and the laws of his state rather than the doctrine of his faith in making his legal decision. He believes in the forefathers' doctrine of separation of state and religion. A few days later, he received a letter from the priest of his church stating that he was no longer eligible for communion services or absolution in the church, which in fact amounts to excommunication. The judge had been a regular parishioner and financial supporter of the church for decades. In my opinion, the priest of that church is an anti-American who hates my 1776 forefathers' America. He is a danger from within our borders.

In another case, a judge was a member and habitual attendee and financial supporter of the Baptist Church all of his adult life. In his ruling regarding the right to abort the unwanted pregnancy of a 13 year old runaway child, the judge considered the opinions of the doctors who stated the child was in great danger as her young body was not mature enough to stand the rigors of childbirth. He listened to the tearful pleading of the youngster asking the judge to permit the abortion and considered the opinions of the child's government-assigned child care official whose stance in court was being directed by theocracy-opinioned politicians. The judge ruled in favor of the distraught youngster despite the posture of his church. He believed the secular laws of America took precedence over his own and his church's pose. A few days later, he received a letter from his Baptist minister advising him that he was no longer welcome to attend his church. The judge dropped out of the church. In my opinion, the minister of that Baptist church is an anti-American who hates my 1776 forefathers' America. He is a danger from within our borders.

There are of course a vast number of similar evil theocracy attacks on our judicial form of government occurring in less conspicuous cases month after month and year after year. The attacks are not limited to just the actions of the leaders of the various religious sects. There are many judges working within the judicial system who are in their positions as the result of the theocracy-minded politicians who have been financially supported in elections by the united religious coalition front.

The most obscene and highest level theocracy judge is the current Supreme Court justice Antonin Scalia who makes it known he answers to a higher power than our manmade laws.

Before any legal matters are presented in any case involving any issue related to religion, this judge's decision is known to all in the case before any action in the courtroom takes place. While the court case is in session, this judge normally never asks a question or pays much attention to the proceedings. He has made his decision and his vote is known before the case commences. He is a disgrace to the Supreme Court, our judicial system and the American government.

The following is an incident with a lower level theocracy-oriented judge's verdict. The plaintiff was a young unemployed women, Ms. Stephanie Collopy, with a 12 year old son who had been fathered by priest Arturo Uribe. The judge was Keith Meisenheimer. In this case, knowing full well that if the scientific DNA procedures were used, he would be proven the father, priest Uribe readily admitted he was the father of the boy. The youngster was in need of health insurance and financial support as he was (is) suffering from several illnesses. Priest Uribe's defense for not providing the necessary financial support was that in the religious order of his faith he had pledged to live in poverty serving God during his career and life as a priest so he could not contribute to his son's care.

(Let's break off here to consider how the boys live while serving as poor priests. Chauffeured cars when traveling, living with all meals prepared by others in first class living accommodations far beyond the level a military officer enjoys aboard a Navy ship. When an upper level poor boy like Cardinal Mahoney of Los Angeles travels to and from Rome, he enjoys the comfort of sitting in the first class section of the airplane with the privileged class. When Cardinal Mahoney stands in front of his flock in his new $278 million Los Angeles cathedral, he is dressed in his magnificent robes, often clutching his jeweled staff, wearing his gorgeous crown and various caches of expensive jewelry. All of this personal adornment is rumored to cost in excess of $150,000. He indeed makes a very impressive looking king-like appearance in all this gorgeous attire. Man, that's the way to live in poverty!)

Judge Meisenheimer ruled in favor of priest Uribe. Ms. Collopy and her son will therefore have to resort to US government programs to survive. Now think about theocracy-minded judge Meisenheimer's decision in this case as related to legal decisions regarding the errors or misdeeds of employees or agents of American businesses.

When I owned my small business, McBride Realty, in San Diego, I had to carry expensive liability insurance to protect me in the event one of my agents or employees made an error or performed some deed that caused any of our clients problems. I was legally responsible for the actions of my agents and employees. Priest Uribe is certainly an agent of his religious order. The Catholic Church is a very wealthy organization supporting the

I cannot think of a superior representation of the decline of the dominance and power of the Christian leaders in America in my lifetime as when seeing this play produced at the Old Globe Theatre in San Diego last year. The very idea of a playwright or producer conceiving such a play in the early years of the 1900s or even up to a few decades ago would have been considered an insane idea by any person with common sense.

Man... let me tell you...the movie producers, playwrights and producers of any type of entertainment in the early 1900s walked on eggshells when they ever touched the subject of Christian religion of any sect in their productions. Even the slightest hint of any kind of criticism of any religion in an entertainment production would bring out the pickets, announced boycott of attendance and heated comments in the newspapers. This "Prince of L.A." performed to sold out audiences from Sept. 24 to Oct. 30th,

. The theme of the production was the scandal and corruption in the Los Angeles hierarchy of Cardinal (Stonewall) Mahoney.

The play gave meaningful insight into the men and women who devote their lives to the worship of God but also in a humorous and funny plot revealed the corruption at the top of the hierarchy. The play received numerous favorable reviews from theater critics; there was never any sign of pickets or protestors and I am sure it will be produced in other theaters across America; but of course not in the Bible belt. I doubt if Falwell, Robertson, any cardinal, bishop, minister or priest would spend any of their momentous tax free funds to attend this play.

WINNER OUTSTANDING NEW PLAY!
L.A. DRAMA CRITIC'S AWARD
THE PRINCE OF L.A.
DAKIN MATTHEWS
photo by John Apicella.
THE OLD GLOBE
(619) 23-GLOBE (234-5623)
www.TheOldGlobe.org
GROUP SALES: (619) 231-1941 x2408

lifestyle of its priests and especially the magnificent and luxurious lifestyle of the cardinals and bishops.

I have no respect for the manner in which Ms. Collopy's lawyer represented her. I am confident that if the attorney had insisted on a jury trial, the 12 American citizens of the jury would have rightfully sided with the youngster and his mother. I forgot to mention earlier; following the decision in the trial, the church transferred priest Uribe from his position in the Whittier, California church to a church in Chicago. I hope Uribe has now gained better control of the zipper in his church robes and now only unzips when it's time to urinate.

History has proven that regardless of the religion, when religion controls the government, the nation's citizens will experience poverty, corruption, elimination of scientific research and the loss of rights and freedoms. The result is a gradual return to the sinister Dark Ages of corrupt religious dictatorship.

K: I can see the actions of the Baptist minister, Catholic priest and the theocracy minded judge really rang your bell!

T: When I witness the actions of the Baptist minister and the Catholic priest mentioned earlier, attacking the judicial system set up by my 1776 forefathers, it makes my blood boil with anger. In my opinion, both the minister and the priest are anti-Americans. They and the many other anti-Americans who share their hatred of our American judicial structure represent a greater danger within our borders to our American form of government than any overseas enemy.

Kelle, the day this book is printed, I will mail one to each of these anti-Americans. I will certainly put a notation with the page number on the package for them to read my comments about them. I try to follow the intelligent philosophy of the genius Baruch Spinoza to control my prejudice and anger but it is hard to control your anger when you read about the evil activity of persons like the above Baptist minister, theocracy judges and Catholic priest.

I have yet to hear of any patriotic Americans taking any action against the Baptist and other Protestant ministers attacking our judicial system and many other aspects of our secular America but I have noticed the activity of the patriotic Catholic lady, Mrs. Haggett in the New England states. Mrs. Louise Haggett founded the CITI in 1992.

Louise Haggett

Probably the least known but most important and overwhelming threat to the power of the popes in Rome over the past two decades was the 1992 establishment of the

American "Celibacy Is The Issue" (CITI) organization founded by dedicated Catholic, Ms. Louise Haggett.

The organization grew slowly until the respect for the hierarchy of the Catholic church was shattered by the past decade's revelations of the world-wide sexual abuse of youngsters and the cover-up by the cardinals and bishops of the church. Since 2001, the CITI organization has grown by leaps and bounds and as of 2006, has a membership of over 2,500 married priests performing in all aspects of the Catholic Church for thousands of Catholic believers. The powers in Rome do not recognize the CITI Catholic priests as a part of their empire but all of their performances in marriages, baptisms, funerals, counseling and church services are legal in America and accepted as authentic (per canon law #843) by the followers. The disaffected Catholics believe their married priests are more understanding and their day-to-day plights are more readily understood than by the celibate priests.

See www.rentapriest.com.

K: What is the Canon Law #843?

T: (See Google and type in "Canon Law 843") As you know, any statement by the pope is the infallible word of God and cannot be challenged. A long time ago, possibly centuries ago, (I have not nailed down the exact date) the pope declared that any individual who is once designated a priest (I am sure soon to be he or she) is morally bound for the individual's lifetime to provide religious services to any individual who requests religious services even if the priest drops out of the church, marries or becomes secular. Therefore, if an individual asks a person who was once a celibate priest, or one of the married protestant ministers who convert and become a Catholic priest, or an individual priest who had left the church to marry, that former priest is morally bound for life to provide the services requested, baptism, marriage, funeral, whatever. So even if you are not a Catholic, you can dial 1-800-PRIEST9 to procure religious services in almost any city in America by a CITI priest…soon this will be true in any large city in most of the world.

The married priests in the New England area perform second marriages, same sex unions, say authentic masses at health care facilities, private homes and rented meeting facilities. The papal hierarchy in Rome never had a problem with very much dissent in America until the post-WW-II founding of the United Americans, American Atheist Society, Skeptics Association, (Humanists established pre-war in 1941). Now the dissent is growing.

The CITI is a much more threatening organization than any of the other organizations because the married CITI practitioners are devout Catholics practicing the identical centuries-old Catholic rituals. There is no question the majority are supporters of women's right to choose, birth control, legal divorce, second marriages, sex education along with all ancient Catholic rituals. They make it clear to their followers that popes, priests, bishops and cardinals of the church were legally married until the pope in the year 1139 made the decision that all in the church's hierarchy had to be celibate. They teach the reason the pope made that decision was because celibacy would eliminate the problem of the priests leaving their property to their wives and children rather than to the Vatican. If the present rate of growth of married priests continues, there will probably be as many as 12,000 married male Catholic priests across America by the end of this decade. No doubt the construction or purchase of the first CITI organization's church is not too far into the future.

Kelle, do you think the Catholic hierarchy is concerned about this CITI organization? In 2006, the congregation of one of the small parishes that was to be closed for financial reasons caused by the more than $100 million settlement of the sex abuse cases in Boston advised the hierarchy they intended to hire a priest on their own from CITI. The next day the hierarchy announced they had found sufficient funds to keep the parish open.

K: You sure do come down hard on many religious leaders but you have to admit the fact the popes ruled the Western World for over 1,000 years after the fall of Rome with discipline equal to the discipline of the previous emperors.

T: True. But all you have to do to understand how the popes managed to maintain that iron fist dictatorship for over the thousand years of the Dark Ages is to refer to James I, Chapter 13-17 in the Gideon's Bible to get the answer to that question. The following is exactly as written:

"Obey those who rule over you, and be submissive, for they watch out for your souls, as those who must give account. Let them do so with joy and not with grief, for that would be unprofitable for you." Unprofitable, meaning we will burn your ass.

Plus the teaching of Psalms 14:1. That is: "The fool says in his heart, 'There is no god' they are corrupt, they do abominable deeds, there is none that does good." PERIOD. In other words, if you peons question any of the dogma that means you are one hell of bad person and for sure on your way to the furnaces in hell. Question: Where in the hell is hell? Illiterate persons during the Dark Ages never asked that question.

So the vast majority of the world's population—illiterate, uneducated, full of superstition, myth, fear and brainwashed from childhood—believed that the only way they could gain God's favors and find salvation in the after life was to obey without question the word of the pope. With this generation after generation of brainwashing maintaining loyalty and discipline was never a problem for the popes. The ancient popes' problems started with the arrival of the brave Martin Luther. The popes of the future will probably also remember the name of Mrs. Haggett and her CITI organization.

Kelle, does the pope really have a direct line of communications with his God?

Our famous American entertainer, Andy Rooney, has asked the following question:

"The Pope traditionally prays for peace every Easter and the fact that it has never had any effect whatsoever in preventing or ending a war never deters him. What goes through the Pope's mind about being rejected all the time? Does God have it in for him?"

Andy capitalizes the word "pope." I suggest Andy send a letter to the pope:

"Dear Pope, we and all of our dedicated and patriotic young men and women fighting and being terrorized by the nutty suicide bombers in Iraq, Afghanistan (maybe here in America someday) and other unilateral American police activity about the world are waiting breathlessly for your message next Easter. Don't be discouraged; remember the Indian rain dancers also often failed to bring about rain in their efforts too."

Spreading the Faith

What is it in the dogma of the Christian religion from about 75 ACE to 2006 ACE, (and continuing), whereby their cult absolutely insists that all persons in the world must believe as they believe? Until the establishment of the Christian religion the Jews and Pagan believers were comfortable living their lives with different beliefs. The hatred of all cultures and religious beliefs, (even of the different sects within Christianity), other than their own specific Christian sect's beliefs has been a fixture of this cult since the earliest days of their arrival in Rome. Unfortunately the Christian's hatred of other beliefs was adopted word for word by the new Muslim cult some 632 years after the establishment of Christianity.

Christian missionaries and priests have been invading all areas of the planet destroying other age-old cultures and religious beliefs since the first century. The Muslim, Jewish and Christian beliefs are all derived from the same one and only God declared by Pharaoh Akhenaton in the 18th Dynasty of Egypt. This hatred and killing of each other in the name of Akhenaton's "One and Only God" is the curse of the Western World. Until the arrival of the militant Christian religion, the many pagan believers and the Jews lived in peace with each other. Sometimes individuals would belong or support several different sects and pagan cults at the same time just to be sure. The following documentation from Isaiah 45:21-22 in the Christian Bible and the similar dogma the Muslims inserted into the Koran some 632 years later set the Western World off into the bloodiest and cruelest 1,400 years in the history of civilization. Millions of innocent humans have been tortured and slaughtered by misled brainwashed believers of their one and only six-day God. Here is the verse that set off the "Curse of the Western World."

ISAIAH 45:21-22

"And there is no other God besides Me...Look to Me and be saved...all of you to the ends of the earth.....For I am God and there is no other." P.S. My other name is "Allah."

Following the creed set forth in Isaiah 45:21-22, the Christian rulers set off to invade and conquer the world. They commenced invading and destroying all other cultures and beliefs on the planet. From Hawaii, to the smallest Pacific Islands, to the vast New World from the Mexican border to the southern tip of South America to many areas of Asia and Africa, the Christians have invaded, conquered, destroyed or attempted to destroy every non-Christian culture they have encountered. And the Christian/Muslim mutual hatred begun during the Crusades continues to this day. All in the name of the one and only god of the different sects, not only between Muslims and Christians, but also between the sects within each of them. Protestants, Catholics, Sunnis, Shiites, all killing each other over the centuries.

K: Many people are of the opinion the Christians dedicated efforts to spread their faith to all areas of the world is for the good of all. You sure have a much different opinion.

T:True. If you want just one example of the harm the missionaries and armies of the Christian empire have caused over the centuries, take a look at what happened in Hawaii. The Hawaiians had their own fictitious gods. A handful of righteous missionaries arrived in the mid-1800s, destroyed their culture, banned their use of their own centuries-old comfortable religion and stole all of their economic wealth. This is just one example of the thousands of similar invasions the Christians have made all over the world over the past 2000 years. Most of the invasions were bloody, cruel and carried out by a combination of Christian religious leaders backed by heavily armed armies. Let's review the mother of all invasions in the history of civilization: Rome!

The Sunday School Rome Stories

Let's discuss the stories we were told in Sunday school about the bad, sinful, sexy, wild Roman citizens who were severely punished by the Christian's God. In Sunday school, we learned how the Christian's angry God put an end to the great but very sinful Roman Empire because of their sinful parties and lifestyle.

So I had to do some Googling, locate some history books and read what credible historians say about the fall of the Roman Empire. The following is now my understanding of how the emperors were eliminated and the Roman Empire collapsed.

When the new militant Christian faith took root in Rome, they immediately declared that they answered only to a higher authority in heaven and not to all the dictates of the less important Roman emperors. Much like the born again types and followers of Jerry Falwell who feel they are right and the laws of our nation granting specific rights to gays, lesbians and women are wrong and sinful. Needless to say, the emperors were not pleased with these declarations and severely punished the offending Christians. History has proven the punishment, persecution and killing of citizens for their beliefs creates martyrs which in turn generates great energy in the flock. (The us against them scenario! The generation of hate). This action of the emperors created an outstanding opportunity for the leaders of the flock to recruit, solicit funds and expand the organization.

From the date of the arrival of Paul to the middle of the third century, the Christians continued to recruit and brainwash the mostly illiterate citizens of Rome.

In Rome, as in all other areas of the ancient Mediterranean world, the Christians had very little competition. The Jews were not that numerous and ignored the activity of the Christian recruiters. The pagan practitioners were no competition as they for the most part were selling only favors from the gods they represented for just a few token coins in the platter. The Christian recruiters had the greatest appealing and salable product mix that an illiterate superstitious peasant or slave could imagine. Once convinced they were born sinners and their sin for being born a sinner could be removed, then getting favors and day-to-day help for whatever they desired and finally to get to live with god when they died, many of the Roman citizens were easily recruited. By 375 ACE the militant Christians in Rome were numerous and actively attempting to take down the emperor. From the earliest days of the founding of the Christian empire they have rarely deviated from their SOP (standard operating procedure). Whether the goal is as small as the taking over a local school board in the year 2005 or the taking over of an empire in early history, they have stuck to the same SOP. That is to lay low until strong enough in numbers to walk, when stronger run, when strong enough, mount up, take over and rule with iron fist discipline. You will do as we order and believe or else.

By 400 ACE, the Roman Empire was in shambles with the disorder and strife within the empire between the militant Christian Romans and the non-Christian Romans fighting an internal war. Weakened Rome fell to the barbarians attacking from northern Europe. The Christians commenced recruiting the superstitious illiterate barbarians. When the Christians were finally strong enough to mount up and rule, the dictator popes took over the supervision of the Roman Empire and plunged the Western World into the most corrupt, cruel, bloody and dreadful 1000 plus years which historically are referred to as the Dark Ages. The popes of the Dark Ages were without question the cruelest dictators in the 10,000 years of known history of civilization. There is nothing in the known history of Babylonia, Greece, Egypt or any other ancient society to indicate that any of the ancient dictators were as cruel and ruthless as the popes of Rome who ruled during the Dark Ages.

K: Are you sure of your concept of the history and downfall of Rome?

T: I might be off a few decades or years one way or the other regarding how and when the Christians took over and eliminated the emperors and government of Rome. The winners write the history books and the Christian spin masters have accomplished a great whitewash about the true history of how the popes took over the Roman Empire. I am comfortable with my understanding of how the Roman emperors were eliminated and the popes took over. It's too bad we cannot get any true information on how the Roman rulers were wiped out by the Christians. Again, remember the victors write (spin) the history.

The Council of Nicaea

I would like to diverge from serious discussions and have some fun with my fictitious story about the 325 ACE Council of Nicaea of Christian leaders called by the Roman Emperor Constantine. Once I heard about the important conference, I went to Google and followed link after link, hour after hour seeking all the information I could find about this important ancient conference. The Christian leaders have maintained a policy of strict secrecy regarding the subjects and decisions arrived at in the conference. But historians have been able to pretty well determine why the conference was called by the Emperor and what was actually accomplished. Then I gathered all of my Google notes and decided to write a story in the same manner as the famous author, James A. Michener, wrote his great books. He would take the history of a nation, state or organization and then stick to the true history but insert fictitious characters which enhanced the story.

I was in my early 60s (about 1983-85) before I learned that it was not until 325 years after the approximate date of Jesus' birth (the popes have changed his date of birth and death several times to coincide with specific holidays adopted from the pagans), that some 318 leading Catholic fathers (now called bishops and cardinals) were ordered to meet on June 19, 325 ACE in the city of Nicaea in ancient Turkey. The conference was to be led and overseen by the powerful Roman Emperor Constantine. In the fourth decade of the century, Emperor Constantine was in a life and death struggle in civil conflict with his adversaries in the Roman Empire. He was in need of military help and was determined to bring in the rapidly growing powerful militant Roman Christians as his allies. Although this was the primary reason for his demand for the conference, the Christian fathers were also interested in a conference due to the turmoil over the status of Jesus in the church. Was he to be declared a great and important moral teacher or divine and the actual son of their one and only God? This determination was full of tension and bitter debate among the 318 church fathers, because Jesus was a Jew and to declare Jesus the son of their God meant they were declaring their one and only God was also a Jew. Imagine the tension, friction, arguing and gut wrenching discussions that took place in that conference! In a close vote, it was determined, once and for all, that Jesus would be declared divine and the son of their God. Since the church fathers are of course infallible, the subject could never be debated again in future years. This is actual Roman recorded history known to our 1776 forefathers, many of whom could read and speak both Latin and Greek.

(See Google: Search words, "Nicaea+Turkey" and follow the links to comparative religious documentation.)

Kelle, in recent years, I occasionally also imagine a literate society existing, rather than the 99%+ illiteracy at that time, and then apply a little 2006 ACE type of journalism. So: a little "playful" fiction here. Why not? The pope, cardinals, priests, Protestant ministers and TV psychics all love fiction!

We are, of course aware, that in the year 325 ACE, the vast number of people in the area of the former Roman empire were illiterate and lived their lives without traveling more than 15 miles or so from their place of birth. They had no source of information other than wandering story tellers. The common citizens had no access whatsoever to the ruling powers' proceedings or knowledge of political activities. But imagine how the proceedings of the all important Nicaea Conference of 325 ACE would have been received by a literate population if the citizens had the education and media exposure the citizens of the world have today. Let's imagine CNN was at work … imagine the state of affairs with modern media coverage. Remember, to this day, expert historians are still attempting to discover what really took place in this important secret conference...but...enough information has leaked out to give a very good indication of what really took place...so on to my imaginary CNN broadcast.

CNN REPORT: NICAEA, TURKEY JUNE 19, 325 ACE (9:15 p.m.)

Aaron Brown the First of CNN: "We now go to Ms. Kurse reporting from Nicaea, Turkey on today's events at the conclusion of Roman Emperor Constantine's mandatory conference attended by the ruling 318 fathers of the Christian Church. Go ahead Ms. Kurse:"

Ms. Kurse: "Dan, as you know, the conference with the mandatory attendance of the 318 fathers of the Christian Church, gathered from all over the empire, was demanded by Emperor Constantine to firm up his alliance with the militant Christians, to aid his loyal forces in the ongoing strife with the activist malcontent non-Christian forces attacking him in his vast Roman Empire. Gathering the news from the conference has been very difficult due to the demands and at the insistence of the church leaders, that all proceedings had to be conducted with the greatest security and secrecy imaginable. However, thanks to our friendly rival, Fox News, planting a bug in the conference center earlier this morning, we can share this taped portion of the proceedings with your viewers...whoops!...a little confusion here, as just a few minutes ago this lady protestor here on the sidewalk gave birth to a little girl...and they have named the little tyke Ms. Happenstance!...Anyway Dan, I'll read you this report from the bug information obtained by Fox News. Here are the comments typed from the taped recording:

'The Emperor made it clear, his number one priority in calling this conference for the church fathers was the firming up support for his forces, with an alliance with the rapidly growing militant Christian believers in his empire. The Christian fathers made it clear they also had many major problems of their own to solve during the conference. The Emperor obtained the assurance of the church fathers of their support early on in the conference, despite the many skeptical comments of several of the fathers, that they knew full well, the Emperor was not one of them, not a true believer, and was still a pagan worshiping the Sun God Atum. The Emperor denied these accusations and claimed he is one of them and deserving of their support. To get their support he had to convince them that he believed as they believe! He was well aware the fathers hold anyone who believes in any belief other than their own as an evil person. Once the Emperor got their support this matter was settled and the fathers then moved on to the issues of importance to them.

The Jesus thing has been a major point of contention among the church's flocks and among many of the church leaders for many decades. The fathers wanted to solve this issue here and now. One major obstacle to solving the problem is the fact that there is no single book of reference addressing the history, dogma and teachings of the church. There are almost as many different books as there are fathers of the church, with each having his own handwritten version of the faith's history and dogma. A committee of nine fathers in the conference submitted an agreed upon version they call the New Bible, which seemed acceptable to the majority. The problem with this solution of having an identical common book universally used by all fathers of the church, is the great cost of labor for a crew handwriting such a large number of identical books. This financial problem was solved by the Emperor when he declared he would personally finance the cost of creating 318 identical new books. It will be named "The True Bible." It was agreed that under no circumstances will anyone other than a church father or priest of the church be permitted to read any of the new books. It is to be declared a great sin for any person who is nothing more than a follower or believer to read the new book. A very serious sin! And an even greater sin, if a female should even touch any of the books.

The members of the conference then moved on to discuss the problems with the individuals of the empire recently adopting the Gnostic Gospels and the sinful pagan priests still practicing in the empire and the rumors of individuals in far away places tinkering with some kind of new religious documentation in the desert areas to the east. They voted and declared these situations and problems were to be laid aside for now and would be discussed and solved at some future date.

However, the church fathers stipulated and made it very clear they would never, ever accept or permit any faith other than their own to exist on this precious earth, created by their own one and only six day God. Obviously they were upset when the Emperor demanded the seventh day of rest and goof off time be named, 'SUNDAY', in honor of the sun and also that the day SUNDAY was to be used by the church for future meetings, collecting money from their flocks and teaching their dogma. This was considered rude of the Emperor by the church fathers as in the past all church meetings have been held on Saturday. And this request of the Emperor (actually a demand), of course made many of the fathers even more suspicious of the Emperor's attachment to the pagans' sun god. Several of the fathers made some very angry comments and attempted to recall the vote to be an ally of the Emperor but were voted down.

They finally consented to the Emperor's desire for the name of the seventh day of rest being SUNDAY when several of the fathers pointed out the fact the Emperor was doing them a great favor financing their new common and identical, 318 or so handwritten secret, (for only church fathers and priests to read), Bibles. Also, the word Sunday has a very nice ring to it when the word Sunday is a part of hymns and put to harp music. Once the conference got into the Jesus thing, the smelly stuff, (can I say those words on CNN TV news, Dan?), really hit the fan. There was near chaos during the debate in the conference room. The question of whether Jesus was divine and a true son of God, or a very moral and great teacher, has been a subject of great passion and friction in the church for over 300 years!

In past years, people (especially many innocent Jewish citizens), have been mauled and even killed in heated demonstrations addressing this subject. Following several hours of heated debate and riotous conduct of the attendees, the Emperor took the podium, demanded absolute silence and ordered the fathers to once and for all solve the problem with a secret vote. All 318 father attendees were given a small stone and ordered to walk up to two boxes, each with a small hole at the top of the box. No one could see which hole the individual father dropped his stone into, but all could hear if the stone was dropped into one of the two boxes. One box was for Jesus being divine, and one box if voting Jesus as a great inspirational and moral teacher. Many of the fathers were weeping and sobbing as they approached the boxes. The only sounds in the emotionally charged room on the tape was the sobbing and the sound of the dropping stones in the boxes.

Imagine the emotion of many of the fathers as they approached the boxes, knowing that Jesus was a Jew so their vote would also declare that his father, "their one and only God", was a Jew. At the completion of the voting, the stones were counted and Jesus was elected as the divine son of their Jewish God by a narrow margin. By a declaration of the majority of the fathers, the conference attendees declared the majority vote on all of the days proceedings, was to be considered the infallible and correct dogma of the church. Further, that none of the subjects acted upon in the conference were ever to be debated again. PERIOD! The fathers are to be considered infallible! The influential church father representing Rome was elected to gather together the notes and documentation of the day's conference proceedings, take them to Rome and deposit them in a permanent safe keeping secret chamber forever and ever in his headquarters.

CNN REPORT: CONSTANTINOPLE JUNE 19, 0425 ACE (9:15 p.m.)

Aaron Brown, the 5th of CNN: "We now go to Ms. Zacred in Constantinople who has been interviewing a very interesting lady celebrating her 100th birthday today. Go ahead Ms. Zacred."

"Hello Dan, I have Ms. Happenstance here with me. I am confident your viewers will find Ms. Happenstance a very interesting person and her life history of the past 100 years observing and living through the so many great events of the past 100 years a very interesting story. She is visiting here with her great granddaughter Mrs. Rene Latinus who is a crew person on the Roman trading boat Seafire.

"Ms. Happenstance, I understand you were born on the sidewalk outside the conference center in Nicaea 100 years ago today, while your mother was participating with a protestor group during the June 19, 325 ACE church fathers conference ordered by Emperor Constantine."

Ms. Happenstance: "That's indeed true Ms. Zacred, a very unusual happening for sure!"

Ms. Zacred: "Ms. Happenstance, you have surely lived through ten decades of some of the greatest events of history. I know our viewers would enjoy hearing what you have personally observed over these past 100 years of your life. Would you please tell us about some of the history you have observed?"

Ms. Happenstance: "I'll start off from my earliest memories as a child. I was orphaned at age 2; my mother had become pregnant again, and since she was not married she did not want to go through the same experience she had with me a second time. She tried to perform an abortion with a coat hanger and died a cruel, painful death. You know, once a teenage young lady makes a sexual mistake like having a child out of wedlock, no man in our Christian society will marry her and she is condemned to a life of poverty and disgrace. I was raised by kind and generous foster parents and spent my early life here in Constantinople, this great city developed by Emperor Constantine. Now I am just visiting with my great granddaughter, Rene, and will be returning to Rome next week, where I now live.

Unfortunately, once the great Emperor Constantine died, life became harsh and cruel under the new leaders of our Roman world. We call these times our "Dark Ages," because of the cruel and harsh treatment of women. Maybe the life of the citizens will improve in the future. Following the conference of June 19 in 325 AD, the church father who returned to Rome gradually became the most powerful of the fathers of our church, and finally begot the name of papa and later changed that name to pope, which all of the later Roman dictators have adopted to this day. The succession of popes who have taken over the empire since that time have made life unbearable for women. The leaders have decreed that the world is filled with evil and sin, because of the conflict between sexuality and spirituality. The fathers teach that women are the cause of the sinfulness of the population, because they are the cause of sexuality. The pope has declared that the woman Eve, of course, was responsible for the original sin. This means that men cannot be good Christians if they become involved with the enjoyment of sinful sex with women. The fathers of the church do not want God to punish them as he punished the Roman Empire leaders for the Roman rulers' sinful degrading lifestyle of parties with sex and drinking.

Until my brute husband died, I lived a life no different than the life of a slave. I had a kind and sincere neighbor boy friend, who I loved dearly but I was forced to marry this ugly older man because he had a large enticing bride price for my hand while my young friend was yet to acquire a career or savings. I, of course became a Christian, because it is now required to be a Christian in my part of the former Roman Empire. I would be persecuted, tortured or declared a witch and be killed if it was learned I do not believe the same as our infallible pope teaches. I...ah...ah...I am sorry I cannot continue, as I am so sad thinking about having to return to Rome and the horrible lifestyle we women endure....I must immediately return, as soon as my great granddaughter and the crew unloads this cargo and loads the goods on the wharf. She is just a member of the crew and treated no different than the slaves owned by her husband, who is the captain of the boat. As you know, a woman has no rights in our Christian society. We are just property of the men. Our only choices are to live the cruel life we are forced to live, catering to these brainwashed brutes, or commit suicide to get away from them. At my old age, my only happiness is the thought - it won't be long now until I get to return to where I belong in the great beyond. Maybe there will be a sense of fairness between the sexes in the great beyond. I dream about a new world like that."

Ms. Zacred: "I am so sorry about the situation, Ms. Happenstance. I wish you the best and like you, I do look forward to the possibility of some decent men in the future who may come forward and develop a more fair and pleasant lifestyle for all citizens in your part of the world. Take care and now I would like to have a few words with your great granddaughter."

"Ms. Rene, I would like to know if the lifestyle of women of your generation has improved since the era of your great grandmother, grandmother, and your mother's generations?"

Mrs. Rene Latinus: "Ms. Zacred, it is very important you do not let any of the crew or my husband learn what we discuss. With this assurance I want you to know the lives of the women of my generation is as dreadful as the women of my great grandmother's generation experienced, and in fact I think even worse than that of our parents and grandparents. Our great Roman Emperors are no more. Now the popes rule the empire. Since the power of the popes has increased, women's lives have become even more painful. There is no sign of the church fathers ever considering us as equals with the men. We are just property and told we are the originators of sin. They consider us so evil we are not permitted to even speak or represent our sex with the pope's God. We are nothing more than a piece of property in the eyes of the men. I have a secret wish that the war the pope is proposing (to destroy some people who do not believe the same as the pope in the eastern deserts) will require my husband to depart with the pope's Army. Then I can live a more decent life. I will be so pleased if he never returns. I was 14 years old when my father accepted a large bride price from this 52 year old nasty sea captain for my hand. Like my great grandmother, I too dream that I may some day depart this land and live in a new world with all citizens being equal, free to think, free to believe in whatever they wish, so long as they obey the laws of the nation and live free of these evil mores. I have had such nightmares since my beloved brother fled to the north following the tragic incident and gruesome slaughter of two of his football teammates last year. The two boys were discovered in an intimate situation in bed, and then killed by the church leaders in the usual method of punishment of gay men. They hung them upside down, with ropes tied to their ankles and then sawed them in half. To this day and every day of my life, I still see that terrible sight and remember their screams of pain. My brother shouted obscenities at the killers and was arrested and taken to the church. The following day my father went to see the priest and negotiated a large contribution to the pope's God to purchase "a forgiveness" from the priest for my brother's conduct, and to obtain his freedom. The next day my brother asked my father for one of his horses and then rode off to the north. All I have now is a letter from him that he is safe near the North Sea and not to worry about him. I will never get to see him again; my nightmares of the cruel deaths of his friends, and the screams of his friends and teammates being killed, still haunt me. When I attend church while the others are doing their prayers, I pray the great Roman Emperors will someday once again arise and take over Rome. Then, hopefully they can return Rome to the old days of the great Roman Empire. Or it may be, if we were to sail to the end of this world, our ships would drop off into a new world of our dreams of living with decent men! All we can do is dream."

Ms. Zacred: "Back to you Dan."

K: Well Tom, who knows, with a little practice you might become a writer.

T:At age 84, I doubt if I have the time to learn to be a writer. Besides, my dog Boris takes up so much of my time I would never get around to it.

My Prayer

Kelle, the Western World is in a very great need of a new, more peaceful God to take over! What do you think about a new rain dance type chant asking, "God, if you are really out there; please, let's get this situation taken care of!"

K: Well the chant, as you call it, is free so why not give it a try?

Kelle, as you know we were taught in Sunday school and in sermons as adults the Christian God is aware and in charge of all things on HIS tiny planet earth. Athletic and military units are blessed before action on the field of battle, God takes note of the activity of each of the billions of people's day to day activity, candles are lit to get God's attention in various times of chaos, danger or need of healing attention. The Christian God is aware of all things! Just like Santa Claus he keeps notes on the day to day activity of each of us. He sure as hell micro manages all events and activity on this planet. So he no doubt is very well aware of the contents of our conversation.

OK...So now I would like to speak directly to God, ask a few questions and relate my thoughts to what is going on in his kingdom. I cannot write a letter to God as I have done to Jerry, Pat and the boys in Rome as we do not have snail mail or e-mail capability to communicate with Him. But of course I can verbally address Him. Here goes:

Dear God,

For Christ's sake, why don't you do something about this dysfunctional family of the Western World meaning the Jewish/Christian/Islamic family of siblings you created who hate each other with such passion. We have had these sibling's followers killing each other for many (most) of the past centuries. We have the Christians killing the Jews and Muslims, Muslims killing the Christians and Jews, also within the sects the Protestants and Catholics killing each other and the Sunnis and Shiites killing each other. All these multi-millions of killings in your name in the Western World has resulted in our western portion of the planet thankfully not being so over-populated as the Far East nations of India and China. But these immeasurable killings are one hell of a price to pay for the luxury of living in a less crowded environment. Could it be you are a bit egotistical and enjoy these sacrificed lives in your name? Or were you so exhausted after working those six tough days establishing this tiny planet that you need some more rest before you do the work of correcting this problem?

If you are now old and too weary to do the job, you could turn the task over to your son Jesus as he exhibited great energy and ability in his short three decades of his life down here. In case you have forgotten, let me remind you that Jesus impressed all on earth with his deeds. Think about this; when your son Jesus was a child lying on Mary's lap beside his father Joe and then Mary said, "I would like some of the fruit on the top of the palm tree." Ole Joe said it was too high up to get the fruit. So Jesus as just a child spoke to the palm tree and the tree bent down so that Mary could pick off the pieces of fresh fruit. Then as a young adult, Jesus fed vast numbers of people with the multiplication of bread from nowhere, providing tons and tons of fish in the same manner, converted thousands of gallons of water to wine to please the multitudes, (and our Baptist ministers are still angry about Jesus providing sinful, evil liquor to the populace) raised dead people to enjoy life again, cured the handicapped and blind, even walked on water and instantly calmed great storms. I suggest you send Jesus back down here to straighten out this dysfunctional family. True, without these mass killings in your name we will eventually suffer the same over population problems of India and China but we can learn to cope with that much lesser evil.

Amen.

Kelle, do you think God may send me an answer via Pat Robertson when he and Pat have their next conversation?

K: Unless you stop riding Pat's butt, Pat is not going to communicate with you! Do you think new gods will be brought to life in this century?

T: I sure do think there will be self-appointed Gods reps popping up from time to time all over the world. But fortunately, because of greater worldwide literacy, modern global communications, increasingly better education, the Skeptics Society and Google they will be both short lived and garner very few believers. Here's what it takes to become a "God Rep" and a few of some of the more recent self-appointed ones.

New Religions

Fortunately, a new self-appointed representative of god, a newly initiated religion or split–off sect of an existing religion will not survive and grow unless most all of the necessary important facets of the venture are in play. In building, making, creating or developing any successful product, organization or career, the element of timing is very important. It has to be at the right place at the right time. In this and future centuries, increasing world-wide literacy and sources of information like Google will limit the number of believers which new self-appointed representatives of god will be capable of recruiting.

Depending on the nature of any type of venture, whether as small as baking a cake, or as large as building a house, establishing a business or creating an organization, the cook, builder or venturer has to have the right recipe or plans to bring the venture to a successful conclusion. The timing of the inclusion of the ingredients is very important. You can't put a roof on a house until the framing has been completed; and of course, the old axiom, to be in the right place at the right time, is a crucial ingredient for creating any kind of organization. Either by plan or luck, the right ingredients must come into play at the right time for a new religious venture to become a long lasting and successful organization.

The Christians were fortunate in coming into being at a time when the vast population in the Middle East was illiterate, extremely superstitious and brainwashed by all kinds of self-appointed psychics with supposed connections to some kind of supernatural power.

The following series of events and insertion of ingredients at the right time will determine whether a newly initiated religious sect will survive or become just a passing event:

(1)   Initiated by a charismatic individual capable of attracting attention with an appealing message or in some cases announcing a catastrophic ending of life on earth at a specific time.

(2)   The timing of the insertion of the important ingredients creating the undertaking is important. In some cases the timing of any one of the ingredients may be a little different than in other similar ventures.

(3)   The initiating person of the venture offers the acquisition of appealing products in an efficient manner. The Christians offered forgiveness of sins, favorable treatment by your maker and a happy afterlife living with your God. These are very appealing and emotional products to promote and sell.

(4)   Persecution of the venture by existing cultures. Persecution creates energy in the herd or flock with the scenario of us against them! Team enthusiasm! Citizen members of Christian churches provided the persecution of the Mormons in the 1800s. The Romans provided the persecution of the early Christians.

(5)   The creation of martyrs from the persecution. This ingredient generates great energy in the movement. The Romans' treatment of Christians is a good example of creating martyrs.

(6)   Marketing symbol. Just like a professional or college sports team, a marketable symbol is important to identify the followers and give them something to proudly display. The cross has become the favorite Christian symbol.

(7)   Leadership with a solid succession program to ensure that disciplined believers are available to replace the organization's leaders on their death or retirement. The story tellers that evolved some several decades after the death of Jesus luckily had all of the ingredients fall timely into place.

Americans have witnessed the initiation of thousands of religious cults and sects of every description in the last two centuries. Each and every day a few persons roll out of bed in America or return from a stroll at night having experienced a dream or hallucination of imagined contact with their God, an angel, or a messenger from God directing them to perform some act or commence some kind of religious or cult venture. Many born again Christians are criminals who have dreams after being locked up in isolation in prison for long periods of time.

Thousands of persons encounter some kind of emotional incident in America every day and become "born again" people. This may result in some of them simply living with the experience for a few days and then forgetting about the event. A few may end up on street corners and in public parks preaching the message delivered to them by the supernatural power or in rare cases starting a life-long dedication to establishing an organization to carry out the work which the God encounter directed them to carry out. Often they simply change their lifestyle without confiding in anyone.

Of the thousands of such incidents in the 1800s, only one cult has grown to a large worldwide organization, thanks to their possessing all of the necessary ingredients and the fortunate timing of events required to establish a lasting religious sect. This, of course, is the Mormon organization. The persecution and the creation of their martyrs was much different than in the time of Jesus since the Mormons had the freedom to believe in whatever they chose to believe thanks to their 1776 forefathers. They did suffer great persecution and had martyrs created through the hatred extended to them by the fanatic brainwashed followers of the mainstream American religious cults. The Mormons are the only surviving major sect of the thousands of religions initiated in the 1800s because they were the only sect to contain all of the necessary ingredients, all of which were added at the right time. As of 2006, it is obvious that no other cults and sects initiated in the 1900s are on their way to equal the success that the Mormons have achieved. This birth of a new sect occurred long before significant literacy in America and of course before massive nationwide communications of all kinds existed.

A brief review of just a few of the more successful newly initiated sects of the 1800s and 1900s follows:

Nation of Islam. In 1930, a black man in Detroit, Mr. Wallace Fard, rolled out of bed one morning following a prophetic vision. During his sleep, he had a meeting with either Allah or one of his messengers. In this vision, Wallace was directed to establish "The

Nation of Islam" for the black people of America. The sect flourished to some extent in his lifetime but the organization lacks all of the necessary ingredients to continue growing. The sect exists today, but is in a declining mode.

The **ISKCON, Hare Krishna** sect. Established in New York City in 1966 by a man of the Hindu faith, it reached its peak in the 1970s and has been in rapid decline since that time. All the ingredients are not in place for long term growth.

The **Transcendental Meditation (TM),** an "exercise-spiritual" like movement was introduced to America by Maharishi Mahesh Yogi in 1959 and still attracts followers, many of whom are also religious believers. Although TM is non-religious, participants experience a "spiritual feeling" similar to what Dr. Goldschmidt teaches at UCLA. There are many practitioners promoting and conducting "paid" sessions. So long as entrepreneurs are earning income and developing a career from such sessions, TM will experience growth and success. Hopefully other similar "spiritual like" movements will develop in the future rather than the offbeat religious cult type sects that are hostile to the judicial branch of our American government.

Santeria. This faith began to root in the USA shortly after the Cuban revolution in 1959. The sect first became noticeable in New York City among some of the many Afro-Cubans and Puerto Ricans who immigrated to America. The faith is considered to be a hybrid religion combination of ancient African and Catholic beliefs and spirits. The movement lacks appeal to the majority of Americans, is limited to just a portion of the total American population, and lacks most of the necessary ingredients to become a mainstream sect in America.

Scientology. This sect founded by L. Ron Hubbard emerged in the 1900s as an attempt to combine the scientific findings of the last two centuries with the Christian faith. In my humble opinion after studying his faith on the many links on Google, the reason many of its participants belong is to combat the onslaught of scientific discoveries in the last century, all of which are the deadly enemies of the Christian faith. In the past, the Christian leaders have used the Bible to explain any event good or bad, prove or disprove any argument, cause of an incident or subject based on unquestioned faith. However, in the 1900s the populations of the first world nations (including America) have become so literate and well educated that the fiction of the ancient storytellers' tales and the fictitious stories in the Bible were no longer holding the believers to the faith. This Scientology sect, which reached its peak in the late 1900s is still attracting followers, but will probably disappear in this century as it lacks most of the essential ingredients for the organization to grow and prosper. They have desperately worked on the idea of creating the impression that the individuals who have made great scientific discoveries debunking the fiction of the Christians, were in fact learning God's work. L. Ron Hubbard made a great fortune with his organization (he sold millions of his books and generated hefty fees in his speaking tours). Since his passing from the scene, Scientology will no doubt join the junk pile of past religions described by Professor Carl Van Doren (see p. 291).

A person could write a wide-ranging book addressing the thousands of new faiths and cults initiated over the past two centuries. I'm limiting my list to just a few.

Here are a few more faiths and beliefs initiated since 1800:

Ms. Mary Baker Eddy fell on an icy pavement in 1866 and was severely injured. When she came to and recovered she was convinced God had taken care of her recovery and later created the **Christian Scientists** organization in 1875. They have established reading rooms in many cities. Often times the parents who practice this belief end up in court for depriving their desperately ill children of much needed medical attention.

The Children of God: This sect, established in Huntington Beach, CA. in 1968, is pornography-tolerant, promotes free love and wife swapping among other offbeat (but maybe enjoyable) ideas.

Many newly initiated faiths are based on predicted apocalypse and Armageddon disasters for mankind. When they fail to occur on schedule, the new cult usually fades away. An exception to this failure is the **Seventh Day Adventists** faith which was initiated in the early 1800s based on the prediction that the apocalypse would occur in 1843. Many left the faith when it did not occur on schedule, but the faith has continued.

Some sects ended tragically such as the group in San Diego which committed group suicide to fly out and ride the passing comet; the Jones group that originated in San Francisco and committed mass suicide after moving to Guiana, South America; and the Dividians who along with innocent children died in the sad Texas confrontation with the government authorities. All tragedies in the name of some fictitious God.

Kelle, few of these inventors of new religions probably ever heard of the genius writer and philosopher Voltaire (1694-1778) but they had a similar idea to what Voltaire stated,

"If God did not exist, it would be necessary for us to invent Him."

I have listed just a few of the newly formed faiths. If you have interest in the subject go to Google and search for Faiths, Apocalypse or Armageddon. Hopefully you will not become a member of any of these faiths or cults!

K: What does it take to start a new religion?

T: You have to take advantage of people's herding instincts. Here are my thoughts.

Herding and God's Reps

MY EGOTISTICAL STATEMENT

All of the information about the herding concept was taken from thoughts I came up with while walking and pondering with my dog Boris late one night around our marina. I have always wondered why no matter how remote a village or society is, that they had a god and a god's representative. He may be the son, close relative, descendent or whatever, but he would for sure be the representative of God to that society. The society could be found on a remote island, in the deepest jungle of Brazil or in a remote hidden valley in New Guinea with none of them ever having had communication with the outside world. But without a single known exception they would have a god and the god's representative in their society. In less than an hour of pondering this scenario with my dog Boris, I came up with our theory "Herding and God's Reps." As soon as we arrived home I sat down and wrote out exactly what Boris and I had pondered. Boris is my only witness.

So I came up with the answer to a question I have struggled with for many years; "Why is it, that no matter how remote or primitive a human society that discoverers have ever come across, the discovered society would have a god and the god's rep in their midst?" More often than not, a god and rep would be very similar to the gods and reps of the known so-called civilized societies. Also the God's reps would govern the society.

To discuss God's reps, first we need to address animals. Perhaps you agree with me that we are the ultimate, most intelligent and most sophisticated animal on the planet. And we are an animal! Maybe you also believe that we are related to all the other living animals possessing the same four letter DNA code of life as all forms of animal life on earth.

The human animal has inherited all of the best and most unique survival characteristics inherent in the animals from which the human has descended.

We are so closely related to pigs that scientists are now raising a type of pig that has organs suitable for transplant into human beings. Scientists are having a tough time with the religious fundamentalists in the US in 2006 with stem cell research programs. Although they are not harmed by these fanatics, they do face considerable criticism from cult-promoted and sponsored politicians. Because of this, America may fall behind the other nations in this field. Christian leaders hate these endeavors.

Other than the rare predator animals such as the Bengal tiger and similar top of the food chain reclusive types of predators, all flocks, herds, packs, groups of animal species survive and successfully propagate by use of the stance of the herd leadership and discipline of the group. Unless most species of animals develop such a herding behavior and so-called "pecking order," the species will become extinct. The human animal is no different from the other warm blooded animals. The behavior and instinct genes are passed on from an earlier primitive animal to the succeeding more adaptable animal with the evolutionary progression of the animals. The herding instinct was/is all important in the evolutionary maturing of the modern human from the earlier primitive hominoids.

Herding Examples

Place a dozen of unrelated chickens that have not seen each other before into a coop and in a relatively short time a leader and pecking order will be developed. The leader will normally be the biggest and strongest rooster. He will rule the roost, mate with the hens and produce strong and healthy chicks. In case of danger, the chickens rally around their herd leader. The pecking order will maintain discipline in the flock when confronting danger. The rooster is the herd (pack, flock) leader. In a very short time each of the chickens will know its position in the pecking order of the flock.

Put a dozen or so horses in a pasture consisting of several stallions and mares who have not seen each other before and the same situation will occur. The strongest and biggest stallion will take the herd leadership position in a matter of hours or days. He will mate, protect the herd and keep any lesser endowed stallions in their inferior position. In any dangerous situation the herd leader will be in charge.

Watch any of the nature films on PBS and you will note the same type of activity with all packs, flocks, herds and groups of animals. Humans have inherited these same survival characteristics from their predecessor animals in the evolutionary process over countless millions of years.

How is the herd leader chosen and how does pecking order and discipline come about? Depending on the type of animal, the leadership position goes to the biggest and strongest, sometimes the animal with the unique and appealing or loudest call, the most impressive color or gorgeous impressive feathers as in peacocks or simply the most aggressive and strongest animal in the group. The group leader then has the pick of the females; the species produces the strongest and best endowed offspring. All of this inherited herding instinct is very important for the survival of the species. The leader of the pack, herd, or flock will also be the one the others look to when danger from any event or from any other species occurs.

The discipline of the pecking order with a herd leader will dictate how the animals will perform to support the leader in time of danger and sometimes in the allocation of food and shelter to the group. With rare exceptions, every successful animal species will produce a herd leader and pecking order or the species will become extinct.

In the earliest periods of hominoid development, the strongest and biggest human animal no doubt took the leadership position in much the same manner as the biggest and strongest stallion or bull takes control of a herd. The biggest and strongest cave man would be the herd leader. Why on earth would he permit a lesser endowed member of the pack be the leader?

As the hominoid species continued to evolve from the earliest primitive hominoids, the efficient grip of the hand with the four fingers and a thumb caused the brain of that specific species of hominoid to gradually grow to become much more important in the selection of the leadership of the herd than the size, looks, or strength. Especially so following the development of speech and writing in the species. Thus, unlike all other animals of the planet, the brain in the human animal became all important in the selection of the herd leadership. Of course the combination of the imaginative and creative brain combined with looks, strength, creativity, imagination, verbal ability, personal charisma, leadership ability, drive, and ambition of the individual were also very important in the selection of the herd leader of the modern human animal societies.

Once the homosapien had finally reached the status of the ultimate animal on earth, with the ability to write and verbally communicate, a person with a large brain coupled with the use of imagination, creativity, ambition, and personal charisma could overwhelm the biggest and physically strongest of the clan. Such an individual, even of small stature, could (and has in the past and will continue to do so in the future), attract a gathering of admirers and followers, (called groupies in present day entertainment and athletic circles; disciples in other circles), which he/she can use to gain influence and the leadership position of the community.

There are various scenarios on how such an individual of the human animal species can, and has, become such a herd leader of a clan, group, village, cult or nation without being driven away by the physically stronger individuals. An ambitious human, especially in the earlier illiterate world, with a believable, concocted, pretended, invented, fictional or in some cases personally imagined or dreamed connection to a supernatural power or god, normally became the most powerful person in the tribe if he, (most always a he), could convince a gathering of groupies he had a connection, communication or relationship with a superpower in the heavens, a god on the top of a far away mountain or some other location none of the other herd or clan members in the herd could reach.

Here are just a few examples:

1.   A person comes down from a stroll in the mountains with a tale of speaking to a god who was masquerading as a burning bush. I believe the man was carrying a stone with some writing on it, a hammer and a chisel when he told his story. BELIEV-ABLE? No one else in the tribe has such a super God relationship. Usually this becomes a story only after many decades or centuries have passed so that the story teller cannot be proven wrong. These story tellers can, and then did, become the agents of that long ago individual, because they have the story. They, just among themselves, would normally select one of their own as the herd leader. They became the supreme power's disciples, teachers, or priests creating careers for themselves in the name of their related association with the current or past icon related to the supreme power, as the herd leaders or pronouncing the supreme powers wish for them to designate someone anointed by them as the herd leader. They then take on the task of teaching the herd members that their responsibilities are to conform and comply with the god agent's instructions and orders so as not to be punished.

2.   An illiterate individual known to have problems with epileptic fits returns

from a stroll in a New York forest with a tale of reading messages from God on golden plates. Illiterate and epileptic but nevertheless he has the charisma to be capable of developing a group of believers who will go on to create a following of believers to grow a cult. Like the stallion or bull uses strength to become the leader, the human uses his imagination, proclaiming his relationship with and/or communication with the supernatural or a God to become the herd leader. Awakening from a fit or dream he may truly believe the story himself.

3.   A camel herder returns from a trip in the desert under a hot sun with a story of speaking with messengers from God and is able to attract a group of believers and groupies.

4.   A few so-called, self-appointed "wise men" locate a newborn baby and declare him the son of God. Or in the case of Tibet, in this day and age they locate a baby and declare him the new representative of God when the current Dalai Lama dies.

In examples 1, 2, and 3 we have to give thought to the fact that all of these individuals were alone, there is never a witness. We have to consider the fact that many humans are subject to delusions, hallucinations, visions, realistic dreams, and many are subject to schizophrenia. Many individuals are very motivated in seeking attention, leadership positions, income and glory. The all important facet when it has to do with religion is, it is almost always a male and always a loner. When a few self-appointed wise men decide a newborn baby is the son of a god (always a male of course) or a representative of a god, who appointed these individuals to have the authority to make that decision? Who designated them as "wise men?"

One of the most important aspects of this scenario is that the story of the person is circulated by an individual or individuals (believers, disciples, story tellers) many years or decades later and also that these story telling persons may be persons with the same goals of leadership (disciples/priests) as the icon of their stories in setting themselves up as the reps of the supernaturally connected individual, seeking a career, status and income.

We see many persons with these ambitions or delusions often standing on boxes and sometimes with a bullhorn in our public parks and on street corners today. They may be innocent of any attempt to deceive and sincerely believe in their story; or they may be seeking attention, herd leadership, career, income or personal glory.

There has never been a witness of God or one of his/her messengers speaking to any person on earth in the 3,500 years of the history of civilization. You either believe or do not believe the story of the lone individual who relates his lonely exciting experience with the supernatural.

The only example I have personally witnessed of an individual making claim to holding personal meetings with God was when I was living in Taiwan off and on in the

1980s and 90s and observed self-elected priests and priestesses doing business from their store front locations. They used self-hypnosis to assist them in their trips to and from heaven to visit with God after collecting a handful of requests from their followers in written notes. First the priest or priestess would stroll among the congregation collecting notes from the members written on paper scrolls that the individual members of the congregation had of course purchased (the selling of religion is a very profitable business) at the entrance of the meeting room. God's rep would then place the gathered colorful scrolls in a pouch on their chest and sit on a chair-like throne and hypnotize themselves. The god's rep would experience much shaking and quivering as he/she made his/her trip up to heaven for the meeting. The rep would then appear almost lifeless lying back in the chair for about eight to ten minutes. Then the God's rep would begin to recover while experiencing more shaking and quivering, and when completely recovered from the trip, the rep would take out the scrolls and commence reading God's answer to the individual congregation member's requests. I attended many of these sessions in Taiwan as, Charlie, my Taiwan business associate's wife was a priestess. Privately, Charlie advised me she was full of you know what but nevertheless he occasionally collected the money selling the colorful paper scrolls at the door. Apparently God is not much of a writer because I occasionally would look over her shoulder after her return from the trip as she read God's response to the believers and never saw any writing on them other than the message of the sending believer. Of course the writing and conversations were all in Chinese and I am not able to either write or speak the language. It may be God writes in an invisible ink so that non-believers can't read his reply. She must have had special powers to read the reply from God to each of the believers' requests. Or maybe she had a great memory so that she could remember God's verbal reply to each of the several dozen requests. This hypnotic travel by God's reps to and from the meeting with God was a thriving business when I lived in Taiwan in the 1980s and 90s.

I understand American TV Bible thumper Pat Robertson holds his conferences with God without the use of self hypnotism or traveling to and from heaven. Having God come to him rather than Pat going to visit God is pretty impressive.

The number 4 scenario above (of a company or a group of individuals) is a very common, age-old approach practiced to this day in creating an icon to promote a personal career, a company PR business, a representative and on-going association of the icon or financial return for the efforts. If an individual is involved, this is true of themselves, or if a company, their company, their cult or their entertainment business. In this mode of operation, you do not promote yourself or your entity such as a public relations firm or political action group. You and your entity get your return for yourself or your firm by being the person, company, cult or business that will get the benefit of association with the icon, idol or person (sometimes a baby) being promoted. You become the "rep" of the icon individual. A "spin master" may be paid for the effort or gain a beneficial association with the promoted icon. In today's society, promoting an individual, a politician, a CEO, an actor, event, religious icon, or a cause is usually accomplished by a PR firm earning money. A good example is how Rockefeller paid spin masters a vast sum of money in the early 1900s to spin stories to counter his ruthless business reputation and promote him as a great and compassionate business leader.

In a similar scenario in ancient times, the storytellers had to have a good story to earn their keep and welcome when they traveled from village to village. Over a period of years they could not entertain and earn their keep with the same story, year after year. They often picked some icon individual dead for some years, decades, or distant time to build stories around the subject and by implication, their association with the icon. In an illiterate community where by 99+% of the inhabitants were born, lived and died without ever traveling much more than 15 miles or so from their place of birth, and with no type of mass communication whatsoever, it was a simple step-up for many of the story tellers to insinuate their personal association in one form or another with the icon of their stories.

Jesus was one of many persons accused of a crime deserving of the death penalty by the Roman leaders and who was killed in the normal Roman method of carrying out a death sentence. The cruel nailing of a convicted person to a cross was nothing new for the Romans at that time. The stories about Jesus, his disciples, and last supper commenced many decades after his death by self-appointed storytellers, some of whom adopted the position as his agents on earth. Many of these people made their entire careers out of spreading the stories as his representative (disciple). Historians have noted that long before, and at the time of Jesus' birth, the known Mediterranean world had countless numbers of male individuals circulating among the populations representing that they were related to or the agent of supernatural powers, pagan gods or the long awaited son of the Jewish God. (Why wasn't it a Jewish daughter? But of course, men wrote the stories.) The Jews at that time were eagerly looking forward to the arrival of the son of their God. Credible historians have noted that the stories of the wise men and the booked up inn with no rooms available were originated and circulated many decades after Jesus died.

The attendees of the storytellers' meetings either believed the stories or did not believe them, but there was no way to prove or disprove the stories. The Jews did not believe the story that Jesus was the son of their one and only God, just as the earlier Egyptians would not accept Pharaoh Akhenaton as the son of the Sun God.

In the later years, many decades after Jesus' death, the storytellers' tales of Jesus walking on water, curing people by touching them, providing vast amounts of nourishment from a hand-held pitcher to multitudes of people without refilling it, calming storms and then his body raising up and going out into space without the use of a rocket are all tales of fiction were not much different from some of the preachers curing people that Francy and I had witnessed in the revival tent shows in the early 1930s.

If Jesus actually rose from the dead and was out there in space, then Hubble or his namesake the Hubble Space Telescope of today would have already located him. Since the Hubble Space Telescope can see a tiny spec of the universe billions of light years away, it sure as hell could spot a man and his parents, (there must also be a mother), circling this tiny planet just a matter of a few millions miles distant.

The other take on this phenomenon of creating an icon or idol for the good of your career is to be involved in the selection of a future religious leader like the wise men of Tibet who will select a newborn baby to be the next representative of God when the current Dalai Lama dies. This is not just a modern story as it is known this has been an ongoing theme in all of our 3,500 years of recorded history. The phenomena and procedures were first initiated in ancient Egyptian stories and are even related to the story of the Roman pagan priest's stories about the wolves raising a baby. Of course once the baby is selected the persons (say a group of self-appointed wise men) making the selection will most certainly expect to be the groupies of the child as he grows to an adult. The story teller's stories of Jesus and the manger in a barn, the booked up inn, the wise men following the bright star were neither original ideas of the time or much different from other stories of that time or of the very similar stories that had been originated in ancient Egypt hundreds of years earlier. Some stories had a baby drifting down the Nile River in a basket which was a much more exciting childhood story taught to me in Sunday school.

In summary, first it was the strength and power of a male which would determine who would lead the clan or a tribe of homosapiens in the same manner as in all other animal species. Then the evolutionary development of the super homosapien brain made the strength of the most powerful male less important compared to an individual with an imagined or concocted connection to a supernatural power. An individual with the ability to create the impression of having a supernatural connection either as a result of being the offspring of a leader who had that God connection (example being the Emperor of Japan) or from a believed or concocted encounter with God, one of his angels, messengers or reading sacred tablets became the basis and most important determining factor to become a leader (herd leader) of a homosapien group.

Since the 1776 forefathers founded this great secular (so far) nation, the herd leaders have been selected by the flock based on their motivation, charisma, speaking ability, leadership abilities, the PR spin masters' ability to create background stories and raise lots of money to win the office of the presidency and to be the herd leader for at least 4 years.

The problem with religious theocracy control of a society develops many years later when the original leaders have passed away (such as the disciples who followed Jesus) and are replaced by those who claim to rule in the name of the original leader(s). They are of course mostly interested in their own personal ambition. They pose in his name as disciples, clerics, priests, popes, selected God's reps of some kind. Sometimes they are related to the long gone individual through a dream of the former leader speaking to them, or messengers contacting them, or of his father speaking to them or any number of other similar stories to justify their relationship with the God. Once they gain this stature, (this is true in many cults, not just in the Christian cult) they gain the ability to rule as they see fit.

Unfortunately, and unlike the pagan cult leaders they replaced, the Christian cult leaders introduced their new militant concepts that if you do not believe as we believe in our one and only God, we will punish or kill you in the name of our God. Plus, it is our God's mission for us to invade other nations and cultures all over the planet and convert all believers of other faiths in the world to accept our God. Our God and our beliefs are superior to all other cultures and beliefs on earth (see Isaiah 45: 21, 22). And you damned well better believe as we believe. Period.

More unfortunate is the fact the Muslims not only copied and adopted much of the Christian's militancy agenda 600 years after Jesus' death but unlike the Christians, they have never lost control and have not become more moderate in their actions. There has never been a person similar to Martin Luther in the Muslim world. In America, the Christians' punishment of a free-thinking individual of any kind is limited to name calling, legal restrictions of non-believers holding public office in some states, career limitations, talk show insults, and restricting people from holding positions in many fields of education and various social groups. The ultimate cruel dictator leadership of killing non-believers or those who commit sinful acts, such as burying a women up to her neck in sand and stoning her to death for committing adultery and cutting off the right hand as punishment for a minor theft, is still very much alive in Muslim-controlled nations.

It is important to review the facets, ingredients, timing, developing of an icon (the originator) in the initiation of a cult or religion. How does it come about? Many believe the following is a common sense answer to the question of how new religions and cults are initiated (very much the same as in the thousands of years when cults and religions were initiated in the ancient Egyptian era).

In the human animal species now and for thousands of years in the past, each and every day multitudes of individuals commence working on an entrepreneurial venture to establish a business, a career, or to obtain the prestigious position of herd leader. Most of the ventures involve business but many are related to religion, entertaining and acting. The instigator of a religious venture may very well be a dedicated believer who has been motivated by a dream directing him to do so, hallucinations, or in many cases simply a strong motivation to create a financially rewarding career in the religious, entertainment or acting business. A significant number of these individuals are simply reacting to the instinct of most all warm blooded animals, the herding instinct, of seeking to be the herd leader or at least having a good position in the herd's hierarchy.

Quick Summary of the Herding Instinct

Scientists studying the human brain have learned that as any species evolved throughout many millions of years that the characteristics and traits of the lower level of the animal are inherited in the brain of the evolving animal. Therefore many of the instincts of the ultimate present day human are related and similar to the traits and characteristics of the ancestors of his species. This includes what I call the herding instinct.

K: Tom, I find your and Boris's "herding instinct" theory very interesting. Have you ever sought the advice of professionals in the field of genetics to learn their opinion of your "herding instinct" theory?

T: No. I wouldn't know where to find such a person and I am content to feel that I have finally found the answer for myself as to why no matter where there is a society of humans, regardless of how remote or separated from civilization, you will find the society has a god and a god-related individual in the society. Also that the religion of that god would be used to control and govern the society.

This control and governing a herd is the same scenario as our lesser-endowed animal species seeking a leader for the safety and discipline of the herd, flock or whatever. Kelle, I would like to tell you my "sheep story" as related to my "herding instinct" story.

K: OK, is it as interesting as the "herding instinct" story?

T: I think you will find it both believable and interesting. Here we go.

First, it is well known since the arrival of the super animal, the human genus, this animal has had the aptitude and talent to accomplish changes in the species of other lesser endowed animals in a matter of just a minimum number of generations as compared to nature requiring millions and millions of years as discovered by Charles Darwin for a species to change through natural selection.

So let's compare my sheep story to what has occurred in the human species over the past 2,000 years.

Of course everyone is aware of how the humans have developed all kinds of dogs in color, size, temperament and specific traits to assist humans accomplishing various work effort, pleasure and tasks. The humans have also domesticated sheep and bred sheep with reference to producing better wool, milk and meat. Scientists have proven that over the many thousands of years the humans have been breeding the domesticated sheep in the qualities and persona they desired they were also unknowingly breeding the sheep with brains that were no longer as large or as street (surviving in the wild) smart as the original wild moufflon ovis sheep living in the wild of south west Asia who were their ancestors. The domesticated sheep accepted the human "shepherd" as their leader to find food, shelter and protection from predators. With the shepherd's leadership they no longer had to think about the perils of surviving free in the wild. Now let's relate this to the human animal.

Historians have written countless volumes of history books about the fantastic engineering undertakings, legal citations (example the invention of legal condominiums democratic rule and judicial documentation), military endeavors and advanced civilization endeavors of the Roman Empire under the leadership of the emperors

Then Christianity arrived in Rome. The leaders of the Christians eventually overcame and replaced the emperors in about 400 ACE and the popes took over the leadership of the known western world. In the next 1,000 years of the Dark Ages, one generation after another generation of humans for the entire evil thousand years of the Dark Ages lived in the same squalor, poverty and corruption as the generations before them. The fantastic inventions comings and goings accomplishments of the former Roman Empire under the leadership of the emperors had come to an end. For hundreds of years, the people of the entire western world suffered through the Dark Ages with the pope as their "shepherd" proclaiming they were born sinners and that the popes could overcome their sin if they did as he dictated, supposedly received help from his God if they prayed to him and a great afterlife with his God if they did not detour from the popes dictates. During these 1,000 years civilization pretty much stood still as compared to the accomplishments of the Roman Empire before the emperors were taken down in the fourth century ACE.

Then once Martin Luther took the first steps that broke the iron grip of Rome over the western world, in less than a century the free northern nations of Europe broke free of the Dark Ages and commenced the great scientific discoveries and steps toward democracy that followed. Kelle, do you also see a parallel of the sheep story with this human story?

K: This is very interesting and I am going to have to do some study and research on my own to see how these two stories correlate.

T: OK, I hope you will give me a summary of your thoughts at the end of our conversation for your book. Now on to a new subject: while most of our citizens are concerned about our enemies outside our borders, as you have observed in our conversations, I am more concerned about the enemies within our borders attacking our form of government. Now I would like to again address the danger to America regarding the activities of those who I consider a great danger to the future of America.

Be Aware: Christian Fanatics Bide Their Time

AGAIN & AGAIN, BE AWARE; READ IT AGAIN!

I have no monetary motivation to write this memoir at my age. I would be so pleased to have the opportunity to go eyeball to eyeball in debates with the likes of the TV Bible thumpers and similar types who are attempting to change the American government to a theocracy dominated government.

I feel it is my patriotic duty to bring to the attention of the younger, next generation what I know to be the truth about organized fictitious man-made religions and cults. I have no reason to believe there is or is not a supernatural entity; I can only hope SHE is out there.

Trust the work effort of your 1776 forefathers. If a person lives a life in accordance with the American Constitution, Bill of Rights, and the laws of America's Supreme Court, that person will be a credit to the human race.

Again, always remember: Christian fanatics bide their time. Counseled by their leaders, they are very patient in working their centuries-old strategy to take control of any sized opponent, whether it is as small as a village, a local school board, a city council, or as large as a state legislature or the federal government. Their strategy is based on laying low and being low key until strong enough to go public, then stand and be noticed. When strong enough, walk; a little stronger, run; when strong enough, mount up, take over and rule with an iron fist. Once they have the power, "You will believe as we believe or else!" PERIOD.

Christians worked this strategy for approximately 400 years before they were able to bring down the Roman Empire. They replaced the emperors with the dictator popes and then plunged the Western World into the over 1000 years of the terrible bloody Dark Ages. With the use of this centuries old, standard Christian strategy of patiently laying low until strong enough to take over the coalition of Protestant and Catholic cults in the last decade in the United States have successfully taken over school boards in California, Texas and several other states. Once they had control of the boards, they immediately set in motion to change the school curriculum whereby the teaching of evolution was downplayed and replaced with teaching of the creationist theory. They removed many science books from the school libraries and harassed any public school teachers who failed to follow their directives.

In the 1800s, just two decades after the death of the last 1776 forefather, they were able to commence getting the state legislators and the governors to sign into law that no one in that state could run for or hold a political office unless he was a Christian believer; many of the states still have this law in force. Meaning, as of today, if alive, many of our 1776 forefathers would not be eligible to run or hold office in these states.

In past centuries they promoted their priests and ministers to be the actual hands-on leaders of any agency, nation or legal body they sought to control. In modern times they have modified their strategy and now use the subtle approach of selecting specific political public figures; believers who they then promote and finance into office. Without being aware of what is going on the top 1% of the wealthy Americans (one third of the wealth of America is in the hands of the top 1% of wealthy persons) who have their own agenda seeking tax benefits and corporate welfare are helping the hard core evil coalition leaders to accomplish their agenda by financially supporting the candidates the coalition selects.

America is as vulnerable now as the Roman Empire was in the second, third and fourth centuries (100 to 400). In America, the attack on the 1776 forefathers "wall of separation of state and religion" commenced just a decade or so following the death of the last of the 1776 forefathers (in 1830 ACE). As they have grown stronger, they have intensified their attacks. The Christian's first major "crack in the wall victory" was the successful accomplishment of printing "In God We Trust," on our currency in the 1860s. As Alan Sears, president of the ADF, (one of the most powerful entities of the religious coalition preaches), "We have removed many of the bricks of the wall and will continue to remove many more of them as the years go by."

They have been pounding on the wall to force the public schools to teach their version of theocracy religious government in the classrooms for over 150 years. Their controlled politicians' new tactic in fighting to brainwash the young is to promote the use of taxpayer funds, financing vouchers to support religious and ethnic schools of all types. They know, just as the tobacco companies know, that to grow their agenda they have to capture the minds of the young before they mature to an age of mature thinking.

Following our victory in WW-II, they were able to have the words,"Under God," inserted into the pledge of allegiance. In recent decades there have been many instances of their attempts to place religious symbols and sculptures in our civic buildings and in our educational facilities, from elementary schools to universities. Only education of our young people can defeat them and support the goals of our 1776 forefathers. History has shown that in every nation, where the education of the citizens improves, the power of the fictitious man-made organized religions and cults significantly decreases.

In America's first census more than two hundred years ago, only 11% of the population reported a significant relationship with an organized religion. The population was then greatly influenced by the actions of the 1776 forefathers (based on statistics maintained by the Smithsonian Institute in Washington, D.C.). The religious fanatics didn't dare attack the wall of separation of state and religion until the last of the 1776 forefathers had died.

In a worldwide poll taken just a few years ago, France reported 14% to the same question regarding religious affiliation. I wonder if Muslims living in France were polled? No nation in northern Europe reported a percentage as large as 30%. The United States of America was the only nation of the world's so-called first world nations, with the population reporting over 50%. The only nations in the world reporting in excess of 85% were illiterate third world nations.

We must promote secular education based on proven facts, science and the 1776 forefathers' provisions of freedom; including the freedom to believe or not to believe in whatever you care to! Just live and obey the laws of the nation.

K: Are you pessimistic about the future welfare of America as related to what you consider the threat of the Christian fanatics?

T:Not in the long run, Kelle. I believe the rise and growth of the fanatic Christian Coalition Movement commencing in the early 1980s reached its peak in 2004 and is beginning to turn down in the last two years. I see a similar situation to what I witnessed in the 1930s when the Christian Temperance Union (CTU) which had commenced growing in strength in 1918 at the end of WW-I, reached its peak in the late 1920s after bringing about Prohibition laws and then declined rapidly in the late 1930s. We rarely hear from the CTU anymore. I believe the majority of American citizens prefer religion be practiced in our churches and in our homes but restricted from becoming a part of our government.

The dominant prestige and power of religion I witnessed in the American society in my youth, especially prior to WW-II, has been greatly diminished in the last 60 years. One example being how the fanatics pushed through the congress the words "Under God" in our pledge of allegiance shortly after the end of WW-II with little if any opposition or publicity.

Kelle, can you imagine the uproar in today's society if the words were not in the pledge of allegiance in 2006 and the fanatics were to try to insert the words now? Think about the battle the pro-American organizations would put up if our money was similar to other first world nations and the fanatics were to try to print "In God We Trust" on our money in 2006!

I am confident the dwindling of the religious fanatic Christian Coalition Movement's visibility and power will continue to decline at an increasing tempo in future decades because of the escalating opposition they are encountering from the many pro-American organizations that have come to life in the last century. The vast majority of parents are very much concerned about the education of their children and I am sure they are going to think about having their children brainwashed with fictitious stories in their youth. A great many parents in the future will be encouraging their children to obtain education in the sciences and to learn about the work of the important philosophers so that they will be able to compete for the best professional jobs in our society. They will for sure look upon the brain washing of youths with fictitious stories in much the same way as they look upon protecting them from becoming smokers, dope addicts or other mendacious practices. I feel sure the continuing decline in attendance of the mainline religious services that has come about in recent years will accelerate in the next few decades. By the end of this century, I am confident America will be as secular as it was when the 1776 forefathers were alive and will be every bit as secular as France, Sweden, Holland and Great Britain by the year 3,005 ACE.

I lived as a young man through the terrible dark days as Hitler's army rolled over the nations of Europe and then witnessed the great speech of Winston Churchill to the tune of, "We will never surrender, we will fight them on the beaches, we will fight them, etc, etc, we will never surrender." I remember having tears in my eyes as he spoke and intended to leave for Canada and join the Canadian Army. My dad put the end to that idea in no uncertain terms. No, I see victory for America in the long run just as I envisioned victory under the leadership of Churchill in 1940. I believe the majority of Americans want the forefathers' wall to stand firm and protect all citizens rights of freedom of and freedom from religion.

AN OPTIMISTIC TREND

The religious fanatics seeking theocracy in our government operated with little or no organized opposition from the time shortly after the death of the last of our 1776 forefathers in 1830 to the formation of the Americans United (AU) organization in 1947. (That's a period of 117 years of little or no opposition in America.) True, many patriotic individuals spoke out against the activity of the religious fanatics prior to 1947, but they were not organized. Since then the American Humanists organization established in 1953 and the American Atheists Organization established in 1963 have joined in the battle to preserve the goals of the 1776 forefathers. The American Civil Liberty Union (ACLU) became very active in the 1900s and has won important legal battles in opposing the Christian fanatics in the last decade. The most powerful organizations fighting the evil theocracy coalition is the Americans United for Separation of State and Religion (www.au.org) established in 1947. Believe it or not the Americans United for Separation of State and Religion has a substantial number of Christian ministers holding important chairs in the organization because they believe the separation of church and state is very important to guarantee freedom of religion to all types of religions; Christians, Jews, Muslims, any kind. It would appear that the advancement of better education of the citizens, investigative aggressive journalists, and wide ranging Google internet information is beginning to turn the tide. Could you image any journalist taking the chance of ending his/her career attacking the wide spread abuse of children in the Catholic Church say back just 50 years ago? The journalist would have been slandered, shamed, disgraced and fired in a matter of days in the 1920s or even into 60s. More and more prominent patriotic Americans are openly and proudly declaring themselves atheists, agnostics and secularists. More and more are coming out of the closet. Now your reader can get involved in honoring the 1776 forefathers! They can join and financially support one or more of the patriotic organizations. I support Americans United full bore! I was once a gunfire warrior for America against foreign powers; now I'm a friendly verbal and memoir-writing warrior for America trying to counter the real danger from within our borders.

THE DECLINE OF CHRISTIAN DICTATORSHIP

This is how I see the past rise and then the commencement of the decline of the imperial rule of the Christian empire. From the time of the pope's defeating and taking over the control of the Roman Empire from the Roman emperors in the fourth century ACE and plunging the Western World into the horrendous Dark Ages, the popes ruled supreme and with a power similar to the former emperors (but with none of the emperors' ability to advance the growth of a learned and civilized society) without challenge until the 1500s ACE. Any questioning of the pope's rule, teachings or beliefs were dealt with as severely or even more so than what we see existing in most of the Muslim nations of today toward any Muslim person who would dare publicly question any of the dictates of an ayatollah or the text of the Koran. In the Christian world during the Dark Ages questioning the tales in the Bible, the pope's rule or dictates would result in torture or a cruel death sentence with burning at the stake or being cut in half. Every bit as painful as a person being buried in sand up to their neck and then stoned to death (as it is now occasionally done in the Muslim world) or hung on a cross in Roman times.

The rebellious actions of Martin Luther in the 1500s did not immediately cause a change in the cruel treatment of any free thinkers or questioners of the pope's supreme power. But his actions and teachings were the first small steps commencing the weakening of the pope dictator's control of the entire European continent. Martin's actions did initiate the eventual and gradual setting free of the northern nations of Europe from the pope's rule, and commenced the growth of free thinking individuals, scientists and their discoveries and psychological discourses by learned persons that would grow exponentially in the following centuries. All of these then led to the weakening of the pope's power and the shattering of the many fictitious tales and dictates of the Bible in the minds of the free thinking persons in the free nations. No longer would intelligent citizens believe the occurrence of severe storms, hurricanes, earthquakes, other tragedies or personal tragedies such as accidents and children born with defects or ugly birth marks were the acts of an angry God. As occurred with the previous beliefs of the great god Zeus and the thousands of the many former pagan Gods and beliefs, the decline of the Christian supreme dictator's control of the minds of the Western World's populations in the free nations, commenced a slow but ever increasing decline in the power of the popes.

Since the early 1600s, the growth in numbers of free thinkers, agnostics, atheists and skeptics of Christianity based on the belief of their one and only "six-day God" of the planet earth has grown at an ever increasing rate. Had the Christian pope captured and killed Martin Luther for his actions in the 1500s in the same manner as the Muslim ayatollahs do today to Islamic heretics, the western Christian populations of the world, would no doubt still be living in the same conditions as they did in the Dark Ages. We would be living in this 21st century in a lifestyle no different than that of the populations of most of today's Muslim-controlled nations. No powerful dictator of any type has ever voluntarily given up his supreme power. Over the past three centuries, the activism, power and influence of the citizens of the free northern nations of Europe and America, "the first great secular nation," eventually forced the moderation of the Christian dictates and cruelty through out all of the Christian areas of the world.

Scientific discoveries of the past three centuries and the development of citizens representative democracy copying our 1776 forefathers' model of government around the world have challenged and diminished the power of not only the pope, his cardinals and priests, but also of all of the multitude of leaders of the offshoot Protestant Christians from the original Catholic sect. In fact, in recent years the antics and silly statements of many of the TV Bible thumpers have become a source of amusement to the majority of American citizens. When Bible thumper Robertson speaks on his Sunday broadcasts about his most recent conversations with God, he may have some of his fanatic followers taking it in but the vast number of Americans are simply amused with his stupidity. The Christian areas of the world have experienced a massive revolutionary wave of intellect and discovery that commenced slowly throughout the 1600s and then exploded exponentially throughout the 1700s and 1800s, and continues to this day. As historians have noted, the geniuses of one generation stand on the shoulders of the geniuses of the previous generations, so we have to admit our 1776 forefathers, the many scientists such as Charles Darwin and Isaac Newton and countless other great intellectuals could not have accomplished their extraordinary work if it had not been for the activity and revolutionary actions of the free thinking citizens of the free nations in the 1600s and early 1700s. Thanks to Martin Luther.

Prior to the northern nations of Europe breaking away from the control of the pope commencing the so-called, "The Enlightenment Period of History," the pope had the power to dictate who would rule under his direction in any nation in the Christian Empire, of both the European and the new world nations. In this 21st century in most all free nations of the Christian areas of the world, it would be the kiss of defeat for any candidate the pope would foolishly openly endorse.

Statements of a Few Noted Nonconformists 1990 – 2006

Looking back to my memory of normal day-to-day conversations in the first half of the 1900s, I can not imagine citizens making public statements like the following in our pre-WW-II era or in the later 1800s or even the mid-1900s following WW-II!

"I don't believe in heaven or hell. I don't know if I believe in God. All I know is that as an individual, I won't allow this life—the only thing I know to exist, to be wasted."

"We were not created by a deity. WE created the deity in our image!!! Life began on this planet when the first amoeba split." (Read this statement again.)

"Mankind will forever be seeking a God. The God they are seeking is only a spirit. They can't see it or touch it. They can only feel it. It's called LOVE."

"Now that I have had some education and exposure to adult minds, I am almost as angry about the God stories as I was when I learned the stories about Santa Claus were a lie."
(I can sure relate to that comment! I was very angry with my parents when I learned the truth about Santa from my older playmates).

"Organized religions and their dogmas only serve to indoctrinate the participants into a dull sheep-like brainwashed flock. Skepticism toward such groups is enriching, intellectual and entertaining."

"There doesn't need to be a God for me. There is something in people that is Godlike. That is all I need."

"I love the idea of Santa Claus and a God. I am an enthusiastic agnostic who would be so very happy if shown there is a God."

"I grew tired of religion in Sunday school. I believe in people. I believe in humans. I don't believe in something that cannot be proven."

"I can't believe in the Christian God. If in fact God created man in his own imagine then he is the image of humans. If this is so, where does he get the nourishment and oxygen to exist out in space?" Who collects the waste and garbage up (where?).

"I love all religions. The celebrations are great fun, the music is beautiful, and the attractive costumes of God's reps are entertaining. The cost is much less than a show on Broadway."

My comment. You can be sure the ayatollahs of the Muslim world have taken note of such statements and the loss of power the popes have suffered by permitting the birth of the free nations in Europe and permitting citizens of the free nations to make such statements. The ayatollahs are not about to permit such statements in the Muslim world. They will continue killing Muslim skeptics, atheists, secularists, agnostics, and free thinkers to make sure they do not threaten their dictatorships; and no doubt the boys in Rome regret letting the northern nations of Europe escape their rule.

Question

Is this great secular nation slowly drifting away from the goals and work of our great 1776 forefathers? Think about it! Also remember, the religious coalition is always engaged.

The Catholic Cardinals of America fought a historic lonely political battle from the mid 1800s to the later years of the 1900s attempting to acquire taxpayer funding for the teaching of Christian religion in private Catholic schools. After failing to succeed in this long struggle, they changed tactics and in recent decades they and selected Protestant sects have successfully organized a quiet united coalition front with the likes of Christian TV ministers Pat Robertson and Jerry Falwell plus powerful Christian religious politicians led by Gary Bauer and Ralph Reed to attack the wall of separation of state and religion constructed by our 1776 forefathers. These individuals and very different Christian sects may dislike, even passionately hate, each other but they are united in their greatest hate and joint aggressive attack on our 1776 forefathers wall of separation of state and religion. The following is the <u>*united coalition agenda*</u> for 2004 and the next decade:

- Secure federal money to fund religious schools and ministries.
- Force public schools to teach religious dogma.
- Eliminate legal obstacles to religious politicing.
- Obtain the right to display religious symbols in public buildings.
- Obtain the right to display religious symbols in all schools.
- Acquire legal denial of specified rights to women, gays and lesbians.
  (Source of above information: see Google, search word, "United Americans" and follow the links.)

Letter to the Vatican

In April of 1988, shortly after reading some of Professor Carl Van Doren's teaching material and at considerable snail mail expense, I sent a letter to the Vatican. I thought it important to remind the boys in the Halloween-like suits over in Rome that they had better start thinking about the hereafter for themselves with regard to how they have been condemning the Jews as Christ killers, persecuting and ostracizing them for the past many centuries. In the letter I asked, "Are you folks aware that Jesus was a Jew so therefore his father is a Jew?"

Then I suggested that when they departed this planet and arrived in the heaven they have been promoting for some 1,900 plus years they might find Jesus' father to be pretty pissed off about their treatment of the Jews on earth over these past many centuries. I also asked them if they thought Hitler would have been able to find enough Jew haters to carry out the Holocaust if the Catholic popes had not been condemning and preaching hatred toward what they have consistently referred to as the "Christ killers" for many centuries. I reminded them that all dictators need an enemy to teach their flocks to hate and despise and although the Jews were obviously an ideal target for the popes, these attacks would not please their Jewish God.

I also suggested they had better think about the manner in which they treat women as less than equals in society. I mentioned that although God had strayed a bit impregnating Mary, we can be sure the Jewish God has a wife up there and she is for sure going to be less than pleased about your dogma with regards to her sex. I doubt if she will be in the mood to serve wafers and a bit of wine to you guys when you arrive at the pearly gates unless you clean up your act. I put my return address on both the envelope and the letterhead but the boys in Rome never replied to thank me for my sincere concern about their future. I have noticed in the news that they have eased up on these evil comments about the Jews in the last few decades. Hell, who knows, maybe my letter was made a part of some of their bull sessions.

Kelle, I regret the fact I sent that letter some months before I became aware of much of the scientific discoveries in recent years by the cosmology scientists. If I had had the latest cosmology scientific information before I sent the letter I would surely have added the following information for the boys in Rome to comprehend:

Recent Cosmology Discoveries

Cosmology scientists have proven beyond any doubt that our tiny speck of matter in the vast universe that we call Earth is located in a rapidly accelerating expanding universe that is approximately 15 billion years old. In just my eight decades of life, actually in just the last 65 years, the cosmology scientists have also proven this one universe contains several hundred billion galaxies each of which contains several hundred billions of stars. In 1995, it was learned that this vast universe is probably only one of billions of vast universes. There are a great many uncounted worlds and tiny planets circling those hundreds of billions of stars in our just one of the billions of galaxies in this universe. The vastness of the universe is mind boggling! Whether any of these billions upon billions of planets are inhabited or not of course remains to be seen. One thing we know for sure is that all of the inhabitants of these many distant planets, if there are any inhabitants, are going to hell because the pope says they were born sinners and he has not cured any of them of their sin. And speaking of real sin, not one of them has ever put money in any of his collection plates. Another question the cosmology scientists have to address: where is "hell?" Could "hell" be located in or on one of those bright red hot icons the scientists are studying in our galaxy?

K: Tom, now I think I would classify you as something akin to a militant agnostic anti-Christian. Does that ring a bell? Does that offend you?

T: I have great respect for the millions of dedicated Christian believers and the good work many of them do. I realize persons who have not really thought about the fiction in the Bible (especially the first five pages) may need a fictional crutch to face the ups and downs they encounter in their journey on earth. They may know it is fiction but get comfort in the fiction in the same manner as I enjoy reading the note in my after meal Chinese fortune cookie.

Hopefully I will never lose my respect for the 1776 forefathers and the words of Thomas Paine and stop supporting their goal of freedom for all to enjoy the right to believe or not to believe, freedom of and from religion. True, I am opposed to the evil theocracy-type elected politicians in our government. They are in cahoots with the Christian coalition intentions of breaking down the wall of separation of state and religion and installing theocracy into our laws. So I am not offended. I welcome the statement as it gives me the opportunity to clarify my opinion of the growing danger of theocracy within our borders.

Professional Magician's Influence

Kelle, let me tell you how and when I changed from a very passive, quiet secular agnostic to a verbally but very friendly and revolutionary "anti-Christian coalition" person. I'm just quietly doing what I can to encourage people to pay attention to what is politically going on in Washington, D.C. with regards to the attacks on the 1776 forefathers' wall of separation of church and state and our judicial branch of government. We will get to what the magician's influence has had on me shortly.

In late 1985 or maybe early 1986, I received a phone call from my brother in Virginia informing me my 86 year old mother, who lived alone in our family home that she and Dad had bought in 1936, was probably terminal with her illness. She had not been doing well for many months and was now in and out of the hospital on several occasions. I told my wife, Karen, that I thought it would be good for both my mother and I if I took a week off from work to go back to Aliquippa, Pennsylvania and spend a week alone with my mother. Just to sit and talk about old times, drive her around to visit a few of her old friends, our old hometown of Carnegie and visit a few of her favorite restaurants. Karen had already lost both of her parents and thought it was a very good idea. I departed LAX for Pittsburgh as an agnostic, secular individual. My mother and I had a very enjoyable week together that I will never forget. I am so thankful Karen and I decided that I should make that trip.

The Sunday morning before I returned to California, I came downstairs about 9 a.m. and joined Mother as she listened to her favorite TV Bible thumper minister. I never ever mentioned my opinion of him or of his sermon. At the end of the sermon, he commenced the strange tongue "thou and thee" stuff with his eyes closed, his right arm and hand pointed upwards, head leaning way back, organ playing softly in the background asking all of his ill and handicapped listeners to pray with him as he prayed for them to have God make them well. He then of course sealed the well performed act with the plea for contributions for God. I then observed my mother put cash, not a check, in an envelope, address it, add the stamp and put it in her purse. On the way to our breakfast at the restaurant, we stopped by the corner mail drop and I deposited the letter for her. God, of course, did not participate in the thousands of dollars that poured into the tax-free coffers of the TV Bible thumper. This mail-in fortune supported his chauffeured luxury car, private plane, yacht and oceanside estate lifestyle.

As a business man, I have often envied the advantage the radio and TV Bible thumpers have over other businesses as they don't have to box, wrap, insure or ship their product. They just verbally sell their fiction and collect the tax-free mailed-in checks and cash.

The next day at the Pittsburgh International Airport for my trip to California, I was no different in my religious thinking and attitude than when I boarded the plane at LAX to go to Pittsburgh. While sitting at the window seat about a half hour after departing the lady in the aisle seat laid a magazine on the empty seat between us. I asked if it would be OK if I read it. She jokingly replied, "It's not mine, it's the airline's."

One of the stories in the magazine reported the activities of professional magicians involved in exposing the outrageous conduct of faith healers, mind readers, psychic practitioners, and TV Bible thumpers deceiving the public with fakery, fictitious stories and mystic activity while picking the pockets of the believers. I was surprised to learn that of all of the categories of professional people, professional magicians make up one of the largest anti Christian-coalition movements in America. Why?

Reading the story, I learned that a great many professional magicians resent the religious practitioners who use much of the same type of recitals and acts the magicians use to entertain, but the Christian practitioners use them to brainwash, control, implant fear, myth and imply false hopes and marginalize their audiences. I was astonished to read about the prominent magician James Randi devoting his life to debunking the fakery of various kinds of practitioners. I urge you to go to www.randi.org or Google and type in James Randi. If you spend some time reviewing the information presented by his organization, you will learn that professional magicians not only resent the practitioners of fakery and brainwashing but they also believe them all to be crooks, white collar criminals and thieves picking the pockets and incomes of the innocent believers.

When I walked off the airplane at LAX that Monday evening, I had become an agnostic, verbal but friendly, rebellious anti-Christian coalition individual. As an ordinary citizen, I realized I could not hope to accomplish what a professional magician could accomplish performing in front of large audiences and earning a six-figure income, but in my own small way, I decided I could make a contribution to the movement. Always acting in a very friendly manner, just pecking away; one by one, talking to persons and writing my memoir. This has been my diminutive contribution over the past two decades.

When one-on-one with an adult, I pay attention for an opening to make a friendly comment that will not upset them. For example: a few days after my return from Pittsburgh, while attending a pops concert sitting at a round table with 12 people, Karen was sitting on my right side and another lady was on my left. During the evening in friendly conversation, the lady and I made comments to each other about the music and the performers. She asked if I was a musician. I told her no I was in the building business and then learned from her that she was a professional organist. She also mentioned the different places she performed including a local prominent church.

When she asked if I had ever attended, I saw my opportunity and mentioned that because of recently reading the first five or six pages of the Bible I was having trouble considering the authenticity of such stories and had not been attending church for some time. After discussing a few of the stories in the first five pages she said, "I have not thought of reading the Bible for years. I agree those stories are nonsense; when I go home tonight I'm going to read them again." No doubt she would relate that story to another person who in turn hopefully would relate it to another, just planting the seed of reason and questioning, spreading the word one at a time in the most friendly and non-confrontational manner.

That was a very friendly verbal encounter and a successful score; admittedly not as exciting as a gunfire combat score but very satisfying. If you want to make a contribution to the effort, simply listen for the opening in a one-on-one adult conversation. When an opening is available, make a noncontroversial friendly statement that will lead to discussing the first five pages of the Bible. Then leave the subject to simmer. Get on to another subject in which the person is interested. Your targeted person will probably mention this conversation to other persons and unknowingly will have become a part of the network spreading the word. Some of the others your targeted person mentions the subject to may also help expand the network by casual conversation with others. Amusingly, this reminds me of how casual statements about information used to be spread rapidly and widely around the ship's crews of over 2,000 men aboard the aircraft carriers in the Navy.

In casual conversation, you will be amazed how few adult persons have read the Bible in the last few decades of their lives. The goal is just to entice them to read the first five pages, the actual underpinning of their six-day God religion. Once they read the first five pages of the Bible in their next church service as they are watching their spiritual leader perform they will have some new thoughts and questions passing through their minds. Remember, a long journey starts with the first step. Also remember "SHE" may be out there and will be very appreciative of your help. The book is a collection of fictitious stories but it is the first five pages that are a riot of sci-fi imaginative yarns that will shock people who have not read the Bible since Sunday school.

*K:	I am sure with this personal program you must have had many stormy encounters with unforgiving Christians since your first efforts in 1986 or 1987.*

T: Sincerely and honestly, I have never had a single angry confrontation with any person with the approach I have been using. I simply make my verbal approach as if I am confused and trying to make sense out of the first five pages of the Bible. I have had a few persons just comment that the best thing to do for my own good was simply to accept what is in the Bible without question as that is the only way to have a comfortable life. Nevertheless, I am sure some of them may have gone home and read the first five pages; thought it over and maybe mentioned the conversation to others. Hopefully the encounter will lead to others to help spread the network.

Kelle, I have to mention the most interesting friendly conversation I have ever had trying to encourage another person to think about the fiction and authenticity of the man-made fictitious religions.

The encounter came about on Catalina Island about 15 years ago. Karen, I and our wire hair terrier dog Barkley (Barkley has departed for the unknown beyond and we now have Boris who is a dead ringer near identical terrier) sailed our Columbia sloop from our Long Beach slip over to the Catalina "Two Harbors" anchorage on a Friday afternoon. While Karen was hunting and gathering in the gift shop, I took Barkley for a walk to take a look at the buffalo (actually American bison) grazing on the hillside. At that time they did not have any fences erected so it was very interesting to watch the buffalo up close grazing near the Two Harbors tourist buildings.

I was wearing my Navy Post Graduate School sweat suit. A man, about a decade or so older than me, wearing a Navy jacket from the Pensacola Air Museum, was also eyeballing the buffalo. We struck up a conversation as the two of us and Barkley returned to the snack patio by the harbor and enjoyed some refreshments together. We discussed the events of WW-II, our boats, my sloop vs. his power boat and current events. As usual, I listened for an opportunity to mention my standard well rehearsed, very friendly comment about my confusion with the authenticity of the story about the six-day God. When I inserted my comment into our conversation he turned to me smiling and asked what I did while in the service. After I answered he said, "Guess what my duties in the service were?" A few seconds later he answered his own question, "I served for over six years as a chaplain!"

Well, that came as a shock to me. Then he told me his story with the comment that he normally never discussed religion with anyone since he was retired. He had at first thought he would make a career serving in the Navy but changed his mind and left the service to return to the civilian church hierarchy about two years after the end of WW-II. A few years after serving in the civilian world, he was assigned to a small church of his own in northern New York State. He enjoyed his civilian service for some years and had no intention to change his career.

One of the duties he performed was counseling people and couples who were having difficulty with their personal lives. A couple having difficulty in their marriage sought his help but after several sessions the husband let it be known he was separating and wanted a divorce. That was the end of their counseling sessions and he never saw the man again. A few months later the wife came to seek counsel in a very depressed mood as she had just learned her ex was living with her former close friend who was also the receptionist at her husband's firm. During these counseling sessions, my new friend learned he was in love with the lady. At the end of one of the sessions he told her he had decided to resign from his position in the church and as soon as he was a free man he intended to try and become her fiancée. He said she smiled and told him you won't have to try very hard because I'll be waiting for you. They laid their plans on the up and up (so he told me), he went about resigning with dignity and with no fanfare. She sold the house she had gained in the separation, put her furniture in storage and rented a furnished apartment. Once he was free to go, they took off in her car as he didn't own a car for a cross-country tour of the US and ended up in California. They set up housekeeping in a rented home and she contacted the New York storage company to send her furniture.

It took awhile living together before she was free to legally marry again. Apparently her ex had never had the divorce legally documented. Once they had this documentation accomplished they went to Las Vegas and were married.

After he told me his story I decided to open up and tell him what I was really about with my so-called seeking help with my feigned confusion with the stories in the Bible. He broke out laughing; we finished our snacks and refreshments and parted as new friends.

On Sunday afternoon, I was packing some gear in our shore boat to take out to the sloop for our sail back to Long Beach when he came up to me, shook hands and said, "Tom, my wife and I made a vow that because of my background we would never ever discuss religion with anyone at any time. You were my one exception. But I want you to know I think America is very much in need of people like you and the many magicians you mentioned. Keep it up." Needless to say that was a great morale booster for me.

Intelligent comedians are also making a major contribution in the verbal battle to combat the insertion of theocracy into our secular government by making fun of many of the silly programs promoted by the Christian coalition. The current silly effort of the coalition to introduce intelligent design (actually Christian creationism) into our public schools as a science along with the evolution discovery of Dr. Darwin is the current comical subject of countless comedians on both the stage and on TV.

K: I must say that is the first time I have ever heard about the role of many of the professional magicians in America. In the last decade or so I too have noticed the increased number of comedians making fun of and ridiculing many of the tactics, statements and programs of the same Christian entities you address in your memoir.

Notre Dame Cathedral in Paris

There's such a contrast between my trips to Guangzhou and Beijing in 2002 and 2003 when I visited the temples crowded shoulder to shoulder every day of the week and what I saw in 2003 visiting the world famous Notre Dame Cathedral in Paris. In Paris, there were hundreds of tourists visiting the great cathedral every day I visited. I entered the cathedral and sat through a mass on Sunday. The attendance was very sparse. There were almost no one in attendance younger than 50 or 60 years old. Needless to say, I was delighted to see the lack of enthusiasm of the French people for the Christian religion. When I was a young adult I would have thought the French people were bad for this lack of support of the cathedral. At age 82 I admired them for their intelligence. The cathedral is an impressive historical edifice and I hope the French will preserve it as a historical attraction.

A Failed Anti-Christian Attack

(A good lesson of how not to combat the Christian Empire.)
In 1917, the new Communist government of the Soviet Union attempted to combat Christianity in their government by setting up a government based primarily on atheist concepts.

Their major misstep was to attempt to control the power of the Christian leaders' influence in the new Communist government by persecuting the Christian practitioners in a manner similar to the procedures used by the Romans of many centuries earlier. Being persecuted is the life blood and creative energy that fuels the growth of Christianity. History has proven tolerance, secular education of the citizens, and the complete freedom of all citizens to believe or not to believe in the Christian six-day God or any other belief is the only effective technique any democratic or any other kind of government can successfully use to combat the Christian empire. The use of control and persecution and the failure to permit freedom of and freedom from religion is essential to combat the Christian empire. Of course the primary cause of the failure of the Soviet communist system of government was that their communist doctrine violated the most basic instincts of the human animal. The power structure of the governing communist party was extremely dictatorial (not unlike the popes of the Dark Ages) including immense widespread corruption and with absolutely no democratic power or representation given to the citizens.

K: Well, I think you are a real optimist, but I am sure a great many people will resent your attitude of wanting to see the decline of the Christian influence throughout the world.

T: So be it, kid! Now on to my daydreaming.

Just a Dream

Of the many thousands of different religions, faiths, sects and cults that have been initiated in the recorded history of mankind, only a few have survived and are now mainstream organizations and prospering at this time in the United States.

Christianity is growing and prospering in the third world illiterate nations, but is very much on the decline in all of the highly literate nations of Europe, especially in France, Sweden and Holland. The United States is the only one of the so-called first world industrial literate nations where the heavily financed Christian promoted politicians are an increasing threat to the nation's existing secular government.

During the months from January 2002 to February 2005 there has been great controversy in America about the subject of gay and lesbian marriages. There is no doubt, I and most of my friends find the sight of two men kissing each other less than a pleasant sight. Two women doing the same does not seem to be as an offensive sight to most of us.

The really worrisome fact of the gay and lesbian controversy is not how each of us feels about the issue, but the fact that the hard core Christian promoted politicians are attacking the 1776 forefather's legal structure of our government based on law, because of this issue. The vicious scandalous religious fanatic Christian politicians attacks on our nation's judges and our secular legal courts as well as the American legal process is a real danger to the future of our government. There is no question that our 1776 forefathers did not want Christian politicians dictating the legal decisions affecting the freedom of our citizens.

Whatever our personal opinions regarding emotional legal controversies, women, minorities, gays, lesbians, stem cell research, or any other situation, it is all important for the future of America that the issues be resolved by our secular judicial system and not by theocracy oriented Christian politicians.

"Forefathers Universalists," a Daydream

Almost all newly initiated cults and religions come about as the result of a single individual having a dream, hallucination, an imagined conversation with God, or meeting a messenger from God or finding messages from God. I have not had a dream or message from any source, but while walking my dog Boris each day, especially around the quiet marina late at night, I often daydream about someone becoming the leader of a new religious society that would promote the dreams and goals of my 1776 forefathers. Pretty ridiculous at my age for me to ever try to be involved! The following is the mental construction of my daydreaming:

As an officer student at the U.S. Navy Post Graduate School in Monterey, California, I learned the Navy procedures to promote your own ideas and the steps to object or modify others' approaches to the same issue in meetings and conferences regarding projects, instruments of war and tactics in the military. Basically:

(1)   You always attend the meeting or conference with your proposal in writing.

(2)   Any verbal contributions you make during the meeting have to be promptly put into writing following the meeting and submitted to your immediate superior for his comments and his forwarding to the senior officer who presided over the meeting. Your senior officer would be expected to add his pro or con comments in his forwarding letter. ("His" because in my Navy there were no women. This happens to be a factual not a derogatory statement.)

(3)   All of your contributions must be in writing and forwarded through the chain of command. There can be no such thing as a later statement such as, "but this is what I verbally proposed or recommended."

We were also taught never to criticize existing situations verbally or in writing of plans, tactics, equipment or operations unless we also submitted a written proposed solution to the subject, plan, procedures, equipment or operation we were criticizing.

Therefore: since I have laid down in no uncertain terms my opinion of the horrible coalition leadership and questionable authenticity of the Christian religion in this story, I feel in my daydreaming I am obligated to prepare a written opinion of a possible solution to do battle with the Christian leaders who are attacking the 1776 forefather's wall, attacking both the present leaders and the teachings of fictitious stories by the Christian leaders.

Again, I have great admiration for the Christian believers and followers who in this day and age are performing good deeds in many venues. But I wish some of them would get around to reading the works of some of the great scientists, philosophers and the biographies of our 1776 forefathers. My anger and anxiety about the future of secular America is sharply and bitterly aimed at the Christian past and present leaders. The vast majority of the current honest hard working Christian believers have never taken the time to review the past history—the true historical background of the fictitious stories and horrific bloody deeds of the leaders of the Christian religion. Nor are the majority of them aware of the great danger of their Christian leaders' current attacks on the wall of separation of state and religion and our judicial system.

THIS IS MY DAYDREAMING PROPOSED SOLUTION

First, the initiation and establishment of a new religion and an overtaking faith to promote scientific research, public education and the goals of our 1776 forefathers.

My suggested name of the new faith (organization or association) to be "Forefathers Universalists." Not to be confused with the existing Universalist sect, which is closely associated with the Unitarians. There is a possibility the two groups may find it advisable to join forces with my proposed "Forefathers Universalists" organization.

A newly initiated religion must have all the necessary ingredients, and also to have them inserted at opportune times in the building of a successful long lasting religion. The required ingredients are:

(1)   The religion must be initiated by a charismatic individual capable of attracting attention with an appealing message. Hopefully such a person will emerge out of the over 300 million citizens of the United States, someone like a new Thomas Paine type with great charisma.

(2)   The timing of the insertion of the important ingredients creating the undertaking would be important. In some cases the timing of any one of the ingredients may

be a little different than in other ventures. The initiating person of the venture would be presenting the acquisition of appealing products in an efficient manner. A good example being forgiveness of your sins, favorable treatment by your maker and a happy afterlife living with your God. These are very appealing and emotional products to promote and sell. A version of this can be incorporated into the new religion because SHE may be out there or at least some kind of cosmic force to associate with. A good spin master should be able to create this scenario.

(3)   Persecution of the venture. Persecution creates energy in the herd or flock with the scenario of "us against them!" Team enthusiasm! We can be sure the Christian coalition will provide all the heat needed to make the new members feel persecuted.

(4)   The creation of martyrs from the persecution. This ingredient really generates great energy in the movement. Just as occurred with the Mormons in the 1800s, the existing fanatics of the man-made fictitious religions will generate the martyrs of the new religion with their verbal abuse.

(5)   Marketing symbol. Just like a professional or college sports team, a marketable symbol is important to identify the followers and give them something to proudly display. The cross has become the favorite symbol of the Christians. The new Forefather Universalists will have a competing symbol they can wear with pride.

(6)   Leadership with a solid succession program to ensure availability of future disciplined believers to follow a program that will ensure a system of efficiently replacing the organization's leaders on their death or retirement.

The story tellers that evolved many decades after the death of Jesus luckily had all of the ingredients fall timely into place. This new "Forefathers Universalists" religion can accomplish the same effect.

Now in 2006, and noting the great success of the Christian initiators of their faith some 2000 years ago, it seems necessary for the proposed overtaking "Forefathers Universalists" new religion to also possess the same important ingredients. So why reinvent the wheel; study and copy the route the Christians took.

So here is the identical list of the important ingredients that must be in the recipe of my daydreaming new Forefathers Universalists religion. The ingredients can be put in place as follows:

(1)   This new religion will attract attention by promoting the greatly admired 1776 forefathers of this great secular nation. The religion will put great emphasis on the

work of the scientists to get beyond the Big Bang to know more about the great God of the universe. The forefathers' goals and accomplishments in founding this nation will be the most important appealing message. The new faith will also adopt the same grand end of the year holiday celebrations, especially the Christmas holiday that the Christians adopted from the earlier pagan religions. Holidays are important in the growing of any religious organization. But the name of the holiday will have to revert back to one of the colorful pagan names.

(2)   The timing of the insertion of the important ingredients can be manipulated with professional promoters. Modern spin masters will do work comparable to the ancient story tellers who took up the promotion of the Jesus stories as a career some five to six decades after Jesus' death. Modern spin masters (story tellers) can efficiently insert the ingredients in a timely manner. The mystery of what is beyond the Big Bang and the search for HER will be emphasized.

(3)   The appealing products of this new faith will be all the benefits of the United States Constitution, Bill of Rights, the ongoing scientific research to fully learn all aspects of the universe, continually searching for the great God of the universe, and the construction of a faith based on humane laws. The great appeal to literate persons of the new faith will be reading about and watching the faith's scientists continuing to search beyond the Big Bang to discover the supernatural being, entity or whatever force responsible for the billions of planets, meteors and other space material discovered in the universe in the last century. The new faith would state without any qualifications that they believe in the law of physics. Therefore there is a cause or action of some kind for the creation of the universe. The followers of the faith will never cease searching for the real supernatural entity or force that created the universe. The followers of the faith will not believe in any stories of any individual having a lonely personal contact with a supernatural force or entity without professional scientifically trained witnesses.

(4 and 5)   The persecution of the new faith and the creation of martyrs will be similar to the historic facts of the creation of the Mormon martyrs in the 1800s. The instigators of the new faith (like the treatment of the Mormons in the 1800s) will be vilified and condemned as heretics by the Christians as they have done to hated free thinkers, skeptics, atheists and agnostics. The TV Bible thumpers and the cardinals dressed in their Halloween get up will verbally condemn and demonize the new faith. The great number of Christian radio talk show hosts will unceasingly condemn and ridicule the followers of the new Forefathers Universalists religion. Unlike the age of torture in the Dark Ages the Christians will be limited to verbal harassment in this secular America. Fat boy, drug addict, radio talking head Rush Limbaugh will have a field day condemning the new faith. All of this will bring great publicity and attention to enhance the growth of the new faith.

The internet chat rooms will be full of pro and con opinions.

(6)   The marketing symbol will be a small red, white and blue colorful medallion, pin or ring with the words "Forefathers Universalists" in a circle around the circumference of the jewelry.

(7)   The leadership of the new faith will be based on the same criteria as the system of public elections for politicians in America. Persons interested in leadership of the new faith will have to prove themselves in promoting the faith and attracting the attention of the faith's voters.

(8)   Since the new faith will not have massive cathedral buildings to hold meetings of its adherents, the faith will be financially supported similar to the existing Christian Scientists method of establishing meeting and reading rooms in strategic locations. The faith's meeting rooms should also have a gift shop and licensing program of appealing products in addition to the medallions, pins and rings to generate income. Products such as books, flags, holiday and greeting cards, bumper stickers, hats, belt buckles, door knockers, license plate frames, key rings, scarves, all types of clothing with insignia, on and on; all with the Forefathers Universalists insignia.

All that's needed to kickstart the new religion is a group of energetic young literate persons to join together and get the ball rolling. The first step would be for one of the computer savvy initiators of the faith to set up and promote a web page. For this new faith to be continually and scientifically searching for the real God of the universe, it must also be constantly in the media, legally attacking the past and present Christian activities through the judicial process in cooperation with the ACLU; such as hard nosed attacks to:

(A)   Eliminate the Christian politically passed laws barring non-believers from holding office in the states that still have these laws on record;

(B)   Stop the printing of "In God We Trust" on all of our currency and replacing it with pictures and comments of our 1776 forefathers;

(C)   Remove the term "under God" from the pledge of allegiance;

(D)   Legally stop any efforts of the Christian politicians to fund private religious schools with public funds;

(E)   Ensure that religious symbols of any kind are never permitted in public schools or government buildings;

(F)   Champion the 1776 forefathers for the documentation of the first great democratic government;

(G)   Constantly legally attack any actions of the Christian politicians to down-grade the rights of women or people "not just like them;"

(H)   Teach tolerance and accept the fact that the gay and lesbian folks deserve the same legal protection and rights as heterosexual people;

(I)   Promote and demand freedom of and from religion;

(J)   Promote the 1776 forefathers' dream and goal of this nation being a nation of laws, administered by a secular judicial body of courts and judges.

At my age, I can only daydream of such a movement and new religion. Maybe some day a patriotic, energetic and charismatic young person will have the same dream and take the steps to develop a following! Anyway, daydreaming about it is a pleasant way to enjoy my daily walks with Boris.

Seeking a New Herd Leader

It costs less than $50 a month (in 2006) for a young energetic web design master and charismatic leader to commence and maintain an informative educational web site that supports the new "FOREFATHERS UNIVERSALISTS" religion.

K: What would represent a palatable religion to you?

T: Millions of Americans are becoming doubters and questioners of the dogma of the religious fanatics and are turning to an alternate more intelligent type of religious experience. I call it a move toward, "Enjoyable Religion"…something very different than a belief in ancient fictitious stories. Here goes.

Enjoyable Religion

In my memoir, I frequently make fun of, ridicule, insult and take to task so many of the current and past dogma, dictates, mean leadership and past and present evil practices of the Muslim and Christian religions. The few persons who have helpfully critiqued my notes have mentioned I am for sure a confirmed mean spirited politically-oriented combatant atheist.

Frankly, I admire the most prominent expounders of atheism for their courage confronting the brainwashed society of believers in the two religions but also feel the atheists are just as guilty as the religious fanatics of dogma holding themselves up as the only persons with the true rejoinder regarding the cosmos, birth of the planet earth and the universe. In my opinion, any person who feels they and they alone have the answer concerning all factors related to the vast universe of the billions of stars (every star in the universe is a sun) with each sun possibly having as many planets and meteors in its system as our sun has to be an egotist. If Albert Einstein with the greatest brain of the past century could not be sure of what "cosmic power" might be behind the existence of this and the possibly many other universes yet to be discovered, then a true atheist has to really be a bit of an egotist to think he/she has the only answer. We can only be sure the stories in the Muslim's Koran and the Christian's Bible are nothing more than creative, sci-fi, imaginative fiction.

Christian and Muslim leaders throughout history have used their holy books to brainwash societies that they as the teachers and self-appointed custodians of the books are the only sources of the true answers to all aspects of society. Using this power of persuasion over the centuries, they have been highly successful in raising vast amounts of money from their brainwashed followers to build empires, impressive cathedrals, and govern societies. Over the centuries they have used every category of propaganda and tactics to enhance their power to brainwash, bind and bend their converts to their beckoning. They use this power to encourage their followers to contribute money and service to fight both real and imagined enemies of their empires.

In America today, Christian leaders are raising vast sums of money to battle the rights of gays and lesbians, the rights of women to be equals and control their own bodies and any and all manmade laws that are not in compliance with the theological dictates in their book of fictitious stories. To maintain their Christian impetus they desperately need to find enemies—evil, real or make believe. For over two thousand years the innocent Jews were their primary make believe enemy but they have eased up attacking the Jews in recent decades.

If you are like many restless citizens trying to decipher truth from fiction with regard to religion, I offer the following philosophy based on my journey over the past 83 years. I too once sat in Christian pews on Sundays watching and listening to various practitioners dressed in sometimes impressive costumes delivering their tomes in various traditions, most often enhanced by the confines of an impressive structure with expensive colored windows and accompanied by an organ and beautiful choir music. All very impressive but nevertheless all based on obviously fictitious stories.

Religion can be enjoyed in many different ways. It need not be based on fictitious ancient stories and manmade mean theocracy dogma.

So if you become bored or impatient just as I had, you can become a quiet questioner, doubting Thomas and accept the "dogma of uncertainty."

There is a social price to pay when you give up the weekly sermons because there will be a sense of loss of community by not attending the colorful and entertaining services.

In the last decade (1995 to 2005) a survey by the highly respected City University of New York, "American Religious Identification Survey," revealed some 27 million adult Americans (one in seven Americans) now reject religious labels of any kind. That is double the number that had the same label in 1994.

If you are restless in the pew, resent the insult to your intelligence of the teaching of fiction as the truth with the practitioner in the robes waving smoking canisters, speaking in strange tongues, sprinkling "holy" water and having you bow, open and close your eyes as you quote mass catechism, you can retain the same sense of community by joining one of the doubter and uncertain communities:

- Skeptics Society: www.skeptic.com

- American Humanist Society: www.americanhumanist.org

- Universism: open-site.org/Society/Religion/Universism (or just Google Universism)

- American Atheists: www.atheists.org (The president is Ms. Johnson, a very attractive intelligent young blonde lady.) Regular meetings are held in most cities in America.

- Americans United: www.au.org. (Americans United for Separation of State and Religion) They also hold meetings in most American cities.

I am sure communicating, blogging and attending meetings with any of these groups of enthusiastic intelligent people will give you a sense of community with dedicated loyal Americans that cannot be equaled in a community teaching fiction. This association will bring about a real sense of comfort and belonging in a "for real" world.

I think the two most spiritual-feeling experiences of my life were watching what many professionals consider the two greatest documentaries ever produced in America. The "Ascent of Man" by Dr. Bronowski and "Cosmos" by Dr. Carl Sagan; the 13 hour Cosmos series is enhanced by beautiful music as Dr. Sagan takes you through the mind-boggling vastness and inscrutability of the vast universe.

Be sure to participate in all of the enjoyable religious holiday events that the Christians have adopted from the earlier pagan religions and then make these holidays a part of your own celebrations. The tooth fairy, the bunny rabbit with the attractive eggs and chocolate treats, Santa Claus and other celebrations are fun and enjoyable for both adults and the youngsters in their lives.

Bibliography Information

T: Kelle, you had mentioned the fact that most books contain a bibliography of the sources of the author. I do not have the background you have in the academic, writing, and story telling field, so I hope it is acceptable for me to substitute an index of all subjects at the end of the book. Much of my memoir is based on the works and discoveries of the great and very intelligent individuals in books I have read, some notes from post college courses I have taken or topics I simply Googled. I'm confident an index of all of the subjects at the end of the book will be sufficient.

In addition to all of the persons mentioned in the index there are the many science and universe documentaries I am addicted to on the Charter Cable Science Station, the many related links I have followed on Google related to science and the many stories of developing and newly discovered science in the Los Angeles Times from time to time.

I'm giving details of sources that helped shape my thinking and life. It may be from a book, from the internet, a visit with a person, an observation of an event or an experience I had. In each case, I note the years the individual lived and worked and cite references where readers can learn more about the individual.

K: I have never seen the substitution of an index for a bibliography done this way but I imagine it is up to you.

T:I will list names and subjects as I think of them.

Google

T: I consider the establishment of the Google Corporation, their worldwide operations combined with the internet to be the second most important addition to worldwide education in the history of civilization. Of course, the first and most important addition to civilization's education being the invention of writing. Historians have written that the invention of the fax machine and the common use of the telephone in Russia was one of the most important technological developments that caused the collapse of the Soviet Union as the new communication tools enabled the population to arrange massive demonstrations to oppose the evil government. These two tools are important for communications but they are insignificant compared to the internet and Google! Some time ago, I think it was in 2001, while attending the annual Linux Conference in San Francisco in the Moscone Convention Center one of the two young founders of Google was a guest speaker. I am not sure now if the speaker partner was Sergey Brin or Lawrence Page. In any event the young executive co-founder who looked about the age of a high school senior delivered a great speech outlining how he and his Stanford graduate partner intended to develop Google into a worldwide information, education and service company. At that time Google was not a major corporation. I was astonished to hear what he and his partner planned to do. I knew that if they accomplished their goals it would change the world in many ways. Obviously they have been successful in accomplishing most of their goals and the now powerful information and educational contributor, Google Corporation, is rapidly changing the world. For the first time in the history of civilization nearly all the information known in the civilized world is just a mouse click away to any person with access to a computer. Medical, science, engineering information, any world government, city, state, province laws, regulations, names and titles of the officials, structure and regulations, geography, whatever you are seeking is just a mouse click away. No longer is it necessary to commute to a library or a book store to acquire research information. Go to Google using any major world language and visit the most important libraries in the world and acquire whatever information you are seeking with a few clicks of the mouse. If you want the book containing the information in the library you just go to Amazon.com and order the book. It makes no difference where you are in the world: all the information available in the civilized world is just a few mouse clicks away.

Education is the deadly enemy of any religion based on dogma of certainty, theocracy-controlled government or dictatorship. The dictator-controlled nations will do their best to censor the information but they will be overwhelmed by the vast flow of information. Darwin delivered the first stiff body blow to the fiction in the foundation of the Christian religion; the world-wide education now available on Google is rapidly developing a knockout blow worldwide to all of the Christians' fictitious stories that will be known to the vast majority of all of the world's populations no later than the end of this century. As proven in Northern Europe, especially since the end of WW-II, the fiction of Christianity cannot stand up to literate educated populations. The Christian religion in literate societies is slipping into a God Zeus type legend at an ever-increasing speed. Like a dying wounded beast that screams the loudest as it is dying, the Christian leaders in America in 2006 are shirking and screaming as they see the American society moving toward a more secular society with Supreme Court decisions favoring the rights of women and minorities. The recent appointment of two neocon Supreme Court justices is just a temporary setback.

Of course Google is just one of a vast number of sources of information on the internet. One indication of the power of the internet with regards to the American public was the very surprising impact it had on the 2004 presidential election. The tremendous amount of money contributed via the net to support the candidates of both parties was amazing. In past elections, average income Americans were not much of a factor in fundraising for the candidates as compared to the lobbyist contributors controlled by the major corporations and the wealthiest 1% of the population. Average income Americans not only contributed multi-millions in small donations over the net they also gained true uncensored information from the thousands of "bloggers" (the word is so new it is not in most dictionaries but it is the nickname of individuals and associations who publish uncensored news and opinions on the net) who published for and against the different candidates. This was a demonstration of true democracy in action. I am an occasional blogger, verbally attacking the evil Christian Coalition members who are trying to destroy the judicial branch of our American Government and replace it with theocracy-minded judges. Major corporations, dictatorships, the Christian Empire being the most expert and very wealthy people in America can censor and adapt news to accomplish their goals by what honest journalists refer to as "censorship-by-omission."

Here is how it works in America. Close to three-quarters of our printed and broadcast media are owned by a handful of powerful people. Much of the income of the media is derived from the advertising income collected from the major corporations. The media executives find it financially beneficial if they pay close attention to any contact by phone, personal visit or letter from one of their major advertising customers regarding how to treat embarrassing or derogatory stories about their firm, products or executives with care. So if the story has to be printed or broadcast, the media executives put their best spin masters on the job of working on "censorship-by-omission" before the story is presented to the public. The Christians use a slightly different approach by the top church leaders by establishing close ties to the members of their faith who hold top executive positions in the media. Not stated but implied, "Do you and your family wish to be in good standing with your church leaders?" In the case of TV Bible thumpers it would be similar to the corporations approach of, "Would you like to continue earning the income you have been receiving from our paid broadcasting?" That is what takes place in much of the American media. In Ireland and Latin nations, "censorship-by-omission" with regards to news about the church or its practitioners is controlled by a heavy hand. But there is no way for the powerful to shut down the internet bloggers. So long as the internet remains free, the bloggers will continue to bring the sunshine of honest disclosure and criticism to the minds of the American public and much of the citizens of the rest of the world.

Of course someday a new source of information other than Google may be borne in Silicon Valley, Tokyo, Beijing, London, Paris or wherever brilliant minds exist. But as of this time, in my opinion, Google is the top dog disseminating worldwide information and education.

As the internet and Google continue to expand and add additional high tech services, imagine the impact this will have on societies around the world with family individuals many thousands of miles apart not only in daily text communications with loved ones but also seeing each other on the screen while communicating. WOW!

K: I'm impressed with Google too, but I must say you come across as an enthusiastic public relations employee of the two young geniuses.

T: Yes, other people I have spoken to about Google and the internet have the opinion it is an impressive organization but not as important as I think it is. I truly believe that people of today's society observing the internet and Google are in a state of knowledge similar to the people in the years 1900-1904 observing the emergence of the telephone, the automobile and the Wright Brothers first flight at Kitty Hawk. How could they possibly imagine how the emergence of these three icons of the early 1900s would affect the world in the balance of the twentieth century? I believe by the middle of this new century people all over the world will be instantly in touch with each other via the internet addressing all forms of marketing, all sources of information and sending messages and pictures to each other with a personal credit card sized cellular device.

They will be capable of instantly communicating from any place on earth to any other spot on the earth. In my youth we listened to Buck Rogers sci-fi radio programs and read comic pages whereby Buck and his associates communicated in a futuristic sci-fi fashion with a device that looked like a wrist watch. At the time I thought this was very entertaining but way out sci-fi nonsense. In 2006, people send words and pictures across the nation in hand held cellular phones they can carry in their shirt pocket. Recently I read in a high tech magazine that in 2007, the first dog and cat collars will be on the market whereby the owner will know the exact location of his wandering pet with in six feet of the pets location and that the same device can be attached to a child, adult, car, boat or any kind of valuable personal property.

Last spring I attended the Elton John Red Piano show at Caesar's Palace in Las Vegas and the man sitting beside me was holding up his new camera cell phone sending pictures of the show to a friend in his hometown. I believe the internet and Google are in about the same time frame era in internet technology and worldwide communications as aviation, automobiles and the telephone were in the time frame of 1900-1910; the citizens then could not imagine the impact of these inventions would have on society in the future years of the century nor can we foresee or imagine what the bright minds will accomplish with this internet and Google technology accomplish in the next 50 years or so.

K: You're right. Just think about what we have witnessed in just the last 15 years on the internet and personal computers.

Tom, I'd like you to tell me about some of the scientists, philosophers and professor's who you studied in your research and most admire; and also what you learned from their works and teachings about the origin of the universe.

T:		OK, Kelle, but as a professional story teller, I think you well know many people reading your book may not be interested in the same kinds of people I admire or the subject matter. Also my interpretation of their findings, work and teachings may be much different than your readers' interpretation if they have studied the works of the same outstanding people.

*K:	That's OK, let's get on with it.*

T:		First let's address the past geniuses I came across and most admire and then get on to the subject of my understanding of the origin of the universe.

People I Admire

K: Tell me more about some of the people you admire.

T:Kelle, there have been so many great thinkers, many which I haven't even included in this memoir. Information about Sigmund Freud, Charles Darwin, Carl Van Doren, Jacob Bronowski, Charles Bradlaugh, Sunand Joshi. Baruch Spinoza and Carl Sagan follows.

Sigmund Freud 1856 – 1939

In his biography of Dr. Sigmund Freud, Dr. C. George Boeree quotes Dr. Freud's 1927 work, *The Future of an Illusion*: "Men (meaning both males and females) cannot remain children forever, they must in the end go out into the hostile life."

It is my understanding that the good doctor was referring to the fact that as persons mature into adulthood, they must grab hold of reality. In gradual steps, a child must mature past belief in the tooth fairy, the Easter bunny, Santa Claus and eventually in adulthood, the super-Christian "Santa Claus-like" six-day God illusion who is an image of a human and keeps tabs on our day-to-day good and bad behavior. My first steps into the region referred to by Dr. Freud as the "hostile life" were when I commenced questioning the fairy tales some five decades ago that were taught to me in my Christian education.

This is my sincere effort to reveal my evolution from child in religion to my entry into what Dr. Freud referred to as the "hostile life" of reality. To me, the reality and truth of what Dr. Freud refers to is not a hostile life or hostile world.

I considerate it a blessing to be free of religious superstition, myths, fear of the unknown as well as the fear of an angry god. I believe Einstein was correct when he said, "We do not know what is out there beyond the Big Bang."

I only know it is not the six-day God.

Now I would like to address Dr. Darwin and his earthshaking discovery in the 1800s.

Charles Darwin *1809-1882*

Dr. Martin Luther (1483-1546), the rebel, genius and religious liberator made the first great break from the dictator popes of the Dark Ages, resulting in the freeing of many of the northern nations of Europe from the dictators of the Dark Ages in Rome. With this freedom, these nations became the foremost nations in the world in science, productivity, literacy, citizens' freedom and military strength. As a result, the citizens of these nations enjoyed a more humane lifestyle and economic well being.

Free thinking persons, such as our 1776 forefathers or scientists like Darwin and Wallace would not have accomplished their great work if it were not for the bravery and actions of Martin Luther.

With the freedom to think and explore the fields of science, history and philosophy in these free nations, scientists made incredible discoveries which made it impossible for a sane, literate person to believe the biblical fictitious miracle stories concerning the origin of life.

(A humorous personal note. When I was a test pilot at the Patuxent Navy Base, I remember testing a new type aircraft at an extreme altitude, and in the long time it took to reach the maximum altitude, I noticed the wings of my airplane became less and less effective to turn or maneuver as I climbed. There was not enough atmosphere to support the lift of the wings. After landing, I joked with one of the engineers, "I don't know how the angels get around, because my plane's wings were no damn good up there." He mentioned, "I wonder how in the hell they breathe or find something to eat up there and where do they bury their crap, urine and garbage?")

Darwin proved that there is no more design by any supernatural power in the variability of organic beings and in the action of natural selection, than in the course which the wind blows from hour to hour. Evolution is completely random.

Random atom scenario: Wow! In ancient Greece in 475 BCE genius Leucippus of Miletus had stated the earth consisted of atoms and that they moved in an uncontrollably random manner. How could this Greek genius know that almost 2,500 years ago? It makes a person wonder how every so often people like this ancient Greek, Darwin, Einstein and the many other geniuses of the past are born with such brains. I wonder whether as evolution continues, whether large numbers of humans will be born with genius brains?

I learned from Professor Walter Goldschmidt of UCLA that the evolutionary process as discovered by Charles Darwin could never take place without the rhythms of birth and death. Evolutionary change comes only as new generations acquire favorable new traits through mutations that render the old obsolete and make the new generation better able to survive and cope with the trials of life. Had first life on earth emerged without this process of evolutionary regeneration, there would only be strings of some kinds of unicellular forms that emerged from the primordial ooze and the planet earth without evolution now would, at best, be covered with a permanent, never-changing blanket of the greens and grays of slime and mold. Understanding that others had to have died for us to emerge and live and the inevitability that we must, in turn, die so that others may be born and live reinforces the sense of our continuity with eternity. Understandably, we shun thoughts of death aside, but death is central to life and evolution. So we must do our best to enjoy the one and only trip we will have on this planet.

Darwin departed England in 1839 in the HMS Beagle as a believer in the mythology of Christianity, and returned from the voyage in 1842 having arrived at his theory of evolution and natural selection; however, he did not publish the findings until 1859. He may never have published the findings because of what he must have felt, that this earth-shaking revelation would bring about great ridicule of himself and the theory. At that time in history, even in the free nations, a person challenging the beliefs of Christianity would be ridiculed and condemned by nearly all in the brainwashed society. In many ways the same is still true in 2006.

Christian leaders have spent a great amount of energy and resources (and still do) to make sure any person challenging their beliefs in "certainty" is smeared as an atheist, heretic, immoral, and sinful person. Apparently Darwin was not willing, in the 1840s, to risk the tranquility of his life by revealing his theory, but in 1859 with information that the scientist, Alfred Russell Wallace, was in the process of publicly revealing his near identical discoveries in South America, Darwin decided to publish.

Once the published theory was in circulation, Darwin did suffer the humiliation of the attacks by the Christians. Fortunately, he was in a free nation and did not suffer any physical harm. He was fortunate not to be living in a Muslim or pope-controlled nation.

The Christians were outraged to have a scientist prove that they were decedents of hominoids; the very same species of animals as the apes and monkeys descended from. Imagine the shock to persons who had been led to believe in the mythology of their religious dogma, that they had been created in a God's image thousands of years earlier in the exact same physical form as they were in 1859. It is difficult to believe that just 145 years ago (just two normal lifetimes), the vast majority of citizens (even in the free nations) believed they were the image of a God who looked just like them (if they were male and Jewish). Did they question where he hung out? Did he have a wife? If he and the citizens were images of each other, then he would have to have food and water. Did they question their God may be a lady rather than a male?

Believe it or not, in the year 2006, the creationists and many of the TV evangelical ministers still insist Darwin is nothing more than a misguided atheist. A tip for creationists and TV ministers: if you go to the internet and type www.flat-earth.org, you can apply for membership in the Flat Earth group on line and add another belief. If you like to travel, you might consider also taking a trip out to New Mexico and visit with the next arrival of the aliens from outer space; and if you are one of the privileged, financially well off American CEOs, please contact me. Although retired, I am still a licensed real estate broker and I have a listing on a great bridge in Brooklyn to sell you.

I suggest you Google Charles Darwin for information about his book and also books about his career and discoveries.

K: While you were discussing Dr. Darwin's discovery of evolution I started to think about my cat. A few days ago as she slept in my lap, I wondered what her tail was for. This brought me back to thinking about the constant evolution that all animals in the world are going through, and that some of it has not been done by God, but by man. For instance dog breeds—man has manipulated dogs to come up with the look they want—this is evolution sped up and molded into the forms desired. Then I thought of the Manx cat that has no tail, and found that it is native to the Isle of Man—these cats for some reason mutated to have little or no tail. Since the cats were confined to an island with no new genetic material introduced into their cat world, the Manx became a breed. This is evolution that happened spontaneously as has happened on many secluded islands all over our planet. So if Christian's don't believe in evolution, I guess I would ask them, "Is God still creating? And is your Bible wrong in how long it took God to create the earth and all its animals?"

T: Well I'll be. My friend Kelle is a Darwinian scientist! Remember Kelle, dedicated Christian supporters of the Christian coalition do not believe in science and only enjoy reading the Bible. Also you are not to ask questions, PERIOD.

K: I enjoy reading the silliness about "Intelligent Design." The Evangelicals' pursuit of this idea is mind boggling to me. If I were an inquisitive person attending one of their conferences, I'd ask, "If the designer was so intelligent, why have so many species gone extinct?"

I've a feeling that they would reply that that's how God designed it, and extinction is the Almighty's will. Then I'd have to reply, "You mean everything is pre-ordained? — in that case what good is it to pray for anything? It's already been pre-ordained! Everyone tries to find that inside track to the "heavenly miracle gifts." Fads come and fads go! I really love this ID statement! "A is for Adam, God made him from dust/He wasn't a monkey, he looked just like us." Oh, yeah, then who were the humanoids that roamed the world before Adam? And where did they come from? They had to be here before Adam because they didn't look just like us. I think intelligent design is a good phrase, but the question is whose

*intelligence? Chaos, nature, or a deity? Most probably some fanatic nut standing on a
soap box with a bullhorn in a public park.*

    T: I'd bet it came from the guy with the bullhorn in the park or from a TV
Bible thumper. Intelligent Design dreams came to life many years ago, in the 1920s, and
then nearly disappeared. Then about 10 to 15 years ago a few individuals added several new
twists to the original creationism story and brought it back. I am sure it will pass from the
scene again just like the once prominent Christian Temperance Union has all but disappeared in our more enlightened society.

Dr. Carl Sagan 1934-1996

    I remember Dr. Sagan for being the author, teacher and documentary film maker
who made me aware of the vastness and beauty of the universe. He is so famous I need not
go into any great detail about his outstanding 13-session Cosmos documentary and the
statement he repeated in every one of the sessions about the billions of stars and planets
in the universe. Until reading his books and watching the documentary, I had no idea of
the vastness of the universe. It's regrettable that he passed away just a few years before the
discovery in the mid-90s that our vast universe is probably just one of many, many vast
universes.

    I remember Dr. Sagan warmly because of a personal incident some years ago at the San
Diego USMC Military Exchange when I happened to meet one of my former USS Leyte
(a WW-II Essex class Navy carrier we both served on in post-WW-II years) shipmates
while my wife and I were shopping at the exchange. Normally when we go shopping, I take
some reading material. After I've had enough shopping, I sit on the exchange's outdoor
patio with my dog, Boris, and spend the time reading material of interest and enjoying a
refreshment while Karen does her "hunter gatherer" thing. On that day, I was reading one
of Dr. Sagan's books, enjoying my snack while sitting on the comfortable sunny patio of the
exchange. My old USS Leyte shipmate friend saw me and we had a chat about old times.
He noticed my Carl Sagan book and we got into a discussion about Dr. Sagan, space, the
universe, where did we all come from, where are we going to go and why are we here. As
it turned out, he and I are both great fans and admirers of Dr. Sagan. He mentioned first
that this kind of science had also shaken his belief in the myths of the Christian religion
and God creating the earth in six days and other fictitious stories from his Sunday school
days. He, his wife, and I had attended many ship company parties together so I asked
about Sally. He then told me he had lost his wife a few years earlier. They had been married
for 50 years and had celebrated the anniversary with the children and grandchildren a
few months before her passing. She had not shown any signs of serious health problems
but one morning when he woke up she was dead lying in bed beside him; a very peaceful

way to go. He went on with the story and the fact he could not face having a pagan-like Christian ceremony followed by a wake party and then have her buried to rot away with the worms underground. So he had her cremated; by prior agreement between the two of them did not have any Christian service performed and arranged a party at his golf club three weeks later to celebrate her life and their marriage with only the family and closest friends attending. Without informing anyone in the family, he bought a rose bush at the local nursery, dug a hole in his front yard and put her ashes in alongside the roots of the rose bush. He told me each day when he goes out to get the morning paper he takes a glass of water with him and waters the bush and says, "good morning." He feels that her "dust to dust" elements of the universe are there in the plant and the beautiful rose bush is more comfort to him than commuting to a graveyard to look at a cold bleak headstone. Every time I pick up a Dr. Carl Sagan book or see the Sagan Cosmos documentary on the science cable channel I think of my shipmate friend and what comfort Sagan's works has brought to him. I know Dr. Sagan would be very pleased if he knew about the comfort his teachings and published works brought to my friend.

DR. SAGAN ASKS, "ARE WE ALONE?"

For thousands of years (at least as long as over 100,000 years), homosapiens have turned their eyes to the lights in the night time sky with wonder and questions. In the last few thousand years with the discovery that the dots of light in the sky were suns and planets, they began to question: what are they? Are they the same as earth? Where did they come from? How did all of this come about? Is God living on one of them?

For thousands of years, religious leaders of all kinds have always placed the God they represent at some location no one could reach. Some far away mountain, across the seas or deep in a forest, so naturally one or many of the would-be representatives of God would place he/she/it on one of the bright lights in the heavens.

After countless thousands of years and the lifetimes of billions of people, suddenly in just the lifetime of one person, ME, almost all of the answers to these questions about the universe have been discovered and verified by scientists.

As Dr. Carl Sagan taught, it is beyond our ability to really grasp the vastness of the universe with its billions of stars, planets, meteors and debris that have been hovering around for the past 15 to 20 billion years.

Try this Dr. Sagan exercise to imagine just this one aspect of the universe. The light reaching planet earth, from a star <u>and traveling at the speed of light</u> for a billion years! A billion years <u>at the speed of light</u>, it finally reaches the Hubble telescope. Earth is not as large in relation to this vast universe as the tiniest grain of sand is in relation to the size of the earth. All of this information discovered, verified and made public in the last 78 years has intensified the interest of people in the question: "are we alone in the universe?" To try and visualize the size of the earth compared to the universe, I tried a Dr. Sagan-type exercise of acquiring a two foot by two foot piece of plain white wrapping paper, laying it on a table and then making a small dot with a pencil on it; then standing back a bit and observing the small dot compared to the huge sheet of paper and realizing that the small dot was actually <u>several million times</u> too large to compare to the size of the universe represented by the large paper to the size of our planet! To properly compare the size of the planet earth to the size of this one universe, it would be necessary to have a dot on the paper so small it would take a microscope to see the dot. It is very difficult to gain a perspective as to just how insignificant the tiny earth planet is in relation to the known universe. Just think, it took this Jewish guy six days to make this tiny thing the size of a grain of sand in the universe! Then he had to goof off and rest on the seventh day. Is he incompetent or just lazy? From end to end the known universe is said to be 156 billion light years in size. With billions of other stars and planets in just this one universe, it would seem very likely life exists elsewhere in the myriad starfields. Without question, whatever form of human-like life that may exist anywhere in the vast universe, they are all going to go to exist in Hell when they die, because the pope on earth claims they are not Catholics. They were born sinful and the pope did not relieve them of their sin and none of them ever put money in the plate. Where in the hell is Hell?

Literate persons know that the story of the six-day God with one day to rest is a fictitious story. What we do not know is from where did the universe come? What brought it about? Where did the atom that burst into the Big Bang come from?

In Physics 101, we were taught there is no such thing as perpetual motion and that there has to be an origin for such an event as the sudden arrival of the original Big Bang atom. It could not have been born in a vacuum of nothing. Some scientists are suspicious the Big Bang atom actually dropped out of the bottom of a giant black hole of an older universe. It has been verified in recent years that we are just one of many galaxies. In the near future it may be verified that our vast universe is just one of many millions of vast universes.

One thing is for sure; you and I are not an image of whatever she/he/it supernatural power is behind the creation of this vast universe, even if you are male and Jewish; and if you are a lady you can be sure your kind were not made from a man's rib.

It would be a real disappointment if I arrive in Heaven and discover "it" is a HE in the image of my Jewish real estate associate, Babe Siener, a 6 foot 2 inch former heavy weight boxer who looks like he lost a few tough fights. On the other hand, if HIS domain includes a sports bar with free cold beer, the Babe and I along with some of our WW-II buddies would find that to be very enjoyable.

Scientists have proven every form of life, everything on earth, and the earth itself all consist of the elements of the universe. The scientists have also proven every discovery of matter (so far) in the universe, consists of the same elements that exist on earth. You, I and every living thing (animal or plant) on earth consist of these elements of the universe and water. Without question, scientifically proven, we are "star stuff." PERIOD.

Thanks to Dr. Sagan and the works and discoveries of many other great astronomical scientists of the past two centuries, we now know who we are, why we are here and where we are going: we are recycled elements of the universe.

Jacob Bronowski 1908–1974

I consider the information I learned in the Jacob Bronowski course at the University of California, San Diego in the early 1970s, and from his book, *The Ascent of Man*, and his documentary based on his famous book, one of the most interesting and exciting educational experiences of my life.

Dr. Bronowski's explanation of how the evolutionary mutation development of a thumb on the hand of the first hominoid species (the development of a grip) would set that species off on a course of evolution that would create the ultimate animal on earth. He took the class step by step through the evolutionary procedure of how the thumb and grip drove and grew the specie's brain to the fantastic level of the likes of Einstein, Darwin, Newton and all the other great geniuses and tool makers of history, as well as the great brain we lesser intelligent persons have.

His scientific studies also proved the Darwinian theory that animals retain much of the primary brain characteristics and brain wired uniqueness of the brains of the animals from which they descended. The herding instinct for the safety and leadership of a species is one of the most important inherited instincts.

Bronowski and his works are well represented on Google.com with search words "Jacob Bronowski." The professor wrote many books and discovered many important scientific manifestations of mankind and civilization, while working at the world famous Scripps Institute adjacent to the University of California in La Jolla, CA.

One of his most memorable quotes was, "Man masters nature not by force but by understanding." Ponder that statement for a few minutes.

In the teaching of the course, "The Ascent of Man," Bronowski made it clear that man is different from other animals because the frontal lobes of the brain continued growth as a result of the hand driving the subsequent education and enlargement of the brain. The species then became primitive tool makers. This growth, through evolution and natural selection, with the survival of the fittest to cope with difficult events, created a human capable of ever more efficient learning including the ability to memorize new experiences and to adapt to new challenges, to eventually develop language and writing. All of this is a result of the thumb and grip of the hominoid's hand exercising and driving the brain.

Bronowski's lifetime of research resulted in the book *Ascent of Man* which is indeed one of the most important intellectual literary achievements of the 1900s. Regrettably this great scientist and teacher died of a heart attack at the age of 66 on Long Island while producing a new documentary, still at the peak of his illustrious career.

Although he had accomplished cutting edge advances in science at the Scripps Institute, he still had a great deal more knowledge to pass on to humanity when he died.

"The hand is the cutting edge of the mind," Dr. Bronowski, 1971.

A dialogue of a lecture given by Dr. Jacob Bronowski

T: Kelle, I first heard this Dr. Bronowski discourse in 1972 in the "Ascent of Man" Bronowski course at UCSD located in La Jolla adjacent to the Scripps Institute where Dr. Bronowski had his office and laboratory. I am sure the reader of your book will believe this is one of the most emotional and thoughtful philosophical dialogues about the conduct of humans ever stated. The Holocaust could not have taken place if the German society of the 1940s had not been led by despots who although not religious, believed they had absolute certainty in what they were doing. Could this happen again?

Dr. Bronowski: "I grew up to be indifferent to the distinction between literature and science, which in my teens were simply two languages for experience that I learned together."

"Dissent is the mark of freedom."

"Sooner or later every one of us breathes an atom that has been breathed before by anyone you can think of who has lived before us: Michelangelo, or George Washington, or Moses."

"The Principle of Uncertainty is a bad name. In science—or outside of it—we are not uncertain; our knowledge is merely confined within a certain tolerance. We should call it the "Principle of Tolerance." And I propose that name in two senses: first, in the engineering sense—science has progressed, step by step, the most successful enterprise in the ascent of man, because it has understood that the exchange of information between man and nature, and man and man, can only take place with a certain tolerance. But second, I also use the word, passionately, about the real world. All knowledge—all information between human beings—can only be exchanged within a play of tolerance. And that is true whether the exchange is in science, or in literature, or in religion, or in politics, or in *any* form of thought that aspires to dogma. It's a major tragedy of my lifetime and yours that scientists were refining, to the most exquisite precision, the Principle of Tolerance—and turning their backs on the fact that all around them, tolerance was crashing to the ground beyond repair. The Principle of Uncertainty or, in my phrase, the Principle of Tolerance, fixed once and for all the realization that all knowledge is limited. It is an irony of history that at the very time when this was being worked out there should rise, under Hitler in Germany and other tyrants elsewhere, a counter-conception: a principle of monstrous certainty. When the future looks back on the 1930s it will think of them as a crucial confrontation of culture as I have been expounding it, the ascent of man, against the throwback to the despots' belief that they have absolute certainty. It is said that science will dehumanize people and turn them into numbers.

That is false: tragically false. Look for yourself. (While showing his documentary film.) This is the concentration camp and crematorium at Auschwitz. This is where people were turned into numbers. Into this pond were flushed the ashes of four million people. And that was not done by gas. It was done by arrogance. It was done by dogma. It was done by ignorance. When people believe that they have absolute knowledge, with no test in reality—this is how they behave. This is what men do when they aspire to the knowledge of gods. Science is a very human form of knowledge. We are always at the brink of the known; we always feel forward for what is to be hoped. Every judgment in science stands on the edge of error, and is personal. Science is a tribute to what we *can* know although we are fallible. In the end, the words were said by Oliver Cromwell: "I beseech you, in the bowels of Christ: Think it possible you may be mistaken." We have to cure ourselves of the itch for absolute knowledge and power. We have to close the distance between the push-button order and the human act. We have to touch people." From the *Knowledge of Certainty* episode from *The Ascent of Man*.

"Fifty years from now if an understanding of man's origins, his evolution, his history, his progress is not in the common place of the school books we shall not exist." This from *The Long Childhood* episode from *The Ascent of Man*.

Note: This dialogue was made in the early 1970s. Will the neocon coalition take over the teaching of subjects in our public schools and prevent the future generations of Americans learning philosophy such as this?

Statement by Albert Einstein:

"All our science, measured against reality, is primitive and childlike-and yet it is the most precious thing we have."

So Kelle, the most brilliant man of the last century believed we have much more to learn and that there is no such thing as any earthbound person or organization qualified to be teaching "certainty" in any subject, religion or field of thought. Humans must forever question, doubt and always search for the truth. If that upsets the practitioners preaching the dogma of certainty so be it.

Charles Bradlaugh 1833-1891

When first elected as a member of the British Parliament, Charles Bradlaugh was not permitted by the members to take office because he would not take the oath of office with his hand on a Bible. In his opinion, the Bible was a book of fiction. Remember, this occurred even in a nation that permitted free thinking! After much controversy that went on for close to a decade, he was finally seated in Parliament in 1886. (Possibly finally seated as a result of the widespread publication of both Darwin and Wallace's works.)

Bradlaugh became disenchanted with fictitious manmade organized religions as a young man and was an outspoken critic of the Church of England throughout his life. In fact, he was a critic of the dogma and fiction of all religions. His views were closely related to the views of the American 1776 forefathers, whom he greatly admired. In his mind, just like the Koran of the Muslim religion, the Christian Bible sanctioned many gruesome acts. He maintained that only secularism and the efforts of free thinkers in the free nations brought about moderation of the inhuman provisions of the Bible. For example: a single sample of atrocities among many cruel dictates the Bible sanctions, the book approves and encourages slavery. It is printed in black and white in all Christian Bibles. Bradlaugh argued that the moderation of the intolerance set forth in the Bible could only be brought about by skepticism of free thinkers, agnostics, secularists, and atheists. The Bible then and now sanctions slavery and killing of women witches. This is printed in the Bible you have at home. The fact that the Christians now ignore that phrase in the good book came about through the actions of the activist secularists of society, not by the Christian leaders.

If you follow the train of thought Bradlaugh was pursuing, you will see that the Christian leaders of today would be little different from the ayatollahs of the Muslim world if it were not for the secularists, atheists, agnostics, skeptics and free thinker activists of the free nations. So let us analyze Bradlaugh's theory as it applies to the Muslim and Christian religions of 2006.

Much of the Koran is derived from the earlier Christian Bible. The Muslim-controlled nations do not have openly secularist citizens. To oppose any rulings of the ayatollahs decisions based on their Koran is cause for execution. Thus, as called for in the Koran, a starving man who steals a loaf of bread will have his right hand cut off when caught. A lady who commits adultery will be buried up to her shoulders and then stoned to death. A man should not commit adultery either, but if he does there is no penalty. Men of course wrote both the Bible and the Koran. This is just one example of the type of punishment printed in the Koran, and these punishments are carried out to this day.

Thanks to the bravery of Dr. Martin Luther in the 1500s, many nations were able to break free of the iron fist of the infallible Catholic popes. With freedom to read, think, and study in these free nations, numerous free thinking skeptics, atheists, agnostics, and secularists, not only became outspoken, they also became activists demanding humanitarian treatment of the citizens. As one example, Bible-sanctioned slavery was abolished peacefully in Britain and later in America with a great war.

Unfortunately, there has never been an individual like Dr. Martin Luther in the Muslim world, so the cruelty of the Koran lives on. Anyone questioning the fact that the Christian leadership would have ever moderated, if the freedom to think, read, question, be a skeptic, a free thinker, an atheist or a secularist had not come about in the free nations, is not very realistic. No dictator ever voluntarily gives up absolute control. Bradlaugh believed the gathering together of the American 1776 forefathers creating the first great secular nation could not have come about if it were not for the acts of the brave Martin Luther.

The real difference between the punishments still carried out under the dictates of the Koran and those now permitted in the Christian nations is due to the result of the heroic activism of the skeptics of every level in the free nations.

Sunand Tryambak Joshi 1958-Still Active in 2006

Mr. Joshi has made the research of the works of many of the most celebrated thinkers, past and present, and also the philosophers in the field of atheism, agnosticism, skepticism, free thinkers and mythology, a major part of his career. His book, *Atheism, a Reader*, is a must read for any adult in a quandary (such as I was) about what they were taught in Sunday school as compared to what they now know as a literate, educated and informed adult; yet fearful of letting go of the "crutch" to face life on their own.

If nothing else, you will learn what some of the greatest minds of both the present and past think and thought about religion. He has researched and summarized the works and teachings of many of the greatest philosophers of the ages. The knowledge you gain reading his book may protect you from drifting into membership of a dangerous brainwashed cult.

Many who have elected to face life without the crutch of religion claim there is a feeling of accomplishment to sit through a Christian performance of marriage, funeral or sermon, and having the feeling that they know the real truth. It's kind of an egotistical feeling similar to sitting in a college class and realizing you know more about a subject than the professor or being a pilot in training and knowing you can fly better than the individual checking you out.

Just relax, enjoy the great sentimental music at a wedding, the social contacts and the warm atmosphere, act humbly and keep your mouth shut, but don't make any financial contribution. At a sad funeral hopefully the sentimental music will help ease the pain. The mumble jumble will no longer help once the transition has been accomplished.

Having studied the work of Mr. Joshi, I came away with the feeling that confirmed atheists also have to be a bit egotistical to be absolutely sure there is no kind of supernatural power. How can they be sure? Einstein was not sure whether some kind of cosmic supernatural "thing" might be out there. I still occasionally take my dog Boris for a walk in the marina late at night and look up at the universe and have a little chat just to be sure. I am sure as hell "IT" (if it exists) doesn't look like me and "IT" never sent any boy down to this tiny grain of sand sized planet of the universe to talk to people. I am also sure "IT" could care less if I eat beef on Friday, dance, have sex with my wife just for enjoyment, drink alcohol, never fast, drink coffee, and eat pork.

Carl Van Doren 1885–1950

T:Now I would like to encourage you to learn more about Columbia Professor Van Doren. Professor Van Doren never taught or wrote any information that would indicate he did not firmly believe that all citizens should enjoy the freedom of and the freedom from religion.

The professor was very critical of any religious sects' use of government powers or any government provisions supporting religious leaders engaged in heavy-handed proselytising and coercion of the citizens. I became keenly aware of the importance of the professor's lifetime work while living in San Diego. The incident that caught my attention was reported in the San Diego Union newspaper stories concerning what happened to the careers of teachers in Poway, a San Diego County Public School system, following the taking over of the school board by a group of dedicated Christians. The stories were shocking and a wake up call for me. Many science books were removed from the schools libraries and the teachers were monitored by members of the school board who were frequently interviewing students about what they were being taught in science classes. Needless to say, Dr. Charles Darwin's scientific discoveries were no longer emphasized in the science classes and none of his books were in the library. Fortunately the fanatics were gone following the subsequent election of school board officials. But remember they are there in the community and they will never cease in their efforts to get back into power and dictate what is to be taught in the schools.

Thanks to Google more and more Americans will become familiar with Dr. Van Doren and his intelligent and thoughtful teachings. At the turn of the last century, Dr. Van Doren addressed the demise of all of the past many thousands of fictitious gods from the earliest known in history to the present day. And in my opinion Charles Darwin, plus the work of all of the many other great scientists, philosophers, educators of the past 150 years and all this vast information available with just a few mouse clicks on Google will have the fictitious Islamic Muslim sects and Christianity with its many sects join the other fictitious gods on what Dr. Van Doren considered to be the trash pile in history. Dr. Van Doren said it another way: "The past thousands upon thousand of gods are now nameless in the compost of civilization."

Professor Van Doren of Columbia University was also a literary critic and author. He published many important books, one of which was the most insightful biographies ever written about Benjamin Franklin. He published eloquent works refuting the belief that atheists were merely negative persons with a bleak outlook on the world and life. He made it clear that atheists were no less virtuous or moral than believers. He may have arrived at this opinion after his intensive study of the life of Benjamin and a few of the other 1776 forefathers.

Professor Van Doren taught and wrote, "When I say I am a non-believer, I do not mean I am not a Methodist, a Mormon, a Catholic, a Baptist, or even that I am not a Christian; I mean I do not believe in any fictitious god that has ever been devised, in any super-natural myths, fiction and doctrine that has ever been revealed or claimed by men or in any mythical scheme of immortality that has ever been expounded. As to gods that have been, there are countless numbers of them in the history of civilization that now lay nameless in the compost of civilization. It would be unreasonable to assume some of them or any one of them is a true God.

Why do I find Professor Van Doren as one of my most influential philosophers? It makes me realize the truth of my belief that the herding instinct of most all animals has been retained through evolution and natural selection in the genes of humans. So, that is the reason for the vast number of thousands of different past and present gods in the known history of civilization. Regardless of how remote a group of humans, throughout the history of the human animal, every isolated group will have a god of some kind in place due to the inherited herding concept in action. The actual reason Van Doren stated, "so many thousands upon thousands of god beliefs have been eventually over taken and trashed."

When I formulated the list of the ingredients that are necessary to initiate a successful new religion, the works of Professor Van Doren depicting the vast number of past gods convinced me that they and the gods of future centuries that will surely come about are the result of the evolutionary inherited "herd instinct" imbedded in the genes of the human animal.

The instinct of an individual using the power of the super homosapien brain to become a herd leader or one of the "groupies" (disciples) of a herd leader. The icon leader may have been still alive or have been dead and then glorified by groupies seeking the leadership of a herd. The herd may be as small as an isolated tribe in the Brazilian forest or as large as a major nation, but a herd leader or the groupies of a past or present herd leader with a connection to a supernatural power will emerge from time to time in this and in future centuries, as they have in past centuries. Fortunately, the rise of worldwide literacy and education will no doubt limit the number of believers in new religions to small cells within large democratic secular societies.

The Christians, of course feel they have their God's doctrine, encouragement and his demand that they travel all over the earth to do away with all of the other gods and herd leaders. See Isaiah 45:21,22 in the Bible. (The same dogma was then copied and printed in the Koran 632 years later.)

Regardless of where the Christian missionaries have gone to do their God's work, they have created havoc in the cultures they have invaded. The Spanish priests destroyed the centuries old culture, gods and religions of the South American Aztecs, Incas and other Indian cultures in the 1400s and 1500s. The American Protestant missionaries in the 1800s not only destroyed the culture, ancient gods and religion of the people of the Hawaiian

Islands, they also stole everything of value on the islands for themselves. The descendents of these Hawaiian missionaries as of 2006 ACE still own a significant amount of the land and wealth stolen from the Hawaiians by their missionary great-grandparents.

*K:	So if you believe the same as Dr. Van Doren, you don't believe in organized religion or their efforts to convert the world to their beliefs?*

T: Absolutely true. The organized Islamic and Christian religions have no right to invade other cultures and societies converting their beliefs to the Christian and Islamic beliefs. It is difficult to be a true atheist knowing Einstein theorized that there may be some kind of cosmic force out there beyond the Big Bang. All we know for sure is that the Christian and Islamic dogma are fiction. See Google. Type in "Professor Carl Van Doren."

Baruch Spinoza 1632-1677

Philosopher Spinoza, considered a genius by historians, made the following statement: "I have made a ceaseless effort not to ridicule, not to bewail, not to scorn human actions (including beliefs), but to understand them."

His extremely naturalistic views on God, the world, the human being and knowledge serve to ground a moral philosophy centered on the control of the passions leading to virtue and happiness. They also lay the foundations for a strongly democratic political thought and a deep critique of the pretensions of scripture and sectarian religion. Of all the philosophers of the seventeenth century, perhaps none have more relevance to today than Spinoza.

I admire Baruch Spinoza and I wish I could live up to the philosophy he expounded at all times; but I must admit I cannot control my anger at some incidents. I truly believe every American must be granted freedom of religion and also freedom from religion. I admire many true Christian believers and sometimes feel it would be comfortable to be able to believe as they do when facing difficult times or incidents. But I cannot believe in the fiction of the religion since the greatest brains of the last two hundred years have proven beyond any doubt that the Christian religion is fiction. As Einstein said, "There may be some supernatural cosmic source or icon out beyond the Big Bang."

We only know it is not a six-day Christian or Muslim God.

Origins of the Universe

Moving Toward Skepticism…We Do Repeat Ourselves!

Reading the works of Professor Van Doren, Dr. Charles Darwin, scientist professor Bronowski, the late Dr. Carl Sagan and the first five pages of the Christian sci-fi Bible is what set me off on my personal drive and research to try and learn who I am, where did I come from, why am I here and where will I be going when my time is up on this planet. At middle age, I had had enough of living and believing in myths, superstition, fictional stories and the lectures of the practitioners of fictitious religion. So far, all I have learned is that no one knows what is out beyond the Big Bang. The atheists have to be egotists to believe they have the answer and the practitioners of manmade fictitious religions know they are purveying fiction.

After reading the fiction in the religious books, I directed my search toward the science behind the universe. This chapter includes not only material on the big bang, but first life on this planet and the theory of evolution. It includes material I learned from reading about the brilliant work of scientists, genius philosophers and deep thinkers of the past who have contributed to the world's knowledge; kind of like a parrot repeating the words of his master. I must admit, much of what I read in the work of these superbrains is over my head.

Because of "Googling" (think of how difficult it was for people to research information before Google) and parroting the information I have found in the works of the great men and women of the past, some of the material I include may be considered plagiarism. Google and the books I learned about on Google have been my sources of information since 1998! There is no way an old military throttle jockey and real estate developer can research the complicated subjects without these tools. In every subject I discuss, it is my intention to note the source and person responsible for the factual matter. If you disagree with the scientific work or history presented by an individual as I understand the subject or the philosophy, so be it. If I put the information in this book, it means I believe in their work and analysis. I also realize that my interpretation may not agree with what you believe. So be it.

K: Tom, I think you have a good reason to study and research. We would all like to know the truth about who we really are, where we came from, why we are here and where we will be going when we complete our journey here on earth.

T: In addition to this curiosity, I also happen to have a quiet resentment about being hustled by propaganda, falsely promoted by advertisers, (when watching television, I often hit the mute button immediately when the ads come on), and above all, I despise being lied to by our politicians or any organization's propaganda, including Bible-thumpers and any of those attempting to convert our secular government into a theocracy-governed nation.

K: Tom, trust the philosophy of Abe Lincoln for the long run of America; they can fool some of the people some of the time but they cannot fool all of the people all of the time. With better education now a national issue, the citizens of America will not be fooled by the religious coalition.

T:Kelle, I think the neocons and religious fanatics who have mounted up and have been on a rampage from the early 1980s to the present time are soon to become well aware of the great Republican's proclamation: "You can fool all of the people some of the time, and some of the people all of the time, but you cannot fool all of the people all of the time."

What a great and meaningful statement! I am confident in the next decade or so, thanks to the educational efforts of the many pro-American organizations we have discussed the citizens of our country will start voting out the kind of religious fanatics now holding many of the important offices in our government.

K: Let's hope so for the good of America's future!

T:I personally only know for sure whatever is out there it is not the six-day God in my or any male's image taught to me in Sunday school.

K: We certainly have a lot of thoughts in common! What got you headed in the direction your philosophy took?

T: When I did some basic research and reading about the works and scientific discoveries by the great minds of the past, it became clear that just about all of the teachings I learned as a young person in Sunday school, later in the sermons in my church, and the verbal baloney fed to us WW-II military people by the military chaplains were for the most part make-believe fiction and lies. I became very, very angry. Not angry just because I was deceived, but also for my friends who didn't survive the wars and went to their deaths believing this fiction.

K: Do you believe something is behind storms? You don't think that conditions can come together in just the right way for hurricanes, tornadoes, or floods to occur spontaneously? Couldn't the Big Bang be the combination of various conditions at the right time to create an explosion creating the universe?

T: I am a believer in the ancient Greek genius Leucippus of Miletus's teaching that all things and events are the result of the random chaos of atoms that are not in the control of any power. A good example of this random chaos of events would be the decade or so ago of atmosphere events that caused the so called "perfect storm" that occurred off of the coast of New England. If Einstein wasn't sure of what is out there a person would have to an egotist to think he/she was more intelligent than Einstein. Until the scientists get beyond the Big Bang I would classify persons like me as an agnostic skeptic.

K: I think I will designate you as a militant verbal skeptic of the Christian coalition! Are you also anti Jewish, Buddhist, Hindi, and Muslim? They are also organized religions.

T: The Jews are not a militant organized religion like the Christians and Muslims. The Jews have never invaded and attempted to convert other society's beliefs to their beliefs. I am not a religious scholar so I am not familiar with all of the religions of the world but if there were any other militant organized religions with a history of mass killings similar to the Christians and Muslims I am sure it would be widely known in the modern world.

Designating me as a verbal skeptic of the Christian coalition is fine with me. All we know for sure is that Christianity, like all the previous manmade fictitious religions, is based on stories with no more credibility than the Haitian voodoo operators I found entertaining in Haiti while in the Navy. Also that none of the Christian leaders today or over the past 2,000 years have any more connection to whatever is out there (if there is something out there) than you or I. In my opinion, Christianity will eventually join God Zeus and the thousands of the other gods on the trash pile Dr. Van Doren called the compost of civilization.

K: There are scientific theories that are now on that civilization compost heap too. Isn't it just the evolution of the human mind and discoveries that make it possible to disprove from time to time widely held scientific principles? Therefore, I'd suggest that it is up to each individual to study the writings of scientists, philosophers, anthropologists, and archeologists to arrive at their own view of things.

T: Yes, I agree with you that evolution in all fields is all important and literate persons need to keep informed of the progress in all the fields you mention. The primary problem with the leaders of the Christian empire is that they are locked into 2,000 year-old fiction of certainty with the inability to reform to and adjust to modern discoveries.

K: So you then became an atheist?

T: No Kelle. I became skeptical of what I was taught being raised in the Christian religion but not a true atheist as I am still wondering what is behind the Big Bang and the reason for the existence of the vast universe. In Physics 101, I was taught there is no such thing as perpetual motion and there can be no such thing as the Big Bang that came from zilch. There has to be something out there but we can be sure the six-day God story of the Christians and Muslims has to be fiction.

SKEPTICS SOCIETY

Living in Long Beach, California, I have the pleasure of attending the Skeptics Society's programs at nearby CalTech (California Institute of Technology) located in Pasadena. The director of the Skeptics Society is Dr. Michael Shermer who is also the author the book, *Why People Believe Weird Things*. I was impressed with a paragraph on page 6 of his book. Here is the paragraph:

"This hope is what drives all of us—skeptics and believers alike—to be compelled by unsolved mysteries, to seek spiritual meaning in a physical universe, desire immortality, and wish that our hopes for eternity may be fulfilled. It is what pushes many people to spiritualists, New Age gurus and television psychics, who offer a Faustian bargain: eternity in exchange for the <u>willing suspension of disbelief</u> (and usually a contribution to the provider's coffers)." (Read the underlined words again.)

Following my reading of that paragraph, I thought about my earlier concept about the inherited "herding instinct" of most all warm-blooded animals with the desire for safety, shelter, food and in the case of the superbrained human animal, immortality. Taking another read of the paragraph and thinking about the imagination and creativity of the ancient writers of the Bible I can see how they played on this inherited instinct of humans to build the myths, fiction, legends, superstition and fear into their leadership of societies.

Read the paragraph again and compare (especially the last sentence) the message to the practice and promises of the leaders of Christian flocks. Is there any difference in their conduct, promises and operations from the fake gurus, spiritualists and television psychics? In my opinion there is little or no difference.

Google: "SKEPTICS SOCIETY" for many hours of interesting information.

K: That is indeed an interesting and thought-provoking paragraph.

T:I knew you would find it very interesting. Although the meetings take place in Pasadena, California, many people join the society from all over America and many foreign countries. As a member, you will also receive a year's subscription of their very interesting magazine. All Skeptics presentations are recorded so that they can be read on the internet by readers all over the world.

So let's take another step related to Dr. Shermer's paragraph 6 in his book *Why People Believe in Weird Things*. The purveyors of fakery of all kinds are well aware that the foremost concern of a vast number of humans is: "Where do I go following my journey on earth?" ...seeking peace of mind. And the fakers pound on that concern to fill their coffers with money.

They well know it is in the inherited genes of all warm blooded animals, including humans, to seek assistance from some quarter, (example, herding with a strong leader for four-footed animals) and from some mystic power, a leader, (a representative of a god in the human species) to protect, comfort and assist the individual animal during its journey on this planet. (Of course the four-footed animals are just seeking security and leadership in their here and now existence.) I discussed the herding instinct and herd leadership earlier.

Let's review the following poll of the American public related to believing weird things:

In a 1991, a Gallup Poll of adult Americans was conducted to learn the beliefs of Americans seeking peace, direction and comfort in their lives. The Gallup Poll established the following regarding the beliefs of the American population:

Believers:

Astrology   52%

ESP (extra sensory perception) 46%

Aliens have landed on earth   22%

Dinosaurs and humans lived simultaneously   41%

Some individuals can communicate with the dead   42%

Of course any human can talk to a dead person; the real problem is trying to get the dead person to answer.

Clairvoyance   59%

Some humans have psychic power   67%

(In the 1980s, First Lady Nancy Reagan arranged Ronnie's (the president's) most important meeting schedules at times recommended by her personal astrologer.)

I wish the poll had also included:
  Reading tea leaves
  Chinese fortune cookies (I am an enthusiastic reader after meals)
  Palm readers
  Haiti voodoo practitioners (I enjoyed visiting with them)

So it has to be foreknown the purveyors of religion based on past centuries of superstition, ancient myths, fear and fictitious stories would have a bonanza harvest of followers. The percentages indicated in the poll of believers in most anything is an accurate poll within 3 to 5%. If they believe any of this fiction, why wouldn't they also believe the stories of the Christian, Islamic practitioners and pagan priests?

THE BIG BANG

The "Big Bang Theory" has been challenged, but the vast majority of reputable and recognized scientists believe it to be one of the most important discoveries of the 1900s.

I was surprised to learn in my research that the discovery of the Big Bang occurred in my lifetime. I was 5 years old when the discovery was published in 1927. We can be sure the leaders of fictitious manmade religions have had to struggle with this discovery. It is in complete and absolute conflict with their teachings and contrary to the very foundation of the Christian dogma.

In my real estate development career I engaged in following my military retirement, I learned that if the foundation of a building is faulty, the completed project will be faulty. The same is also true if the source documentation of any organization is faulty or untrue. In ancient times, when the vast majority of the populations of the known Western World were illiterate, were born and died without ever traveling more than a day's walking distance from their place of birth, with no access to any form of media or information, it is understandable they would believe in myths and make believe stories. What I find difficult to comprehend is the fact that millions of individuals, even though many just have an elementary education in today's world but have the ability to read, will read the fiction in the first 5 or 6 pages of the Bible (Genesis 1:2 through Genesis 6:22, the very foundation of the Christian dogma) and still financially support this make believe infrastructure and lifestyle of the leaders of the Christian church. Why not just take a walk in the evening and have a chat with the possible great God of the universe for free?

Fortunately, the scientists who discovered the Big Bang have not been treated very much like the treatment of Galileo in 1633. Galileo was sentenced to a lifetime of house arrest by the pope because Galileo validated the discovery made by the genius discoverer of the Copernican Theory. That theory states that the earth is not the center of the galaxy and is just a planet orbiting around the sun. Of course at that time, nothing much was known about the fact the galaxy was just one of billions of galaxies. Galileo's validation of the fact that the earth rotated around the sun and that the earth was not the center of the known universe as the religious leaders dictated resulted in his arrest.

In our secular nation, the scientists of the Big Bang discovery and those who verified it were praised and rewarded. This discovery has not been fought by any major religious cult to date, but there are many other scientific findings of this century that they are fighting to the bitter end.

The following Big Bang information has been derived from various sources on the internet at http://liftoff.msfc.nasa.gov/academy/universe/b_bang.html.

"The Big Bang Theory is the dominant scientific theory about the origin of the universe. According to the Big Bang discovery, the universe was created sometime between 10 billion and 20 billion years ago from a cosmic explosion that hurled a mass of matter in all directions.

In 1927, the Belgian priest, Georges Lemaître was the first to propose that the universe began with the explosion of a primeval atom."

I wonder if the brilliant priest, Lemaître, was aware at the time of his discovery that he was in fact, confirming much of the ancient Greek scientist, Leucippus of Miletus's "atomism theory."

Lemaître's proposal in 1927 came after observing the red shift in distant nebulas by astronomers, to a model of the universe based on relativity. I must admit, I have read and re-read the Einstein relativity theory too many times and still cannot understand the subject, so I just accept the fact it exists.

http://www.discussionforums.us/forum/archive/index.php/t-4208.html

"Edwin Hubble later on found experimental evidence to help justify Lemaître's theory. He found that distant galaxies in every direction are going away from us with speeds proportional to their distance. The Big Bang was initially suggested because it explains why distant galaxies are traveling away from us at great speeds. The theory also predicts the existence of cosmic background radiation (the glow left over from the explosion itself).

The Big Bang Theory received its strongest confirmation when this radiation was discovered in 1964 by Arno Penzias and Robert Wilson, who later won the Nobel Prize for this discovery and verification of the theory."

It is important to review the scientific work of Edwin Hubble, (1889 – 1953), so as to verify and help prove the Big Bang Theory. www.pbs.org/wgbh/aso/entries/bahubb.html.

"Edwin Powell Hubble is renowned for determining that there are other galaxies in the universe beyond the Milky Way, and for observing that the universe is expanding at a constant rate.

Hubble was a tall, elegant, athletic, man who at age 30 had an undergraduate degree in astronomy and mathematics, a legal degree as a Rhodes scholar, followed by a Ph.D. in astronomy. He was an attorney in Kentucky, (joined its bar in 1913), and had served in WW-I, rising to the rank of major. He was bored with law and decided to go back to his studies in astronomy.

In 1919, he began to work at Mt. Wilson Observatory in California, where he would work for the rest of his life. He was researching nebulae, fuzzy patches of light in the sky and in 1924, he announced the discovery of a Cepheid, or variable star, in the Andromeda Nebulae. Since the work of Henrietta Leavitt had made it possible to calculate the distance to Cepheids, he calculated that this Cepheid was much further away than anyone had thought and that therefore the nebulae was not a gaseous cloud inside our galaxy, like so many nebulae, but in fact, a galaxy of stars just like the Milky Way; only much further away. Until this date, scientific people believed that the only thing existing outside the Milky Way were the Magellanic Clouds. The universe was much bigger than had been previously presumed. Later studies in the 1990s now indicate the universe we now know is probably just one of many vast universes.

Hubble wanted to classify the galaxies according to their content, distance, shape, and brightness patterns, and in his observations he made another momentous discovery: by observing red shifts in the light wavelengths emitted by the galaxies, he saw that galaxies were moving away from each other at a rate constant to the distance between them (Hubble's Law). The further away they were, the faster they receded. This led to the calculation of the point where the expansion began, and confirmation of the Big Bang Theory."

This fantastic Hubble discovery was also made in my lifetime. I was about 4 years old then. It is hard to grasp the fact that in one person's lifetime a discovery of this magnitude would reveal to the world that our galaxy is just one of a great many galaxies in this known universe and then in the 1990s that our universe is probably just one of a great many vast universes. All of the more than 100 billion of people who have inhabited the earth over the past 50,000 years never even imagined they existed. Billions of stars, planets and bits and pieces of the universe just floating around for billions of years. And now there is speculation that our gigantic universe is just one of many yet to be discovered other universes. Wow!

The scientists of the major corporation, Bell Laboratories, also contributed to the effort of confirming the Big Bang Theory.

www.bell-labs.com/hhistory/laser/invention/cosmology.html.

"Murray Hill, N.J. — When the intellectual history of the 20th century is written, very few achievements will tower over these discoveries. Einstein's theory of general relativity will be one, the laws of quantum mechanics will be another. The so-called Big Bang Theory of the origin of the universe will be a third."

My comment, "Maybe these achievements of the 20th century tower over all scientific discoveries of the past 10,000 years!" No doubt our descendents will be visiting some of these far off planets in the next century.

"The discovery in 1963 by Arno Penzias and Robert Wilson of the cosmic microwave background of the Big Bang set the seal of approval on the theory and brought cosmology to the forefront as a scientific discipline. It was proof that the universe was born at a definite moment, some 15 billion years ago, some scientists say 10 to 20 billion years ago. The only facet of the Big Bang Theory that remains to be determined is the exact time of the Big Bang. Some scientists believe it occurred about 15 billion years ago; some have come to the conclusion it occurred as little as 10 billion years ago and still others, as long ago as 20 billion years ago. But no reputable scientist has ever challenged the fact that the Big Bang did occur some 10 to 20 billion years ago."

So now we consider the past great thinkers' works addressing the birth of planet earth and its evolution, knowing full well that all major events such as scientific discoveries, important political and historical occurrences, assassinations of important figures, and similar great events will create a cottage industry of critics and skeptics with careers in challenging the findings or verifying the facts of any major event. The vast majority of scientists have set the date of the "Bang" at 15 billion years ago.

We can be sure the Big Bang did occur. Creationists will have to suffer through with this knowledge in much the same way as the "flat earth proponents" have had to suffer through the fact the planet has been proven to be round and not flat.

www.flate.org or www.flatearth.com

First Life

The subject of first life is one of the most contentious subjects in society. The evangelicals, creationists and many religious believers of all types challenge the scientists to show them how to create life. So they claim that if the scientists cannot create life, then only their creator could have accomplished this feat. In this argument they forget that their God was supposed to have created the earth and all life on it in one week of six days of hard work. So why do they even argue the fact there was no life on earth until about 4 or 5 billion years ago? Obviously they believe their God created life in just six days less than 10,000 years ago because their book tells them so.

In the late 1900s, noting that now mostly literate citizens of the nation were overwhelmingly accepting the scientific work of Darwin as a proven scientific fact the neocon fanatics came up with a new term called *Intelligent Design* that in their minds some how connects evolution to the work of their God. And of course with the use of their interpretation of the fictional stories in their Bible they can prove anything they wish to prove. As we discussed earlier, you can use the Bible to prove anything.

Dr. J. Bronowski, in a lifetime of scientific study, proved beyond any question of doubt, how first life developed from the simple microscopic sized spec cells of the Universe. A short time after completing the Bronowski Ascent of Man course at the University of California San Diego I was visiting the giant General Sherman tree in Sequoia National Park that was then 275 feet tall, 102 feet circumference and several thousand years old. A man was standing near me with his dog. I noticed some small insects fluttering about the grass around the tree and started to think about what I had learned in the Bronowski course. All the life in that area evolved from the tiny cell of the first life on earth. The great tree with a life span of thousands of years, the man with a life span of maybe four score and ten, the dog with a life span of maybe ten to fifteen years, the grass maybe a season or two and the tiny insects with some a life span of just a day or so. Knowing for sure that every living thing on earth evolved from the same microscopic sized first life cell and also that every living thing on earth will eventually return to the elements of the universe to be recycled as "star stuff."

Google has a great amount of information using the search words, "First Life and Evolution", that will keep the reader busy for several hours.

We can combine some of the Google information into a simplistic analysis. Let's concentrate on this tiny microbe-like critter, too small to see without a microscope that somehow emerged from the warm sea some 4 billion years ago. Leading scientists have discovered fossils over 3 billion years old, indicating colonial structures formed by photosynthesizing cyannobacteria were building reefs billions of years ago very similar to the way coral reefs are currently developing. It has been scientifically proven that this simple life form that first existed some three to four billion years ago commenced the evolutionary process of mutations, natural selection and survival of the fittest (meaning most capable to adjust to changing conditions), resulting in all of the forms of animal and plant life that now exist on earth. This was the only living, yet to be visible, object on earth resembling single cell life form for a period of at least 2 billion years.

Some scientists feel they have proven these tiny microbe-like critters were so inexhaustible and abundant all over the earth, that their excrement of oxygen for over billions of years created the oxygen atmosphere of the planet. The evolutionary process then brought about a single cell that prospered in the oxygen atmosphere, energy from the sun and nourishment from the smaller tiny microbes. Further evolution developed a cell that divided and commenced continued propagation. About this time in the evolutionary process, a human would have been able to see a slimy, probably green, substance on the rocks around the sea similar to what is seen around a neglected swimming pool or aquarium.

In 2002, British researchers discovered a shrimp-like creature about two-tenths of an inch long (two-tenths of an inch long and the biggest and most important animal on earth for millions of years!) which lived some 425 million years ago. So there was a period of at least 3 billion years or more of evolution from the earliest cell development to the age of this small creature. Nature's evolutionary program indeed moves very slowly . These are of course my amateurish observations from reading the works of the professionals working in this scientific field.

Internet. Search word "First Life"

http://www.ecology.com/origins-of-life/earths-beginnings/

"First introduction to life on earth, formed about 4.6 billion years ago. Other life followed. First there were Archaeans, 1000th the size of a sand grain. They started at the ocean floor vents, (black smokers), and ate metal ions to survive. The world was extreme, and they were extremophiles. Recently one was found in 250 degree water, but others like ice just as well. Then bacteria came along—it also ate metals. Some didn't like the taste of metal and started manufacturing food from the sun. Other bacteria didn't like metal, but were too lazy to manufacture food. They decided to eat the photosynthic bacteria. So, we had consumers (of metal), the first producers (photosynthesis), and the first predators. Sometime thereafter, eukaryotes (like amoeba) came along. All reproduced by division, which basically meant if not eaten, they never really died. The eukaryotes learned a new trick. Instead of dividing when food sources ran out, some eukaryotes bunched together and moved to greener pastures. Cells became specialized for moving, taking in or making food, and other functions, like reproducing by spores. Cell specialization prevented division, and led to death of the aggregate. Dead cell aggregates became a food source. Fungi developed to take advantage of it. That made a complete, self-sustaining ecosystem.

Some definitions:

Life as we know it cannot exist without RNA (a genetic messenger). At first it was a RNA world. Later DNA (carries genetic code) and more efficient proteins (carry out the chemistry of reproduction) evolved.

Microbes are the smallest form of life on Earth. Nearly all are microscopic. They can be found anywhere and include:

1.   viruses (sort of living and sort of not),
 2.   prokaryotes (kingdom: monera, types: bacteria and archaeans),
 3.   eukaryotes (kingdom: protoctista, also called protists, or protista types: forams, diatoms), and
 4.   fungi (kingdom: fungi, types: mushrooms and molds).

Viruses are the smallest and simplest microbes. They do not meet the requirements of "life," so they are not part of the kingdoms of life, but they do reproduce by injecting their genes into the cells of others, so they sort of live. The earliest of all life might have been similar to a virus.

Prokaryote. The word prokaryotes indicates: RNA unicellular (single cells) and mostly anaerobic (oxygen intolerant). They did not have a nucleus. They reproduced by splitting. These cells appeared on earth at least 3.5 billion years ago. They probably evolved in or around sea vents which release steam and sulfide-rich gasses. On land they may have begun around volcanic vents in a mass of steaming lava or boiling mud, or in a swirl of methane, ammonia and other gases. No one knows for certain.

Eukaryotes. Unlike prokaryotes, eukaryotes have DNA in a nucleus. They are aerobic (they liked oxygen). Their nutrient utilization also differs from prokaryotes. Some were autotrophs (able to make own nutrients by photosynthesis, like plants). Some were consumers of autotrophs (like grazing animals). Early eukaryotes were unicellular. Early on there were multi-cellular eukaryotes, and as time passed some developed into more complex multi-cellular structures."

T: Kelle, after reviewing these scientific findings to this point, the thought came to my mind of at what stage in the development of life on the planet did sex as we know it come into existence? Not just the less than exciting scientific revelations about living cells just splitting and dividing. We know it took millions and millions of years (no doubt over a billion years) from the first microscopic cells to first divide and through Darwinian evolution to become separate independent life forms. Then I read an article about British scientists discovering a tiny fossil in 2002, only two-tenths of an inch long (would be more understandable if they had said about one-eighth of an inch long) that, based on scientific analysis, lived about 450 million years ago. The little guy was referred to as an ostracode.

K: Tom, are we going to get into a disicussion about the evolution of sex?

T:Kelle, we can't touch that subject. Imagine the frustration and angst we would cause your devout Christian and Muslim readers if we had a conversation about the evolution of sex over the past billions of years. Their sacred books were written centuries ago when the authors had little or no knowledge about birth control, women's right to freedom of choice, family planning, the use of condoms and over-the-counter day after pills that prevent conception. They would be so frustrated not finding instructions on these subjects set forth in their ancient books. Let's just discuss this little sexy ostracode guy.

Os-

tracode. Illustration by Laguna Artists Collections

The scientists also believed this type of animal had flourished on the planet for 400 to 500 million or more years before this discovered ostracode fossil had lived. The intriguing part of the story was the fact this fossil was in such excellent condition that the scientists could determine and identify many parts of the ancient fossil's body including the fact the ostracode was a male with a penis. Which of course means there also had to be female ostracodes to keep the males company. So now we know sex among animals as we understand it has been going on for at least a billion years. Wow, no doubt the few Baptists and Catholic leaders who actually believe in evolution have to consider this ostracode animal the cause of the invention of sinful sexual lifestyles. Of course we also know the vast majority of them believe only in intelligent design and that God had Noah put two ostracodes in his boat some 6,000 years ago.

Imagine what the shock would have been to the Christian population of England if this discovery had been made in the mid-1800s shortly after Darwin's evolution discoveries. They were so enraged about the fact Darwin had proved we were the descendents of hominoids that looked like apes. Now they would have had to struggle with the scientific proof that the human animal and all the other animals on the planet were decedents of this ugly little ostracode. No doubt if the great dinosaur tyrannosaurus rex had become aware of this, he/she too would have been very upset to learn this.

In recent years scientists have conclusively learned how the evolutionary process works and have validated Darwin's work. The discoveries of Darwin and Wallace caused a sensation in the mid-1800s and panicked the leaders of the fictitious manmade religious organizations of Europe and America. Had Darwin been born at the same time as Galileo, he would have no doubt been burned at the stake or hung by his ankles and sawed in half.

From the time of the ostracodes, the evolutionary process moved into larger and more complex creatures of many kinds, to the arrival of the dinosaurs approximately 225 million years ago Needless to say, the story tellers of 3000 BCE to 400 ACE had no knowledge of dinosaurs, but they did produce one fictitious story about a large animal which was of great interest to me as a child, about the big fish swallowing a homosapien. It is one of the Sunday school stories I found spellbinding and I believed every word of it.

The Dinosaurs

A period of approximately 500 to 600 million (maybe as close to a billion years) of evolution occurred from the time of the tiny shrimp like critters to the beginning of the dinosaur age. A total of over a billion years since the first signs of life and the first signs of life did not appear until some 3 to 4 billion years after the earth was formed from elements resulting from the Big Bang. A mind boggling difficulty to grasp this time frame!

Scientists have learned that until 300 to 290 million years ago, there was only one land mass on earth, called Pangea, the super continent. About 290 million years ago, the greatest mass destruction in the history of the earth occurred on Pangea killing 90% of all marine life and over 70% of all land animals and plants. This was a far greater catastrophe than the mass killings of the dinosaurs about 65 million years ago. Of course the existence of Pangea and then the drifting apart of the land masses into separate continents was not known by the early story tellers. Scientists believe the dinosaur age was between 225 million to 65 million years ago. Now compare this 160 million year time frame of dinosaur development to the just miniscule 200,000 years of the known existence of the modern homosapien animal. How long will this species last? If global warming continues on its current rate, this species is not long for this planet as compared to the time the dinosaurs ruled supreme.

These killing of masses of life occurrences, such as the extinction of the dinosaurs 65 million years ago, the greater destruction of life about 300 million years ago, and the crash of a meteor the size of Mars into earth and creating the moon, can give one cause to wonder what and when there will be another major and similar catastrophic happening.

As frequent visitors to Yellowstone National Park, my wife and I are aware of some of the scientists' concern that the thin crust over the Yellowstone Park has the potential of erupting in such a blast, as to cause an atmospheric blackout of the sun and a major cooling of the earth for several years. The earth's history indicates there has been and will be a mass killing event, occurring about every 100 to 150 million years; but, why worry, at the rate of increase of the world's human population, and with the continued destruction of the planet's environment it is doubtful if humans will be around as long as even a half a million years.

Why think about that when we in California can always be looking forward to our next earthquake, forest fires, mudslides, tornadoes and hurricanes; all because God is angry about our sinful conduct, according to Bible thumpers, TV evangelists Pat Robertson and Jerry Falwell. Personally, I think God should only be angry with Hollywood and comedians, because they sometimes make fun of him.

Thousands of different types and sizes of dinosaurs evolved between 225 million years ago and their extinction 65 million years ago. During this period, many types of small furry, warm blooded animals also made their appearance. The dinosaurs evolved into thousands of different species ranging in size from a sparrow-sized bird to the largest multi-ton animals ever to walk the earth. Actually, that little sparrow in your front yard is the nearest animal relative on earth to a dinosaur.

There are countless numbers of studies about the extinction of the dinosaurs. My personal favorite of the many studies is that of scientist Donald L. Blanchard of the Morrison Natural History Museum in Colorado. Mr. Blanchard's dissertation covers not only the extinction, but also some of the other major extinctions of life in the history of planet earth. Here is part of Mr. Blanchard's dissertation, "Life in the Ocean."

See www.town.morrison.co.us/dino-colo/extinction/extent.php

"One of the foremost problems that any successful theory of dinosaur extinction must explain is the fact that not just dinosaurs were affected. In fact, dinosaurs represent but a small portion of the animal species and plants that became extinct, at or near the end of the Cretaceous Period. The extinction event that brought the Cretaceous Period to a close (called the K/T extinction; K stands for Cretaceous, and T for the Tertiary Era: the Age of Mammals) was truly a "mass extinction," in that a wide variety of taxonomic groups from many different habitats were wiped out essentially at the same time."

"Many of the groups of organisms that were hit hardest by the K/T extinction lived in the ocean. Ammonites and belemnites, shelled cephalopod mollusks related to the octopus and squid, were abundant in the seas of the Cretaceous Period, but had disappeared entirely by its end. Another squid relative, the nautiloids, were also severely affected; only two species, the Chambered Nautilus and the King Nautilus, have survived to the present. Plesiosaurs, long necked, fish-eating marine reptiles, and mosasaurs, ferocious giant sea-going lizards, also vanished from the seas at this time, although their smaller land-dwelling reptilian cousins survived mostly unscathed.

Bivalve mollusks and other shelled invertebrates of the sea floor also suffered greatly at the end of the Cretaceous. Rudists, bivalve mollusks and the dominant reef builders of the Cretaceous seas, declined sharply towards the end of the Period, and disappeared entirely at its close. Brachiopods, which are bivalved but not mollusks, also suffered greatly, but managed to survive in severely restricted numbers to the present.

Perhaps the most dramatic extinctions in the sea were among the nannoplankton, minute calcium-secreting algae, and the foraminiferans, calcium-secreting protozoans. Their abandoned shells piled up in immense thickness to form the great chalk cliffs that give the Cretaceous Period its name. ('Cretaceous' comes from the Latin word for 'chalk'.) Marine sediments during the Cretaceous Period were comprised almost entirely of this chalk, with only a small percentage of clay particles. Sediments deposited immediately after the K/T boundary is dominated by clay particles, with only 20 to 40% being chalk. This clay layer, known as the "Fish Clay" in Europe, is widely accepted worldwide as the boundary between Cretaceous and Tertiary sediments. It ranges in thickness from less than one-half inch (~1 cm) to over three feet (~1 m) in thickness.

Thus the K/T boundary exhibits a drastic reduction in the abundance of calcium-secreting organisms. Assuming that the clay particles, derived from the erosion of nearby continents, continued at the same rate across the K/T boundary, this represents approximately a 97% reduction in the abundance of marine calcareous algae.

Life on Land

Dinosaurs were the undisputed rulers of life on land, right up to the catastrophic K/T event, but they were not the only creatures to suffer. Although fossil birds are rare during the Cretaceous (due more to the scarcity of preservation than to a lack of abundance), there were apparently several distinct lineages of Cretaceous birds, only one of which survived the extinction event, to give rise to the birds of today. However, many species within that one lineage survived, as many of the modern bird orders were represented prior to the close of the Cretaceous.

Many species of mammals also survived the extinction, as many mammalian orders also have Cretaceous representatives. Cretaceous mammals, however, tended to be quite small, and probably were predominantly nocturnal. Freshwater animals and the smaller terrestrial cold-blooded vertebrates, reptiles and amphibians, were largely unaffected by the K/T extinction.

Land plants were for the most part unaffected by the extinction event. One prominent plant community, however, was nearly obliterated at the end of the Cretaceous. This assemblage of predominantly angiosperms (flowering plants) and conifers, is technically known as the Aquilapollenites botanical province, which flourished right up to the end of the Cretaceous Period in, among other places, Western North America. Western North America was separated from the rest of the continent throughout the Cretaceous by a body of water known as the Great Interior Seaway. The Aquilapollenites plant community occurred along the western margin of this seaway, the same location as some of the richest dinosaur finds in the world. These deposits are found from New Mexico through Wyoming,

Montana, and Alberta. At the end of the Cretaceous Period in this region, above the Aquilapollenites sediments and the inevitable clay layer (which is reminiscent of the Fish Clay of Europe, and here one half (~1 cm) to over one inch, or ~3 cm thick) is found a layer of coal, which represents the remains of a fauna made up almost exclusively of ferns. After the coal layer, angiosperms return to the scene, but this time a different assemblage of species is found.

Requirements for a Successful Extinction Theory

Clearly any successful extinction theory must explain not only why the dinosaurs became extinct; it must also explain what happened to the marine ecosystems, that so many lineages of plants and animals were wiped out. It must also explain why so many organisms were able to survive the catastrophe. It is estimated that somewhere in the range of 20% to 25% of all species living at the beginning of the Late Cretaceous were extinct by its close.

Even more, a really good extinction theory should explain more extinction events than just the K/T. The terminal Cretaceous event was just one of well over a dozen mass extinction events that have occurred over the last 600 million years—and not the most recent nor the most severe. The most recent mass extinction, not counting extinctions attributable to mankind, occurred during the Miocene Epoch of the Tertiary Period, a mere 12 to 14 million years ago. This was a fairly mild extinction, as mass extinction events go.

The most severe mass extinction occurred during the Late Permian to the end of the Permian Period, between 248 and 256 million years ago. Where the terminal K/T event wiped out perhaps 20% to 25% of known species, the end Permian event eliminated a whopping 95% to 96% of known species. This appears to have been a rather protracted extinction event, occurring in waves over a span of several million years. The apparent suddenness of the K/T extinction contributes significantly to its mystery, but a number of researchers are questioning whether it was all that sudden after all.

The second greatest mass extinction occurred near the end of the Ordovician Period, somewhere around 438 to 448 million years ago. Again, this appears to have been a more gradual extinction, wiping out over several million years an estimated 40% of the plant and animal population. The K/T event thus currently stands as the third most severe mass extinction known.

The longest interval between identified mass extinction events is on the order of 110 million years, between the Late Permian event and one at the Frasnian/Famennian boundary during the Late Devonian, around 367 or 368 million years ago. The Frasnian/Famennian event was probably the fourth worst extinction on record. The shortest interval between events, excluding the 12 to 14 million years since the last extinction, was around 24 or 26 million years, between the most recent Miocene event and one at the end of the Eocene, approximately 38 million years ago. Another 27 million years before that was the terminal Cretaceous event."

So, with that brilliant professor's dissertation, we will now move past the next 40 million years and the many animals that evolved, some thriving because of some advantageous mutation to better cope with the environment, some to become extinct not being able to cope during that period and then take a look at the hominoids.

For more, see Google. Search for "hominoid."

Lucy

Who is Lucy? Lucy is the fossil skeleton of a 3ft, 6 inch, 65 pound or so adult woman who lived in the area of Africa now called Ethiopia. She was bipedal, (walking on two legs), and lived some 3 to 4 million years ago. This would be about 4 to 5 million years from the time the first hominoids stood, walked and foraged for food using their former front legs as arms and hands; a total evolutionary time frame of 8 to 10 million years.

There is controversy in the scientific community regarding whether Lucy was truly a beginning of the homosapien species, but the majority of scientists consider her one of our earliest ancestors. I located the following information about Lucy on Google using the search word, "Lucy."

www.asu.edu/clas/iho/lucy.html

The following article by professional anthropologists at the Institute of Human Origins at the Arizona State University provides sufficient information to bridge the gap from the earliest hominoids to the time of Lucy's life. Here is their summary:

When and where was Lucy found?

Lucy was found by Donald Johanson and Tom Gray on the 30th of November, 1974, at the site of Hadar in Ethiopia. They had taken a Land Rover out that day to map in another locality. After a long, hot morning of mapping and surveying for fossils, they decided to head back to the vehicle. Johanson suggested taking an alternate route back to the Land Rover, through a nearby gully. Within moments, he spotted a right proximal ulna (forearm bone) and quickly identified it as a hominid. Shortly thereafter, he saw an occipital (skull) bone, then a femur, some ribs, a pelvis, and the lower jaw. Two weeks later, after many hours of excavation, screening, and sorting, several hundred fragments of bone had been recovered, representing 40% of a single hominid skeleton.

How did Lucy get her name?

Later in the night of November 30th, there was much celebration and excitement over the discovery of what looked like a fairly complete hominid skeleton. There was drinking, dancing, and singing; the Beatles' song "Lucy in the Sky With Diamonds" was playing over and over. At some point during that night no one remembers when or by whom the skeleton was given the name "Lucy." The name has stuck.

How do we know she was a hominid?

The term hominid refers to a member of the zoological family Hominidae. Hominidae encompasses all species originating after the human/African ape ancestral split, leading to, and including all species of Australopithecus and Homo. While these species differ in many ways, hominids share a suite of characteristics which define them as a group. The most conspicuous of these traits is bipedal locomotion, or walking upright.

How do we know Lucy walked upright?

As in a modern human's skeleton, Lucy's bones are rife with evidence clearly pointing to bipedality. Her distal femur shows several traits unique to bipedality. The shaft is angled relative to the condyles (knee joint surfaces) which allows bipeds to balance on one leg at a time during locomotion. There is a prominent patellar lip to keep the patella (knee cap) from dislocating due to this angle. Her condyles are large, and are thus adapted to handling the added weight which results from shifting from four limbs to two. The pelvis exhibits a number of adaptations to bipedality. The entire structure has been remodeled to accommodate an upright stance and the need to balance the trunk on only one limb with each stride. The talus, in her ankle, shows evidence for a convergent big toe, sacrificing manipulative abilities for efficiency in bipedal locomotion. The vertebra show evidence of the spinal curvatures necessitated by a permanent upright stance.

How do we know she was female?

Evidence now strongly suggests that the Hadar material, as well as fossils from elsewhere in East Africa from the same time period, belong to a single, sexually dimorphic species known as Australopithecus afarensis. At Hadar the size difference is very clear, with larger males and smaller females being fairly easy to distinguish. Lucy clearly fits into the smaller group.

How did she die?

No cause has been determined for Lucy's death. One of the few clues we have is the conspicuous lack of post-mortem carnivore and scavenger marks. Typically, animals that were killed by predators and then scavenged by other animals (such as hyaenas) will show evidence of chewing, crushing, and gnawing on the bones. The ends of long bones are often missing, and their shafts are sometimes broken (which enables the predator to get to the marrow). In contrast, the only damage we see on Lucy's bones is a single carnivore tooth puncture mark on the top of her left pubic bone. This is what is called a peri-mortem injury, one occurring at or around the time of death. If it occurred after she died, but while the bone was still fresh, then it may not be related to her death.

How old was she when she died?

There are several indicators which give a fair idea of her age. Her third molars (wisdom teeth) are erupted and slightly worn, indicating that she was fully adult. All the ends of her bones had fused and her cranial sutures had closed, indicating completed skeletal development. Her vertebra show signs of degenerative disease, but this is not always associated with older age. All these indicators, when taken together, suggest that she was a young, but fully mature, adult when she died.

Where is the "real" Lucy?

IHO has replicas of Lucy's bones which were produced in the Institute's casting and molding laboratories. The "real" Lucy is stored in a specially constructed safe in the Paleoanthropology Laboratories of the National Museum of Ethiopia in Addis Ababa, Ethiopia. Because of the rare and fragile nature of many fossils, including hominids, molds are often made of the original fossils. The molds are then used to create detailed copies, called casts, which can be used for teaching, research, and exhibits.

How old is Lucy?

The hominid-bearing sediments in the Hadar formation are divided into three members. Lucy was found in the highest of these—the Kada Hadar, or KH—member. While fossils cannot be dated directly, the deposits in which they are found sometimes contain volcanic flows and ashes, which can now be dated with the 40Ar/39Ar (Argon-Argon) dating technique. Armed with these dates and bolstered by paleomagnetic, paleontological, and sedimentological studies, researchers can place fossils into a dated framework with accuracy and precision. Lucy is dated to just less than 3.18 million years old.

How do we know that her skeleton is from a single individual?

Although several hundred fragments of hominid bone were found at the Lucy site, there was no duplication of bones. A single duplication of even the most modest of bone fragments would have disproved the single skeleton claim, but no such duplication is seen in Lucy. The bones all come from an individual of a single species, a single size, and a single developmental age. In life, she would have stood about three-and-a-half feet tall, and weighed about 60 to 65 pounds.

The analysis indicates Lucy was an adult, bipedal, near human animal going about her daily routine and no doubt a part of a pack or clan. As a female, she no doubt had a male mate who was probably responsible for the hunting of game for protein, while Lucy and her female kind did the foraging for plants, berries and roots. I base this conclusion on the fact that professional researchers have indicated any successful ongoing species had to have leadership, cooperation within the pack, herd, or flock or the species would not survive. We discussed leadership and the herding concept earlier.

To this very day, the genes of our early ancestors are evident when a man and his wife go shopping. The average man, like a hunter, will walk into a department store, take dead aim at the part of the store where he intends to buy something, purchase it and head for home or some other activity. The majority of women will enjoy wandering about the store eyeballing different goods and services and like an earlier hunter-gatherer of roots and berries, eventually buying what she came for plus other items of interest. We indeed carry the genes we inherited from our early ancestor hominoids.

It is approximately 3 million years from the time of Lucy's life on earth to the time of the arrival of the true look-alike homosapiens of today that came about some 200,000 years ago. During this 3 million year span, as well as in the 4 million year period between the first bipedal hominoids, many scientists believe as many as 15 to 25 different species of bipedal hominoids developed and then became extinct for failure to cope with the environment, a superior similar species, or some other events. The survival of the fittest characteristic of the evolutionary process has no preset plan; it is random occurrences of mutations, natural selection, and survival of the fittest that determine which species will be successful. I believe Lucy is one of our ancestors and now I move on to the ultimate creation of nature's evolutionary process, the modern homosapien. THAT'S YOU! You, the bipedal animal that lacks the speed of the predator animals, the strength to do battle with the stronger animals or the ability to fly like a bird or dive deep in the sea like a dolphin. You are the animal that has a nearly three-pound brain developed over the ages. The human animal, as Dr. Jacob Bronowski taught, has been driven over several million years by a hand consisting of a thumb and four fingers. The all-important grip and the brain of this homosapien are just two of the things you have inherited among all of the uniqueness and survival characteristics of the animals from which we have descended.

The grip of the hand, working together with the brain is responsible for developing sophisticated tools to overwhelm the other animals, building machines to fly faster than birds, to travel faster than the speediest animal predators, even to reach beyond the speed of sound, dive to the deepest areas of the seas, and even construct a machine to rocket off to other planets.

Great Minds Consider Creation

EINSTEIN

Recently the Los Angeles Skirball Museum presented the grand Einstein Exhibition depicting the great man's life and his fantastic scientific discoveries. I was struck with his formula of $E=MC^2$ along with his statement that there may be some kind of supernatural force behind the Big Bang. Could that possible supernatural force be some kind of god? If you reverse Einstein's formula, there may have been a supernatural cosmic energy force resulting in the Big Bang and that caused the development of all the matter, planets and stars that make up the universe we now know and the possibly many other universes the scientists now believe are yet to be discovered. As yet, no one knows what is behind or what caused the Big Bang.

Incidentally, I recently learned that the top brain scientists in the world including Dr. Thomas Harvey and Dr. Sandra Witelson have completed a thorough analysis of Einstein's brain and concluded that as compared to hundreds of other human brains, that Einstein's brain is a one-in-a-billion of human brains even though it is only a little over 3/4th the size of many human male brains. They also published the fact that the differences in his brain from normal people's brains existed at his time of birth. That makes me wonder if in the evolution of animal species as described by Charles Darwin, whether the human species will give birth to this kind of brain more often than one in a billion in future centuries.

Just think of the genius of this man. Einstein joined light to time and time to space, energy to matter, matter to space and space to gravitation. He said: "We do not know… there may be a supernatural cosmic force beyond the Big Bang."

So with that statement we know for sure the greatest brain of the last century is stating without qualification that the six-day Jewish God stories are fiction. Am I, you, Pat Robertson, Jerry Falwell, the pope, the ayatollahs as brilliant as Einstein? Lay the memoir down, lean back, relax, close your eyes and contemplate the contents of this paragraph for a few moments. OK Kelle, just a few minutes of contemplation, don't snooze. Let's get on with it. So for now, we can only hope SHE is out there.

We surely now know no six-day God taking a whole week to create this tiny speck of dust in the vast universe was ever involved with the Big Bang and the billions of stars and planets that were born. I think the religious leaders should watch the 13-hour Cosmos documentary by Dr. Carl Sagan whereby they will learn how the Big Bang created the vast universe in a split second!

K: I am not a physicist but that statement seems to ring true. And I too understand Einstein was quoted as saying the universe may have been created by some form of a supernatural cosmic force.

T: True. That was one of his most famous comments regarding religion. From my decades of research and study, I am convinced no one knows what is behind the Big Bang, how or why the universe came about, and as of the 1995 discoveries, whether there is only our one vast universe or possibly untold millions of vast universes. The one thing any individual must know who has the ability and interest to read about the works of the present and past scientists, their fantastic works and discoveries plus the works of the great minds in psychology and philosophy is that what we were taught in Sunday school and our Christian churches is nothing more than man-made fiction.

Hopefully a god is out there somewhere beyond the Big Bang but I am convinced beyond any doubt that if God exists, "SHE," (remember men wrote the Bible) is not an image of any of us and SHE never created this very tiny grain-sized planet located in one of the remote locations of the vast universe in six days.

Kelle, you'll enjoy this bit of information.

Billy Graham, Larry King, Albert Einstein

Billy Graham is without a doubt the most beloved, credible, intelligent and wealthiest evangelist of the 1900s and possibly in the history of America. It would be difficult to find any one who does not admire the gentleman. I personally admire him, I think he is a real gentleman, although I do not believe in his past teachings. He is no country bumpkin clown like Jerry Falwell, Pat Robertson and the many other TV Bible thumpers.

Larry King is the famous and popular CNN talk show host.

Albert Einstein was the most brilliant scientist with the one of a kind brain. The brain scientists claim was born with a one in a billion super brain mutation possibility of the animal species. That's one brain like his out of every billion births.

Then we have me, an ordinary 83 year old senior citizen, over the hill retired Navy throttle jockey and real estate promoter.

As we discussed, over 60 years ago the most brilliant scientist, Albert, of the 1900s said there possibly may be some kind of supernatural cosmic force that caused the existence of the universe. In other words the tiny microscopic spec of matter in the universe called earth was not made in six days by a god who was/is in the image of a male Jewish person.

And I claim because of the teaching of my Physics 101 teacher, Mr. Hartley, that if nothing can come about from zilch (nothing) then there has to be something behind the Big Bang that caused the birth of the universe. In December 2005, Billy, even older than me, on the Larry King show told Larry, "I don't know what it was but there has to be some kind of beginning (and he held up either a pencil or his pointed finger)."

Seems to me the two famous men and I are all of the same opinion. There must be some kind of "thing" as Billy said out there.

This means that obviously the thousands upon thousands of manmade gods created by imaginative earth bound men over the past 10,000 years of known history as Professor Van Doren taught were not addressing whatever it is out beyond the Big Bang that both Albert and Billy are addressing. Columbia Professor Dr. Carl Van Doren claims every god invented by imaginative and creative men over the past 10,000 years of known history are all based on fiction. For the past two thousand years the militant, intolerant, bigoted, prejudiced and aggressive man-conceived Christian religion has been one of the most dominant of the current religions. Hopefully the next major conceived religion by sci-fi, creative and imaginative men or women will be a more kind, tolerant and peaceful religion.

K: How can you admire Billy as being such a distinguished honest gentleman if he has the same thoughts as Albert regarding the birth of the universe but nevertheless goes before hundreds of thousands of people preaching about the six-day God constructing the earth in just one week? How could a person believe the same as genius Einstein and still preach about a fictional six-day God?

T: The old guy is now retired and no doubt now has the time to be reading some 1850 and later years' science books. I was shocked when he made the statement with no reference to a six-day God. I admire him for coming clean about his current thoughts about the birth of the universe. It also makes me feel good that I now know my beliefs are about the same as two of the most famous men of the last century. And now I will make an egotistical statement: "I arrived at that belief before I learned what Albert had stated and many, many decades before Billy expressed the same belief on the Larry King show." There must be something out there.

Comfort and Peace, at Last

So now you know my thoughts as to who I am, where I came from and where I will be going. No more superstition or foolish thoughts about wandering around out in space with a set of wings playing a harp, joining up with loved ones and old shipmates out yonder, knowing full well the practitioners of make believe are preaching fiction and nonsense. I have a very comfortable feeling of being at peace with the world and I must admit a bit of an egotistical feeling when in a group of people discussing the hereafter; just standing there silently knowing the truth and being above it all. We are all "star stuff." Enjoy the trip.

K: Tom, when we crossed paths and commenced our conversation, I was hoping to get a good story to add to my story telling collection. I have enjoyed our conversation, e-mail messages and also getting to know Karen and Boris. I look forward to our future meetings and conversations.

I would like to summarize what I am taking away from our tête-à-tête as I understand your motivation in writing your memoir. I would like to know your opinion of my understanding.

T: Let's hear it, Kelle.

K: I think you are one of the WW-II generation who saw the great war coming and prepared yourself as best you could to do your duty when called to do so. You followed through in the naval service and then in later life came to believe that America may have been successful in defeating the overseas military enemies but America was and is now in danger from enemies of our form of government residing in our country. In your memoir, you make it clear that you believe that fictitious manmade religions of one kind or another have been used throughout the history of civilization to rule and control societies and nations.

No matter how remote the societies unknown to each other from Egypt, the ancient nations of the Middle East to the tribes in Africa, the isolated islands of the world, the Incas of South America or the Aztecs of what is now Mexico, a "god related" individual would emerge to rule the population and then his "self appointed agents" would rule in his name after his death. You see the Christian religion as one of these many religions. You see many of the leaders of the Christian religion as enemies of our 1776 founders (you call them your forefathers) of our American type of government constructed with the wall of separation of church and state. You have noted that the Christians did not dare touch the founders' wall while they were alive but in the 1830s following the death of the last of the 1776 founders, they have steadily chipped away at the wall; successfully having "In God We Trust" printed on our money, laws in many states to this day that unless a person believes as they do they cannot hold public office, constantly lobbying to teach religion in our public schools, to put Christian propaganda memorabilia in our schools and public buildings, then putting "under God" in our pledge of allegiance at the end of WW-II and constantly attacking the judicial branch of our government.

At first I thought you were overly pessimistic about America sliding down a slippery slope into a theocracy ruled nation. But you seem to believe the many pro–1776 founder organizations that have been born since the end of WW–II promoting the strengthening and preserving the wall of separation of church and state are beginning to curb the Christian activists attacking the wall. Now in your mid–80s, you have a burning aspiration to warn as many as you can to be aware of this danger to the existence of the America designed by our 1776 founders (your forefathers).

T: I like your summary. You are a part of the generation that will be the elders in the next couple of decades. I hope many members of your generation will support the numerous post WW-II pro-American organizations that are battling the evil doers chipping away at the wall. We discussed many of these patriotic organizations in our conversation.

And Kelle, I am optimistic about the future of America because until post WW-II the Christian leaders attacking the wall had little if any organized opposition from the 1830s to 1945. As I mentioned, the Smithsonian historical records reveal only 11% of the American population indicated a church affiliation in America's first census; by the end of this century with the ever-increasing improvement in our education system, I am sure our population will again approach this same low percentage of church affiliated families. Hopefully the scientists studying the universe in this century will get beyond the Big Bang and truly discover what the hell is really out there.

T: Let's end your story and this conversation with a message from our forefathers.

K: *OK, the founders are some of my favorite people too. What is the message?*

T: Here it is:

A MESSAGE FROM YOUR 1776 FOREFATHERS

Congress shall make no law respecting <u>an establishment of religion,</u> or prohibiting the free exercise thereof; or abridging the freedom of speech, or of the press; or the right of the people peaceably to assemble, and to petition the Government for a redress of grievances.

"Eternal vigilance is the price of liberty," Thomas Jefferson

Dear Reader,

Thank you for reading my story,

MY CONVERSATIONS WITH A WW-II CORSAIR FIGHTER PILOT
His story through the decades

Since you completed reading the book, I will now ask you a great favor which, if you do, will make you feel you have made a significant contribution to the future wellbeing of America. It is a significant step to help ensure your children and grandchildren will also get to enjoy living in the same kind of America you have enjoyed in your lifetime. Please go to www.au.org or if you are not using a computer use the snail mail address:

Americans United for Separation of Church and State
518 C Street, N.E.
Washington, DC 20002

Please make a contribution of just $25 (as of 2005) to become a member and a recipient of the Americans United publication of "CHURCH & STATE."

Thank You,
Kelle

PS: I did not contact the Americans United organization for permission to print this message in my book nor have any members of the organization been contacted about the contents of my discussions with Tom…we both admire the organization and are simply interested in promoting their good work.

About The Author...

Kelle Metz was born in 1944, in Kansas. She has moved most of her life, first as the daughter of a Shell Oil employee and later as the wife of a career Army officer. She has lived all over the United States and in Europe and Asia. For the past 26 years, Kelle has lived in a log house she and her family built on a self-sufficiency farm a few miles from Oakville, Washington. Among the variety of animals on her 25 acres are pigs, goats, chickens, bees, and several cats. Kelle describes herself as a "Jacqueline of all trades, master of none." She has tried many of the skills homesteaders of the past had to learn; quilting, soap making, gardening, butchering, and food preservation.

During her lifetime, Kelle has worked at a variety of jobs: long distance and PBX operator, receptionist, medical records secretary, medical insurance billing clerk, teacher's aide, school bus driver, office manager for an historical seaport, bookkeeper, and library circulation assistant. She retired from working for others in 2004 and has been running her own business since that time, selling honey.

Kelle's current hobby is doing historical and genealogical research. She is a member of the Olympia Storytelling Guild and loves writing and telling the historical stories she uncovers. Kelle wrote a history of her community from 1850 to 1900 and has compiled and merged with photos the 115 letters her father wrote her mother during World War II. In 2000, she began researching the history of the aircraft carrier that her father served on from August 1944 to November 1945, and to date has gathered information about the ship's history, from its commissioning until the end of the war.

Kelle's plans for the future include writing a book covering her mother and father's lives from the end of WW-II until their deaths, an autobiography of herself, and a compilation of first person stories of WW-II.

Index

Kelle Metz was researching her father's World War II naval experiences when she met Tom McBride, who served on the same aircraft carrier, the USS Bennington. It gave her the opportunity delve into questions she would have asked her father, were he still living. Expecting to hear personal observations about the war, she got much more than she bargained for. With her passion for history, genealogical research, and storytelling, she has crafted a compelling "conversation" with Tom, a retired WW-II fighter pilot. She says it's wonderful to see how one person's life, ideas, and philosophies change over a lifetime. WW-II was the only war, since the Revolution, which involved the entire nation and every citizen working toward one goal—victory. Kelle's conversations with Tom will be of great interest to Americans who remember the war and to those who are too young to have experienced it.

My Conversations with a
WW-II Corsair Fighter Pilot

Tom McBride, who served on the USS Bennington as a Corsair fighter pilot, shares his memories of pre-war life in Carnegie and Aliquippa, Pennsylvania, remembrances of wartime adventures, post-war flying experiences, and much, much more, including the origins of the universe, first life on earth, and where we are headed as a civilization.

This old warrior may no longer be involved in gunfire wars, but he is hell bent in verbally attacking those he calls the "enemies within" who are attacking his beloved 1776 founders' goals and dreams for America as well as their attacks on the judicial branch of our government. He is now as dedicated to the goals of the Americans United for Separation of Church and State as he once was as a warrior fighting America's enemies overseas.

*Be prepared: this is **NOT** your average war story.*